Christmas, 2008

Love, Mom + Bill

THE COMPLETE BOOK OF
SEWING

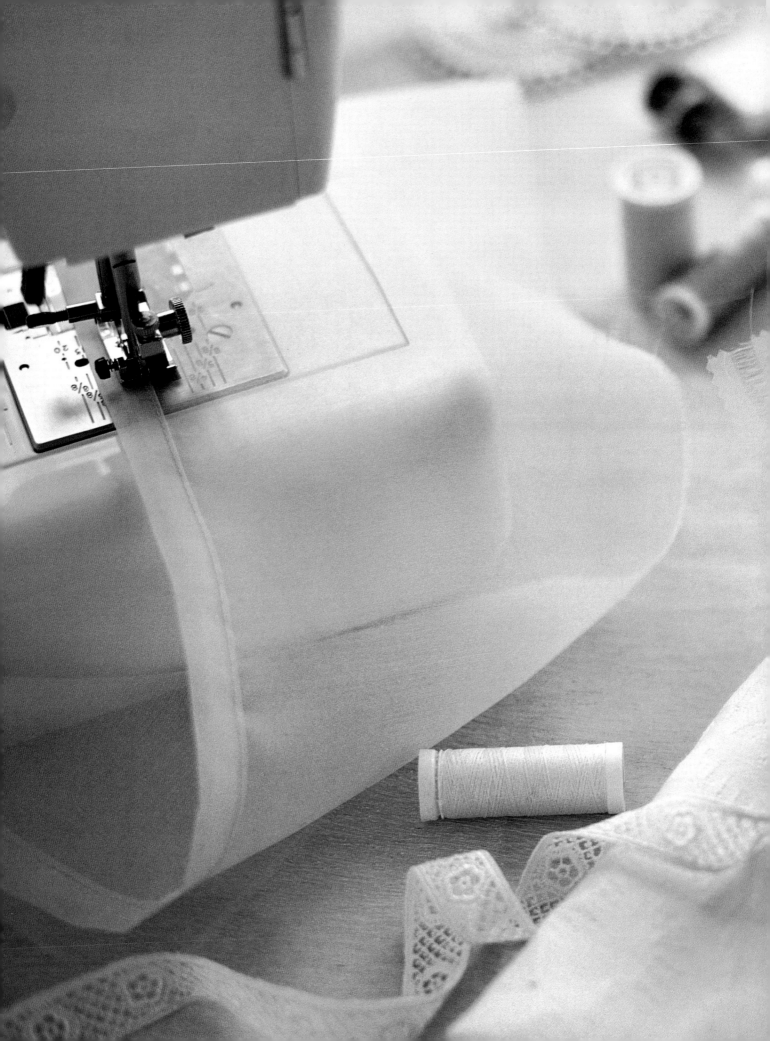

THE COMPLETE BOOK OF
SEWING

DORLING KINDERSLEY

LONDON, NEW YORK, MELBOURNE, MUNICH AND DELHI

REVISED EDITION
Editor Betsy Hosegood
Art Editor Jane Forster

Managing Editor Stephanie Farrow
Managing Art Editor Karen Sawyer
DTP Designer Sonia Charbonnier
Production Controller Louise Daly

Photography Laura Knox
Styling Jane Forster, Martin Short
Fashion Drawing Terry Evans

DORLING KINDERSLEY INDIA
DTP Coordinator Pankaj Sharma
DTP Designers Umesh Aggarwal, Balwant Singh,
Ajay Verma, Narender Kumar
Editor Sheema Mookherjee
Managing Art Editor Aparna Sharma

ORIGINAL EDITION
Senior Editor Penelope Cream
Senior Art Editor Cathy Shilling

Editors Joanna Bellamy, Tracey Beresford,
Colette Connolly, Linda Gibson,
Samantha Gray, Vivien Ruddock
US Editor Laaren Brown

Designers Ellen Harris, Dawn Terry
Assistant Designers Helen Benfield, Nathalie Hennequin

Managing Editor Stephanie Jackson
Senior Managing Editors Josephine Buchanan, Krystyna Mayer
Senior Managing Art Editor Lynne Brown
Production Controller Meryl Silbert
Photography Andy Crawford, Steve Gorton

First American edition, 1996
6 8 10 9 7

Published in the United States by DK Publishing, Inc.,
375 Hudson Street
New York, New York 10014

Copyright © 1996 and 2003
Dorling Kindersley Limited, London

Library of Congress Cataloging-in-Publication Data

The Complete book of sewing. – 1st American ed.
p.   cm.
Includes index.
ISBN 0-7894-9658-5
ISBN 978-078949658-4
1. Sewing   2. Dressmaking   I. DK Publishing, Inc.
TT705.C744 1996   96-10834
646.4 – dc20   CIP

Printed and bound by Neografia, Slovakia

CONTENTS

INTRODUCTION

CONTAINING a wealth of information on fabrics, basic sewing equipment and skills, The *Complete Book of Sewing* enables you to create almost any garment, and many home-furnishing items. Once you have mastered the basic techniques, you can progress to creating elegant couture garments, using professional methods. Sixteen comprehensive sections provide detailed advice on tools, fabrics, notions, and techniques. Step-by-step color photographs, accompanied by full instructions, clearly show you how to get perfect results.

HOW TO USE THIS BOOK

THIS BOOK consists of 16 major sections, each dealing with a different category. Beginning with the equipment you will need, the sections progress through sewing basics, including using fabrics and patterns, working stitches, and making seams. There follow comprehensive sections on sewing and styling specific garment parts.

Chapter opener with contents list

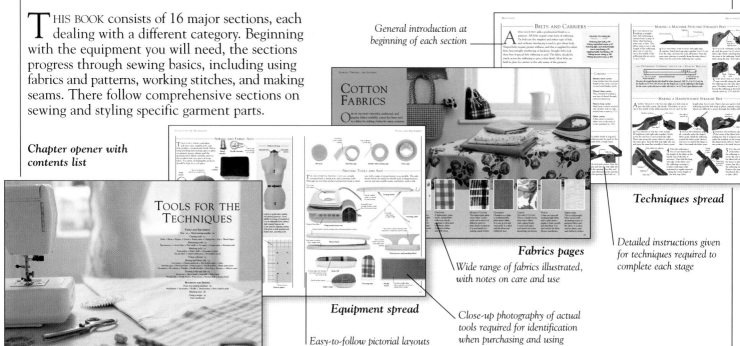

General introduction at beginning of each section

Techniques spread

Detailed instructions given for techniques required to complete each stage

Fabrics pages

Wide range of fabrics illustrated, with notes on care and use

Equipment spread

Easy-to-follow pictorial layouts

Close-up photography of actual tools required for identification when purchasing and using

FINDING INFORMATION ON THE PAGE

INFORMATION IS PRESENTED in an easily accessible way, with introductory text on each technique and its applications, followed by clear, step-by-step photographs and text instructions explaining every stage of the sewing process. Where relevant, tips and variations are also featured, and cross-references direct you to related methods.

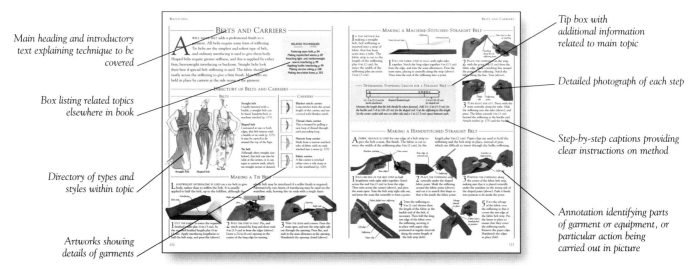

Main heading and introductory text explaining technique to be covered

Box listing related topics elsewhere in book

Directory of types and styles within topic

Artworks showing details of garments

Tip box with additional information related to main topic

Detailed photograph of each step

Step-by-step captions providing clear instructions on method

Annotation identifying parts of garment or equipment, or particular action being carried out in picture

HOW THE STEP-BY-STEP SEQUENCES WORK

THE NUMBERED STEP-BY-STEP SEQUENCES explain how to accomplish all the stages of each sewing technique. Close-up pictures of the action show clearly how the method is carried out. Often a tip box gives additional information or hints on related topics. The number of steps in the sequence depends on the complexity of the technique.

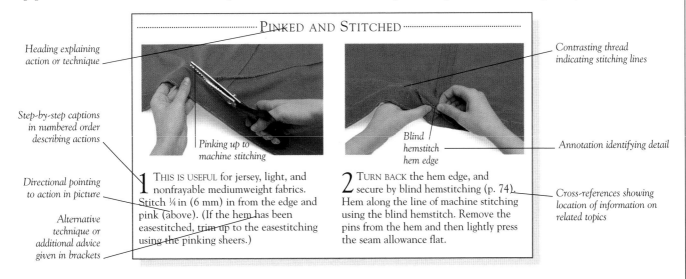

PINKED AND STITCHED

Heading explaining action or technique

Step-by-step captions in numbered order describing actions

Directional pointing to action in picture

Alternative technique or additional advice given in brackets

Pinking up to machine stitching

1 THIS IS USEFUL for jersey, light, and nonfrayable mediumweight fabrics. Stitch ¼ in (6 mm) in from the edge and pink (above). (If the hem has been easestitched, trim up to the easestitching using the pinking sheers.)

Contrasting thread indicating stitching lines

Blind hemstitch hem edge

Annotation identifying detail

Cross-references showing location of information on related topics

2 TURN BACK the hem edge, and secure by blind hemstitching (p. 74). Hem along the line of machine stitching using the blind hemstitch. Remove the pins from the hem and then lightly press the seam allowance flat.

USING THE BOOK

THE COMPLETE BOOK OF SEWING is designed to be used by sewers at all levels of ability. It can be followed section by section as a beginner's course in home sewing and dressmaking, and can also be consulted by more experienced sewers requiring help with specific techniques. It includes a glossary of sewing terms and an index.

Sewing items

This book is intended as a technical sourcebook with the emphasis on a clear explanation of the technique required to make an item following a selected pattern. For this reason,

Picture showing specific action – in this case, cutting

Color of fabric used is an example only

pictures of finished items are not generally included. Below are some guiding principles that should be noted when working through the techniques described in the book.

Equipment section

The basic requirements when starting to sew are a sewing machine, an iron, and an adequate sewing kit, including sharp scissors and a measuring tool. The equipment section (p. 8–19) suggests the minimum required, as well as describing items for more advanced sewers.

Pattern section

The photographs show pattern pieces specially made for this book. It is assumed that a commercial paper pattern will be used, and no instructions are given for constructing pattern pieces. There is, however, detailed information on altering a basic paper pattern. Although right-side pattern pieces are mainly shown, the instructions apply to both right and left sides.

Fabrics and threads section

The section on fabrics and notions (p. 40–69) examines a variety of fabrics and their uses, and gives information on aftercare. Notions, such as different threads, are also described.

Techniques

The choice of style and fabric shown here is intended as a guide only. Thread and fabric should generally match as closely as possible, but to make the techniques easy to follow, the thread in the photographs is often contrasted with the fabric.

Easily visible contrasting color thread

Professional techniques section

This section (p. 280–303) explains how to make garments that have a professional finish. Relatively advanced techniques are covered here, including constructing and fitting a custom-tailored jacket, and mastering couture dressmaking techniques such as boning a bodice, cutting fabric on the bias, ruching, and making decorative rosettes and bows.

COMMON TERMS USED IN THE BOOK

Stitch Usually, to be stitched by hand or by machine.
Machine stitch To stitch using a sewing machine.
Handstitch To stitch by hand, using the desired stitch.
Baste To secure temporarily with running stitch.
Staystitch Row of machine stitching along raw edges.
Easestitch Large machine stitches used for gathering.
Seam allowance ⅝ in (1.5 cm) is the standard amount.

TOOLS FOR THE TECHNIQUES

TOOLS AND EQUIPMENT

A COMPREHENSIVE but basic range of tools and equipment is an excellent starting point for any sewer. More specialized pieces of equipment may be purchased later. Small pieces of equipment, such as pins, needles, and cutting implements, are relatively inexpensive items, while a sewing machine is more costly but indispensable. A steam iron and an ironing board are both essential, and a sleeve board is helpful. Tools such as hem markers, stitching tapes, and fabric markers are useful for specific purposes.

PINS

PINS ARE AVAILABLE in several different thicknesses and lengths, and in brass, stainless steel, and nickel-plated steel. Standard dressmaker's pins are 1¹⁄₁₆ in (2.6 cm) long, while shorter, fine lace pins, used on lightweight fabrics, are 1 in (2.5 cm) long. Glass-headed pins are easy to handle, and T-pins will stay in position on open-weave fabrics.

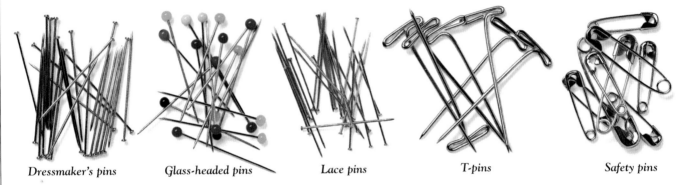

Dressmaker's pins   *Glass-headed pins*   *Lace pins*   *T-pins*   *Safety pins*

HAND-SEWING NEEDLES

THE RANGE OF NEEDLES used for handstitching varies in size, length, and point shape. The most common needles are known as "sharps." Specialized tasks are handled with specific needles, in a variety of lengths and widths. When choosing a needle, be guided by the structure and weight of the fabric and of the thread being used.

Sharps are widely used for general hand-sewing purposes. Medium-length with a round eye, they suit most fabrics.

Betweens are short needles with a round eye. They are used to make close, fine stitches, as in quilting.

Ballpoint needles are very similar to sharps, but have a rounded point that penetrates between knit yarn fibers.

Straws are longer needles than betweens. They are also known as milliner's needles, and are often used for tacking.

Chenille needles are thick and sharp, and have a wide eye. They are larger than embroidery crewel needles and are suitable for use with heavy yarns.

Beading needles are very long and fine, with a sharp point. They are used for decorative work, particularly for attaching beads and sequins.

Tapestry needles are strong, thick needles that have a sturdy, blunt point. They are suitable for working tapestry and needlepoint projects.

Long darners are long, thick needles, suitable for mending holes in heavy fabrics. Used with thick, woolen yarns, they form a closely worked mesh for covering large holes.

Embroidery or crewel needles are sharp, medium-length needles with a long eye through which strands of embroidery floss are threaded.

Cotton darners can vary in length and diameter. Traditionally used for darning, they are also suitable for delicate yarns such as cotton and silk because of their fine points.

Curved needles are available in a variety of sizes. They are used in mattressing and upholstery work, where straight needles are unsuitable.

Glovers are sturdy needles with a round eye and a triangular point. They are suitable for piercing both leather and strong plastic fabrics.

CUTTING TOOLS

ALWAYS BUY GOOD-QUALITY cutting tools made of high-grade steel, and keep them sharp, since dull blades can damage fabric and slow the cutting process. Bent-handled shears are used for cutting out, and sewing scissors for trimming seams and facings. Pinking shears are used to form fray-resistant edges, and embroidery scissors are designed for needlework. Leather shears cut leather and suede, as do cutting knives, and rotary cutters produce precise, straight edges. Awls are used for piercing small holes in fabric for eyelets and buttonholes. Thread clippers snip thread, while seam rippers open seams and are used for detailed work such as undoing buttonhole stitching. Stitch rippers are smaller than seam rippers and can cut stitches close to the fabric.

Thread clipper

Spring-action blade

Bent-handled shears

Angle of lower blade allows fabric to lie flat while being cut

Sharp point should be covered for safety when not in use

Awl

Blunt point on upper blade prevents fabric from tearing while being cut

Sewing scissors

Adjustable screw allows even pressure along blades

Sharp, replaceable blades in snap-off sections

Cutting knife

Heavy, serrated edges

Hook removes stitches and opens seams and buttonholes

Leather shears

Seam ripper

Ball acts as guide through fabric

Zigzag blades for finishing seams and raw edges

Stitch ripper

Pinking shears

Sharp, pointed blades

Embroidery scissors

Handle

Blade **Rotary cutter**

Cutting mat

Grid for precise measuring and cutting

Rotary cutter and blade
The rotary cutter is available in several sizes with different blades. It has a mechanism that retracts the blades. When using a rotary cutter, work on a cutting mat to protect the blade and the cutting surface.

Straight-edge rotary blade

1 2 3 4 5 6 7 8 9

MEASURING TOOLS

USING A RANGE OF SUITABLE TOOLS for taking measurements helps produce successful results on your sewing project. Measuring tools are needed for obtaining both pattern and body measurements in order to make any adjustments that are necessary on pattern pieces. Making these adjustments ensures that the finished item will be a good fit. Some tools are designed for a variety of general sewing purposes and are required every time you sew. Others are useful for more specific purposes, such as making adjustments to necklines and other curved pattern pieces, adjusting hemlines, or measuring pleats.

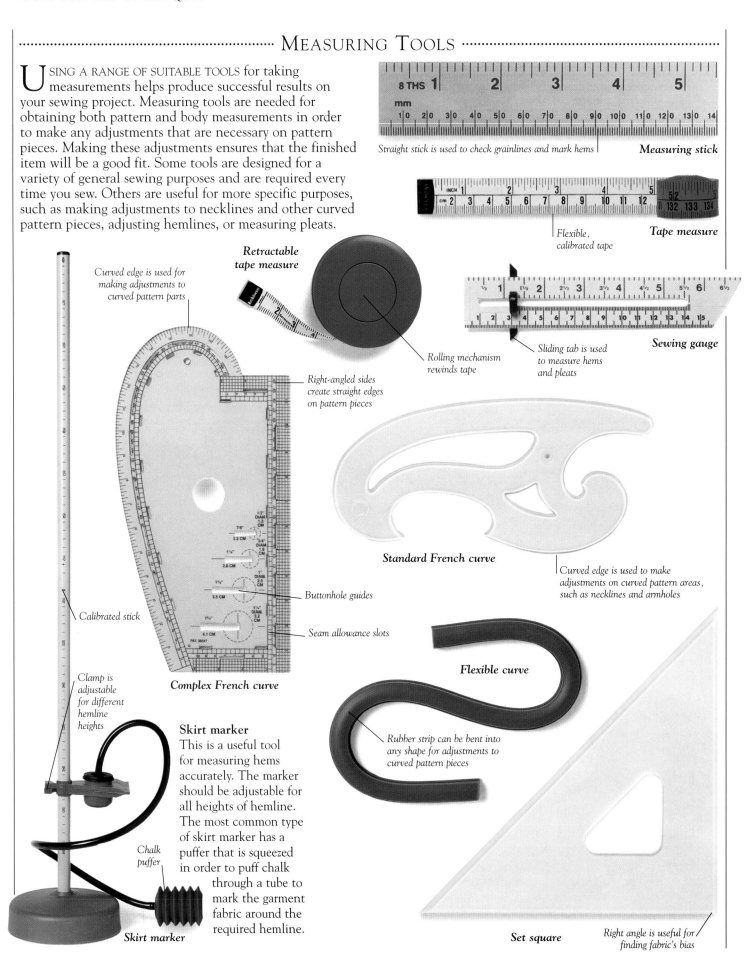

Straight stick is used to check grainlines and mark hems | **Measuring stick**

Flexible, calibrated tape | **Tape measure**

Retractable tape measure

Curved edge is used for making adjustments to curved pattern parts

Rolling mechanism rewinds tape

Sliding tab is used to measure hems and pleats | **Sewing gauge**

Right-angled sides create straight edges on pattern pieces

Standard French curve

Curved edge is used to make adjustments on curved pattern areas, such as necklines and armholes

Calibrated stick

Buttonhole guides

Seam allowance slots

Complex French curve

Flexible curve

Clamp is adjustable for different hemline heights

Rubber strip can be bent into any shape for adjustments to curved pattern pieces

Skirt marker
This is a useful tool for measuring hems accurately. The marker should be adjustable for all heights of hemline. The most common type of skirt marker has a puffer that is squeezed in order to puff chalk through a tube to mark the garment fabric around the required hemline.

Chalk puffer

Skirt marker

Set square

Right angle is useful for finding fabric's bias

MARKING TOOLS

ONE OR MORE MARKING TOOLS will be required for transferring pattern markings to garment fabric pieces and for marking alterations on garments. There are various types of marking tool to choose from. The best choice for specific jobs has much to do with personal preference, so it is a good idea to try out the different options.

Marking wheel

Tailor's chalk

Wax chalk

Dressmaker's carbon
This type of marking paper is widely available in a number of colors, including white. It is used for marking all types of fabric in combination with a tracing wheel (below). The instructions given on the package should be followed, since these vary between brands.

Seam marker
This plastic holder contains powdered chalk, which is released through a small wheel at the base. It is used for marking seam allowances.

Chalks
Tailor's chalk is available in a range of colors and is removed by brushing. Wax chalk is black or white and is used for wool fabrics. Pressing will remove it.

Tailor's chalk
This pencil is used to mark garment details, such as pleats and darts, because it makes finer lines than a block of tailor's chalk.

Tracing wheel
Used with dressmaker's carbon, this tool is used to transfer pattern markings to the wrong side of the fabric.

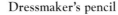

Liquid marking pen
There are two main types of liquid marking pen. One makes marks that disappear after 48 hours, and the other washes out.

Dressmaker's pencil
Available in white or pastel shades, this chalk pencil is used to make fine lines on fabric. It has an erasing brush at one end.

USING A PLEATER

A PLEATER IS A TIMESAVING DEVICE that is used for gathering fabrics for smocking or elasticizing. A row of needles, threaded with either thread or elastic, passes through the garment fabric as it is wound around a series of rollers. The rollers are activated by turning the handles on the side of the pleater; they have grooves to guide the needles forward evenly. The number of needles used depends on the area of garment fabric that is to be pleated.

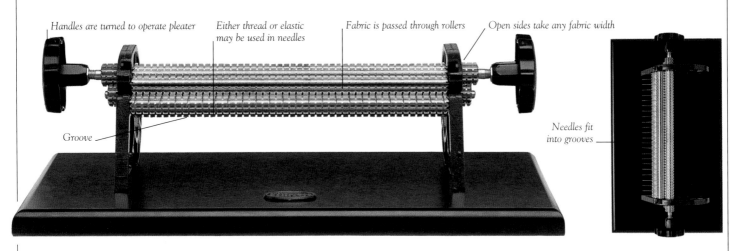

Handles are turned to operate pleater

Either thread or elastic may be used in needles

Fabric is passed through rollers

Open sides take any fabric width

Groove

Needles fit into grooves

Side view

Top view

SEWING AND FABRIC AIDS

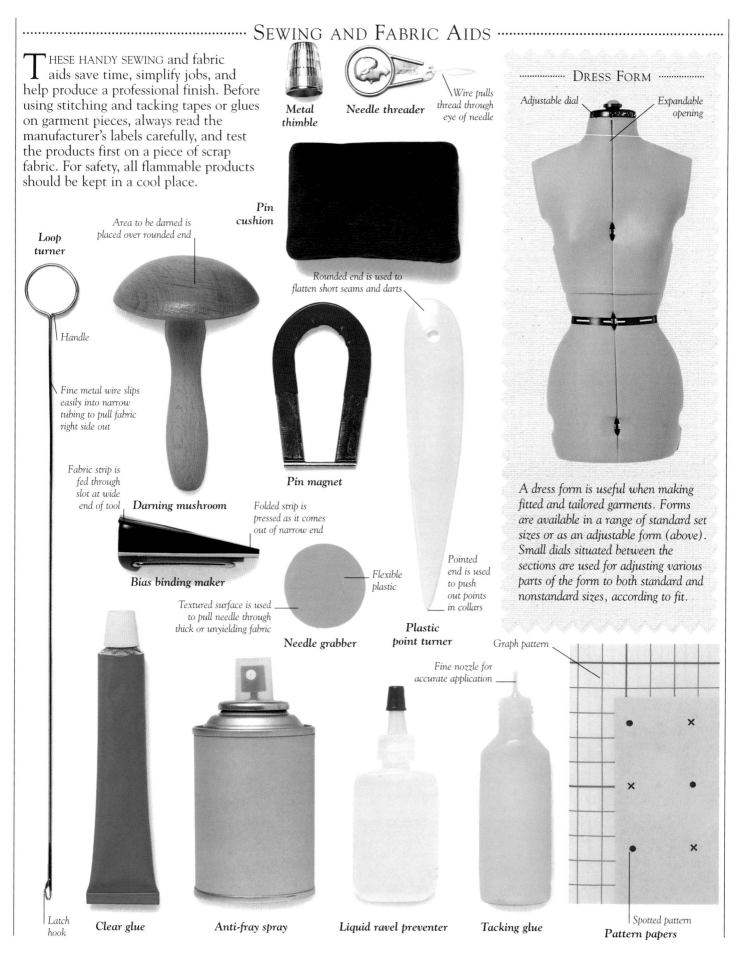

THESE HANDY SEWING and fabric aids save time, simplify jobs, and help produce a professional finish. Before using stitching and tacking tapes or glues on garment pieces, always read the manufacturer's labels carefully, and test the products first on a piece of scrap fabric. For safety, all flammable products should be kept in a cool place.

Metal thimble

Needle threader

Wire pulls thread through eye of needle

DRESS FORM

Adjustable dial

Expandable opening

A dress form is useful when making fitted and tailored garments. Forms are available in a range of standard set sizes or as an adjustable form (above). Small dials situated between the sections are used for adjusting various parts of the form to both standard and nonstandard sizes, according to fit.

Pin cushion

Loop turner

Area to be darned is placed over rounded end

Handle

Rounded end is used to flatten short seams and darts

Fine metal wire slips easily into narrow tubing to pull fabric right side out

Fabric strip is fed through slot at wide end of tool

Darning mushroom

Pin magnet

Folded strip is pressed as it comes out of narrow end

Bias binding maker

Textured surface is used to pull needle through thick or unyielding fabric

Needle grabber

Flexible plastic

Pointed end is used to push out points in collars

Plastic point turner

Graph pattern

Fine nozzle for accurate application

Latch hook

Clear glue

Anti-fray spray

Liquid ravel preventer

Tacking glue

Spotted pattern

Pattern papers

14

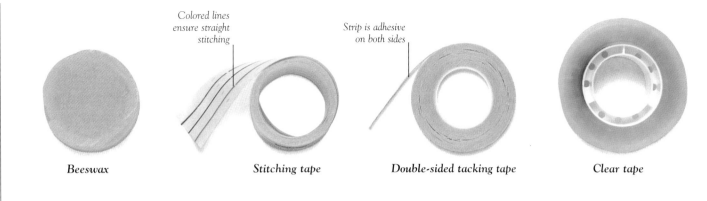

Colored lines ensure straight stitching

Strip is adhesive on both sides

Beeswax

Stitching tape

Double-sided tacking tape

Clear tape

PRESSING TOOLS AND AIDS

THE ONLY ESSENTIAL PRESSING TOOLS are a sturdy ironing board, a steam iron, and a pressing cloth. Although an iron that produces pressurized steam is ideal, one with a surge-of-steam feature is acceptable. The aids shown below are useful for details such as shaped pieces, narrow and inaccessible seams, and fabrics with a pile.

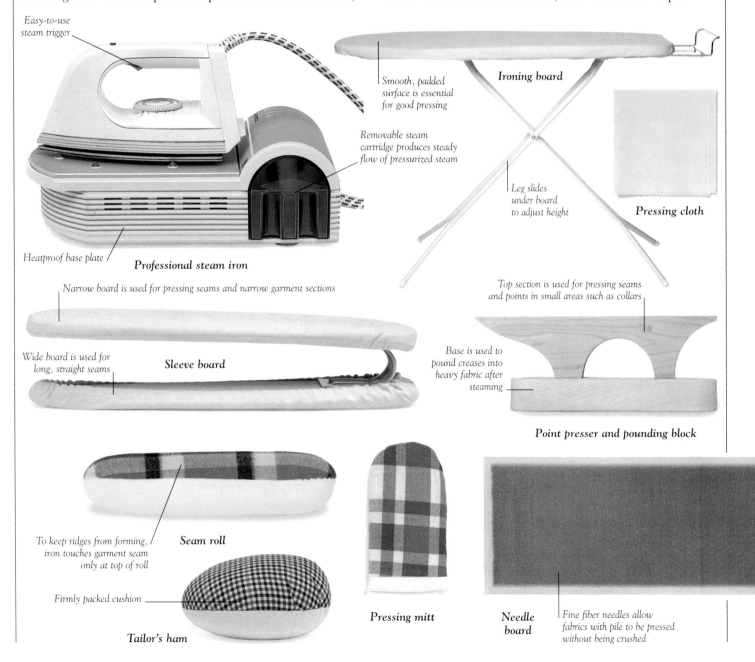

Easy-to-use steam trigger

Smooth, padded surface is essential for good pressing

Ironing board

Removable steam cartridge produces steady flow of pressurized steam

Leg slides under board to adjust height

Pressing cloth

Heatproof base plate

Professional steam iron

Narrow board is used for pressing seams and narrow garment sections

Top section is used for pressing seams and points in small areas such as collars

Wide board is used for long, straight seams

Sleeve board

Base is used to pound creases into heavy fabric after steaming

Point presser and pounding block

To keep ridges from forming, iron touches garment seam only at top of roll

Seam roll

Firmly packed cushion

Pressing mitt

Needle board

Tailor's ham

Fine fiber needles allow fabrics with pile to be pressed without being crushed

MACHINES FOR SEWING

A SEWING MACHINE or serger allows the operator to produce garments and home furnishing items with a professional finish quickly and with ease. Many different types of machine are available, from the manually operated to the computer programmed, and it is important to purchase a machine with at least the minimum of functions required, usually straight and zigzag stitches. Sewing machines and sergers have special machine feet and other attachments that are designed for specific tasks. These can generally be purchased separately. Both sewing and serger machines are available in a range of styles, depending on their brands and ages, but as long as the functions, attachments, and feet have the same names as on the following pages, the results will be the same as those demonstrated.

PARTS OF A SEWING MACHINE

THE TYPICAL electric sewing machine used in the home is a compact unit that can be adapted for a variety of tasks. The mechanisms of the machine are housed within a strong, molded body that allows easy access by means of hinged cases, a removable needle plate, and storage compartments for bobbins, needles, and accessories. The machine may have a hard, protective cover and a built-in handle.

Spool attachments
These attachments hold the spool of thread on the spool pin, enabling the thread to be fed through the machine and down to the needle.

Spool pin felt

Spool stand

Spool holder

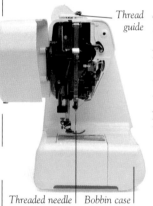

Thread guide

Threaded needle | *Bobbin case*

Foot holder clip

Presser foot

Plastic bobbin

Metal bobbin

Thread view
From the spool, thread passes through the tension control and the take-up lever, down to the needle. In the lower part of the machine, thread is wound on the bobbin (see below). Thread guides assist the flow of thread through the sewing machine.

Machine feet
The choice of machine foot is determined by the stitch required. A foot holds the fabric flat, guides the needle smoothly over the fabric, and is changed by means of a foot holder, clamp, clip, or screw.

Bobbins
The thread required to make a stitch is wound around a bobbin, which is inserted under the machine needle plate. Some machines have plastic bobbins; others have metal ones.

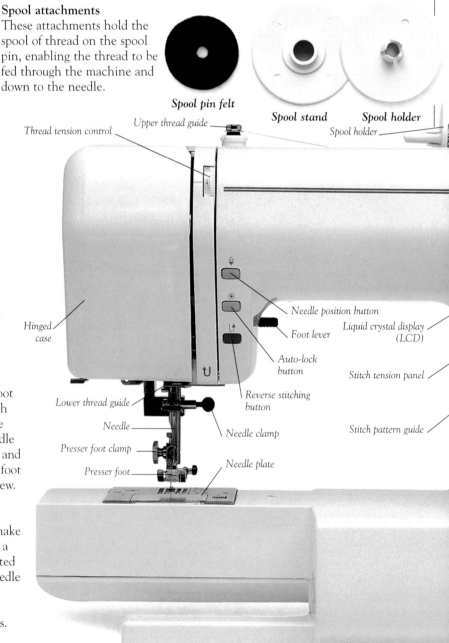

Thread tension control

Upper thread guide

Spool holder

Hinged case

Needle position button

Foot lever

Liquid crystal display (LCD)

Auto-lock button

Stitch tension panel

Lower thread guide

Reverse stitching button

Needle

Needle clamp

Stitch pattern guide

Presser foot clamp

Presser foot

Needle plate

ATTACHMENTS

Circular sewing guide
This guide is used to stitch a perfect circle or a combination of circles, using either straight or decorative stitching.

Seam gauge
Used as a straight seam guide, a seam gauge is attached to the needle plate and adjusted to the required measure.

Pintuck foot and cord guide
To make corded pintucks, a cord is fed through the guide on the plate. The foot sits over the fabric and the cord.

Ruffler
This foot produces tucked pleats from flat fabric and stitches the pleats into place in a single operation.

HOW A STITCH IS MADE

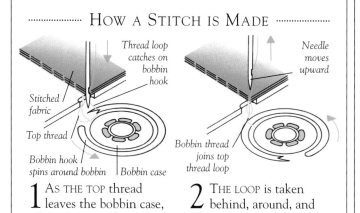

Thread loop catches on bobbin hook

Stitched fabric

Top thread

Bobbin hook spins around bobbin | *Bobbin case*

Needle moves upward

Bobbin thread joins top thread loop

1 AS THE TOP thread leaves the bobbin case, a loop forms and is picked up by the bobbin hook.

2 THE LOOP is taken behind, around, and off the bobbin, joining the top thread as a stitch.

STITCH TENSION

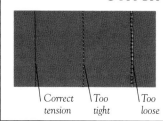

Correct tension *Too tight* *Too loose*

STITCH TENSION controls the amount of thread in a stitch. If the tension is too tight, there is too little thread for a stitch; if it is loose, there is too much.

Thread

Spool pin

Bobbin pin

Balance wheel

150

ACCESSORIES

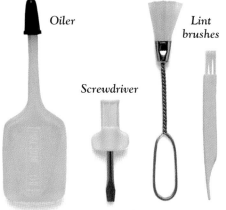

Oiler

Lint brushes

Screwdriver

A SEWING MACHINE needs frequent cleaning to prevent dust and residue left by fabrics and thread from clogging up the inner workings. Many machines are self-oiling, especially the drop-in bobbin models, but they still require cleaning.

Machine movement
A sewing machine is belt driven. The speed of the belt is controlled by a foot pedal, which turns the belt. This enables the moving parts to synchronize, forming both threads into stitches at a chosen speed.

Foot pedal

NEEDLES

Sharp-point needle for woven fabrics

Ball-point needle for knits

Wedge-point needle for leather

Twin needle for topstitching and decoration

Twin needle for stretch fabrics

Triple needle for decoration

Wing needle for detailed decoration

Blue-tip scarfed needle for synthetics and silks

Topstitching needle for thick threads

Denim needle for thick denims and canvas

NEEDLES ARE AVAILABLE in a range of sizes to suit fabrics of different thicknesses. Needles are also made for specific fabrics; for example, a ball-point needle is used for stitching knitted fabrics. Needles should be changed after each item is finished, as blunt needles can often mark fabric.

MACHINE FEET

MACHINE FEET allow a sewing machine to be used to full advantage. Each foot enables the machinist to sew an item, or piece of a garment, in a specific manner. While some machine feet can be used for a number of tasks, many cannot. Practicing with each foot on scraps of fabric allows the machinist to become familiar with the feet.

Quilter guide bar
This adjustable quilt guide stitches accurate quilt patterns.

All-purpose foot
This all-purpose foot is used for zigzag or straight stitch.

Overedge foot
When overedge stitching, this foot prevents flat fabric edges from curling.

Blind hem foot
Blind hems and tucks are formed with this foot.

Zipper foot
This foot allows the needle close to the zipper teeth.

Concealed zipper foot
This foot is used only for inserting an invisible zipper.

Piping foot
This foot is used for making and applying corded piping.

Pintuck foot
This uses twin needles to sew evenly spaced pintucks.

Narrow hemmer foot
A narrow hem is formed and stitched with this foot.

Quarter-inch seam foot
This foot sews a ¼-in (6-mm) seam allowance quickly.

Satin stitch foot
This foot outlines appliqué with dense zigzag stitches.

Gathering foot
This foot quickly creates soft gathers.

Automatic buttonhole foot
Using its sizer, this foot sets the buttonhole length.

Quilter guide bar

All-purpose foot

Overedge foot　*Blind hem foot*

Zipper foot

Concealed zipper foot　*Piping foot*　*Pintuck foot*

Narrow hemmer foot　*Quarter-inch seam foot*　*Satin stitch foot*　*Gathering foot*

Automatic buttonhole foot　*Sliding buttonhole foot*　*Button sew-on foot*

Beading foot

Embroidery foot

Fringe foot

Ribbon and sequin foot

Binder foot　*Roller foot*　*Nonstick foot*　*Walking foot with quilter guide*

Sliding buttonhole foot
This is ideal for stitching a four-step buttonhole to the required size.

Button sew-on foot
This foot holds flat buttons in place when stitching.

Beading foot
This has a deep groove for attaching decorative strings of beads to fabric.

Embroidery foot
A special foot, this is used for machine embroidery.

Fringe foot
This foot creates a decorative fringe using a continuous thread.

Ribbon and sequin foot
A special foot, this is used for applying ribbons and stitching sequins.

Binder foot
This foot folds, binds, and stitches bias binding.

Roller foot
This foot gives more control and less friction than the nonstick foot.

Nonstick foot
A nonstick coating makes this foot suitable for synthetic fabrics.

Walking foot with quilter guide
This foot helps match stripes and prevent slipping, and it stitches leather easily.

USING A SERGER

THE MAIN PURPOSE OF A SERGER is to clean finish or overlock seams, which it achieves by trimming while sewing. It is not a replacement for a sewing machine, which is needed for straight stitching, making buttonholes, and attaching zippers. However, a serger sews faster than a sewing machine, and there are attachments available that enable it to be particularly useful for a range of purposes, including stitching rolled hems, gathering, and attaching bindings. A serger is useful for finishing seams on knits such as jersey, since its unique, multithread stitching prevents the fabric from stretching along the seam.

Working a serger

When fabric enters the machine, it is moved through the feed dogs. These small, moving tracks push the fabric toward the blades, that then trim the fabric. The fabric is then stitched by the loopers and needles, and pushed out of the machine. Thread is fed from spools or cones, not bobbins, at the back of the machine which enables up to five threads to operate at once. A serger uses a two-blade cutting system, which works like a pair of scissors. The top blade moves, cutting against the under blade, trimming both the fabric and the thread.

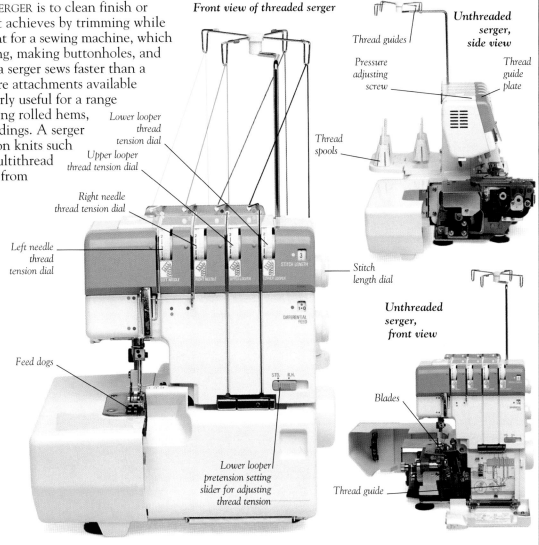

Front view of threaded serger

Thread guides

Unthreaded serger, side view

Pressure adjusting screw

Thread guide plate

Lower looper thread tension dial

Upper looper thread tension dial

Right needle thread tension dial

Thread spools

Left needle thread tension dial

Stitch length dial

Feed dogs

Unthreaded serger, front view

Blades

Thread guide

Lower looper pretension setting slider for adjusting thread tension

SERGER ATTACHMENTS

Stitching and trimming seam

Standard foot
This foot trims and overlocks a seam. The pin on the foot is placed under the groove of the foot holder, and the foot holder is lowered to lock the foot in place. The foot should be raised to check that it is secured.

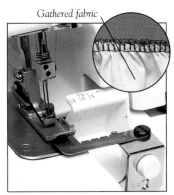

Gathered fabric

Gathering attachment
A gathering attachment is used for quick gathering, or to separate two layers of fabric while gathering, such as ruffles on hems or home furnishings, when one layer is gathered and the other is not.

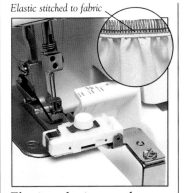

Elastic stitched to fabric

Elastic gathering attachment
An elastic gathering attachment is used for quick and easy sewing of elastic or decorative tape onto areas of fabric, such as waistbands. The elasticity of the tape can be changed by turning a screw.

Taping reel

Taping attachment
The taping attachment and reel is used for sewing tape onto a shoulder or armhole line to protect it from stretching, or for decoration. It works well when used with the taping or cording foot.

PATTERNS

WORKING WITH PATTERNS

A PATTERN has three main parts: the envelope, the guide sheet, and the pattern tissue. The envelope, which contains the other two components, is printed with a photograph or illustration of the garments, plus the information required to select the appropriate size of pattern and purchase the correct amount of fabric and notions. The guide sheet (or sheets) explains how to use the pattern and what the different pattern markings mean. It also gives cutting diagrams and sewing instructions. The tissue sheets are printed with full-size pattern pieces. Single-size patterns contain a one-size pattern only. Multisize patterns are marked with lines to cut three or four different sizes. Patterns are shown completed in catalogs, from which a selection can be made.

READING A PATTERN ENVELOPE

THE ENVELOPE FRONT illustrates the finished garment produced from the pattern. Different versions of the same garment are called views. On the envelope back, shown here, there are usually charts detailing the fabric amount required for each view. Size charts, recommended fabrics, and drawings of the garment detail are also given.

Number of pattern pieces

Design number for ordering pattern

Description of garment giving details of style and any different views included in pattern

Lists of pattern sizes in metric and imperial measurements for bust, waist, and hips in each size

Suggested fabrics suitable and unsuitable for garment

Notions required for each view

5678
15 PIECES

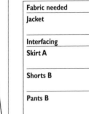

MISSES' UNLINED JACKET, SKIRT, SHORTS, AND PANTS.
Unlined, semi-fitted, V-neck jacket has short sleeves, front buttons, optional waistline darts, and optional breast pocket. Straight skirt, above mid-knee, and trousers or shorts with straight legs, have waistband, front pleats, side seam pockets, and back zipper.

FABRICS: Jacket, skirt, shorts, and trousers: wool crepe, soft cottons, sheeting, linen, silk, silk types, and lightweight woollens. Skirt, shorts, and trousers also challis, jacquards, and crepe.
Unsuitable for fabrics printed with obvious diagonals. Allow extra fabric in order to match plaids, stripes, or one-way design fabrics.

Use nap yardages/layouts for shaded, pile, or one-way design fabrics.
* with nap. **without nap
NOTIONS: Thread. Jacket: three ⅞ in (1.2 cm) buttons; ¼ in (6 mm) shoulder pads. Skirt, trousers: pkg of 1¼ in (3.2 cm) waistband interfacing; 7 in (18 cm) zipper; and one hook and eye closure.

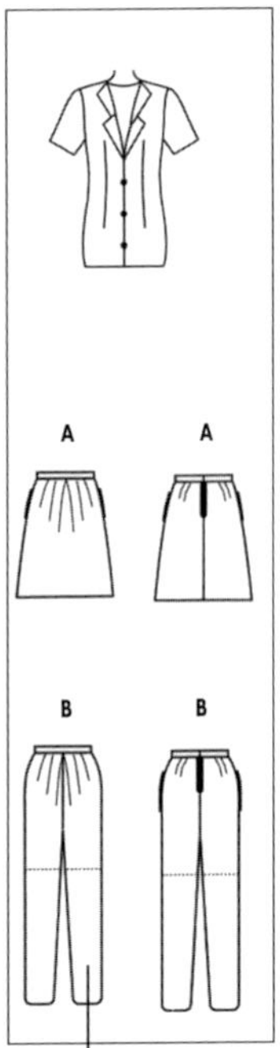

METRIC

Body measurements	(6	8	10)	(12	14	16)	(18	20	22)	
Bust	78	80	83	87	92	97	102	107	112	cm
Waist	58	61	63.5	66	71	76	81	86	94	cm
Hip	81	84	86	91	96.5	102	107	112	117	cm

Fabric needed		(6	8	10)	(12	14	16)	(18	20	22)	
Jacket	115 cm*/**	1.70	1.70	1.70	1.80	1.80	2.10	2.20	2.20	2.20	m
	150 cm*/**	1.30	1.30	1.30	1.40	1.70	1.70	1.70	1.80	1.80	m
Interfacing		1 m of 55–90 cm lightweight fusible or non-fusible									
Skirt A	115 cm*/**	1.6	1.6	1.6	1.6	1.9	1.9	1.9	1.9	2	m
	150 cm*/**	1.2	1.2	1.3	1.3	1.3	1.3	1.4	1.4	1.5	m
Shorts B	115 cm*/**	1.6	1.6	1.6	1.6	1.9	1.9	1.9	1.9	2	m
	150 cm*/**	1.2	1.2	1.3	1.3	1.3	1.3	1.4	1.4	1.5	m
Pants B	115 cm*/**	2.4	2.4	2.4	2.4	2.4	2.4	2.4	2.7	2.7	m
	150 cm*	2	2	2	2	2.1	2.1	2.2	2.3	2.3	m
	150 cm**	1.6	1.6	1.8	2	2	2.1	2.2	2.3	2.3	m

Garment measurements	(6	8	10)	(12	14	16)	(18	20	22)	
Jacket bust	92	94.5	97	101	106	111	116	121	126	cm
Jacket waist	81	83	86	89.5	94.5	100	105	110	116	cm
Jacket back length	73	73.5	74	75	75.5	76	77	77.5	78	cm
Skirt A lower edge	99	101	104	106	112	117	122	127	132	cm
Skirt A length	61	61	61	63	63	63	65	65	65	cm
Shorts B leg width	71	73.5	76	81	86.5	94	99	104	109	cm
Shorts B side length	49.5	50	51	51.5	52	52.5	53.5	54	54.5	cm
Pants B leg width	53.5	53.5	56	56	58.5	58.5	61	61	63.5	cm
Pants B side length	103	103	103	103	103	103	103	103	103	cm

IMPERIAL

Body measurements	(6	8	10)	(12	14	16)	(18	20	22)	
Bust	30½	31½	32½	34	36	38	40	42	44	in
Waist	23	24	25	26½	28	30	32	34	37	in
Hip	32½	33½	34½	36	38	40	42	44	46	in

Fabric needed		(6	8	10)	(12	14	16)	(18	20	22)	
Jacket	45 in*/**	1⅞	1⅞	1⅞	1⅞	2	2⅜	2⅜	2⅜	2⅜	yd
	60 in*/**	1⅜	1⅜	1⅜	1½	1⅞	1⅞	1⅞	1⅞	2	yd
Interfacing		1⅛ yd of 22–36 in lightweight fusible or non-fusible									
Skirt A	45 in*/**	1¾	1⅞	1⅞	1⅞	2	2	2	2	2⅛	yd
	60 in*/**	1¼	1¼	1⅜	1⅜	1⅜	1⅜	1½	1½	1⅝	yd
Shorts B	45 in*/**	1¾	1¾	1¾	1¾	2	2	2	2	2⅛	yd
	60 in*/**	1¼	1¼	1⅜	1⅜	1⅜	1⅜	1½	1½	1⅝	yd
Pants B	45 in*/**	2⅝	2⅝	2⅝	2⅝	2⅝	2⅝	2⅝	2⅞	2⅞	yd
	60 in*	2⅛	2⅛	2⅛	2⅛	2¼	2¼	2⅜	2½	2½	yd
	60 in**	1¾	1¾	1⅞	2⅛	2⅛	2¼	2⅜	2½	2½	yd

Garment measurements	(6	8	10)	(12	14	16)	(18	20	22)	
Jacket bust	36¼	37¼	38¼	39¾	41¾	43¾	45¼	47¾	49¾	in
Jacket waist	31¾	32¾	33¾	35¼	37¼	39¼	41¼	43¼	45¼	in
Jacket back length	28¾	29	29¼	29½	29¾	30	30¼	30½	30¾	in
Skirt A lower edge	39	40	41	42	44	46	48	50	52	in
Skirt A length	24	24	24	24¾	24¾	24¾	25½	25½	25½	in
Shorts B leg width	28	29	30	32	34	37	39	41	43	in
Shorts B side length	19½	19¾	20	20¼	20½	20¾	21	21¼	21½	in
Pants B leg width	21	21	22	22	23	23	24	24	25	in
Pants B side length	40½	40½	40½	40½	40½	40½	40½	40½	40½	in

Line drawing of garment, including back views showing darts and zipper position

Garment measurements box gives actual size of finished garment

Chart to follow for required fabric quantity, indicating size across top, and chosen view and correct width down side

UNDERSTANDING PATTERN MARKINGS

PATTERN MARKINGS are the lines, dots, and other symbols printed on a pattern to provide information. Often the most important are the straight arrows, which mark the grainline, and the bent arrows, which indicate where the pattern edge should be placed to the fold of fabric. One or other of these markings appears on each piece.

Pattern markings

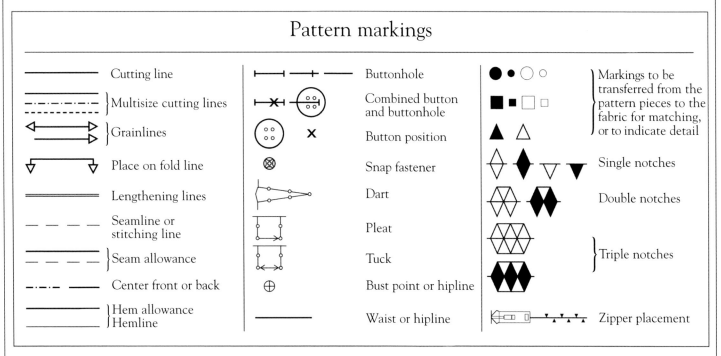

Cutting line	
Multisize cutting lines	
Grainlines	
Place on fold line	
Lengthening lines	
Seamline or stitching line	
Seam allowance	
Center front or back	
Hem allowance / Hemline	

Buttonhole	
Combined button and buttonhole	
Button position	
Snap fastener	
Dart	
Pleat	
Tuck	
Bust point or hipline	
Waist or hipline	

Markings to be transferred from the pattern pieces to the fabric for matching, or to indicate detail	
Single notches	
Double notches	
Triple notches	
Zipper placement	

MULTISIZE PATTERNS

THESE PATTERNS have the cutting lines for different sizes printed on the same pattern piece. The lines for each size are labeled, and are often drawn with a different type of line.

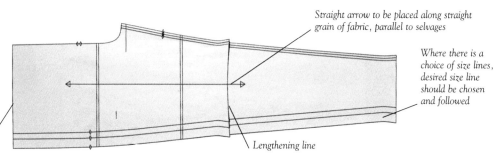

Straight arrow to be placed along straight grain of fabric, parallel to selvages

Where there is a choice of size lines, desired size line should be chosen and followed

Where there is one line only, it applies to all sizes

Lengthening line

SINGLE-SIZE PATTERNS

SINGLE-SIZE patterns are printed with a single cutting line that is appropriate to the size purchased.

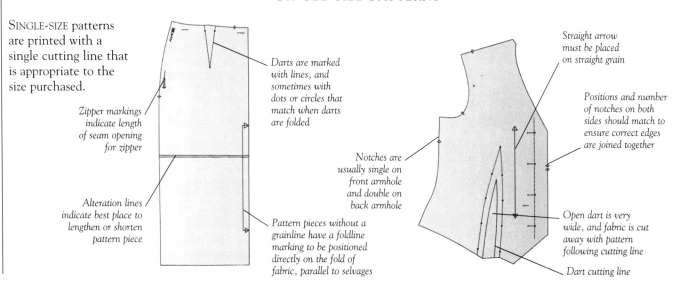

Zipper markings indicate length of seam opening for zipper

Alteration lines indicate best place to lengthen or shorten pattern piece

Darts are marked with lines, and sometimes with dots or circles that match when darts are folded

Notches are usually single on front armhole and double on back armhole

Pattern pieces without a grainline have a foldline marking to be positioned directly on the fold of fabric, parallel to selvages

Straight arrow must be placed on straight grain

Positions and number of notches on both sides should match to ensure correct edges are joined together

Open dart is very wide, and fabric is cut away with pattern following cutting line

Dart cutting line

TAKING AND COMPARING MEASUREMENTS

Accurate measurements are needed for choosing a pattern size. A perfect fit is ensured by comparing your own measurements to those of the pattern, taking ease into account (see below), and then by making any adjustments (p. 26–33). Pattern pieces are measured between the seamlines, not from edge to edge.

CHOOSING A PATTERN SIZE

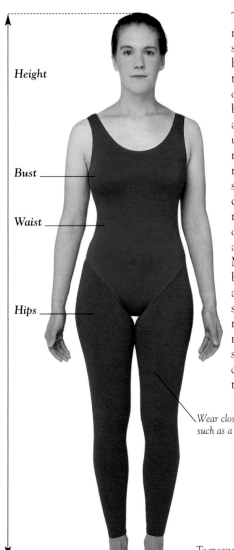

Height

Bust

Waist

Hips

THE BODY measurements needed for choosing a pattern size are the bust, waist, hips, height, and the back of neck to waist. Wearing a leotard or underwear and standing barefoot and straight, have a friend measure you. It is unlikely that your body measurements will exactly match a specific pattern size, so choose the size that comes closest to your largest measurement. Keep a record of your body measurements, and update them regularly. Measure height by standing barefoot with your back against a wall or similar flat surface, and by placing a ruler flat on your head and marking the height on the surface. Then measure the distance from the floor to the mark on the wall.

Wear close-fitting clothes, such as a leotard and leggings

To measure height accurately, it is important not to wear shoes of any type

MINIMUM WEARING EASE

Ease is included in pattern measurements, and is the difference in size between a body measurement and a pattern piece. It varies according to garment style and should be taken into account when adjusting the fit. Below is the minimum basic "wearing" ease for a close-fitting garment.

Bust	3 in (7.5 cm)	Crotch depth	⅝ in (1.5 cm)
Waist	1 in (2.5 cm)	Front crotch length	⅝ in (1.5 cm)
Hips	2 in (5 cm)	Back crotch length	⅝ in (1.5 cm)

HIPS

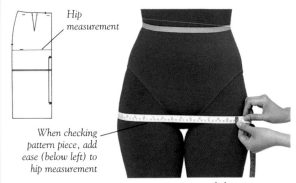

Hip measurement

When checking pattern piece, add ease (below left) to hip measurement

MEASURE AROUND THE FULLEST PART of the hips, 7–9 in (18–23 cm) below the waist (above), depending on height. Choose a pattern for pants or a skirt by hip size rather than waist size.

WAIST

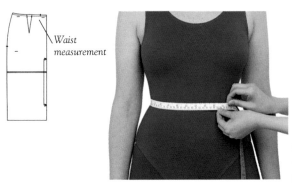

Waist measurement

TIE A RIBBON (or string) loosely around the waist, and move to let it settle at the natural waistline. Measure around this marker with a tape measure (above). Do not pull the tape measure tight. Leave the marker in place for taking other measurements.

BUST

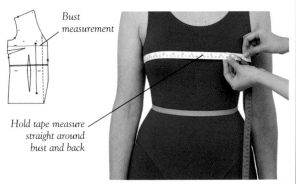

Bust measurement

Hold tape measure straight around bust and back

KEEPING THE TAPE MEASURE straight, measure around the fullest part of the bust and the widest part of the back (above). When using a pattern for a top only, choose your size by the bust measurement.

HIGH BUST

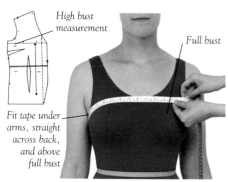

High bust measurement

Full bust

Fit tape under arms, straight across back, and above full bust

MEASURE THE HIGH BUST above the full bust (above). If the high bust is more than 2 in (5 cm) bigger than the full bust, choose the pattern size by the high bust.

BUST POINT

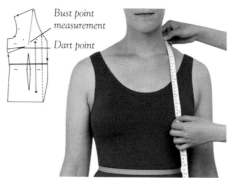

Bust point measurement

Dart point

FROM THE EDGE of the shoulder seam at the neck base, measure to the full bust (above). Measure to 1 in (2.5 cm) from the dart point, and compare to the pattern.

BACK OF NECK TO WAIST

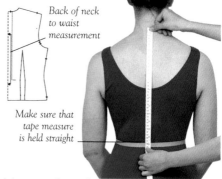

Back of neck to waist measurement

Make sure that tape measure is held straight

MEASURE from the protruding vertebra at the neck base to the waistline marker (above). This measurement should be compared to the pattern piece for fit.

SHOULDER LENGTH

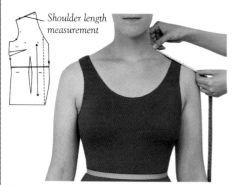

Shoulder length measurement

FIND THE BASE of the neck by shrugging the shoulders. Measure from the base of the neck to the shoulder edge (above). Compare to the pattern shoulder seam.

SLEEVE LENGTH

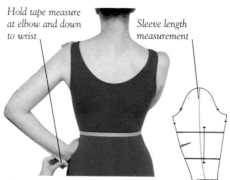
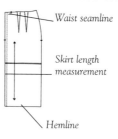

Hold tape measure at elbow and down to wrist

Sleeve length measurement

PLACE HAND ON HIP, and measure from shoulder to elbow, then down to the wrist (above). Check the sleeve pattern length and the position of any elbow shaping.

SKIRT LENGTH

Waist seamline

Skirt length measurement

Hemline

MEASURE down the back from the waistline marker to the desired skirt length (right). Compare to the pattern piece down the center back, from the waist seamline to the hemline.

PANTS LENGTH

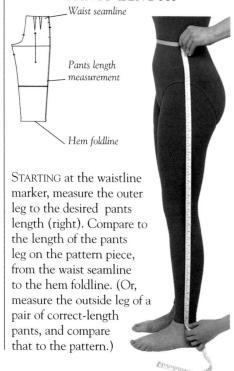

Waist seamline

Pants length measurement

Hem foldline

STARTING at the waistline marker, measure the outer leg to the desired pants length (right). Compare to the length of the pants leg on the pattern piece, from the waist seamline to the hem foldline. (Or, measure the outside leg of a pair of correct-length pants, and compare that to the pattern.)

CROTCH LENGTH

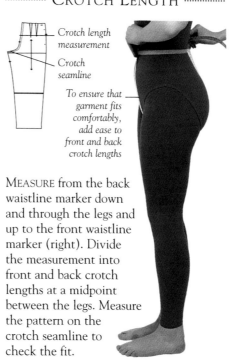

Crotch length measurement

Crotch seamline

To ensure that garment fits comfortably, add ease to front and back crotch lengths

MEASURE from the back waistline marker down and through the legs and up to the front waistline marker (right). Divide the measurement into front and back crotch lengths at a midpoint between the legs. Measure the pattern on the crotch seamline to check the fit.

CROTCH DEPTH

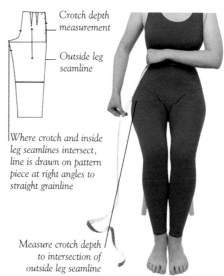

Crotch depth measurement

Outside leg seamline

Where crotch and inside leg seamlines intersect, line is drawn on pattern piece at right angles to straight grainline

Measure crotch depth to intersection of outside leg seamline

SIT DOWN, and measure from the waistline marker to the seat (above). Measure the pattern crotch depth from the waist seamline down the outside leg seamline.

LENGTHENING AND SHORTENING PATTERNS

THE SIMPLEST PLACE TO LENGTHEN or shorten a pattern is at the hemline, but this is not always practicable. Often a pattern needs to be altered while retaining the original width at the hemline or at a design feature such as a kick pleat. Sometimes a specific area of a pattern needs lengthening or adjusting, between bust and waist, or waist and hips. If a pattern does not have printed lengthening and shortening lines, follow the guidelines below.

Always alter the front and the back the same amount and at the same places.

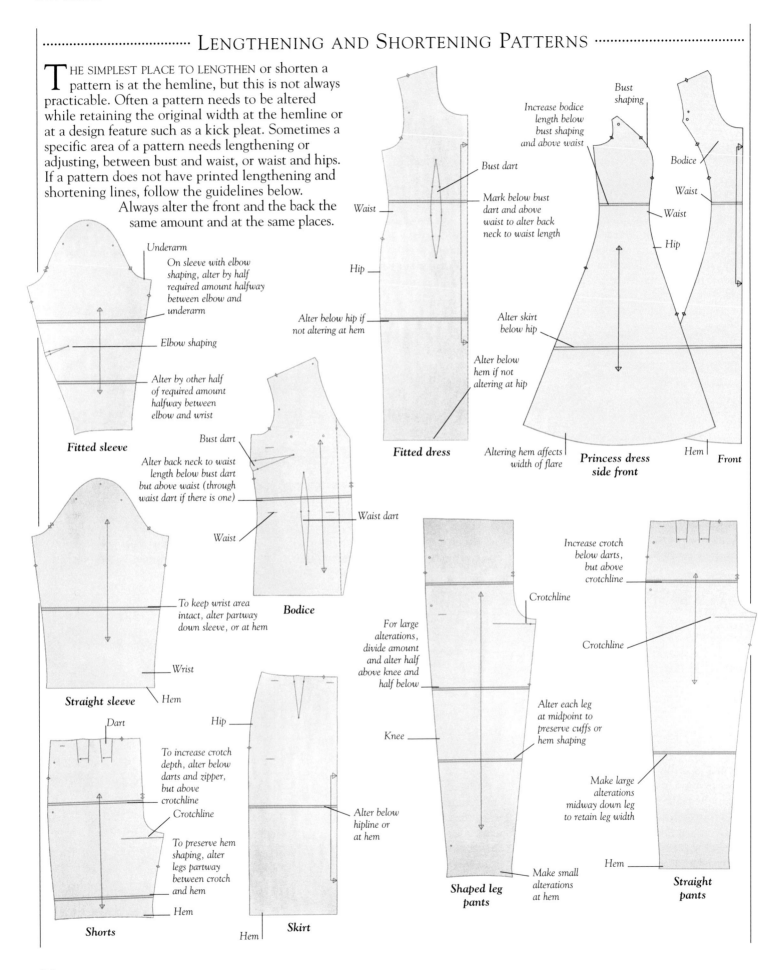

Fitted sleeve

Underarm

On sleeve with elbow shaping, alter by half required amount halfway between elbow and underarm

Elbow shaping

Alter by other half of required amount halfway between elbow and wrist

Straight sleeve

To keep wrist area intact, alter partway down sleeve, or at hem

Wrist

Hem

Shorts

Dart

To increase crotch depth, alter below darts and zipper, but above crotchline

Crotchline

To preserve hem shaping, alter legs partway between crotch and hem

Hem

Bodice

Bust dart

Alter back neck to waist length below bust dart but above waist (through waist dart if there is one)

Waist

Waist dart

Skirt

Hip

Alter below hipline or at hem

Hem

Fitted dress

Waist

Bust dart

Mark below bust dart and above waist to alter back neck to waist length

Hip

Alter below hip if not altering at hem

Alter below hem if not altering at hip

Princess dress side front

Bust shaping

Increase bodice length below bust shaping and above waist

Waist

Alter skirt below hip

Altering hem affects width of flare

Front

Bodice

Waist

Hip

Hem

Shaped leg pants

Crotchline

For large alterations, divide amount and alter half above knee and half below

Knee

Alter each leg at midpoint to preserve cuffs or hem shaping

Make small alterations at hem

Straight pants

Increase crotch below darts, but above crotchline

Crotchline

Make large alterations midway down leg to retain leg width

Hem

LENGTHENING A PATTERN

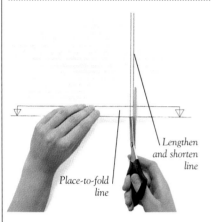

1 TO LENGTHEN a pattern piece, determine the change needed, then cut the pattern along the lengthen and shorten line, across the foldline or the grainline, depending on the pattern piece (left). Extend the straight grain arrow, if there is one, across the lengthen and shorten line.

Lengthen and shorten line

Place-to-fold line

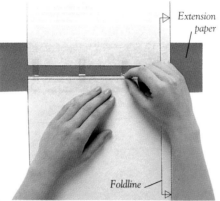

2 ON A STRIP of scrap paper, draw two parallel lines equal to the required increase. Position the cut edges of the pattern on these lines. Use a ruler to check that the foldline or the straight grainline is equal on all the pieces of paper. Tape or pin the pattern to the spare paper (left), then trim at the sides.

Extension paper

Foldline

SHORTENING A PATTERN

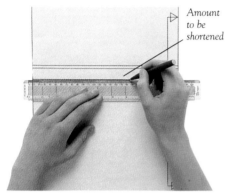

Amount to be shortened

1 EXTEND the foldline, if there is one, across the lengthen and shorten line. Draw a line across and parallel to the lengthen and shorten line, the amount to be shortened away from it (above).

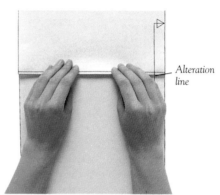

Alteration line

2 FOLD the lengthen and shorten line down to the newly drawn line, folding a pleat in the pattern paper (above). Check that the straight grainline, or the foldline, is lining up correctly.

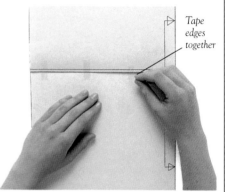

Tape edges together

3 SECURE THE FOLD with tape (above) or pins. (If the shortening causes jagged side edges, draw the cutting edges again to rejoin the original lines smoothly before cutting out the pattern.)

LENGTHENING ACROSS DARTS

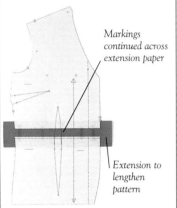

Markings continued across extension paper

Extension to lengthen pattern

CUT ACROSS the pattern and lengthen it the required amount by inserting a strip of paper (see above). Draw the dart stitching line so that it continues across the paper, ensuring that there are no jagged side edges.

SHORTENING ACROSS DARTS

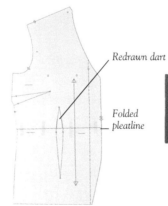

Redrawn dart

Folded pleatline

DRAW a line across the pattern piece, and fold down to shorten the pattern (see Shortening a Pattern, above). Trim the side edges. Redraw the dart stitching lines across the alteration to eliminate any jagged lines.

LENGTHENING A HEM EDGE

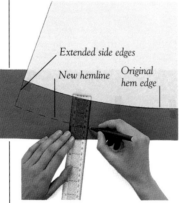

Extended side edges

New hemline *Original hem edge*

ATTACH PAPER to the lower hem edge. Measure the hem extension, and mark it on the paper at intervals (above). Mark more closely on the curves. Smoothly connect the marks. Extend the side edges, and cut along the new lines.

SHORTENING A HEM EDGE

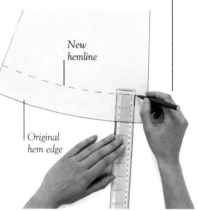

New hemline

Original hem edge

MEASURE UP from the lower hem edge, and mark in the new hemline the required amount up from the hem edge (above). The more curved the hem, the closer the marks should be. Connect the marks and cut along the hemline.

MAKING BUST ALTERATIONS

Bust shaping can be repositioned or altered. When a small alteration is made to raise or lower the bust shaping, the dart remains basically in the same place with only the point being moved. For large alterations, the whole dart is raised or lowered to improve the garment fit. For increases or decreases, the waist dart must be altered too.

RAISING A BUST DART

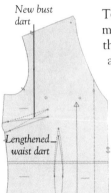

New bust dart

Lengthened waist dart

To raise a bust dart, mark the position of the new dart point above the original dart point. Redraw the bust stitching lines from the new point to meet the original base seamline points. Waist darts can be lengthened in the same way.

RAISING A BUST DART SUBSTANTIALLY

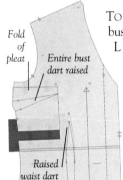

Fold of pleat

Entire bust dart raised

Raised waist dart

To raise the whole bust dart, cut a reverse L shape below the dart and up past the dart point. Press in a pleat across the pattern above the dart. Tape paper over the gap, and adjust the waist darts.

INCREASING AN UNDERARM BUST DART

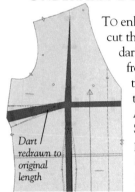

Dart redrawn to original length

To enlarge a bust dart, cut through the bust dart to the center front. Cut through the waist dart up to the shoulder. Add the paper. Spread apart the pattern, tapering into the shoulder and the waist. Redraw the darts.

LOWERING A BUST DART

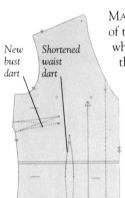

New bust dart

Shortened waist dart

Mark the position of the new dart point, which will be below the original one. Redraw the bust stitching lines from the new point to the original base seamline points. Shorten the waist darts correspondingly.

LOWERING A BUST DART SUBSTANTIALLY

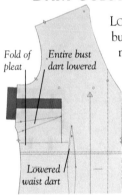

Fold of pleat

Entire bust dart lowered

Lowered waist dart

Lower the entire bust dart with this method. Cut across the pattern above the dart, and down past the dart point. Pleat below the dart to lower it. Tape paper behind the gap, and shorten the waist dart.

INCREASING A DIAGONAL BUST DART

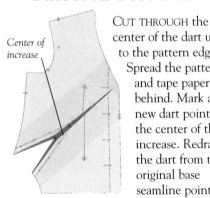

Center of increase

Cut through the center of the dart up to the pattern edge. Spread the pattern, and tape paper behind. Mark a new dart point at the center of the increase. Redraw the dart from the original base seamline point.

RAISING A CURVED BUST SEAM

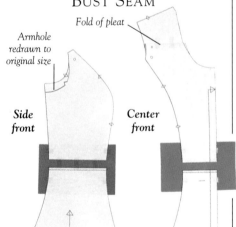

Fold of pleat

Armhole redrawn to original size

Side front

Center front

Fold a pleat across the center front between the shoulder and armhole. Add the same amount above the waist to the front and side front. Lower the armhole on the side front by the same amount.

LOWERING A CURVED BUST SEAM

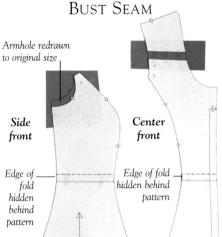

Armhole redrawn to original size

Side front

Center front

Edge of fold hidden behind pattern

Edge of fold hidden behind pattern

Cut across the center front halfway between the shoulder and underarm. Spread the pieces, and pleat up the center front and side front by the altered amount. Add paper. Redraw the armhole.

ADJUSTING A CURVED SEAM

New line tapered into old lines above and below alterations

Side front

Center front

To add up to a 2 in (5 cm) bust increase, divide the required increase by four. Add this quarter amount at the center of the bust shaping on a paper extension. Taper the increase to join the original seamline.

MAKING SHOULDER ALTERATIONS

THESE SIMPLE ALTERATIONS adjust the angle of the shoulderline, which can be raised to accommodate square shoulders, or lowered for sloping shoulders. Before either alteration, the armhole must be traced and redrawn afterward by a compensating amount so that the sleeve or facing fits. Both front and back are altered in the same way.

SHOULDER ALTERATIONS FOR SQUARE SHOULDERS

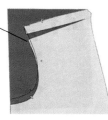

Armhole redrawn to compensate for sleeve or facing alteration

CUT across the pattern pieces 1¼ in (3 cm) below and parallel to the shoulderline from the armhole to the neck seamline. Add paper, and open out the pattern at the armhole edge. Redraw the armhole.

SHOULDER ALTERATIONS FOR SLOPING SHOULDERS

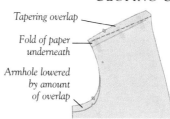

Tapering overlap

Fold of paper underneath

Armhole lowered by amount of overlap

CUT across the pattern 1¼ in (3 cm) below and parallel to the shoulderline from the armhole to the neck seamline. Overlap the cut edges by the required amount. Lower the armhole by the same amount.

PREPARING A SHOULDER PATTERN FOR ALTERATION

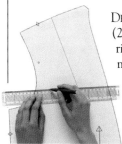

DRAW A LINE 8 in (20 cm) long down at a right angle from the middle of the shoulder. Draw a second line from the middle of the shoulder across to the armhole notch (left).

ADJUSTING TO FIT BROAD SHOULDERS

Shoulderline redrawn

CUT from the shoulder edge to the armhole seamline along the marked lines. Add new paper. Angle the shoulder corner outward, and tape in place. Redraw the shoulderline.

ADJUSTING TO FIT NARROW SHOULDERS

Shoulderline redrawn

CUT along the marked lines, and angle the shoulder corner inward to form an overlap. Tape paper behind the pattern, and redraw the new shoulderline.

ALTERING CROTCH LENGTH

ALTERING THE CROTCH LENGTH accommodates a large stomach or a prominent or flat bottom. Altering at the crotch point, the intersection of the crotch seam and the inner leg seam, increases or decreases the top of the legs. When altering just for the stomach or bottom, the crotch seam method is used to increase or decrease where necessary.

INCREASING A CROTCH POINT

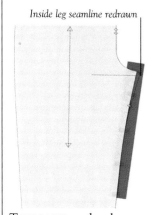

Inside leg seamline redrawn

TAPE PAPER under the pattern to extend the crotch length. Mark a new point outside the seamline. Redraw the inside leg seam from the new crotch point, tapering it smoothly to join the original seamline.

DECREASING AT CROTCH POINT

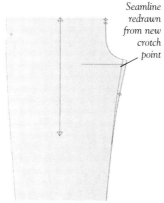

Seamline redrawn from new crotch point

MARK the new crotch length on the pattern inside the old crotch length. Starting at the new crotch point, redraw the inside leg seamline, tapering it to join the original seamline. Trim the pattern.

INCREASING AT CROTCH SEAM

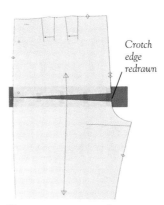

Crotch edge redrawn

CUT THE PATTERN along the alteration line from the crotch across to the outside leg seamline. Add paper, and open out the pattern at the crotch seam. Tape, and redraw the crotch edge.

DECREASING AT CROTCH SEAM

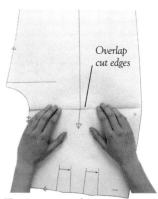

Overlap cut edges

TO DECREASE the crotch length, cut the pattern piece along the alteration line from the crotch to the outside leg seamline. Overlap the cut edges (above) to reduce the seam and tape in place.

INCREASING WAISTLINES

Waistlines can be increased by up to ¾ in (2 cm) by adding to the side seams. A quarter of the increase is added to each side seam, front and back, and the new lines are tapered smoothly into the original at hip level. For larger increases, the alteration is spread around the waist by reducing the side seams and the width of the darts.

INCREASING AT A SEAM

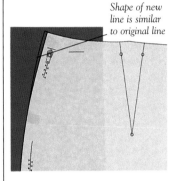

Shape of new line is similar to original line

ADD NEW PAPER to the edge of the pattern, and tape in place. Extending the waistline, measure the increase from the pattern edge, and mark. Draw a new line from the mark, tapering the line gradually to rejoin the original line smoothly at hip or bust level. Alter both the front and back by the same amount.

INCREASING AT A DART

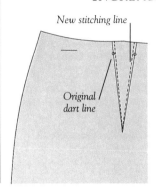

New stitching line

Original dart line

TO INCREASE the size of a waistline at the darts, the darts have to be reduced in width. Mark the new stitching line inside the original dart line at the waist, joining it to the original point. Fold the dart, and recut across the waist edge. The distance between the old line and the new line at each side of the dart is the amount of increase. Alter all darts equally.

FITTED SKIRT

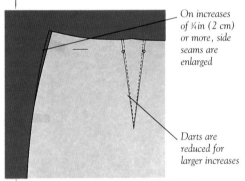

On increases of ¾ in (2 cm) or more, side seams are enlarged

Darts are reduced for larger increases

ON INCREASES of up to ¾ in (2 cm) overall, add a quarter of the total increase required to the front and back of each side seam. On larger increases, reduce the width of the darts as well as the side seam to accommodate some of the increase.

GORED SKIRT

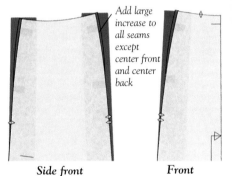

Add large increase to all seams except center front and center back

Side front   **Front**

ADD SMALL INCREASES of up to ¾ in (2 cm) overall to side seams only, in the same way as on a fitted skirt. For larger increases, divide the amount evenly between all the seams (above), except the center front and center back seams.

FULL CIRCLE SKIRT

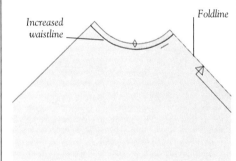

Increased waistline

Foldline

TO INCREASE the waist measurement on a full circle skirt, lower the waistline so that the seamline (not the edge) is a quarter of the total increase required, not including the seam allowance. Increase the length at the hem edge to compensate.

PANTS

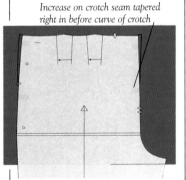

Increase on crotch seam tapered right in before curve of crotch

MAKE small increases of up to ¾ in (2 cm) overall at the side seams. Larger increases can be divided between the side seams, darts, and crotch seam (above). Alter the front and back equally at the side seams.

FITTED DRESS

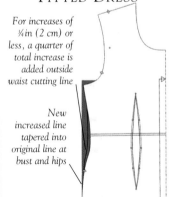

For increases of ¾ in (2 cm) or less, a quarter of total increase is added outside waist cutting line

New increased line tapered into original line at bust and hips

FOR INCREASES of more than ¾ in (2 cm), reduce the width of the darts to release some of the increase before increasing at the seams (above). Alter the front and back equally.

PRINCESS SEAMS

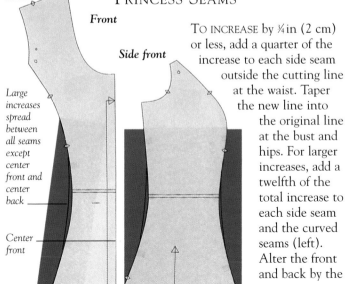

Front

Side front

Large increases spread between all seams except center front and center back

Center front

TO INCREASE by ¾ in (2 cm) or less, add a quarter of the increase to each side seam outside the cutting line at the waist. Taper the new line into the original line at the bust and hips. For larger increases, add a twelfth of the total increase to each side seam and the curved seams (left). Alter the front and back by the same amount.

DECREASING WAISTLINES

SMALL WAISTLINE decreases can be made at the side seams. For large decreases, it is best to alter both side seams and darts to distribute the alteration around the garment. If this makes the darts too large, two smaller darts can be made on either side of each original dart position. In general, the front and back are altered by the same amount.

DECREASING AT A SEAM

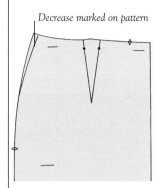

Decrease marked on pattern

MEASURE THE AMOUNT of the required decrease in from the pattern edge, and mark. Draw a new line from the mark, tapering gradually to rejoin the original pattern line smoothly at the hip or the bust. Keep the shape of the new line similar in shape to that of the original line. At the side seams, alter the front and back seam by the same amount.

DECREASING AT A DART

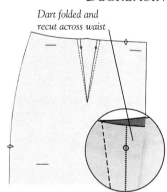

Dart folded and recut across waist

TO DECREASE the waistline at a dart, each dart must be made wider. Mark the new stitching line outside the original at the waist, and join to the original point. Add new paper to the waist edge, fold the dart, and recut. The distance between the old and the new dart lines is the amount of the decrease. Alter all the darts equally.

FITTED SKIRT

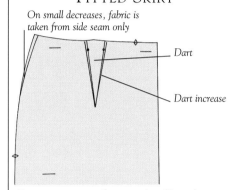

On small decreases, fabric is taken from side seam only

Dart

Dart increase

ON DECREASES of up to ¾ in (2 cm) in total, take a quarter of the total decrease off each side seam (above). Alter the front and back equally. On decreases of more than ¾ in (2 cm), also increase the width of the darts to take in some of the alteration.

GORED SKIRT

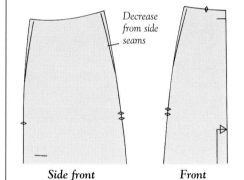

Decrease from side seams

Side front   **Front**

ON DECREASES up to ¾ in (2 cm) overall, take a quarter of the total decrease off the side seams only (above). For larger decreases, divide the amount of alteration evenly between all the seams except the center front and center back.

FULL CIRCLE SKIRT

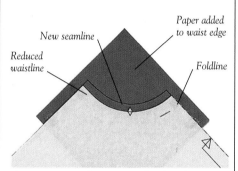

New seamline

Reduced waistline

Paper added to waist edge

Foldline

ADD PAPER to the waist edge for the alteration. Raise the waistline so that the seamline (not the edge) is a quarter of the total measurement required, not including the seam allowance. Reduce the hem length to compensate.

PANTS

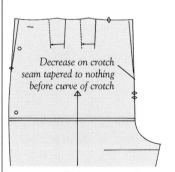

Decrease on crotch seam tapered to nothing before curve of crotch

MAKE small decreases of up to ¾ in (2 cm) overall at the side seams. Alter the front and the back equally at the side seams. Divide larger decreases between all of the side seams (above), darts, and crotch seam.

FITTED DRESS

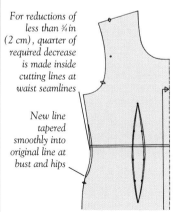

For reductions of less than ¾ in (2 cm), quarter of required decrease is made inside cutting lines at waist seamlines

New line tapered smoothly into original line at bust and hips

FOR DECREASES of more than ¾ in (2 cm), increase the width of the darts to accommodate the extra fabric taken from the alteration at the side seams.

PRINCESS SEAMS

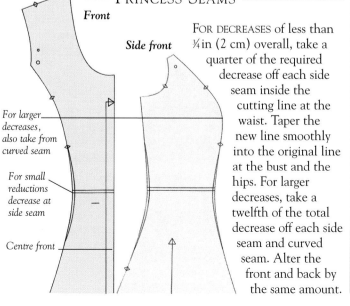

Front

Side front

For larger decreases, also take from curved seam

For small reductions decrease at side seam

Centre front

FOR DECREASES of less than ¾ in (2 cm) overall, take a quarter of the required decrease off each side seam inside the cutting line at the waist. Taper the new line smoothly into the original line at the bust and the hips. For larger decreases, take a twelfth of the total decrease off each side seam and curved seam. Alter the front and back by the same amount.

WIDENING A PATTERN AT THE HIPLINE

To widen the hipline by up to 2 in (5 cm), a quarter of the increase is added to each front and back side seam. To widen the hipline by more than 2 in (5 cm), the increase is spread across all the seams by cutting the pattern and spreading it a quarter of the increase apart on both front and back pieces. The new hiplines taper into the waistline.

FITTED SKIRT

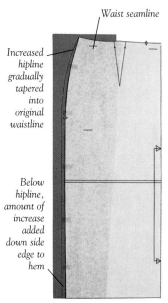

Waist seamline

Increased hipline gradually tapered into original waistline

Below hipline, amount of increase added down side edge to hem

TO INCREASE up to 2 in (5 cm), add a quarter of the increase to each side of the front and back hipline. Below the hip, continue the increase down the side seam to the hem.

FITTED SKIRT FOR LARGE HIPS

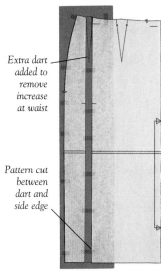

Extra dart added to remove increase at waist

Pattern cut between dart and side edge

TO INCREASE by more than 2 in (5 cm), cut between the dart and side edge. Add paper, and space each pattern edge a quarter of the total increase apart. Add any darts needed.

FITTED SKIRT FOR PROMINENT HIP BONES

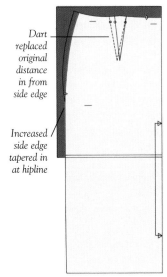

Dart replaced original distance in from side edge

Increased side edge tapered in at hipline

ADD THE INCREASE into the front and back side seams, as for a fitted skirt. Position the dart the original distance from the side seam. Increase the dart width to take in the alteration.

FITTED SKIRT FOR LARGE BOTTOM

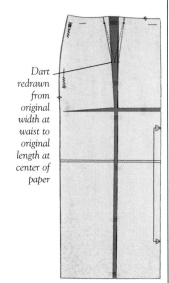

Dart redrawn from original width at waist to original length at center of paper

CUT the skirt back from the dart center to the hem. Cut across the hipline from the center back to, but not through, the side seamline, and spread. Redraw the dart.

GORED SKIRT OR PRINCESS DRESS

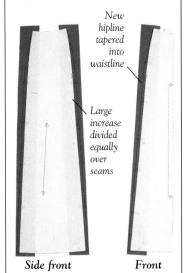

New hipline tapered into waistline

Large increase divided equally over seams

Side front   **Front**

FOR INCREASES up to 2 in (5 cm), alter the side seams. To alter by more than this, spread the increase across the seams, except the center front and back. Taper into the waistline.

PANTS

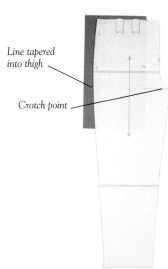

Line tapered into thigh

Crotch point

ADD a quarter of the increase to all the side seams at the hipline, and taper the line into the waist and thigh. On straight pants, continue the increase down the side seams.

PANTS FOR LARGE BOTTOM

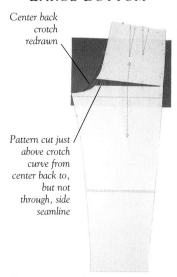

Center back crotch redrawn

Pattern cut just above crotch curve from center back to, but not through, side seamline

CUT ACROSS the pattern at the hipline, just above the curve of the crotch point. Add paper, spread out the pattern, and stick down with tape. Redraw the crotch edge.

LARGE INCREASE ON FITTED DRESS

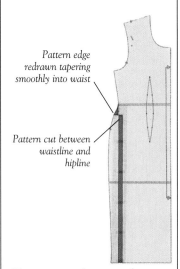

Pattern edge redrawn tapering smoothly into waist

Pattern cut between waistline and hipline

TO INCREASE by more than 2 in (5 cm), cut between waist and hip, and down to the hem. Add paper. Spread the edges a quarter of the increase. Alter the back in the same way.

DECREASING A PATTERN AT THE HIPLINE

THE HIPLINE CAN BE DECREASED just at the hip area when the reduction required is small and on styles where the original width around the hemline is needed.

For large alterations, the garment has a smoother line if the decrease is tapered in from the waistline to the hip, and the same reduction continued down to the hemline.

FITTED SKIRT

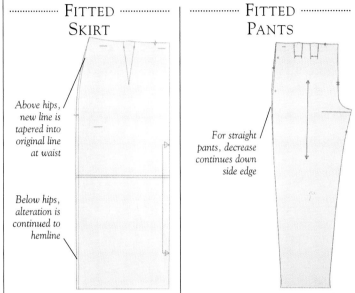

Above hips, new line is tapered into original line at waist

Below hips, alteration is continued to hemline

TO DECREASE up to 2 in (5 cm), take a quarter of the decrease from the front and back hipline. Above the hips, taper the line into the waist. Below, continue to the hem.

FITTED PANTS

For straight pants, decrease continues down side edge

DECREASE BY A QUARTER of the reduction required on the hipline at each side. Taper out smoothly to the original seamline just below the waist and around the thigh.

GORED SKIRT OR PRINCESS DRESS

Small increases at side seam

Increased spread over seams

Side front   **Centre**

MAKE DECREASES up to 2 in (5 cm) as for Fitted Skirt (see left). To decrease by more, divide the amount between the seams, except center front and back. Taper into the waistline.

ALLOWING FOR A SWAY BACK

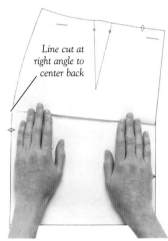

Line cut at right angle to center back

DRAW A LINE across the hipline from the center back up to, but not through, the side seam. Fold along the line, pleating the excess to nothing at the side seam (above). Tape.

MAKING ALTERATIONS TO FITTED SLEEVES

SLEEVES THAT FIT the arm closely may need alteration. When the alteration increases the sleeve cap, the excess can be eased into the armhole, or the armhole size can be increased by lowering the underarm. If the sleeve cap is reduced, the underarm must be raised. Any extra fabric added at the elbow is eased into the sleeve seam.

ENLARGING A SLEEVE

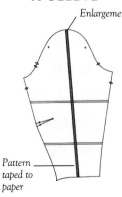

Enlargement

Pattern taped to paper

CUT the sleeve pattern down the center, parallel to the grainline. Add paper, and spread the pattern edges apart. Tape to the paper.

ENLARGING A SLEEVE CAP

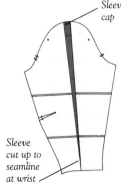

Sleeve cap

Sleeve cut up to seamline at wrist

CUT the sleeve pattern down the center, parallel to the grainline, leaving the wristline intact. Spread the edges apart. Tape to the paper.

ENLARGING AT AN ELBOW

Line drawn centrally

Armhole edge

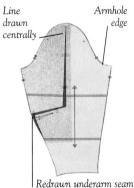

Redrawn underarm seam

DRAW and cut the lines in a backward L shape. Spread the pattern, leaving the armhole edge intact. Redraw the underarm seam.

FOR TIGHT UNDERARMS

Sleeve cap cut to seamline

Sleeve cut across at base of sleeve cap

CUT the pattern as shown above. Spread the pattern edges the required distance apart. Redraw the underarm from the new corners.

SLEEVES FOR THIN ARMS

Fold of pleat

Pleat edges taped together

TO DECREASE a sleeve width, make a pleat down the center of the pattern, tape, and cut out. Decrease the armhole to fit (p. 29).

CUTTING FABRICS

BEFORE CUTTING OUT a pattern, examine the fabric. A fabric is woven by using lengthwise (warp) and crosswise (weft) threads. The selvage is the woven, nonfrayable edge that runs parallel to the lengthwise grain. A diagonal line intersecting both grainlines is called a bias. The true bias is at a 45-degree angle to both grainlines, and has the most stretch. Check the fabric for a nap and one-way designs. If the fabric looks different from one direction, select one fabric end as the top, and follow the "with-nap" layout included in the pattern envelope. Look over the fabric to see if there are any flaws that need to be avoided when cutting, and, if it is very creased, press it before laying out the pattern. Prepare a clean surface on which to cut out the fabric, and assemble the equipment that will be required.

LOOKING AT FABRIC GRAIN AND NAP

FABRICS WITH A NAP, as well as those with any one-way design, are described as being "with nap." Nap indicates that the fabric has a pile or brushed surface that can be smoothed in one direction only. Fabrics without a nap can be cut out at any angle because the direction will not show. "With-nap" fabrics are cut out using a "with-nap" layout.

WOVEN FABRICS

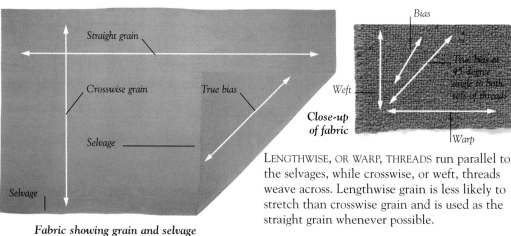

Straight grain

Crosswise grain

True bias

Selvage

Selvage

Fabric showing grain and selvage

Bias

True bias at 45-degree angle to both sets of threads

Weft

Close-up of fabric

Warp

LENGTHWISE, OR WARP, THREADS run parallel to the selvages, while crosswise, or weft, threads weave across. Lengthwise grain is less likely to stretch than crosswise grain and is used as the straight grain whenever possible.

JERSEY FABRICS

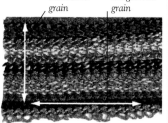

Crosswise grain

Lengthwise grain

KNITTED JERSEY fabrics have ribs of stitches lengthwise and stretchier rows of stitches crosswise. Some jersey fabrics are tubular and must be cut down a lengthwise rib.

CHECKING FABRIC DESIGNS

Fabric is darker on one side

Pattern appears different on each side

Stripes run horizontally on fabric length

Designs with nap
Velvets, corduroy, and velour fabrics have a visible color difference on one side when they are held upside down.

One-way designs
These have a pattern, often floral, that appears different depending on the direction from which it is viewed.

Stripes and checks
To test these for unevenness, grasp the fabric in the center of the length. See whether the pattern matches on both areas.

NAP DIRECTION ON FABRIC

Deciding which direction the nap should run on a fabric depends on the effect desired from the fabric. Short naps, such as those on corduroy, are generally cut with the nap running down, which feels smoother to the touch and gives a soft look to the fabric. Long piles, such as on fur fabric, should be cut with the nap running down.

OBTAINING STRAIGHT EDGES ON FABRIC

IF A FABRIC HAS NOT BEEN CUT PROPERLY from the roll, that is, at a right angle to the selvage, the ends must be straightened by cutting across the crosswise grain. To check grain, the fabric is folded in half lengthwise, with selvages together and cut ends even. If the ends are hard to even up, fabric can be stretched diagonally to correct the distortion.

PULLING THREADS

Pull thread close to edge

ON LOOSELY WOVEN, even-weave fabrics, clip the selvedge and separate a crosswise thread. Pull the single thread right out (above) then cut along the thread line.

CUTTING ON A LINE

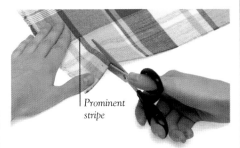

Prominent stripe

ON WOVEN CHECKS and crosswise stripes, cut along one of the most prominent stripes (above). Avoid any fabrics with horizontal patterns printed off the grain.

CUTTING JERSEY KNITS

ON JERSEY KNITS with large stitches, cut across following a row of stitches (above). On finer jerseys, it may be necessary to mark the line with basting before cutting.

PREPARING PATTERN PIECES

WHEN A FABRIC IS READY for cutting, the pattern tissue should be removed from its envelope and the guide sheets opened out. The pieces must be chosen and separated, then smoothed out flat, since any creases or tucks in the tissue will distort the shape. If the pattern is very crumpled, it can be pressed flat with a warm dry iron.

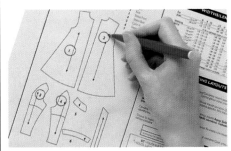

1 FIND THE PATTERN PIECE identification section, with drawings of the pattern pieces, on the guide sheet. Identify and mark the pieces required (above).

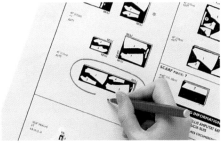

2 SELECT THE CUTTING layouts on the leaflet. Circle the correct layout for the garment view, size, fabric width, and with or without nap (above).

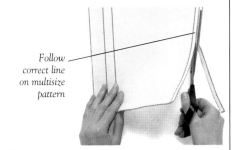

Follow correct line on multisize pattern

3 CUT the pieces from the pattern tissue (above). Cut single-size pieces roughly. Cut multisize pieces accurately to the chosen size to avoid confusion.

SINGLE-SIZE PATTERNS

Single-size pattern pieces do not need to be cut exactly to shape. Cut roughly around them before pinning them to the fabric and cutting out (above).

EASY MULTISIZE PATTERN ALTERATIONS

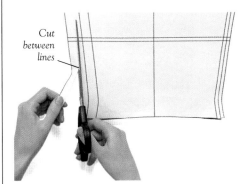

Cut between lines

Between sizes
For body measurements between sizes, cut the pattern between the two size lines. Cut accurately between the lines (above).

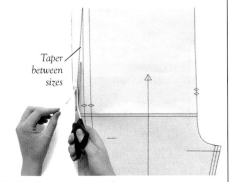

Taper between sizes

Individual pattern adjustments
With, for example, large hips and a small waist, cut to the hips on the larger size. Taper to the next size down to the waist.

INTERPRETING A CUTTING LAYOUT

PATTERN PIECES USUALLY REPRESENT the right side of a garment. When placed right side up on a double fabric layer, the right and left sides are cut at the same time.

When it is necessary to cut the right and left pieces separately using the same pattern piece, one must be cut printed side down and the other with the printed side up.

GENERAL GUIDE TO LAYING OUT A PATTERN

WHEN POSITIONING pattern pieces with straight arrows, keep the arrows parallel to the selvage so the fabric will be straight when cut. Pieces with a straight line and bent arrows should be cut double on the fabric. For a fabric with a nap, the layout must run in the same direction and so a pattern piece can be reversed, placed printed side down, and cut on a single layer.

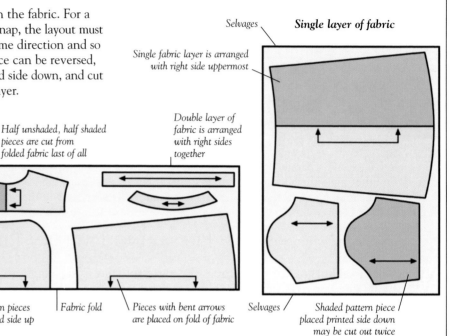

Single layer of fabric

Single fabric layer is arranged with right side uppermost

Double layer of fabric is arranged with right sides together

Folded piece of fabric

Selvages

Half unshaded, half shaded pieces are cut from folded fabric last of all

Pattern pieces extending across fold are cut last from single fabric layer

Unshaded pattern pieces are placed printed side up

Fabric fold

Pieces with bent arrows are placed on fold of fabric

Selvages

Shaded pattern piece placed printed side down may be cut out twice

LAYOUTS FOR FABRICS WITH NAP OR ONE-WAY DESIGN

FABRICS with a nap or one-way design must be laid out in one direction. Decide on the "top" of the fabric, and follow this direction when placing the pattern pieces, so that the nap will run in one direction. One-way designs are arranged on the fabric according to the pattern or the garment design.

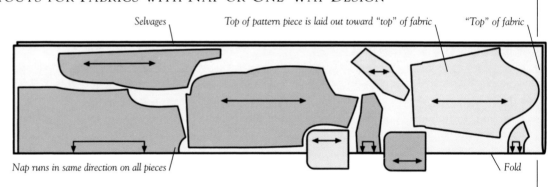

Selvages

Top of pattern piece is laid out toward "top" of fabric

"Top" of fabric

Nap runs in same direction on all pieces

Fold

CROSSWISE FOLD

THERE ARE two reasons for the garment fabric to be folded crosswise at the layout stage. Often, this type of fold is made to accommodate the widest pattern pieces. Alternatively, it may be needed to fit those pattern pieces that have a complex shape onto the fabric area.

Selvages

Fold

Crosswise fold

CROSSWISE FOLD WITH NAP

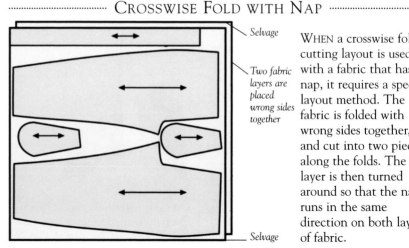

Selvage

Two fabric layers are placed wrong sides together

Selvage

WHEN a crosswise fold cutting layout is used with a fabric that has a nap, it requires a special layout method. The fabric is folded with wrong sides together, and cut into two pieces along the folds. The top layer is then turned around so that the nap runs in the same direction on both layers of fabric.

PARTIAL FOLD

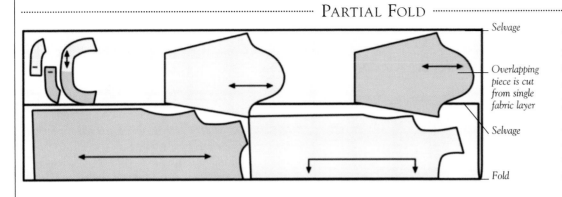

Selvage

Overlapping piece is cut from single fabric layer

Selvage

Fold

THE FABRIC is folded partway for this layout, so that one section of the fabric forms a double layer on a fold and the other forms a single layer. Where a pattern piece to be cut from a single layer overlaps the double layer, cut out the piece from the single fabric layer only.

PINNING A PATTERN TO A FABRIC

BEFORE PINNING PATTERN PIECES to a fabric, fold the fabric in half lengthwise with right sides together, unless the cutting layout shows otherwise. Each pattern piece has a straight grainline arrow or a bent arrow for an edge placed on the fold. Straight grainline arrows must be parallel to the selvage or fold. Pin the pieces to the fabric.

WORKING IN A SMALL SPACE

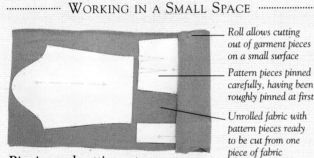

Roll allows cutting out of garment pieces on a small surface

Pattern pieces pinned carefully, having been roughly pinned at first

Unrolled fabric with pattern pieces ready to be cut from one piece of fabric

Pinning and cutting out
With the pattern pieces pinned to the fabric, loosely roll up the fabric and the attached pattern pieces. Cut out the pieces in one area at a time, unrolling the fabric section by section.

Pins should be spaced about 3¼–4 in (8–10 cm) apart on straight edges and closer on curves

Fold

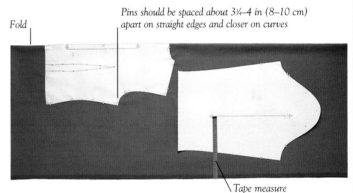

Tape measure

CHECK THAT THE DISTANCE from each grainline arrow end to the selvage is the same measurement. Check also that the fold edge of the pattern pieces aligns with the fabric fold, otherwise the piece will be smaller or larger than the correct size. Pin each of the arrow ends to the fabric, then pin around the pattern pieces.

CUTTING

TO CUT OUT PATTERN PIECES, the scissors should be slid along the cutting surface, making long cuts on the straight edges and shorter cuts at the curves. Care should be taken to cut smoothly to avoid making jagged edges. A pair of sharp sewing scissors (p. 11) must be used – never blunt ones, which would make the fabric edges look ragged.

CUTTING METHOD

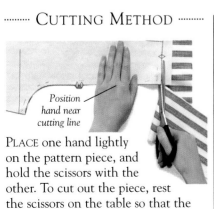

Position hand near cutting line

PLACE one hand lightly on the pattern piece, and hold the scissors with the other. To cut out the piece, rest the scissors on the table so that the fabric is slightly raised, but not lifted high up. Cut smoothly (above).

NOTCHES

Double notch

CUT AROUND the notches. Cut across from notch point to point on double notches rather than trying to cut around each notch separately.

SLEEVE CAPS

Make small clip at marking at top of sleeve

TO MARK the center of the shoulder on a sleeve, clip into the seam allowance at this point (above), or make a tailor's tack at the marking.

CLIPS

Clip edge of fabric at pattern marking

PATTERN markings such as foldlines, center front lines, and darts can be marked with small clips at the edges of the fabric (above).

WORKING WITH CHECKS AND STRIPES

IF STRIPES RUN ACROSS THE WIDTH of a fabric when a garment is cut out, they will run across the finished garment. If the stripes run along the length of a fabric parallel to the selvage, they will run down the finished garment. Checks combine lengthwise and widthwise stripes. Stripes that make up a check are called bars.

CHECKING FABRIC ON A ROLL

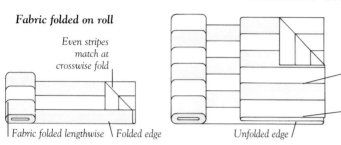

Fabric folded on roll

Even stripes match at crosswise fold

Fabric folded lengthwise   Folded edge

Fabric not folded on roll

Right sides uppermost

Fabric folded back on itself

Unfolded edge

WHEN BUYING FABRIC, find out if a check or stripe is even or uneven by checking on the roll. If the fabric is folded lengthwise on the roll, fold back one corner diagonally to compare the right side of the fabric areas. If the fabric is unfolded on the roll, double it back to form three layers. With the corner of the fabric folded back, it is possible to compare the two fabric areas right side up.

STRIPES

FOLD BACK the corner of the fabric diagonally to check if stripes are even or uneven. Even stripes are symmetrical on both areas of the fabric, and uneven stripes do not match.

Even stripes   **Uneven stripes**

CHECKS

FOLD CHECKS across a corner through the center of a repeat. Even checks are symmetrical on both fabric areas. Uneven checks may be uneven lengthwise, widthwise, or both.

Even checks   **Uneven checks**

MATCHING FABRICS

ON EVEN CHECKS AND STRIPES, fold the fabric in half lengthwise, centering a large stripe along the fold. Pin the two layers together near the selvages (above).

MATCHING POCKETS

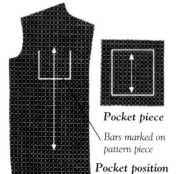

Pocket piece

Bars marked on pattern piece

Pocket position

WHEN POSITIONING patch pockets, place the pocket pattern piece on the fabric, and mark the main bars or stripes of the fabric on the pattern piece. Pin, matching the markings to the bars or stripes.

MATCHING PATTERN SEAMS

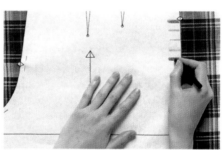

1 FOR A CHECK FABRIC, place the pattern so that the dominant bars are on, or close to, the garment edge. Pin on the pattern. Using a pencil or crayon, mark the positions of the bars near a notch on the pattern side seam (above).

3 ON THE FRONT pattern piece, mark the position of a prominent bar or stripe where it crosses the armhole seam marked on the pattern piece at, or just above, the front armhole notch (above).

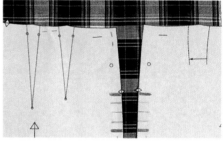

2 LAY OUT the adjoining pattern piece with notches matching and side seams even. Trace the pencil or crayon markings across to the wrong side of the pattern. Match the markings to the dominant bars as before.

4 POSITION THE SLEEVE pattern pieces next to the front pattern piece, aligning the front armhole notch. Trace the marked line on the bodice pattern piece across to the sleeve piece.

LAYING OUT CHECKS AND STRIPES

ON EVEN CHECKS and stripes, the fabric is folded in half with a prominent bar running along the fold. Consideration must be given to where the stripes will look best on the finished garment. On uneven checks and stripes, the fabric is opened out to a single layer. Each pattern piece is laid out and, if necessary, turned over to make a pair.

EVEN CHECKS

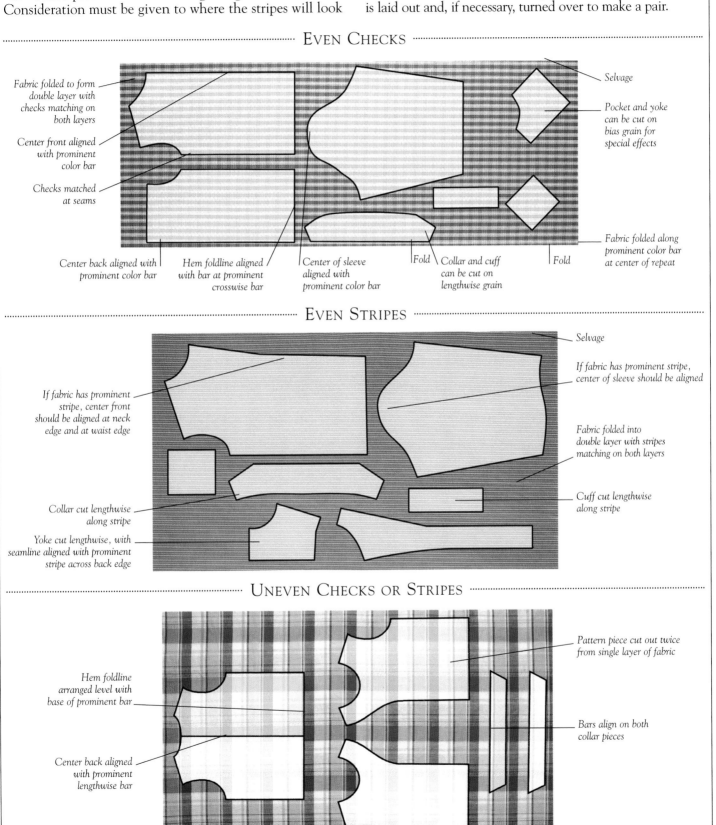

Fabric folded to form double layer with checks matching on both layers

Center front aligned with prominent color bar

Checks matched at seams

Selvage

Pocket and yoke can be cut on bias grain for special effects

Center back aligned with prominent color bar

Hem foldline aligned with bar at prominent crosswise bar

Center of sleeve aligned with prominent color bar

Fold

Collar and cuff can be cut on lengthwise grain

Fold

Fabric folded along prominent color bar at center of repeat

EVEN STRIPES

Selvage

If fabric has prominent stripe, center front should be aligned at neck edge and at waist edge

If fabric has prominent stripe, center of sleeve should be aligned

Fabric folded into double layer with stripes matching on both layers

Collar cut lengthwise along stripe

Yoke cut lengthwise, with seamline aligned with prominent stripe across back edge

Cuff cut lengthwise along stripe

UNEVEN CHECKS OR STRIPES

Pattern piece cut out twice from single layer of fabric

Hem foldline arranged level with base of prominent bar

Bars align on both collar pieces

Center back aligned with prominent lengthwise bar

Selvage

FABRICS, THREADS, & NOTIONS

COTTON FABRICS

ONE OF THE MOST VERSATILE, traditional, and popular fabrics available, cotton has been used as a fabric for making clothes for many centuries. It is a natural material, made by twisting together the long, fibrous hairs that cover the seed pods of the cotton plant. These fibers vary in length and thickness, and have an absorbent quality, making cotton both soft and comfortable to wear. The longest, finest, and most lustrous fibers, such as Egyptian and Sea Island, make the best-quality cottons. Cotton varies greatly in weight and quality, ranging from lightweight, loosely woven sheers to heavy, napped fabrics such as velvet. Other fibers, such as silk, are often blended with cotton to produce a durable, mixed-fiber fabric. Many easy-care, crease-resistant fabrics are blends of cotton and synthetic fibers. Cotton fabrics are widely used for dressmaking, as well as for bed linen, and upholstery and other home-furnishing fabrics.

TESTING FOR CREASING ON FABRIC

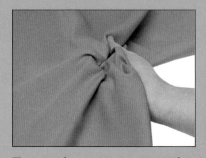

TO TEST the crease resistance of a fabric before purchasing it, crush a piece of the fabric in one hand. Release the fabric, and check how much it has crushed and how quickly the creases fall out.

PRESSING TO MARK FOLDLINES

Fold wrong sides together

Foldline

TO FORM A FOLD in a lightweight cotton, use the pattern markings as a guide, and fold the fabric with wrong sides together. Press along the foldline. This should hold the fold without the need for pinning.

JERSEY
The quality of jersey varies. A good-quality jersey has fine, knit stitches, drapes well, and is crease resistant. It is used for sportswear, dresses, and T-shirts.

GINGHAM
A lightweight, plain-weave, strong fabric with even checks, gingham is often used for blouses, skirts, children's clothes, and table linen.

MADRAS COTTON
This lightweight, plain-weave fabric creases easily and is woven in different colors to form checks or patterns. It is used mostly for making casual clothes.

CHAMBRAY
Chambray is a light- to mediumweight, plain-weave fabric. It is easy to sew and wears well. It is often used for shirts and children's wear.

**CHINTZ
(GLAZED COTTON)**
This is a closely woven, plain-weave fabric with a glazed finish. It wears well and is used mainly for home furnishings and dresses.

POPLIN
A fine and cross-rib mediumweight fabric with a plain weave, poplin is both versatile and absorbent. It is used mainly for shirts, blouses, and dresses.

SEERSUCKER
This is a lightweight fabric woven with alternating stripes of puckered fabric and flat fabric. It is often used for shirts, suits, and children's clothes.

LAWN
A lightweight, crisp, and plain-weave fabric, lawn is smooth and absorbent. It is often used for sewing blouses, soft collars, cuffs, baby dresses, and underwear.

MUSLIN
This cotton-blend or cotton fabric has a plain, open weave. It is used as an interlining in tailoring, for window treatments, and when sewing test garments.

CRINKLE COTTON
Also called crepon, this is pure cotton but may contain other fibers. It is soft and absorbent, and comfortable to wear. It is used mostly for dresses and blouses.

SPORTS NET
This is a see-through mesh fabric with large holes formed between thick, interlinking threads. It is used mainly for sports and fashion garments.

VOILE
A fine and sheer fabric with a plain weave, voile can be either plain or printed. It is often used for children's clothes, blouses, dresses, blinds, and curtains.

LACE
This decorative fabric is made from knotted, looped, or twisted thread. It is used as a trimming on items such as dresses, curtains, and table linen.

CAMBRIC
A fine, smooth, firm, plain-weave fabric that is closely woven, cambric is often used for children's and baby clothes, blouses, and handkerchiefs.

CHEESECLOTH
A soft, loosely woven fabric, cheesecloth has a plain weave, a rough finish, and a crinkled appearance. It is mostly used for blouses, shirts, skirts, and nightwear.

EYELET
A plain-weave cotton or cotton–synthetic mix, this fabric has shaped, embroidered eyelets punched in it, and is used for dresses, nightwear, and table linen.

CALICO
This is a coarse, lightweight fabric that has a plain weave. It is used for mattress covers and sheeting. It is also used in tailoring to make test garments.

DAMASK
A double-sided, woven fabric, damask has a satin weave against a plain background. It is used mainly for jackets, vests, curtains, linens, and upholstery.

DENIM
This is a strong and washable, densely woven, twill-weave fabric. It is used mainly for casual clothes such as jeans, jackets, shirts, and work clothes.

TICKING
This twill-weave cotton or cotton-blend fabric has even stripes. It is used mostly for covering pillows and mattresses, as well as for making home furnishings.

MOLESKIN
A mediumweight, firm fabric, moleskin has a fine nap on one side, giving a brushed surface. It is used mainly for work clothes, casual shirts, and children's pants.

WINCEYETTE
This is a soft and warm, brushed-cotton fabric with a plain weave. It is easy to handle and is commonly used for bed linen and nightwear. It is highly flammable.

DRILL
This is a strong, cotton fabric with a drill weave. When dyed an olive color, it is known as khaki. It is often used for uniforms, casual wear, and work clothes.

TERRY CLOTH
This fabric has uncut loops of cotton on the surface. High-quality terry cloth has loops on both sides of the fabric. It is used mainly for towels and bathrobes.

CORDUROY
A hard-wearing fabric, corduroy has lengthwise "wales" of pile that brush smoothly one way. Wales vary in size. The cloth is often used for sportswear, shirts, and childrenswear.

BRUSHED COTTON
This warm, plain or printed cotton has surface fibers that are brushed on one side. It is used mostly for casual shirts, warm linings, and children's clothes.

COTTON VELVET
Velvet is a woven fabric with a silky pile or nap on the right side. The pile brushes smoothly one way. It is often used for evening wear and home furnishings.

WOOLEN FABRICS

WOOL IS A NATURAL ANIMAL FIBER spun from the fleece of sheep. The finest wools are made of short fibers, with the longer fibers producing a coarser fabric. There are several types of specialty wools. These include mohair, angora, and cashmere, spun from the hair of certain breeds of goats, and alpaca, which is produced from the hairs of the alpaca, a close relative of the llama. Specialty wools are very soft and tend to be expensive because they are produced in relatively small quantities. They are often mixed with sheep's wool to add luster and to improve the drape of the fabric. Wool is a versatile fabric and is available in several different weights, textures, and weaves, plain and twill weave being the most common. It is comfortable to wear and absorbs moisture well. It is also flame resistant, water repellent, and elastic. Wool is usually easy to clean, but it can be permanently damaged by sunlight, moths, bleach, and incorrect pressing.

········ PRESSING WOOL ········   ········ PRESSING DARTS ········

Pressing cloth

Dart

TO AVOID A SHINE when pressing woolen fabrics, use a damp pressing cloth, and press on the wrong side of a garment. Do not use a sliding motion during ironing, since this may stretch the fabric out of shape.

TO PRESS A DART, particularly on thick woolen garments, place the point of the iron under the dart or the seam allowance to avoid producing indentations on the right side of the garment.

WORSTED
This high-quality fabric is made from tightly woven woolen yarns. It is hardwearing, does not sag easily, and is used mainly for suits, coats, and upholstery.

FLANNEL
A strong fabric with a plain or twill weave, flannel has a napped finish on one or both sides. It is commonly used for suits, jackets, skirts, and pants.

CASHMERE
Obtained from
the Kashmir goat,
cashmere is a very fine,
soft fabric that is warm
and comfortable to
wear. It is often used
for scarfs and coats.

TARTAN
Tartan is a checked
twill-weave fabric.
Careful pattern layout
is needed to match the
fabric designs. Tartan is
used mainly for dresses,
coats, skirts, and kilts.

CREPE
This is a fine, soft fabric
with a slack weave and
textured surface. Crepe
is springy to handle,
but soft types drape
well. It is often used
for dresses and suits.

COATING
A bulky fabric usually
woven on its outer
surface, coating often
has a prominent nap. It
is used for large, loosely
fitted garments such as
coats and capes.

GABARDINE
A variety of fibers and
wool blends is used to
make this fabric, which
has a close twill weave.
It is water repellent
and is used mainly for
coats, skirts, and pants.

MODERN TWEED
This tweed is a thick woven fabric that is produced in a wider range of colors and patterns than traditional tweeds. It is mostly used for jackets and pants.

TRADITIONAL TWEED
This rough, thick woollen fabric has a distinct woven pattern. It is named after the area of origin, as in Harris tweed, and is generally used for suits.

DOUBLE COATING
A bulky, reversible fabric made from two layers woven together, double coating is best suited to simple designs. It is often used for coats, capes, and sportswear.

CHALLIS
A plain-weave wool, challis is lightweight, soft, and easy to handle. It is often printed with floral or paisley designs, drapes well, and is used mainly for dresses.

VENETIAN
Any fabric with a shiny twill finish is called Venetian. Made originally from silk in Venice, it is now made from worsted yarns and is often used for jackets.

50

NO-CREASE WOOL
Developed to be crease-resistant and to breathe well, this lightweight fine wool drapes and gathers easily. It is used mainly for full skirts, dresses, and blouses.

SINGLE JERSEY
Plain-knit single jersey has vertical ribs on the right side. It is used mostly for sportswear, children's wear, and casual clothes. Can be loose, as shown, or fine.

DOUBLE JERSEY
This has vertical ribs on both sides and is firmer than single jersey. It is too bulky for gathers, but takes dyes well and holds in body heat. It is used mainly for women's suits.

MOHAIR
A plain-weave fabric with a fluffy texture, mohair is produced from the fibers of the angora goat. It is usually mixed with wool and is used mainly for coats.

ALPACA
A soft, smooth, silky fabric that has a loose weave, alpaca is often mixed with other fibers to give a lustrous finish. It is generally used for coats and suits.

LINEN & SILK FABRICS

Linen and silk are both derived from natural fibers and are traditionally associated with high-quality luxury fabrics, although today they are becoming much more competitive in price. Linen is produced from the fibers of the flax plant, while silk is woven from the threads that are spun by the silkworm. Both these fabrics are available in a variety of weights and qualities and can be woven together to produce linen-and-silk mixes. Linen is cool and highly absorbent, making it a particularly comfortable fabric to wear in hot climates. It takes color well but may crease easily, so it is often mixed with other fibers, such as cotton, to increase crease resistance. Silk is available as a mix, or in its pure form, in which it is woven in varying weights.

CHECKING PIN MARKS ON SILK

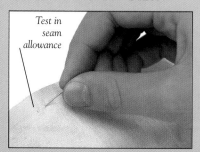

Test in seam allowance

ALWAYS TEST a piece of fabric before you begin sewing to check whether pins leave permanent marks (above). Use fine pins that are specially made for use on silks. Pin within the seam allowances.

CUTTING SLIPPERY SILKS

Slippery silk

PLACE A PIECE of cotton fabric or an old sheet under slippery silk to keep it from moving while the fabric pieces are being cut. (If the under layer is not needed, cut through both fabrics together.)

SUITING LINEN
This type of linen is a strong, absorbent fabric with a crisp finish. It creases easily but is comfortable to wear. It is often used for shirts, skirts, and jackets.

HANDKERCHIEF LINEN
This is a fine, sheer, lightweight fabric with a plain weave. It drapes well, forms tucks better than gathers, and is used mainly for handkerchiefs, lingerie, and blouses.

NOIL
This raw silk is made from the waste created during spinning. It has small flecks of cocoon woven in with other fibers. It is used mainly for dresses and blouses.

SILK-AND-WOOL MIX
In a silk-and-wool mix the wool adds softness and body to the silk, while the silk adds luster to the wool. The fabric is used mainly for suits and jackets.

SILK-AND-COTTON MIX
A soft and lightweight fabric, this has the luster and drape of silk, but with a cotton weave. It is often used for blouses and dresses.

SILK-AND-LINEN MIX
In this mix the linen crispness is softened by silk, forming a shiny, dense fabric. It is easy to handle and is used mainly for suits, skirts, dresses, and pants.

SILK SATIN
This silk has a smooth, lustrous surface and is available in different weights. It is often striped and is generally used for dresses, jackets, and evening wear.

53

TAFFETA
A smooth, crisp plain-weave silk fabric, taffeta has fine ribbing and a lustrous finish. It creases easily. It is used mainly for dresses, jackets, and bridal and evening wear.

ORGANZA
This is a very fine, transparent, stiff plain-weave fabric. It is often used for trims, collars, facings, and fabric flowers, as well as for evening and bridal wear.

WASHED SILK
This is a silk that has been washed in fabric softeners to make it soft and slightly faded in appearance. It drapes well and is used mainly for shirts and dresses.

CREPE DE CHINE
A mediumweight, smooth silk fabric, crepe de Chine drapes well. If bias cut, it gives extra drape to evening wear. It is also used for blouses and lingerie.

DEVORÉ VELVET
This textured fabric is treated with an acid that burns away the nap to reveal a pattern. It has a luxurious feel and is used mainly for evening wear.

CHIFFON
An open-weave, sheer silk fabric, chiffon is made from tightly twisted yarns. It drapes well and is commonly used for evening wear, blouses, and lingerie.

HABUTAI
This silk is a soft cloth that originates from Japan. It is available in several weights and is used mainly for dresses, blouses, and jackets, and for lining garments.

DUPION
Made from double strands of silk, dupion has an uneven surface. Its edges tend to fray. It is generally used for dresses, jackets, and evening and bridal wear.

GEORGETTE
A loosely woven, sheer fabric with highly twisted yarns, georgette is often used for blouses, dresses, and evening wear. It is also produced as a polyester.

SHANTUNG
Woven from irregular yarns, shantung is a mediumweight plain-weave silk fabric with a rough texture. It is used mainly for shirts, dresses, and pants.

SYNTHETIC & SPECIAL FABRICS

FABRICS MADE FROM FIBERS that are not grown naturally fall into two categories: synthetic and rayon. The synthetic fibers, such as polyester, nylon, acrylic, and elastane, are produced chemically from combinations of gas, petroleum, alcohol, water, and air. Rayons, such as viscose and acetate, are made from plant cellulose, which is regenerated to form fibers. Like the fabrics formed from natural fibers, most rayons are absorbent and comfortable to wear, but they crease easily and tend to shrink and ravel. Synthetic fabrics are durable, hardwearing, and crease resistant, but they are not absorbent. Special fabrics include unusual and experimental textiles, as well as fabrics, such as leather and suede, that require special sewing techniques.

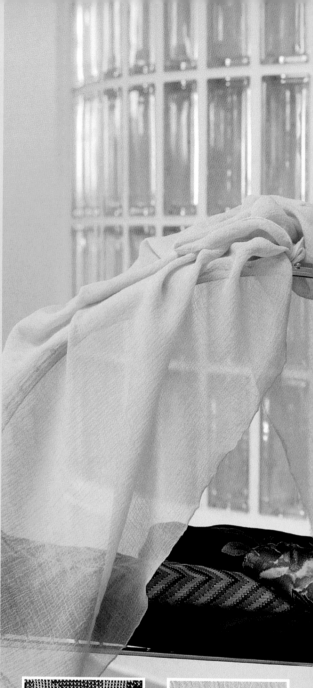

BASTING SLIPPERY FABRICS

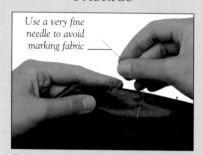

Use a very fine needle to avoid marking fabric

ON SLIPPERY FABRICS such as crepe or satin, use small basting stitches placed close together. This will stop the fabric layers from slipping against each other when they are machine stitched together.

TESTING IRON TEMPERATURE

Test on fabric edge or scrap

MANY SYNTHETICS are sensitive to heat. If the iron is too hot, it can set creases in a fabric, and may even melt it. Always test a scrap of fabric first, increasing the temperature gradually as needed.

ACRYLIC
Acrylic is a lightweight, woven or knitted fabric that was developed as a wool substitute. It tends to retain static. Acrylic is used mainly for sportswear.

CREPON
A fabric made from chemically crimped yarns, this is soft and pliable, which makes it comfortable to wear. It is often used for blouses and evening wear.

FAILLE
A fine, cross-rib fabric, faille is similar to grosgrain (right). It creases easily. Made from acetate, polyester, or viscose, it is used mainly for dresses.

VISCOSE
This fabric is made from wood pulp or cotton waste. Soft, absorbent, and mothproof, it drapes well. It is often used for dresses and skirts.

GROSGRAIN
This is a heavy, closely woven, stiff fabric that has a pronounced crosswise rib. Grosgrain is usually used for formal garments and evening wear.

POLYESTER CREPE
A soft, synthetic fabric, this is crease resistant and hardwearing. It drapes very well and is used mainly for lingerie, blouses, dresses, and evening wear.

MICROFIBER
This is a densely woven, durable fabric made from very fine fibers, usually polyester. Some types are water repellent. It is used for all types of clothing.

BOUCLÉ
This loosely woven or knitted fabric has looped or curled threads for a bulky look. Made from polyester, viscose, or wool blends, bouclé is used mainly for suits.

POLY LINEN
A polyester fabric, this is made to look and handle like linen, but has the crease resistance and ease of care of polyester. It is often used for suits and dresses.

CHARMEUSE
A delicate, satin-weave fabric, charmeuse has a shiny face and a matte back. Made from rayon, viscose, polyester, or blends, it is used mostly for blouses and lingerie.

POLAR FLEECE
This is a lightweight coating with a soft, brushed surface. It is usually made from bulked acrylic fibers and is used mainly for outdoor wear.

CREPE-BACKED SATIN
A reversible fabric with a satin face and a crepe back, this is made from rayon, polyester, and silk. It drapes well and is often used for dresses, blouses, and lingerie.

FLOCK
A synthetic or mixed fabric, flock has short fiber tufts attached with an adhesive to form a pattern. It is used mostly for dresses, jackets, and evening wear.

PURE NYLON
This strong, lightweight fabric takes dye well. It is nonabsorbent, but tends to build up static and to pill. It is used mainly for rainwear, underwear, and skiwear.

JACQUARD FABRIC
This has a patterned finish that is reversed on the wrong side. The pattern may vary from fabric to fabric. Jacquard is often used for making suits, jackets, and skirts.

TULLE
A meshlike fabric net made from nylon, tulle is too abrasive to wear next to the skin. It is often used for full petticoats, ballet skirts, wedding gowns, and costumes.

ACETATE
Similar to viscose but with a different chemical composition, acetate is lustrous and drapes well. It is used mainly for dresses, lingerie, and sportswear.

VINYL
A heavy, synthetic, nonwoven fabric, vinyl looks similar to leather but does not breathe as well. It is generally used for upholstery and outerwear.

CRINKLE FABRIC
This is a synthetic, transparent, stiff fabric that is finely pleated with a crinkle finish. Care is needed when sewing. It is often used for evening wear.

PVC
A woven or knitted, lightweight fabric that is coated with polyvinyl chloride, PVC is tough and nonporous, and is used mainly for trims, rainwear, and aprons.

RUBBER
This is produced from latex, the sap of the rubber plant. Rubber is flexible and waterproof. It is used generally for rainwear, work clothing, and novelty garments.

SEQUIN FABRIC
Sequins are attached to sheer fabric during production. These are heat sensitive and tarnish easily. The fabric is often used for evening wear.

SPANDEX
A lightweight fabric made from elastomeric fibers, spandex can be combined with other fibers to add stretch. It is often used for casual clothes and sportswear.

LAMÉ
A smooth and shiny, knitted or woven fabric made with metallic yarn. Knitted lamé drapes better than woven lamé. Both are used mainly for evening wear.

FUR FABRIC
A fur fabric made from synthetic fibers (usually modacrylic) attached to a firm, woven backing, this is often used to make coats, jackets, hats, and bags.

LIQUID GOLD
This is a synthetic, metallic fabric with a very shiny, decorative surface. It is soft to handle and drapes well. It is used mainly for evening wear.

LEATHER
This is the tanned and finished outside of an animal skin, most commonly sheepskin or cowhide. Sold by the skin, it is used mostly for outerwear and luggage.

FABRIC CARE

Fabric Type	Washing Instructions	Pressing Temperature	Other Pressing Information
Acetate (Sp)	℗	cool iron	Press on wrong side while damp.
Acrylic (Sp)	hand wash or **40°**	warm iron	—
Alpaca (W)	℗	warm iron	—
Bouclé (Sp)	**40°** or ℗	warm iron	Press on wrong side using a damp cloth.
Brushed cotton (C)	**60°– 95°**	warm iron	Press on wrong side.
Calico (C)	**60°– 95°**	warm iron	—
Cambric (C)	**60°**	warm iron	Press while damp.
Challis (W)	hand wash	warm iron	Use a damp cloth.
Chambray (C)	**60°**	warm iron	—
Charmeuse (Sp)	hand wash or **40°**	cool iron	Press on wrong side.
Cashmere (W)	hand wash or ℗	Avoid pressing.	—
Cheesecloth (C)	hand wash	cool iron	—
Chiffon (S)	**40°** or ℗	cool iron	Do not use steam.
Chintz (C) (Glazed cotton)	℗	warm iron	Press on wrong side.
Coating (W)	℗	warm iron	Press on wrong side using a damp cloth.
Corduroy (C)	hand wash or **40°**	warm iron	Press on top of a towel; use steam only to revive pile.
Cotton velvet (C)	℗	warm iron	Use a pressing cloth or needle board; press on wrong side; use steam only to revive pile.
Crepe (W)	hand wash or ℗	cool iron	Press on wrong side.
Crepe-backed satin (Sp)	hand wash or ℗	cool iron	—
Crepe de Chine (S)	℗	cool iron	Use a pressing cloth.
Crepon (Sp)	℗	cool iron	Press on wrong side using a pressing cloth.
Crinkle cotton (C)	**60°**	warm iron	Press on wrong side using a pressing cloth.
Crinkle fabric (Sp)	℗	cool iron	Press on wrong side.
Damask (C)	hand wash or ℗	warm iron	Use a pressing cloth.
Denim (C)	**40°**	warm iron	Press while damp.
Devoré velvet (S)	℗	warm iron	Do not use steam; press on wrong side.
Double coating (W)	℗	cool iron	Press on wrong side using a damp cloth.
Double jersey (W)	hand wash or ℗	cool iron	Press when damp or use a pressing cloth.
Drill (C)	**95°**	warm iron	—
Dupion (S)	℗	warm iron	Do not use steam.
Eyelet (C)	**60°– 95°**	warm iron	Press on wrong side.
Faille (Sp)	**40°** or ℗	cool iron	Press on wrong side using a damp cloth.
Flannel (W)	hand wash or ℗	warm iron	Press on wrong side.
Flock (Sp)	hand wash or ℗	cool iron	—
Fur fabric (Sp)	**40°** or ℗	cool iron	Press on wrong side on top of a towel.
Gabardine (W)	℗	warm iron	Press on wrong side using a damp cloth.
Gingham (C)	**60°**	warm iron	—
Georgette (S)	℗	cool iron	Do not use steam.
Grosgrain (Sp)	℗	cool iron	Press on wrong side using a pressing cloth.
Habutai (S)	hand wash or ℗	warm iron	—
Handkerchief linen (L)	**40°** or ℗	warm iron	Press on wrong side while damp.
Jacquard fabric (Sp)	℗	cool iron	Press on wrong side using a pressing cloth.
Jersey (C)	**40°**	warm iron	Use a damp cloth.
Lace (C)	℗	warm iron	Use a dry iron and a pressing cloth.
Lamé (Sp)	℗	cool iron	Press on wrong side using a pressing cloth.
Lawn (C)	**40°**	warm iron	—

Fabric Type	Washing Instructions	Pressing Temperature	Other Pressing Information
Leather (Sp)	℗	cool iron	Do not use steam; press on wrong side using a pressing cloth.
Liquid gold (Sp)	℗	cool iron	Press on wrong side.
Madras cotton (C)	hand wash	warm iron	—
Microfiber (Sp)	**40°**	cool iron	Press on wrong side.
Modern tweed (W)	hand wash or ℗	warm iron	Press on wrong side using a damp cloth.
Mohair (W)	hand wash or ℗	cool iron	Press with a dry cloth on the mohair and a damp cloth next to the iron.
Moleskin (C)	**40°**	warm iron	Press on wrong side.
Muslin (C)	**40°**	warm iron	—
No-crease wool (W)	℗	warm iron	—
Noil (S)	℗	warm iron	Do not use steam; press on wrong side.
Organza (S)	hand wash or ℗	cool iron	—
Polar fleece (Sp)	**40°**	cool iron	—
Polyester crepe (Sp)	hand wash or **40°**	cool iron	—
Poly linen (Sp)	hand wash or **40°**	warm iron	—
Poplin (C)	**60°** or ℗	warm iron	Use a pressing cloth.
Pure nylon (Sp)	hand wash or **40°**	cool iron	—
PVC (Sp)	℗ or wipe clean.	cool iron	Press on wrong side.
Rubber (Sp)	Do not wash or dry-clean; wipe with a damp cloth.	Do not press.	—
Seersucker (C)	**60°** or **95°**	Usually needs no pressing.	—
Sequin fabric (Sp)	℗	Do not press.	—
Shantung (S)	℗	warm iron	Do not use steam; press on wrong side.
Silk-and-cotton mix (S)	**40°** or ℗	warm iron	Press on wrong side.
Silk-and-linen mix (S)	℗	warm iron	Press on wrong side.
Silk satin (S)	**40°** or ℗	warm iron	Do not use steam; press on wrong side using a pressing cloth.
Silk-and-wool mix (S)	℗	warm iron	Press on wrong side using a pressing cloth.
Single jersey (W)	hand wash or ℗	Do not press.	—
Spandex (Sp)	**40°**	warm iron	—
Sports net (C)	**60°**	warm iron	Avoid snagging with point of iron.
Suiting linen (L)	hand wash or ℗	warm iron	Press on wrong side while damp.
Taffeta (S)	℗	warm iron	Do not use steam; press on wrong side.
Tartan (W)	℗	warm iron	Press on wrong side.
Terry cloth (C)	**60°– 95°**	warm iron	—
Ticking (C)	**95°**	warm iron	Press on wrong side while damp using a pressing cloth.
Traditional tweed (W)	℗	warm iron	Use a damp cloth.
Tulle (Sp)	hand wash	cool iron	—
Venetian (W)	℗	warm iron	—
Vinyl (Sp)	Do not wash or dry-clean; wipe with a damp cloth.	Do not press.	—
Viscose (Sp)	hand wash or **40°** or ℗	warm iron	Press on wrong side while damp.
Voile (C)	**40°**	warm iron	—
Washed silk (S)	℗	warm iron	Do not use steam; press on wrong side.
Winceyette (C)	**60°– 95°**	warm iron	Press while damp.
Worsted (W)	℗	warm iron	Use a damp cloth.

NOTE The instructions given for each fabric in this chart are correct. However, the garment-care instructions inside ready-made garments should always be checked before washing. When buying lengths of fabric, a note should be taken of the manufacturers' care and cleaning labels; these are usually attached to the fabric bolts.

KEY

(C)	Cotton fabric	**95°**	Hot machine wash		Hot iron
(L)	Linen fabric	**60°**	Medium machine wash		Warm iron
(S)	Silk fabric	**40°**	Cool machine wash		Cool iron
(Sp)	Special fabric	**40°**	Gentle cycle machine wash		Hand wash
(W)	Woolen fabric			℗	Dry-clean

THREADS

THREADS ARE USED for hand- and machine stitching, and for both temporary and permanent stitching. Basting thread is relatively inexpensive, and not as strong as other threads. Cotton thread is best for cotton and wool fabrics, while silk thread is best for silk. Polyester thread can be used on both synthetic and natural fabrics.

Basting thread
This loosely twisted cotton thread can be pulled and broken off easily when the stitches are removed. It is always used for temporary work and is not strong enough for permanent stitching.

Polyester cotton
The most common all-purpose thread, this is used on all types of fabric, especially synthetics and jersey fabrics. It is stronger and has more elasticity than other threads.

Silk thread
Fine yet strong, silk thread is used with wool and silk, as well as for basting and tailoring.

Spool fits over spool pin on serger

Buttonhole twist
Strong, thick silk or polyester thread is used for handstitching buttonholes and attaching buttons. Its smooth finish makes it especially suitable for heavy fabrics.

Metallic thread
This is silver or gold decorative thread that can be stitched by hand or machine. Metallic threads are heat- and steam-sensitive, and should be pressed with a cool, dry iron.

Upholstery thread
This very strong thread is used when upholstering chairs and other furniture. It is reinforced to prevent breakage when stitching and pulling tightly.

Cotton thread
Used for handstitching and machine stitching, cotton thread is mercerized for extra sheen and strength, and sold in many colors.

Invisible thread
A very fine, strong thread made from nylon for sewing light- to mediumweight synthetic fabrics, this may melt when pressed.

Spooled thread
All popular threads can be bought on spools (above), which fit over the spool pin on the sewing machine.

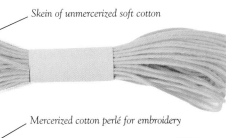

Skein of unmercerized soft cotton

Soft cotton
This thick embroidery thread, with its soft texture, is used mainly for decorative needlepoint on open-weave canvas fabric.

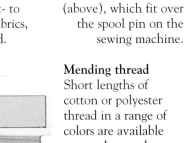

Mending thread
Short lengths of cotton or polyester thread in a range of colors are available wrapped around cardboard. This is an economical way to buy thread when only a small amount of any one color is required. The threads are the same as those on spools and are often used for minor repairs.

Mercerized cotton perlé for embroidery

Cotton perlé
This twisted thread has a lustrous finish and is sold in two thicknesses.

Thick tapestry wool for open-weave canvas work

Tapestry wool
Available in a wide range of colors, this thick wool can be used in dressmaking for blanket stitching a decorative edge.

Mending yarn
A thick, hardwearing wool thread, this is used for strengthening and darning. It is available in small amounts with one or two colors wrapped around cardboard.

Six-stranded thread; for fine work one or two strands only may be used

Stranded cotton
This has six fine strands, which may be separated before use.

NOTIONS

NOTIONS ARE THE ITEMS other than fabric required to make a particular garment. They are listed on the backs of most pattern envelopes. Zippers (p. 250), buttons (p. 234), and interfacing fabrics (p. 95) are classified as notions. Tapes and bands are used to support seams, and to finish and stiffen waistbands. Bindings and ribbons are used for practical as well as decorative purposes. There is a wide range of elastics (p. 66) – some are threaded through casings, while others are stitched to fabric edges. Trimmings (p. 67) include decorative items ranging from delicate lace to sturdy rickrack. Other notions include shaping shoulder pads and money-saving patches (p. 68). The basic curtain-making notions are covered in Notions for Home Furnishings (p. 69), while threads are shown on p. 63.

TAPES

THESE ARE USED to support, stiffen, or hold together various parts of a garment or other item. They are hidden within or on the wrong side of a finished garment. Cotton and twill tapes stabilize seams that might otherwise stretch. Fusible webs and tapes eliminate basting and handstitching; others give firmness to waist finishes.

Curved grosgrain
Grosgrain tape is used for finishing and facing waist edges. The curved type is made for use with skirts.

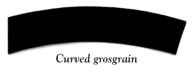
Curved grosgrain

Straight grosgrain
Used like curved grosgrain to face waist edges, this tape has interwoven rubber strips to grip the waist.

Straight grosgrain

Mending tape
This adhesive-backed, fusible fabric strip is used to repair and strengthen garments. The edges of a tear may be overstitched before the tape is applied.

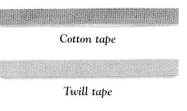
Mending tape

Slotted waistband
This precut stiffening gives a crisp edge to a garment. It is fusible, with premarked foldlines and stitching lines.

Slotted waistband

Belt backing
A hardwearing, fusible tape that is used to form the backing on fabric belts, this is sold in a range of widths.

Belt backing

Waistband stiffening
Made in both fusible and sew-in forms, this stiffening can be bought in widths of up to 2 in (5 cm).

Waistband stiffening

Cotton tape

Twill tape

Fusible web

Bonding web

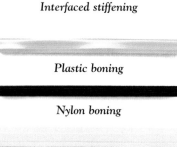
Interfaced stiffening

Plastic boning

Nylon boning

Covered boning

Cotton tape
This woven tape is sewn onto fabric in order to stabilize hems and seams.

Twill tape
Used to stay and strengthen seams, twill tape is made in black, white, and cream.

Fusible web
Sold in a strip, this web is used to finish hems without stitching.

Bonding web
Used for bonding fabrics, this soft web is sold on a sheet of backing paper.

Interfaced stiffening
This strip of firm stiffening is attached to a wider strip of fusible interfacing.

Plastic boning
Boning adds shape and support to bodices.

Nylon boning
This is inserted in a casing to avoid piercing the garment.

Covered boning
Enclosed by tape, this type of boning can be used without a fabric casing.

BINDINGS

BINDINGS ARE USED mainly for practical purposes such as finishing raw edges and strengthening seams. Wide bias binding, when unpressed, makes an economical covering strip for use as piping in home furnishings. Ribbons are more decorative and can be topstitched flat to fabric or formed into three-dimensional flowers or bows.

Satin bias binding
Cut on the bias grain of the fabric, bias binding gives a neat finish to hems and seam allowances.

Satin bias binding

Textured grosgrain
This is a stiff, hardwearing ribbon with a textured rib effect in its weave.

Textured grosgrain

Grosgrain ribbon
Available in a wide variety of colors, this ribbon has prominent vertical ribs.

Grosgrain ribbon

Wire-edged ribbon
The wire edge holds the ribbon in place when it has been shaped.

Wire-edged ribbon

Satin ribbon
Sold in many colors, this can be satin on both sides or on one side only.

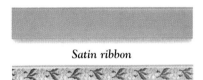

Satin ribbon

Woven Jacquard ribbon
Available in a range of patterns, this ribbon is used as a decorative trim.

Woven Jacquard ribbon

Seam binding
Available in woven (left) or decorative lace form, this tape gives a straight edge to hems and other seams.

Seam binding

Wide bias tape
This bias binding, used for hem facing, is available in widths of up to 2 in (5 cm).

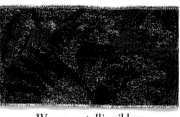

Wide bias tape

Woven metallic ribbon
Sensitive to heat and steam, wire threads should be pressed with a cool, dry iron.

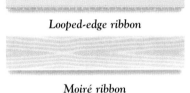

Woven metallic ribbon

Looped-edge ribbon
This lightweight, decorative ribbon is used mainly on children's clothes.

Looped-edge ribbon

Moiré ribbon
The watermarked texture is created by pressing fabric between heated rollers.

Moiré ribbon

Velvet ribbon
If the pile is in one direction only, all pieces should be stitched the same way up.

Velvet ribbon

CLASPS AND BUCKLES

BUCKLES ARE THE TRADITIONAL FASTENINGS for stiffened belts. They can be purchased finished and ready for use or as kits to be covered with the garment fabric. Some buckles have a prong; others simply slide on. Specialized fastenings include the bikini clasp, which is used to fasten two narrow edges, and the overall clip.

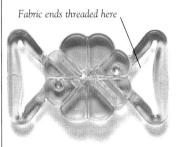

Fabric ends threaded here

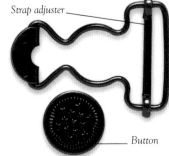

Strap adjuster

Button

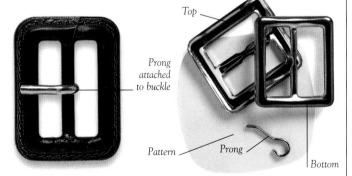

Top

Prong attached to buckle

Pattern

Prong

Bottom

Bikini clasp
This clasp has a slot at each side through which the fabric ends are threaded before the clasp is stitched in place.

Overall clip
The clip has a strap adjuster threaded onto the strap. The button is often attached to the garment bib by a rivet.

Ready-made buckle
A buckle can be made from leather-covered plastic. The prong is inserted through a metal or handstitched eyelet.

Buckle kit
The double-sided adhesive backing sold with this buckle kit allows the buckle to be covered in any fabric (p. 177).

ELASTICS

CORDED ELASTIC is the most common type of elastic. It has lengthwise cords and is usually threaded inside a casing. Some other types are stitched at the fabric edge and left visible. Lingerie elastic has one fluffy, soft side, which is worn next to the skin, while elasticized ribbing forms decorative cuffs and waistbands on casual jackets.

Waistband elastic
This folds over to the inside to finish a waist edge. Rubber strips give the garment a good grip.

Waistband elastic

Elasticized ribbing
A knitted elastic, this can be cut to the required width for neckbands, cuffs, and waistbands.

Elasticized ribbing

Corded elastic
Hardwearing and braided, with a strong grip, corded elastic is available in a range of different widths.

Corded elastic

Grosgrain elastic
A variation on standard grosgrain (p. 64), this is used for skirt waists. It has limited stretch.

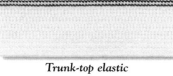
Grosgrain elastic

Trunk-top elastic
Used for underwear, this is strong, woven elastic with a soft finish.

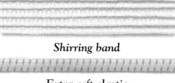
Trunk-top elastic

Shirring band
This open-weave band is used to give a shirred effect without stitching.

Shirring band

Extra-soft elastic
Gentle elastic such as this shapes to the skin and is used on baby clothes.

Extra-soft elastic

Lingerie elastic
An edging for underwear with one soft side that is worn against the skin.

Lingerie elastic

Lace elastic
Soft and flexible, lace elastic shapes to the body on outerwear and lingerie.

Lace elastic

Sports elastic
This elastic is extra-strong to withstand washing, perspiration, and chlorinated water.

Sports elastic

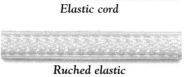
Flat (nonroll) elastic

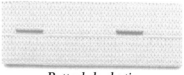
Elastic cord

Ruched elastic

Belting elastic

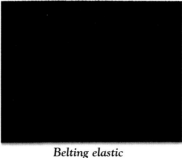
Drawstring elastic

Buttonhole elastic

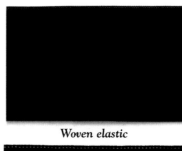
Woven elastic

Threaded elastic

Flat (nonroll) elastic
This is threaded through waist casings on garments in which ordinary elastic would tend to roll and fold in half during wear.

Elastic cord
Also known as hat elastic, round elastic cord can be threaded or zigzag stitched in place.

Ruched elastic
This decorative and practical elastic is used to gather in fabric edges on lingerie and underwear.

Belting elastic
Ribbed and roll-resistant, belting elastic is sold in widths up to 2 in (5 cm) and is used for making belts and suspenders.

Drawstring elastic
A drawstring is inserted along the center of this elastic, which is used at the waist on sportswear and casual pants.

Buttonhole elastic
This has buttonhole slots at 1-in (2.5-cm) intervals for adjusting waists on maternity and children's wear.

Woven elastic
Soft and sheer, this lightweight elastic is 1¾ in (4.5 cm) wide and supple enough to be worn next to the skin.

Threaded elastic
A woven band with rows of elastic threaded through and pulled up to create gathers. The rows of elastic also provide a stitching guide.

TRIMMINGS

THERE ARE MANY DECORATIVE TRIMMINGS used in both dressmaking and home sewing. Trimmings such as rickrack and Russian braid may be applied by machine, while bulkier braids should be stitched by hand, using a fine needle and short stitches. Some trims can be stitched to the fabric surface; others are inserted in seams or at hems.

Eyelet (broderie anglaise)
An open-work, embroidered cotton trim finished at one or both edges, this is often used on children's clothes and bed and table linens.

Beaded lace edging
This is a fine lace border finished on both edges and threaded with small pearl beads. It is used for surface decoration, mainly on bridal wear.

Netted lace edging
Used for lingerie and bridal wear, lace edging is usually sold in black or white. It has a net backing and is machine-made from nylon fiber.

Feather edging
Also known as maribou, feather edging is a fluffy strand formed around a central cord. It should be applied by handstitching over the central cord, stitching carefully to avoid catching the feathers in the stitching.

Cotton piping cord
White cotton piping cord is used as a filler when making fabric-covered piping.

Rayon piping cord
This lustrous cord is sold by length. It is used for drawstring casings and as decorative bathrobe cord.

Thick piping cord
Uncovered piping is sold in a range of thicknesses, from ⅛–½ in (3–12 mm).

Eyelet

Beaded lace edging

Netted lace edging

Feather edging

Cotton piping cord   *Rayon piping cord*

Crocheted lace edging

Silken braid

Rickrack braid

Russian braid

Ready-made welting

Beading strip

Sequin strip

Crocheted lace edging
This thick edging, usually made from cotton yarn, must be stitched with a strong cotton thread.

Silken braid
A light, glossy braid, this can be stitched by hand or machine and is used for a range of trimmings.

Rickrack braid
Made in polyester or cotton, decorative rickrack is sold in widths of up to ⅝ in (1.5 cm).

Russian braid
Mainly used for home furnishings, this corded braid should be stitched along the center groove.

Ready-made welting
The decorative edge of this welting is attached to a flat tape, which is inserted into a seam.

Beading strip
This edging may be stitched either by hand over the join between the beads, or by machine using a beading foot.

Sequin strip
The sequins are stitched together to form a strip that can be attached by hand or machine.

Thick piping cord

DECORATIONS

THERE ARE MANY TYPES and sizes of beads, but the most common are round rocaille beads and tubular bugle beads. Both types are stitched on by hand. Narrow ribbon can be purchased pretied into tiny bows, and ribbons of different widths form rose and other flower shapes. These are handstitched at the back so that no stitching is visible.

Small beads are often used to decorate evening bags

Bow is handstitched behind knot

Tightly coiled layers

Rocaille beads
These are stitched by hand. The stitching under each bead is narrower than the bead.

Bugle beads
These are attached either by threading and couching, or by stitching individually.

Ribbon bow
Bows are often used as decorations on bridal wear and children's clothing.

Ribbon rose
These decorative roses can be applied either with a needle and thread or glue.

READY-MADE ACCESSORIES

NOTIONS INCLUDE ready-made items that can be added to garments as they are being made. Other notions can be used to lengthen the life of a garment. Ready-made lace collars are often attached to a binding that is stitched to the garment. Patches can be either sewn on or ironed on, while shoulder pads are handstitched in place.

Binding trimmed at neck edges

Stitching holes

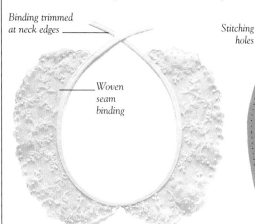

Woven seam binding

Nonadhesive outer fabric side

Pointed tip rests inside collar point

Collar stays
These are plastic strips for strengthening and stiffening the points of collars. The stays should be removed before washing.

Cuff binding patch
Used to cover worn cuffs on garments that receive a lot of wear, this leather binding should be removed before washing or dry-cleaning the garment.

Machine-made lace collar
Ready-made using machine-woven lace, this collar is attached to the neckline by handstitching the binding to the inside of the finished neck, or by catching it between the facing and the garment.

Suede patch
Used to reinforce elbows on jackets, this patch has prepunched stitching holes.

Pants patch
This type of fabric patch has a fusible adhesive bonding and is cut larger than the worn area.

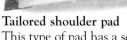

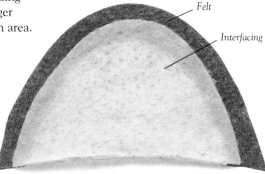

Felt

Interfacing

Covered shoulder pad
This ready-made foam shoulder pad, covered in nylon fabric, is used on unlined garments to shape and support the shoulders.

Uncovered foam pad
A lightweight shoulder pad, this is placed between the fabric and the lining, or it can be covered and inserted in an unlined garment.

Tailored shoulder pad
This type of pad has a soft padding sandwiched between layers of felt or nonwoven interfacing. It is used to give shape to jackets and coats and is inserted between the garment fabric and the lining.

NOTIONS FOR HOME FURNISHINGS

CURTAIN PLEATS MAY BE FORMED manually or created by using heading tape stitched to the top of the curtain. Hooks are then attached to the heading to hang the curtain on the rail. Braids and fringes can be used to decorate a cornice and tiebacks. Fringes are also used to trim upholstered furniture and lampshades.

CURTAIN FINISHES

Steel pin hook
This curtain hook is used where pleats have been stitched by hand. The sharp point of the hook is pushed up through the back of the pleat.

This end is inserted in tape trim

Steel pin hook

Standard hook
Made from nylon or plastic, these simple hooks are used with standard heading tapes and with sheer curtains.

Standard hook

Solid brass hook
A simple, one-pronged hook, this is often used with handmade headings. Unlike other types of curtain hooks, brass hooks are sewn into the tape.

Solid brass hook

Weight is attached to curtain fabric by stitching through holes **Lead weight**

Curtain weights
To make a curtain hang evenly, lead weights are inserted into the hem at the corners and at the bases of any joining seams. Chain weights are inserted along the stitched hem fold, and are used with lightweight fabrics.

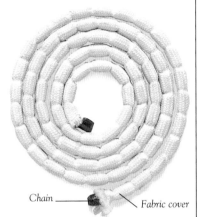
Chain *Fabric cover*
Chain weight

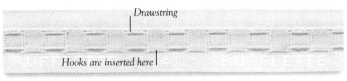
Drawstring
Hooks are inserted here

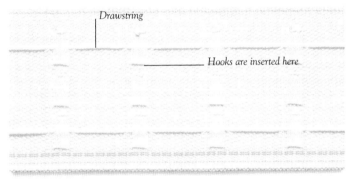
Drawstring
Hooks are inserted here

Standard heading tape (above)
This 1-in (2.5-cm) wide tape is used in order to make softly gathered pleats. The strings are drawn up, and curtain hooks inserted into the loops.

Pinch pleat tape (right)
A variation on standard curtain heading tape, this requires a greater width of fabric. The hooks must be evenly spaced on the tape.

FRINGES AND BRAIDS

MANY different fringes and braids are available as trims for home furnishings. Fringes add decorative touches to many items. Braids can be used on cushions to outline cornices and tiebacks, and to hide tacks on covered chairs.

Chenille fringe
This long, softly rolled fringe is ideal for trimming the lower edges of all types of upholstered furniture.

Metallic braid
A sparkling braid trim can be used to accentuate a fabric that contains metallic thread.

Chenille fringe

Metallic braid

Tasseled fringe

Looped fringe

Narrow braid

Tasseled fringe
This is a silky edging that combines a braid effect at the top with a short, looped fringe as well as longer, tied tassels in a contrasting color.

Looped fringe
Both long and short loops are combined in this lightweight, silky fringe, that usually features a textured braid decoration along its upper edge.

Narrow braid
This is used to cover upholstery tacks and to define the outlines of tiebacks and cornices.

BASIC STITCHES

HANDSTITCHES

MODERN SEWING MACHINES and new stitching methods have all but eliminated the need for hand sewing. However, there are still many situations in which good handstitching is necessary for a high-quality finish. Handstitches can be temporary or permanent. Temporary handstitches include basting, which is used in garment construction but is removed before a garment is finished. Permanent handstitches are part of a garment's structure. Handstitches are used in most stages of a garment's construction, from transferring the pattern markings with tailor's tacks, to joining the ends of elastic and stitching the final hems. There are many different types of hemstitches, and the stitch chosen should be the one that best suits the edge being stitched and the fabric thickness.

SECURING A THREAD

IT IS IMPORTANT TO SECURE THREAD ENDS firmly when starting and finishing handstitching, especially if the stitching is permanent. Basting also needs to be secured firmly if the basted garment is to be tried on. On permanent stitching, the securing stitches must be as small as possible, and worked on the wrong side, invisibly.

TYING A KNOT

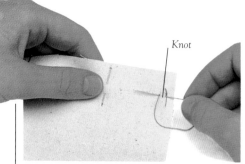

Pass short thread end behind loop
End of thread being knotted

1 THIS KNOT is used for basting as it can be undone by pulling the short end. Thread a needle. Form a loop near the thread end, passing the short end over the long end and behind the loop (above).

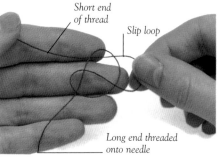

Short end of thread
Slip loop
Long end threaded onto needle

2 PULL THE THREAD through the loop, forming another loop (above). Then pull the needle end of the thread until it forms a knot, taking care not to pull the short end or the slip loop through.

ROLLING A KNOT

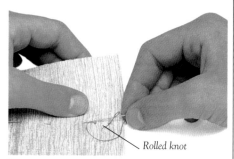

Rolled knot

WRAP THE THREAD around a forefinger. Roll the crossed threads between thumb and forefinger, then slide the loop off the finger and, pinching it, pull the other end to tie the knot. Begin stitching (above).

KNOT AND BACKSTITCH

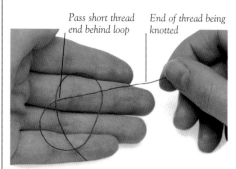

Knot

FOR A SECURE START TO BASTING, or to begin permanent stitching, make a knot, insert the needle, and bring it out ⅛in (3 mm) away from the knot. Insert the needle again at the knot, and make a backstitch (above). Begin stitching.

DOUBLE BACKSTITCH

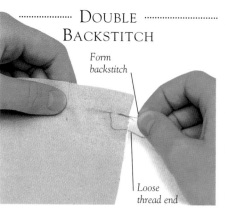

Form backstitch
Loose thread end

TWO BACKSTITCHES make a firmer and flatter start than a knot on permanent stitching. Begin by making a ⅛-in (3-mm) long stitch, leaving a loose end. Make a backstitch in the same place (above), and make a second backstitch over the first.

FINISHING OFF

Loop

For a strong finish to permanent stitching, take a small backstitch over a few threads, leaving a small loop. Make another stitch in the same place (above), and pass the needle through the loop of the first stitch. Pull tight.

WORKING BASTING STITCHES

B ASTING IS USED TO HOLD FABRIC in place prior to permanent stitching. A contrasting color thread is often used for basting so that it is easy to distinguish from permanent thread when being removed. Use silk thread to baste as it pulls out quickly and smoothly. Avoid poor-quality thread for basting; the dye can mark fabrics.

BASIC BASTING

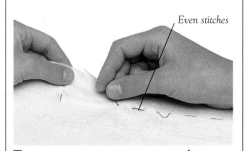

Even stitches

THIS IS A TEMPORARY STITCH used to hold two or more layers of fabric together prior to stitching. Bring the needle in and out, making large stitches of the same length on both sides of the fabric (above).

LONG AND SHORT BASTING

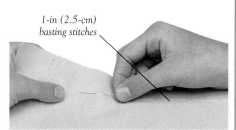

1-in (2.5-cm) basting stitches

NOT AS FIRM AS BASIC BASTING, this is used to cover long, straight areas quickly. Make a 1-in (2.5-cm) stitch, leave a ¼-in (6-mm) space, and bring the needle up again to make the next stitch (above).

LONG DIAGONAL BASTING

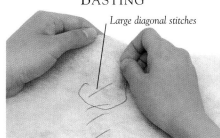

Large diagonal stitches

THIS IS USED to hold two layers of fabric together over a large area. Take a stitch about 1 in (2.5 cm) long, then move up, and make another stitch to form a long diagonal stitch. Repeat (above).

SHORT DIAGONAL BASTING

THIS TYPE of basting is a fast way to hold a number of fabric layers together, for example, in a pleat, prior to pressing. Form the stitches in the same way as long diagonal basting (see above), but make them smaller and closer together (left).

SLIP BASTING

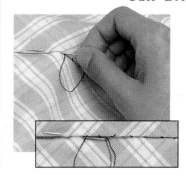

SLIP BASTING is used to join a folded fabric edge to a flat fabric piece so that motifs, checks, or stripes can be matched exactly. Take a short, straight stitch through the flat piece of fabric next to the folded edge, and another short stitch along the inside of the fold alternately (left).

WORKING TAILOR'S TACKS

S INGLE TAILOR'S TACKS are used to mark circles, dots, the ends of buttonholes, and other single pattern markings on a double or single layer of fabric. Continuous tailor's tacks are used to mark pattern line markings, such as a center front line or a pleat foldline. Tailor's tacks are made with doubled thread in a contrasting color.

SINGLE TAILOR'S TACKS

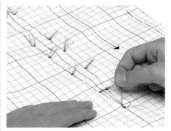

1 TAKE a small stitch through the pattern and both layers of fabric, leaving ⅜-in (1.5-cm) long thread ends. Stitch again in the same place, leaving a 1¼-in (3-cm) loop of thread (above).

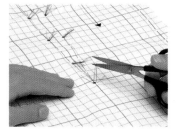

2 CHECK that the stitching has gone through the bottom layer of fabric. Snip the thread, leaving ⅜-in (1.5-cm) long thread ends. Then snip the thread at the center of the loop (above).

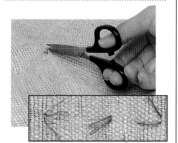

3 PULL the pattern away, and separate the layers of fabric so that the tacks can be seen between them. Then snip the tacks between the layers, leaving tufts of thread in each layer (above).

CONTINUOUS TAILOR'S TACKS

With the pattern pinned in place, stitch along the pattern line, using long stitches but leaving a large, loose loop on each stitch. Cut through the loops. Pull the pattern away, and separate the fabric so that the threads can be seen between the layers. Cut these threads.

HAND SEWING STITCHES

THESE STITCHES are permanent and frequently used in constructing a garment or other item. Some, such as running stitch and backstitch, can be used as a substitute for machine straight stitch on small areas. Others, such as overcast stitch and blanket stitch, are used to finish raw edges on intricate areas that are difficult to reach by machine.

RUNNING STITCH

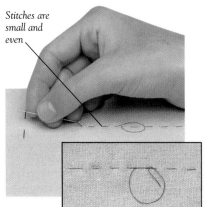

Stitches are small and even

USED FOR SEAMING and gathering, this stitch can be sewn quickly, but is not as strong as backstitch (see right). Work from right to left, taking the point of the needle in and out of the fabric, and picking up a number of stitches before pulling through (left). Each stitch should be about ⅛in (3 mm) long.

BACKSTITCH

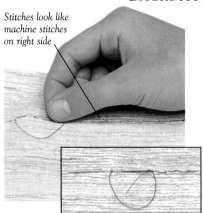

Stitches look like machine stitches on right side

THIS STRONG STITCH is used mainly for seaming. Working from right to left, take a small stitch. Insert the needle at the end of the previous stitch, and bring it out beyond the point where the thread emerges. Continue, always inserting the needle in the end of the previous stitch (left).

WHIPSTITCH

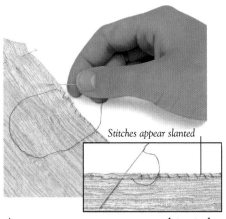

Stitches appear slanted

A STRONG OVEREDGE STITCH, whipstitch is used for joining two flat edges together. Working from right to left, bring the needle through the fabric layers from the back to the front about ⅛in (2–3 mm) from the edge. Continue in this way, moving to the left for each stitch (above).

PRICKSTITCH

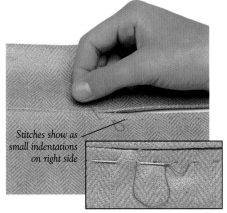

Stitches show as small indentations on right side

THIS SPACED BACKSTITCH is used mainly to stitch in zippers when stitching should be invisible. Working from the right side, make a small backstitch, bringing the needle out ¼–⅜in (6–10 mm) to the left. Continue stitching, making tiny spaced backstitches in this way (above).

QUICK SLIPSTITCH

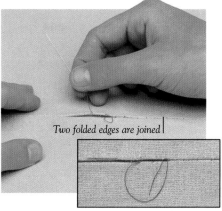

Two folded edges are joined

ALSO CALLED EVEN SLIPSTITCH, this stitch is used to join two folded, abutting edges together. Working from right to left, take a ¼-in (6-mm) stitch through one folded edge. Make a stitch of the same length through the other folded edge. Continue stitching (above).

OVERCAST STITCH

Stitches are evenly spaced and slanting

THIS OVEREDGE stitch is used to finish a raw edge. Working from right to left, bring the needle through the fabric from back to front ⅛in (2–3 mm) from the raw edge. Move the needle along to the left, and bring it out again through the fabric from back to front. Continue to stitch in this way (left).

HALF BACKSTITCH

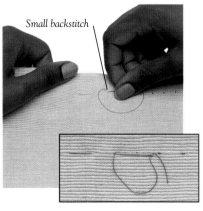

Small backstitch

A DECORATIVE surface stitch, this is used in place of topstitching, usually on collars. Working from right to left on the right side, take a small backstitch over a thread or two of fabric. Bring the needle out ¼–⅜in (6–10 mm) away, catching the top layer of fabric only. Continue (left).

LOCKSTITCH

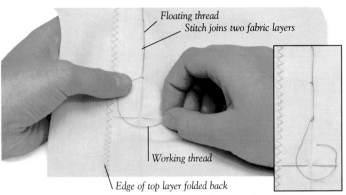

Floating thread
Stitch joins two fabric layers

Working thread

Edge of top layer folded back

ALSO KNOWN AS LOOP STITCH, this stitch is used to join two fabric layers. Fold back the edge of the top fabric layer. Working from top to bottom, start by taking a tiny stitch, picking up both layers. Make the next stitch 1 in (2.5 cm) below the first stitch, picking up both layers and passing the needle over the working thread. Leave the floating thread loose as you stitch (above).

HEAVY-DUTY STITCH

Edge of top layer folded back

A VERY STRONG STITCH, this is used for the same purpose as lockstitch, but on heavy fabrics. Fold back the edge of the top layer. Working from bottom to top, take a tiny stitch through both layers of fabric. Make one or two more in the same place. Make the next two or three stitches through both layers about 1 in (2.5 cm) above. Leave the floating thread loose (above).

BUTTONHOLE STITCH

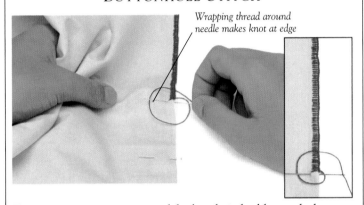

Wrapping thread around needle makes knot at edge

THIS OVEREDGE STITCH is used for handstitched buttonholes. Secure the thread on the wrong side. Then, with the right side facing upward, insert the needle from back to front through the fabric ⅛in (3 mm) from the edge. Wrap the working thread around behind the eye end of the needle, then behind the point. Pull the needle through, bringing the knot to the fabric edge. Continue, making closely spaced stitches and knots (above).

CROSS STITCH

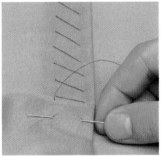
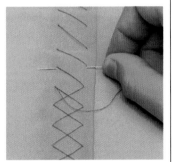

1 CROSS STITCHES have decorative and practical uses, including holding pleats in place. Working downward from right to left, make spaced horizontal stitches – forming diagonal stitches on the right side – until the line of cross stitches is complete (above).

2 WITH the same thread, work back upward and insert the needle at the bottom of the stitch above, bringing it out at the top of the stitch below. Continue working from bottom to top in this way until the crosses are complete (above).

BLANKET STITCH

Thread loops

1 WORKED along the edge of fabric, blanket stitch is used to decorate or finish the edge. Secure the thread on the wrong side. With the right side facing upward, bring the needle through from back to front ¼in (5 mm) from the fabric edge, passing the tip of the needle over the thread loop. Make the next stitch ¼in (5 mm) along the edge from the first (left).

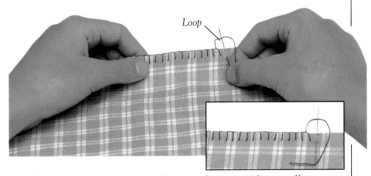

Loop

2 CONTINUE STITCHING in this way, bringing the needle through from back to front and passing the tip of the needle over the thread loop. Keep the stitches evenly spaced and of an even depth, with the loops sitting neatly along the edge (above).

WORKING HEMMING STITCHES

Hemming stitches can be used for purposes other than hemming. Slipstitch and hemstitches are also used for stitching along the inside edges of collars and cuffs, catchstitch is used for joining the edges of facings or interfacing to the inside of a garment, and the blind stitches are used for joining two layers of fabric.

VERTICAL HEMSTITCH

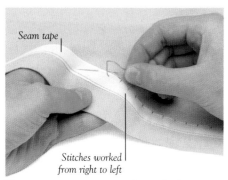

Seam tape

Stitches worked from right to left

BRING THE NEEDLE OUT through the hem edge, and pick up one thread of the underneath fabric directly above where the thread emerged. Then bring the needle through the hem at an angle. Continue stitching in this way (above).

SLANTING HEMSTITCH

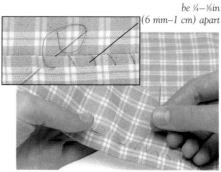

Stitches should be ¼–⅜in (6 mm–1 cm) apart

THIS STITCH is less stable than vertical hemstitch but is quicker to work. Form the stitches in the same way as vertical hemstitch, but pick up a thread of underneath fabric to the left of where the thread emerges from the hem (above).

CATCHSTITCH

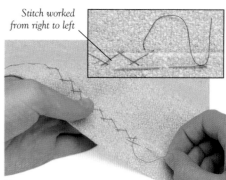

Stitch worked from right to left

BRING THE NEEDLE out through the hem. Move to the right, and stitch through the underneath fabric from right to left. Move to the right and stitch in the same way but through the hem allowance.

BLIND HEMSTITCH

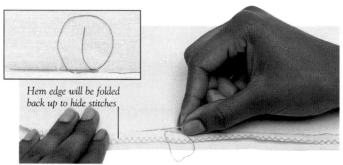

Hem edge will be folded back up to hide stitches

FOLD THE HEM EDGE BACK about ⅜in (1 cm). Working from right to left, take a tiny stitch through the hem and another through the underneath fabric, spacing the stitches ⅜in (1 cm) apart. Continue, leaving the stitches fairly loose (above).

SLIPSTITCH

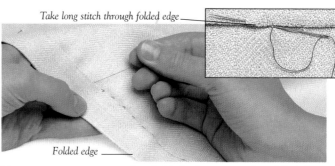

Take long stitch through folded edge

Folded edge

USE THIS STITCH to attach a folded edge to another fabric layer. Bring the needle out through the folded edge. Pick up a thread of underneath fabric, then take a ¼-in (6-mm) long stitch through the folded edge from right to left. Continue (above).

BLIND CATCHSTITCH

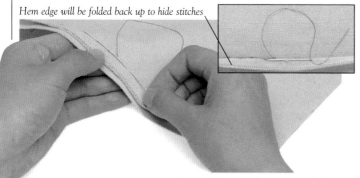

Hem edge will be folded back up to hide stitches

WORK BLIND CATCHSTITCH as for catchstitch (see top right) from left to right of the garment, but first fold the hem edge back ⅜in (1 cm). Work the catchstitches between the inside of the garment hem and the underneath fabric (above).

REINFORCING BLIND HEMSTITCH

Work from right to left

Stitch the hem (see above), but reinforce it with a tiny backstitch on top of the stitch worked through the hem (above). Reinforce every stitch or every few stitches. This stops a large section of the hem from unraveling if snagged.

MACHINE STITCHES

THESE STITCHES can be divided into two types: functional and decorative. Functional machine stitches are used in the construction of items, while decorative stitches are used entirely for embellishment. The number of stitches a sewing machine can make varies tremendously, and when purchasing a machine it is worth considering how many of the available stitches will be used regularly. The stitches below are the main functional stitches that even the most basic sewing machines can produce. Some of these stitches can be used for decorative purposes as well. For example, blind hemstitch is used to stitch hems invisibly, but can also be used to produce delicate shell tucks. Feather stitch is used to join two abutting fabric edges, and it can also be used as a decorative embroidery stitch.

WORKING MACHINE STITCHES

THESE STITCHES ARE USED in sewing construction. Straight stitch is used for seams, understitching, staystitching, and simple topstitching. Zigzag stitch and three-step zigzag stitch are used for clean finishing raw edges. Zigzag stitch is also used for buttonholes. Blind hemstitch is ideal for working a long, straight hem.

STRAIGHT STITCH

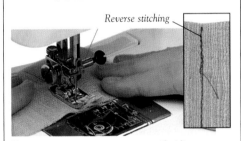
Reverse stitching

BEGIN STRAIGHT STITCHING ⅜–⅝in (1–1.5 cm) from the fabric edge. Reverse stitch to the edge, then stitch forward on top of the reverse stitching. Stitch to the end (above), and reverse stitch to finish.

ZIGZAG STITCH

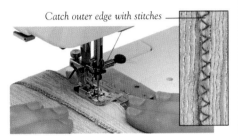
Catch outer edge with stitches

FOR CLEAN FINISHING a raw edge, adjust the machine zigzag stitch settings to medium width and medium length. Stitch along the edge so that the outer swing of the stitch falls outside the raw edge (above).

THREE-STEP ZIGZAG STITCH

ALSO CALLED tricot and multistitch, this is used in the same way as zigzag stitch but gives a flatter finish. It is also used to mend tears (p. 305). For raw edges, stitch close to, but not over, the edge (above).

STRETCH STITCH

Stitches overstitched three times

THIS STRONG, straight stitch is worked with two stitches forward and one backward so that each stretch stitch is stitched three times (left). Stretch stitch is difficult to remove, so test it before use.

FEATHER STITCH

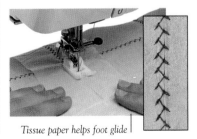
Tissue paper helps foot glide

THIS IS USED to join two nonfraying edges that are butted together, for example on suede. Stitch along the butted edges so that the left stitch catches one edge and the right stitch the other (left).

BLIND HEMSTITCH

THIS CONSISTS of two or three straight stitches, then one wide zigzag stitch. On the wrong side, fold the hem back under the main fabric with the hem edge projecting, and stitch in place (right).

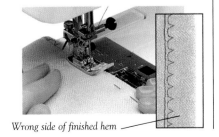
Wrong side of finished hem

ZIGZAG BLIND HEMSTITCH

SIMILAR to blind hemstitch, this consists of three narrow zigzag stitches, followed by one wide zigzag stitch (right). Use for knit fabrics, and work same way as blind hemstitch (see left).

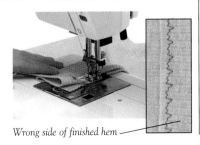
Wrong side of finished hem

FINISHING TOUCHES

T HE TECHNIQUES shown below are not widely used on all garments. They are fine, hand-finished details required at specific points on a garment as a means of reinforcement, or to join parts of a garment without using a seam. French tacks are like fine cords, and usually link a free-hanging lining hem to the main hem to prevent the lining from swiveling around or riding up. The tacks are worked between the two hems on the inside so that they are not visible, and they are usually worked at the side seams of garments. Bar tacks are reinforcing stitches, usually used on work or sports clothes. They are formed at points that may be subject to a great deal of strain, for example at the bases of openings and across the top corners of pockets. An arrowhead is a fine detail, used on garments to add decoration and strengthen seams.

MAKING FRENCH TACKS

F RENCH TACKS HOLD TWO LAYERS of fabric loosely together, usually the hem of a free-hanging lining and a garment. There are several types: a blanket-stitch tack has long threads covered with blanket stitches, a thread chain tack is made by hand from a chain of loops, and a machine chain tack uses machine straight stitch.

BLANKET-STITCH TACKS

1 TAKE A SMALL STITCH through the garment seam near the top of the hem, then through the lining hem at the seamline, leaving a loose thread 1–2 in (2.5–5 cm) long between the stitches. Make five or six stitches this way (above).

2 STARTING AT ONE END, make a small blanket stitch over the ends of the threads and through the fabric. Then blanket stitch over the loose threads only, keeping the stitches close together. Work the last stitch through the fabric (above).

THREAD CHAIN TACKS

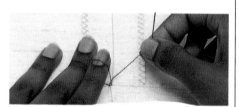

1 FIRMLY FASTEN a long thread to the seamline on the garment hem. Make a small stitch, leaving the thread loose to form a loop and placing two fingers inside the loop to hold it open (above).

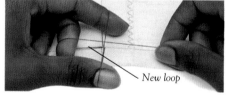

New loop

2 REACH THROUGH THE LOOP, and pull the thread through the loop to form a new loop in the thread (above). Then pull the new loop to tighten the first loop into a chain next to the fabric.

Lining *Thread chain tack*

3 CONTINUE to make chain loops in this way until the chain is the desired length. Finish by pulling the thread end through the final loop and stitching it firmly to the lining hem (above).

MACHINE CHAIN TACKS

Tissue paper

1 USING medium-length straight stitch, reverse stitch on the lining to fasten the thread. Stitch down a piece of tissue paper for the desired length of the tack (above) so that it is not attached to the lining. Leave long thread ends.

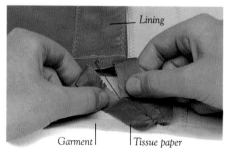

Lining

Garment *Tissue paper*

2 HANDSTITCH the loose thread ends firmly to the garment hem. Gently tear away the tissue paper from the machine stitching to reveal the tack (above). (Chain tacks can also be made using a serger.)

MAKING BAR TACKS

THESE SHORT, STRAIGHT ROWS of reinforcing stitching are used to strengthen points of strain on a garment, and can be made by hand or machine. Bar tacks are used across two adjoining areas of fabric that may be strained or split during wear, for example at the ends of zipper openings, on belt loops, and at the tops of pockets.

HANDSTITCHED BAR TACKS

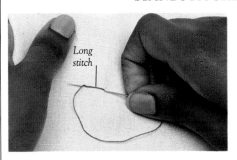

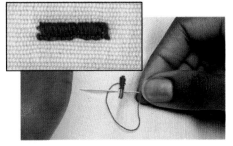

1 FASTEN THE THREAD to the wrong side of the fabric at one end of the placement for the bar tack. Then work two or three stitches the length of the required bar tack, working the stitches side by side and close together (above). Pass the thread to the back of the fabric.

2 BEGINNING AT ONE END of the long stitches, work blanket stitches over the long stitches, picking up the fabric underneath them (above). Make the stitches equal in length, and work them close together so that the long stitches are completely covered.

MACHINE BAR TACKS

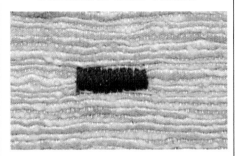

MARK THE POSITION of the tack with a fabric marker. Set the machine stitch to a short zigzag. Leaving long, loose thread ends, stitch along the marked area. Make the tack ¼in (6 mm) long. Pull the thread ends to the wrong side, then knot together and slip them under the stitching.

MAKING ARROWHEADS

THESE SMALL, TRIANGULAR TACKS are worked by hand or machine across a seam to strengthen it at a point of strain, for example at the tops of pleats with an underlay on a tight-fitting skirt. It is best to use a matching color thread and, for a handstitched arrowhead, a thick thread such as buttonhole twist can be effective.

HANDSTITCHED ARROWHEADS

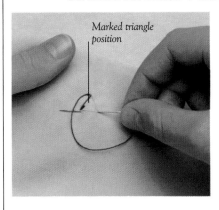

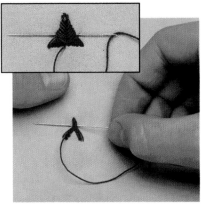

1 TAKE a tiny stitch to secure the thread at the lower left corner. Take a stitch across the top of the triangle from right to left. Insert the needle at the lower right corner, and bring it out at the lower left corner just next to and inside the first stitch (left).

2 AT THE TOP of the triangle, stitch across from right to left just under the previous stitch. Continue stitching down from the point, and across the base (left) until the stitches meet at the center of the base (inset). Secure the thread firmly.

MACHINE ARROWHEADS

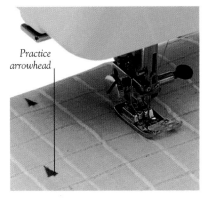

1 SET the machine to a short, narrow zigzag stitch. It may be necessary to practice first on some scrap fabric. Begin stitching slowly at the narrowest end of the arrowhead and, while stitching, increase the stitch width until the base is reached (left).

2 PASS the thread ends from the right side to the wrong side (inset), knot them together, and slip them into the back of the stitching (left). (Alternatively, if the machine has a preset program, select and isolate a single repeat from a suitable embroidery stitch.)

SEAMS

SEAMS AND SEAM FINISHES

THE MOST WIDELY USED type of seam is a plain seam, which is suitable for nearly all fabrics and for different styles of garments. There are other kinds of seams that can be used when appropriate for the fabric, or to add decorative detailing. French seams, and other self-finished seams that conceal all raw edges, are ideal for sheer fabrics. The flat fell seam, with its distinctive double stitching, adds style to casual clothes made from denim or twill cotton. Topstitched seams add definition and sharpness, particularly on jackets and coats.

RELATED TECHNIQUES

Hand sewing stitches, p. 74
Sewing seams in interfacing, p. 98
Making an edge-to-edge lining, p. 103
Staying a gathered seam, p. 121
Making a mock casing, p. 163
Cutting and joining bias strips, p. 214
Mending a seam, p. 305

MAKING A PLAIN SEAM

OF ALL THE SEAMS, a plain seam is the most basic and easiest to use. Its seam allowances are usually pressed open, although on lightweight fabrics they can be trimmed and finished together. To ensure absolutely straight seams, it is advisable to practice stitching while keeping the fabric edge aligned with the seam guideline.

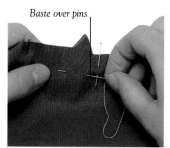

Wrong side of fabric

1 PLACE THE FABRIC edges together with right sides facing and raw edges even. Pin the edges together so that the pins are placed at a right angle to the seamline (above). Match any pattern markings and notches.

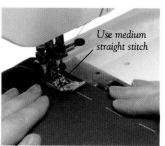

Baste over pins

2 IF NECESSARY, baste the pinned seam close to the seamline (above). The seam allowance is usually ⅝in (1.5 cm), so the basting should be just short of this distance from the edge. After basting, remove the pins.

Use medium straight stitch

3 POSITION THE NEEDLE on the seamline, ⅝in (1.5 cm) from the edge. To reinforce, reverse stitch to the edge, then stitch forward along the seamline, guiding the fabric with both hands (above). Reverse stitch to finish.

Seam allowances

4 REMOVE all the basting. Open the seam allowances, and press flat (above). If desired, seam finish the raw edges of the seam allowances to prevent them from fraying, using a method suitable for the type of fabric (p. 85).

USING SEAM GUIDES

Guidelines

Using seam guidelines on a sewing machine
1 The plate beneath the machine foot has a central hole for the needle and etched lines for seam guides.

Aligned edge

2 Align the edge of the fabric with the correct guideline, and keep parallel to this line during stitching (above).

Masking tape

Masking tape guide
If an unusual seam width is required, use a tape measure and masking tape to mark a new seam guide.

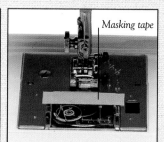

Masking tape

Corner guide
For accurate stitching at corners, attach masking tape in front of the foot at a right angle, ⅝in (1.5 cm) from the needle.

STITCHING A CORNER

ACCURATE STITCHING around corners can create sharp points on collars and cuffs, and add neat detailing to topstitching. Pivoting the fabric with the needle down is the basic technique that is used at all corners. Corners can be reinforced on the wrong side by reducing the machine stitch length for a short distance on each side of the corner.

PIVOTING AT A CORNER

Needle in fabric at corner point

1 USING THE SEAM GUIDE to produce an even seam, stitch toward the corner ⅝ in (1.5 cm) from the edge. Stop ⅝ in (1.5 cm) short of the end, with the needle lowered in the fabric (above).

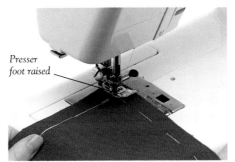

Presser foot raised

2 LIFT THE PRESSER FOOT, and pivot the fabric around the needle so that the second edge lies parallel to the ⅝ in (1.5 cm) seam guideline on the sewing machine needle plate (above).

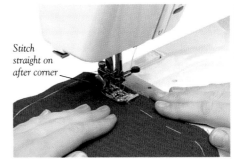

Stitch straight on after corner

3 LOWER THE FOOT, and continue stitching, again keeping the edge of the fabric aligned with the ⅝ in (1.5 cm) seam guideline (above). Continue in this way to the end of the seam.

STITCHING AN INWARD CORNER TO AN OUTWARD CORNER

Staystitching at corner

1 USING small- to medium-length machine straight stitch, staystitch the inward corner to reinforce it, stitching just inside the seamline for ¾ in (2 cm) on both sides of the corner. Pivot at the corner (above) (see Steps 1–3, above).

Pin protects corner staystitching

2 CLIP INTO THE CORNER to a thread or two from the stitching. If preferred, pin across the corner just inside the stitching so that the stitching cannot be accidentally cut through (above). (If this happens, stitch again, over the cut.)

Keep excess fabric away from needle

3 PIN the inward corner to the outward corner, matching the fabric edges and opening out the clip at the inward corner to fit it around the outward corner. With the inward corner uppermost, stitch the seam, pivoting at the corner (above).

MAKING A NEAT POINT ON AN OUTWARD CORNER

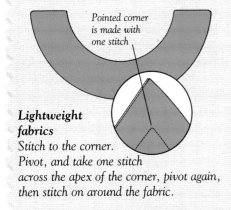

Pointed corner is made with one stitch

Lightweight fabrics
Stitch to the corner.
Pivot, and take one stitch
across the apex of the corner, pivot again,
then stitch on around the fabric.

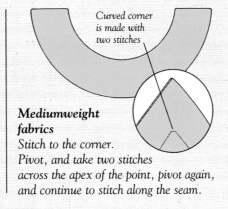

Curved corner is made with two stitches

Mediumweight fabrics
Stitch to the corner.
Pivot, and take two stitches
across the apex of the point, pivot again,
and continue to stitch along the seam.

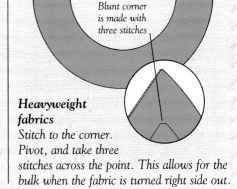

Blunt corner is made with three stitches

Heavyweight fabrics
Stitch to the corner.
Pivot, and take three
stitches across the point. This allows for the
bulk when the fabric is turned right side out.

REDUCING SEAM BULK

SEAM ALLOWANCES THAT ARE ENCLOSED within a finished part of the garment should be trimmed to reduce bulk. On medium- to heavyweight fabrics, layering or grading is required to reduce the bulk further. On curved seams, the trimmed or layered seam allowances should also be either clipped or notched to make them lie flat.

TRIMMING

Seam allowance

TRIM BOTH seam allowances together to about half the original seam width (above) before pressing. This is usually sufficient for seams on light- to mediumweight fabrics.

LAYERING

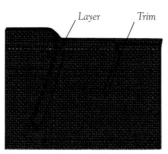

Layer *Trim*

TO LAYER (or grade) the seam allowances, trim the fabric layers to different widths to avoid a thick ridge at the edge (above). The widest layer should sit nearest the garment.

CLIPPING

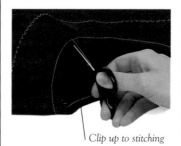

Clip up to stitching

INWARD curved seams, as on collars, require clipping. Cut into the seam allowances up to the stitching to allow the fabric to open out and to fit around the curve (above).

NOTCHING

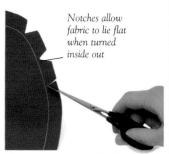

Notches allow fabric to lie flat when turned inside out

NOTCHES are small, V-shaped wedges that are cut out of the seam allowances on outward curves. To form a notch, first cut one side of the V shape, then cut the other (above).

CLIPPING AND NOTCHING

WHERE AN INWARD CURVE is stitched to an outward curve, clip one seam allowance so that the edge lies flat, and notch the other to remove excess fullness (above).

CROSS SEAMS

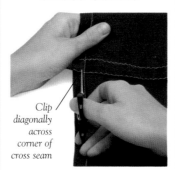

Clip diagonally across corner of cross seam

WHEN AN EXISTING SEAM is stitched across by a new seam, this is called a cross seam. On medium- or heavyweight fabrics only, clip across the corners at an angle (above).

UNDERSTITCHING

TO HELP AN EDGE SEAM roll naturally to the wrong side, press the seam allowances and facing away from the garment. With the facing uppermost, stitch through both the facing and the seam allowances close to the seam (above).

UNDERSTITCHING BY HAND

ON THIN FABRICS and areas that are difficult to reach by machine, a seam can be understitched by hand. Work as for machine understitching (see left), but work prickstitch (p. 74) through the facing and seam allowances (above).

TRIMMING A POINT

Point of seam

1 ON CORNERS where the seams are stitched along both sides, it is important to trim the seam allowances well to achieve a sharp point when the corner is turned right side out. Trim across the point just a few threads outside the seam stitching (above).

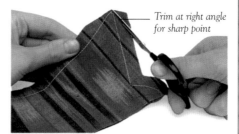

Trim at right angle for sharp point

2 TRIM both seam allowances at an angle toward the corner point (above). The sharper the point, the closer to the stitching the trimming needs to be. When the corner is turned right side out, the seam allowances should sit neatly inside the point without overlapping.

TRIMMING CORNER ANGLES

Clip diagonally across seam allowance

ON A CORNER where one side is formed by a seam and the other is formed by a fold, trim across the seam allowance at an angle (above). To achieve a sharp point, the seam allowance should be trimmed at an angle close to the seam, just a few threads outside the seam stitching.

SEAM FINISHES

A SEAM FINISH NEATENS A SEAM ALLOWANCE while also protecting the seam from wear and tear. The type of finish chosen depends on the design of the garment, the fabric weight, the amount of wear, tear, and laundering expected, and whether or not the seams will show. Zigzag stitch is the most widely used finish for seams.

ZIGZAG-STITCHED

THIS FINISH IS SUITABLE for most types of fabric. Work along the edges of the seam allowances, using a medium-length stitch on light- to mediumweight fabrics and a wider stitch for thicker fabrics (above).

TRIMMED AND ZIGZAGGED

Trimmed seam allowances zigzag stitched together

THIS IS A NEAT FINISH for lightweight fabrics on which the seam shows through. Trim the seam allowances to half the original width. Zigzag stitch the edges together, and press to one side (above).

TURNED AND STITCHED

Turned-under edge

SUITABLE FOR COTTON FABRICS, this finish is used when zigzag stitch is not available. Fold ⅛ in (3 mm) to the wrong side along each raw edge. Machine stitch along each folded edge to finish (above).

BIAS-BOUND

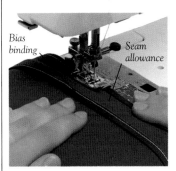

Bias binding

Seam allowance

PRESS A CREASE along the ⅝-in (1.5-cm) wide bias binding, with one side slightly wider. Sandwich the fabric edge in the binding with the wider part underneath. Stitch through all the layers (above).

HAND OVERCAST

AN ALTERNATIVE to zigzag stitch, overcasting is used for small areas and on thick fabrics when zigzag stitch is not available. Overcast the seam edges by hand, using small, loose stitches (above).

PINKED

Pink the edges

USED on fray-resistant fabrics such as wools, this is not a hardwearing finish. Trim the edges of the seam allowances with pinking shears (above), cutting away as little fabric as possible.

STITCHED AND PINKED

MACHINE straight stitching makes this a hardwearing finish. Stitch along the seam allowances about ¼ in (6 mm) in from the edge. Trim the edges with pinking shears (above).

HONG KONG FINISH

Stitch ¼ in (5 mm) from raw edge

Right sides together

1 This is a less bulky alternative to the bias-bound finish. Cut ¾-in (2-cm) wide bias strips from a lightweight fabric. With right sides together and raw edges even, stitch the bias strip to the seam allowance ¼ in (5 mm) in from the raw edge (left).

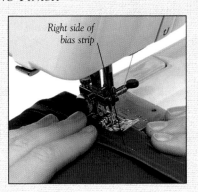

Right side of bias strip

2 Fold the free edge of the strip under the seam allowance. Stitch-in-the-ditch of the first stitching on the right side through all of the layers (left). Repeat on the other side. Press the seam open. For a luxurious finish, use a silk fabric for the strip.

MAKING SELF-ENCLOSED SEAMS

SELF-ENCLOSED SEAMS INCLUDE a variety of seams, such as French seams, that are strong, neat, narrow, and ideal for sheer fabrics. Simple to make on straight edges, these seams are not suitable for curves, where mock French seams should be used instead. Flat-fell seams are hardwearing, and self-bound seams are useful for lightweight fabrics.

FRENCH SEAM

Right side

1 PLACE the two fabric pieces with wrong sides together and raw edges even, and pin. Stitch the pieces together, making a seam ⅜in (1 cm) in from the fabric edge. Then trim both seam allowances to ⅛in (3 mm) (above).

Press seam open

2 PRESS THE SEAM OPEN (above). Fold the right sides of the fabric together, positioning the seam centrally along the fold. Re-press the fabric. Baste the two layers together, stitching close to the ridge formed by the raw edges.

Wrong side

3 ON THE WRONG SIDE, stitch ¼in (5 mm) in from the folded edge (above). Press the seam to one side. (If a narrower seam is required, trim the seam allowances shorter and stitch the final seam closer to the folded edge.)

MOCK FRENCH SEAM

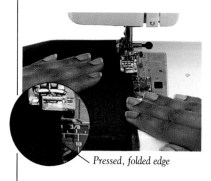

Pressed, folded edge

STITCH an ordinary plain seam (p. 82), and trim the seam allowances to ⅜in (1 cm). Fold in ¼in (6 mm) along both seam allowances. Press the folded edges together. Stitch the seam allowances along the pressed edges (left).

GATHERED SELF-BOUND SEAM

This technique is used where a gathered edge is stitched to a straight edge. With right sides together, stitch a ⅝-in (1.5-cm) seam. Trim the seam allowance on the gathered edge to ¼in (5 mm). Complete as for a self-bound seam (see below).

FLAT-FELL SEAM

Right side

1 THIS STRONG, flat seam is used mainly on sportswear. Stitch a plain seam (p. 82), wrong sides together. Trim one seam allowance to ¼in (6 mm) (left). Opening out the fabric, press the untrimmed seam allowance over the trimmed allowance.

2 TUCK the untrimmed seam edge under the trimmed edge, and press. Stitch the seam allowances onto the garment close to the fold (left). The finished seam width can measure from ¼in (6 mm) to ⅜in (1 cm), depending on the fabric, but it must be the same width throughout.

Stitch seam allowances to garment

SELF-BOUND SEAM

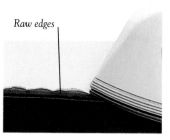

Raw edges

1 THIS SEAM WORKS best on fine, lightweight fabrics that do not fray easily. With right sides together, stitch a plain ⅝-in (1.5-cm) seam. Trim one seam allowance to ¼in (5 mm). Press in ⅛in (3 mm) along the untrimmed edge (left).

Tucked in raw edges

2 FOLD the pressed edge over the trimmed seam allowance, so that it is aligned with the previous row of stitching. Be sure that all the raw edges are enclosed. Stitch along the pressed edge through all thicknesses (left).

MAKING TOPSTITCHED SEAMS

Topstitched seams have a line or lines of stitching on the finished right side of the garment. In the case of topstitched and edgestitched seams, the stitching is purely decorative and adds a crisp finish. With the other seam types shown, the surface stitching is also part of the structural stitching that holds the seam together.

TOPSTITCHED SEAM

Right side

STITCH A PLAIN SEAM (p. 82), zigzag finish the edges together, and press to one side. Stitch through the fabric and both seam allowances, keeping the edge of the presser foot parallel with the seamline (above).

DOUBLE TOPSTITCHED SEAM

PRESS a plain seam allowance open. Working on the right side, stitch down both sides of the seam through the fabric and the seam allowance, an equal and even distance from the seamline (above).

EDGESTITCHED SEAM

Zigzag-stitched edges

ZIGZAG STITCH the edges of a plain seam together, and press to one side. Working on the wrong side, stitch close to the seamline through the fabric and both of the seam allowances (above).

WELT SEAM

Topstitch through fabric and wide seam allowance

ON A PLAIN SEAM, trim one seam allowance to half its original width. Press both allowances to one side with the trimmed edge underneath. Topstitch through the fabric and seam allowance (above).

CURVED TUCKED SEAM

Seam allowance has been clipped before stitching

STAYSTITCH JUST INSIDE the seamline on the top seam allowance of a plain seam, and press the seam allowance so that the staystitching just rolls over to the wrong side. Clip the seam allowance. Topstitch the seam (above) in the same way as for a straight tucked seam (see right).

STRAIGHT TUCKED SEAM

PRESS ONE SEAM ALLOWANCE on a plain seam to the wrong side. With right sides facing upward, lap the pressed edge over the unpressed edge with the raw edges aligned. Pin, and baste if needed. Topstitch along the pressed edge, either near the edge or ¼ in (5 mm) in (above).

CHANNEL SEAM

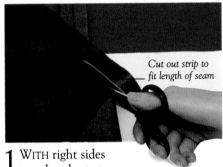

Cut out strip to fit length of seam

1 WITH right sides together, baste to form a ⅝-in (1.5-cm) seam. Press the seam open. Cut out a 1¼-in (3-cm) wide strip of matching or contrasting fabric the length of the seam (above). Place the strip centrally over the seam allowances.

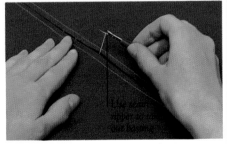

2 PIN, AND BASTE if required. Keeping the machine foot parallel with the basted seamline, topstitch through all thicknesses along both sides of the seam. Remove the basting (above).

DECORATIVE TOPSTITCHING

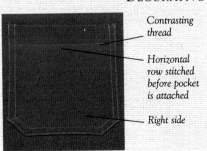

Contrasting thread

Horizontal row stitched before pocket is attached

Right side

For pronounced topstitching for a decorative effect, thread extra-thick buttonhole twist or contrasting thread on the top of the machine, and wind ordinary thread onto the bobbin. Use matching or contrasting colored thread. Working on the right side, stitch as many rows of topstitching as required to achieve the desired decorative effect.

STITCHING CURVED SEAMS

A PRINCESS SEAM is formed by joining inward and outward curves. The curved seam is shaped out over the bust, fitted in at the waist, and shaped out toward the hips. A garment with princess seams usually has a front panel, or two front panels for a center opening, and two side panels. There may also be back princess seaming.

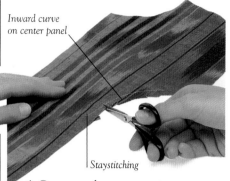

Inward curve on center panel

Staystitching

1 CUT OUT the pattern pieces. Staystitch the center panel, or panels, just inside the seamline from above the top notch to below the second notch under the bust shaping. Clip the curve between the notches (above).

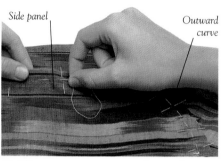

Side panel

Outward curve

2 WITH RIGHT SIDES together and raw edges even, place the side panel and center panel together, with the side panel uppermost. Pin the seam, opening up the clips on the center panel to fit around the side panel shaping. Baste (above).

STITCHING CURVES

Foot raised

On gentle curves, stitch slowly, turning the fabric while stitching. On sharper curves, stop the machine often with the needle down, raise the foot, and turn the fabric (above).

3 REMOVE THE PINS. Working with the center panel uppermost, stitch the seam (above). At the bust shaping, stitch a little at a time, stopping with the needle down to check that the underside of the seam is flat before continuing.

Stitch slowly, checking underside

Notch outward curve

4 REMOVE THE BASTING. Open out the seam. Cut out small notches from the side panel seam allowance (above) so that the panel lies flat. Stagger the notches between the clips already on the center panel seam allowance.

Clipped and notched seam

5 PRESS OPEN the clipped and notched seam using the curved part of a sleeve board or the edge of the ironing board (above). Press carefully, section by section, taking care not to press in unwanted creases around the princess seam.

STITCHING CROTCH SEAMS

Inside leg seam

1 Stitch the leg seams to make two separate legs. Turn one leg right side out, and place it inside the other leg. Pin and baste (above) from the waist edge across the inside leg seams to the zipper.

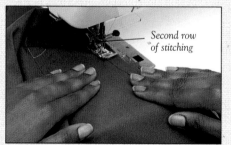

Second row of stitching

2 Remove the pins. Stitch, leaving the zipper opening unstitched. Remove the basting. Reinforce the crotch area of the seam by stitching a second row of small, straight stitches just inside the previous row (above).

3 Zigzag stitch the raw edges. Press the seam open along the straight part of the seam only, leaving the crotch area unpressed. Press seam allowances to the wrong side at the zipper opening (above).

TAPING SEAMS

SOME SEAMS REQUIRE TAPING to prevent them from stretching. On soft knit fabrics, the seams on the main garment may need taping, especially shoulder seams that are cut across the fabric, and those seams that may stretch with wear, such as a hip pocket edge. Twill tape and seam tape make firm seams, and bias binding gives a soft finish.

USING TWILL TAPE

THIS TECHNIQUE is used to strengthen a pocket opening and to keep it from stretching. Position twill tape centrally over the pocket seamline on the wrong side of the garment. Baste then stitch it to the garment.

USING BIAS BINDING

Bias binding

USE BINDING at shoulder seams on knits. Pin the seam. Cut the binding in half lengthwise, open out, and pin the fold along the seamline (above). Stitch.

FINISHING A BOUND SEAM

PRESS THE BINDING away from the seam allowances. Zigzag stitch the binding and the seam allowances together. Trim (above).

STITCHING SEAMS WITH EASE AND BIAS

WHEN TWO EDGES BEING JOINED are not the same length, the longer edge may be eased in to fit. The ease may only be slight – for example, on the back edge of a shoulder seam. Moderate ease is on sleeve caps and at the elbows on fitted sleeves. Stitching bias edges to straight edges is necessary when stitching insertions into garments.

SLIGHT EASE

PIN THE RAW EDGES together, matching notches and distributing the fullness evenly (above). Stitch slowly, taking care to avoid forming tucks.

MODERATE EASE

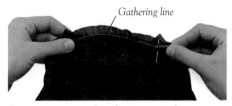

Gathering line

STITCH A LINE of gathering stitches between the notches. Pin the edges, and match the notches. Pull the bobbin thread to ease the fullness (above). Stitch.

BIAS TO STRAIGHT EDGE

WHEN PINNING a bias edge to a straight edge, insert pins closer together than normal (above). This helps to prevent stretching during stitching.

STITCHING SEAMS ON KNIT FABRICS

THERE ARE A NUMBER OF WAYS to stitch a seam on stretchable knit fabrics. Stretching while sewing allows the stitches some elasticity, while a machine overedge stretch stitch produces a strong seam. These seams should be trimmed and the edges zigzag stitched together. Seams on knits are not pressed open because they will not lie flat.

STRETCHING WHILE SEWING

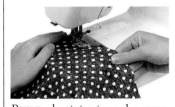

BUILD elasticity into the seam by holding the fabric taut while stitching. Place a hand on either side of the machine foot when stitching (above).

OVEREDGE STRETCH STITCH

THIS strong, preset stitch combines a straight stretch stitch with an overedge stitch. Stitch without stretching the fabric (above).

MACHINE STRETCH STITCH

This stitch is formed by working two stitches forward and one stitch back, so that each stitch is worked three times. Reduce the pressure on the presser foot to prevent the fabric from stretching. Stitch (left).

STITCHING SEAMS ON SHEER FABRICS

SEAM ALLOWANCES are visible through sheer fabrics, so a neat, narrow seam is preferable. Trimmed seams with the edges zigzag stitched together, and self-enclosed seams, such as French seams and flat-fell seams (p. 86), can be used as alternatives to the methods shown here. The enclosed hairline seam is ideal for babies' clothes.

MACHINE OVEREDGE STITCH

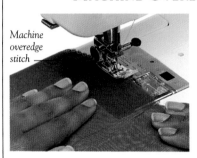
Machine overedge stitch

THIS is a preset machine stitch that stitches and finishes a very narrow seam all in one. Before stitching, trim the seam allowance to the same width as the stitch. Stitch so that the stitching overlaps the edge (left).

ENCLOSED HAIRLINE SEAM

Zigzag stitching

SHEER FABRICS, even enclosed seams, require a neat finish. Stitch the seam, then work narrow zigzag stitch through both seam allowances at once just outside the stitching. Trim close to the stitching (left).

STITCHING SEAMS ON SYNTHETIC FABRICS

SUEDE, VINYL, AND PLASTICS often get hung up under the sewing machine foot. A roller foot, nonstick foot, and walking foot are designed to overcome this problem. Or the fabric can be sandwiched between two strips of tissue paper. Before stitching, these fabrics can be held together with paper clips, double-sided tape, or fabric glue.

PLAIN SEAM ON SYNTHETIC SUEDE

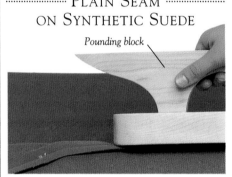
Pounding block

STITCH A PLAIN SEAM. Check for fit. Finger press the seam open, and hammer, using a pounding block to flatten the seam (above). Stick the seam allowances down with an appropriate glue (p. 14).

LAPPED SEAM ON SUEDE

1 TRIM THE SEAM ALLOWANCE from the overlapping edge. Mark the seamline on the right side of the other edge. Stick double-sided tape (p. 15) along the seam allowance, and overlap the edges (above).

First row of topstitching

2 WORKING on the right side, topstitch close to the overlapping edge. If desired, stitch a second row of topstitching, aligning the side edge of the presser foot with the first row of stitching (above).

PLAIN SEAM ON FUR FABRIC

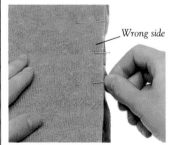
Wrong side

1 PUSH THE FUR PILE away from the seam allowance, to prevent it from getting caught in the seam. With raw edges even, pin the seam edges together (above).

Right side

2 STITCH the seam, and open it out gently. On the right side, use the point of a needle to pick out any pile that has become caught in the stitching (above).

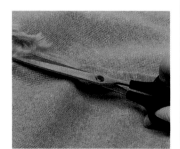

3 WORKING on the wrong side, trim the fur pile away from the seam allowances (above). This reduces bulk and helps the fur fabric seam allowances open out flat.

FLAT FUR SEAM

PIN THE SEAM right sides together. Stitch with a wide, short zigzag stitch, positioned so that the raw edges are covered. Pull gently apart until the edges meet (above).

MAKING PIPING

THERE ARE TWO TYPES OF PIPING, flat and corded, and both are made with bias-cut strips of fabric. For flat piping, the bias strip (p. 214–215) is folded in half and inserted in the seam, while corded piping has a cord inside the bias strip. The cord is available in different thicknesses. Piping can also be bought ready made.

FLAT PIPING

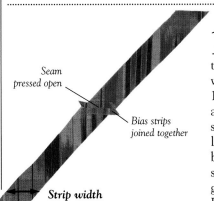

Seam pressed open

Bias strips joined together

Strip width

1 CUT the bias strips to a width that is twice the required finished width of the piping, plus 1¼ in (3 cm) for the seam allowances. Cut enough strips to cover the required length of piping. Join the bias strips with seams stitched on the straight grain the required length. Press the seams open.

Wrong sides together

2 With wrong sides together, fold the entire bias strip in half lengthwise. Press along the center fold. Stitch the strip ½ in (12 mm) in from the raw edges (left). The pressed piping is now ready to be inserted between the two fabric edges of the seam as required.

CORDED PIPING

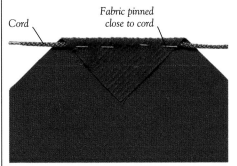

Cord

Fabric pinned close to cord

1 TO DETERMINE the required width of the bias strip, fold a corner of the fabric, or a piece of tissue paper, around the piping cord, encasing it tightly. Pin next to the cord (above). Measure ⅝ in (1.5 cm) away from the pins, and cut across the fabric or tissue at this point, parallel to the pins. Remove the pins.

2 USING the measured piece as a pattern, cut out a cardboard template. Use the template to measure the strip width, and mark out the bias strips to the required width on the fabric (above). Cut out the strips, and join them end to end to make up the required piping length. Press the seams open.

Stitch between pins and cord

Zipper foot

3 WRAP THE BIAS STRIP around the cord with wrong sides together. Place the raw edges together, and pin near the cord. With the zipper foot positioned to the left of the needle, stitch close to the cord (above), leaving enough room to stitch two more rows when it is attached to the garment. Then remove the pins.

PIPING A CURVE

Clipping allows edges to open out

PIN THE PIPING to the right side of one seam allowance, with the cording to the inside. At a curve, clip the piping seam allowance, opening out the edges to ease around the curve (above). The deeper the curve, the closer the clips need to be. Stitch the piping in place.

PIPING A SHARP CORNER

Clip opened to fit around corner

Right side

AFTER PINNING THE PIPING to the seam allowance on one side of the corner, measure ⅝ in (1.5 cm) from the corner, and clip the piping seam allowance almost to the stitching here. Open the clip to fit the piping around the corner. Finish pinning (above). Stitch, pivoting at the corner.

JOINING CORDED PIPING ENDS

Excess to be trimmed level

LEAVE THE PIPING unstitched for ¾ in (2 cm) on each side of the join, and allow excess at the ends of the piping. Overlap the ends at the seamline, and mark with a pin. Pull back the covering, and trim the cords. Overlap the covering at an angle, and stitch across the join (above). Trim.

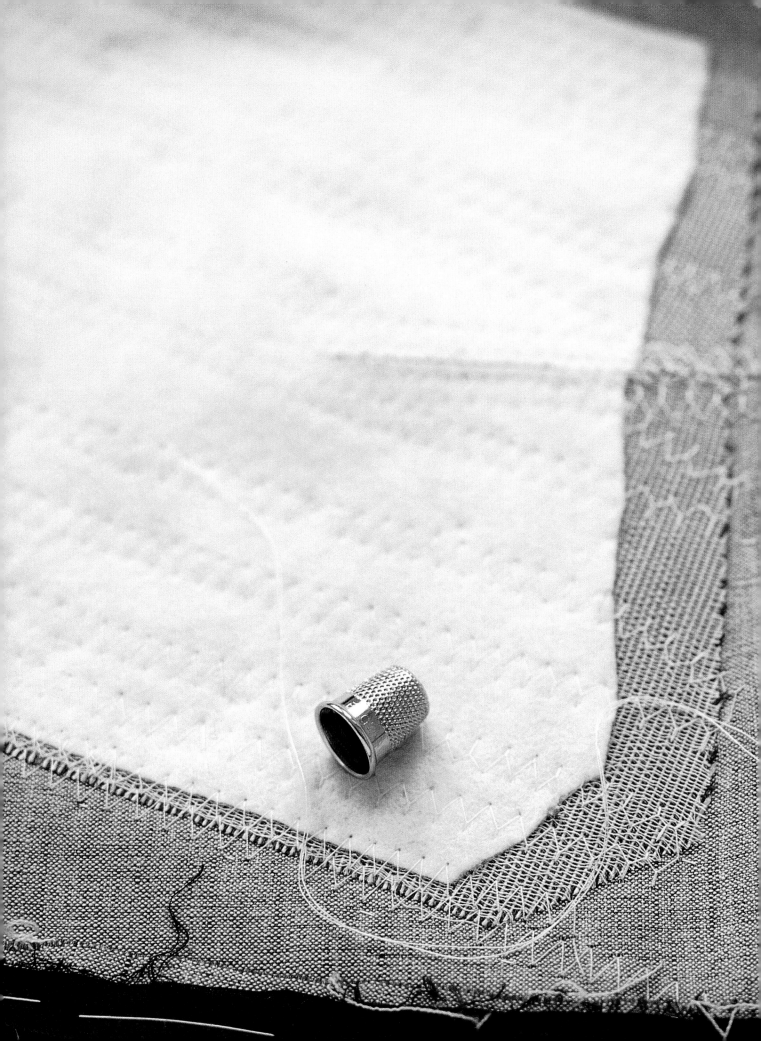

INTERFACINGS & LININGS

UNDERLYING FABRICS

THE UNDERLYING FABRIC LAYERS inside the garment are the lining, underlining, interfacing, and interlining. The lining hides raw edges and the construction details on the inner garment, and it provides a slippery surface that makes the garment comfortable to wear. Sandwiched between a facing and the garment fabric, the interfacing gives additional strength, durability, and stability to collars, cuffs, waistbands, and openings. Underlining and interlining are not used as widely as interfacing and are found mainly in tailored garments.

RELATED TECHNIQUES

Preparing two layers
as one, p. 96
Sewing seams in
interfacing, p. 98
Attaching a lining by
machine, p. 103
Attaching interlining to a
garment, p. 105

DIRECTORY OF UNDERLYING FABRICS

Underlining stitched to garment fabric

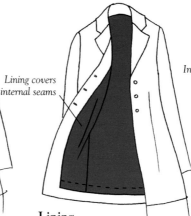

Lining covers internal seams

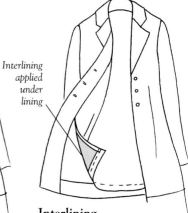

Interlining applied under lining

Interfacing
Applied to the wrong side of facings and to the top collar only (p. 98), interfacing is used to stabilize and stiffen the garment fabric in the areas where this is required.

Underlining
Stitched to the inside of a garment (p. 96), underlining prevents darts and seams from showing on the right side of sheer fabrics, and adds support to loose-weave fabrics.

Lining
A separate layer of silky fabric, lining is sewn inside a garment to hide internal seams and darts (p. 102). It also helps tailored wool clothes to slip on and be worn comfortably.

Interlining
A separate layer of soft fabric that is inserted between the inside of the garment and the lining, interlining is used most often on jackets and coats to add warmth (p. 105).

USING LININGS AND UNDERLININGS

LININGS ARE AVAILABLE in a wide range of colors. The chosen color should complement the garment unless a contrast is desired. If a good match cannot be made, a similar shade that is duller, rather than brighter, than the fabric color should be used. Visible underlinings may match or contrast, but hidden ones must be a neutral shade.

LININGS

LININGS USUALLY HAVE a silky texture. Silk linings are used on woolen and luxury garments. On everyday garments, polyester, acrylic, or fine rayon linings are more suitable. Nonstatic linings are also available. The laundering or dry-cleaning requirements of lining and garment fabrics should always be compatible.

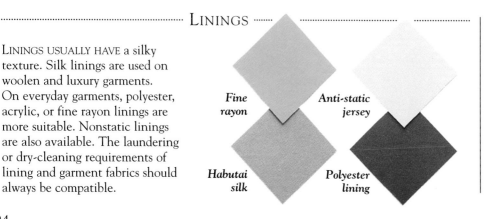

Fine rayon

Anti-static jersey

Habutai silk

Polyester lining

UNDERLININGS

THE CHOICE of an underlining fabric depends on the purpose for which it will be used. Generally, an underlining should be lightweight and should not hinder the natural drape of the garment fabric. If the underlining is backing a lace fabric, then satin, crepe de Chine, or a lining fabric is the ideal choice. When working with a flimsy fabric, it is best to choose a soft underlining.

CHOOSING INTERFACINGS AND INTERLININGS

INTERFACINGS CAN BE WOVEN OR NONWOVEN, sew-in or fusible, and are available in a choice of weights to suit different fabrics. Most types are made in neutral shades of white, cream, gray, or black, but some woven interfacings are available in other colors. Used in a garment to add padding and warmth, interlinings often have a fluffy texture.

WOVEN INTERFACINGS

French canvas
A stiff linen used to interface collars, this is also used in millinery work.

Organdy
This light cotton fabric is suitable for use on both fine and transparent fabrics.

Holland
A mediumweight linen or cotton fabric, this is used as an interfacing on woolen fabrics.

Hair canvas
This is a heavyweight canvas that is used mainly in the tailoring of coats and jackets.

Lawn
A lightweight cotton, this is used on both lightweight wool and cotton fabrics.

Batiste
Batiste can be used on silk, lawn, and cotton. It is a woven fabric that is available in a range of colors.

Organza
Like organdy, this silk fabric is used as an interfacing on very fine fabrics.

Mull muslin
A light, open-weave cotton, this is used on silk, lawn, and cotton fabrics.

Fusible cotton
This is used on cotton and woolen fabrics. It comes in different weights, in black or white.

NONWOVEN INTERFACINGS

Light fusible
This forms a soft but firm base for lightweight cottons, wools, and polyesters.

Medium fusible
This is best for light- to mediumweight crisp cottons and cotton blends.

Firm fusible
Ideal for waistbands, this is used on medium- to heavyweight cotton fabrics, and blends.

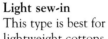

Light sew-in
This type is best for lightweight cottons, velvets, polyesters, and metallic fabrics.

Medium sew-in
This is used for light- to mediumweight corduroys, velvets, and metallic fabrics.

Heavy sew-in
This is suitable for heavyweight wool, gabardine, and coating fabrics.

Soft fusible
An interfacing with a luxurious feel, this is suitable for soft and delicate fabrics.

Stretch fusible
This is used for stretchy fabrics – cotton and polyester jersey, and knits.

Knitted fusible
A knitted fabric, this is used to give extra body to soft crepes and silk fabrics.

INTERLININGS

Wool
Cream-colored pure wool is used as an interlining on wool jackets and coats.

Polyester batting
A bulky, lightweight padding, this is used for quilting and as a stuffing for pillows.

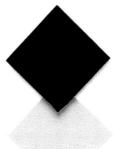

Fleece
Made of a variety of fibers, this is used to add warmth to fabrics or to pad quilting.

Flannel
This interlining is soft and lightweight; flannelette is thinner. Both add warmth.

Jersey calico
This calico supports jersey fabrics without impairing the special qualities of jersey.

Wool fleece
This lamb's wool is used to add warmth, or as a padding under hair canvas.

UNDERLININGS

UNDERLINING IS A LAYER OF FABRIC that is cut to the same shape as, and placed directly underneath, the garment fabric before any seams are joined or any interfacing is applied. It can be used to cover fabrics with an open weave, to add support to a loosely woven fabric, to prevent any construction details from showing through on sheer fabric, or to add weight to light fabrics. The two methods for attaching underlining are shown in detail here. A lightweight lining fabric is usually the most suitable fabric for underlining.

RELATED TECHNIQUES

Marking tools, p. 13
Working basting stitches, p. 73
Working tailor's tacks, p. 73
Using linings and
underlinings, p. 94
Plain darts, p. 109

PREPARING TWO LAYERS AS ONE

IN THIS METHOD, THE UNDERLINING is attached to the wrong side of the garment fabric before any construction detail is worked. This type of underlining reinforces the garment fabric and prevents stitching, seam allowances, and facings from showing through on the right side. This is useful for lace, sheer, and loosely woven fabrics.

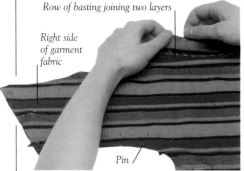

Row of basting joining two layers

Right side of garment fabric

Pin

1 CUT OUT the garment fabric and underlining pieces. Place the two layers together, wrong sides facing. (On lace, place the layers together with right sides uppermost.) With the garment fabric uppermost, baste down the center or, if the piece is narrow, near one edge. Pin around the outer edges (above).

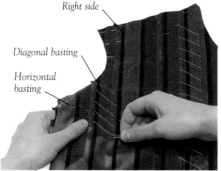

Right side

Diagonal basting

Horizontal basting

2 BASTE HORIZONTALLY across the center of the garment piece, then work two or four rows of diagonal basting down the piece to hold the underlining and the garment fabric securely together (above). Remove the pins and, if needed, trim the edge of the underlining to make it even with the edges of the garment fabric.

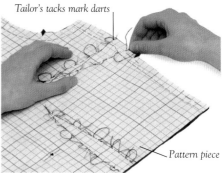

Tailor's tacks mark darts

Pattern piece

3 REPOSITION THE PATTERN PIECE on the inside of the underlining. Transfer the dart markings (above) and other pattern markings to the underlining, using the desired method (p. 13). If any markings, such as a pocket placement, are required on the right side of the garment, use tailor's tacks to mark both layers.

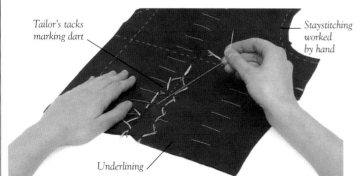

Tailor's tacks marking dart

Staystitching worked by hand

Underlining

4 STAYSTITCH THE FABRIC EDGES TOGETHER where required, for example, around the armholes and neckline, or the sleeve caps. This will prevent the layers from slipping. Staystitch along the center of any darts (above), extending the stitching by two or three stitches beyond the point of each dart. The staystitching can be worked either by hand or by machine.

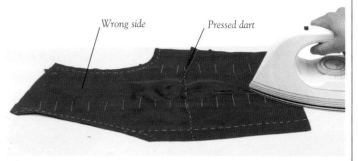

Wrong side

Pressed dart

5 FOLD EACH DART ALONG THE CENTER, then pin and baste. If tailor's tacks were used to mark the darts, remove them. Check that the darts are well formed on the right side. Stitch the darts. Remove the staystitching that extends beyond the dart points, and remove the basting. Press the darts flat, then to one side in the required direction (above) (see Step 3, opposite).

PREPARING TWO LAYERS SEPARATELY

Enclosing the darts between the garment fabric and underlining gives a neat finish on the inside. The darts are first stitched separately on each layer, and the two layers are then treated as one. This method is used to give body to a lightweight fabric; however, it cannot be used on sheer fabrics, because the darts would show through.

1 Cut out the garment fabric pieces, and transfer the pattern markings to them, using tailor's tacks (left). Cut out the underlining pieces, and transfer the markings in the same way. (Alternatively, mark the darts on the wrong side using any method [see p. 13], and use tailor's tacks for other markings so that they show on the right side.)

Dart marked with tailor's tacks

Pattern piece

2 Just inside the seamline, staystitch any edges that may stretch on both the garment fabric pieces and on the underlining pieces, treating each piece separately (left). (On a fitted skirt, staystitch the waistline edges. On a bodice, staystitch the neckline and armholes.)

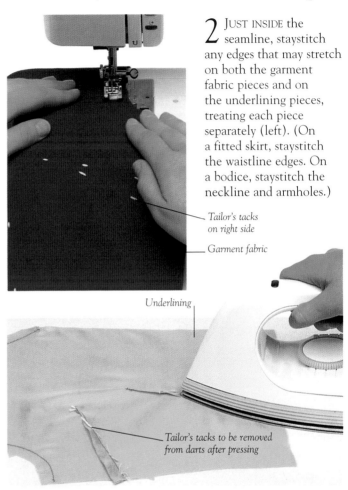

Tailor's tacks on right side

Garment fabric

Underlining

Tailor's tacks to be removed from darts after pressing

3 Working on the garment fabric pieces, fold each dart with right sides together, and stitch from the wide end of the dart to the point (left). Press the darts in the directions given on the pattern. (A bust dart is usually pressed downward, and a waist dart is usually pressed toward either the center front or the center back.)

Folded dart

4 On the underlining pieces, fold each dart with right sides together, and stitch from the wide end of the dart to the point. Press these darts in the opposite directions to those used on the fabric pieces (above) so that they do not create excess bulk once the garment fabric and underlining are joined.

5 Place the prepared underlining piece on top of the prepared garment fabric piece, with wrong sides together. Baste the pieces together down the center front or center back. Pin the pieces together around the outer edges (left).

Pins hold fabric pieces in place

Underlining sits on top of garment piece

6 With the right side of the garment piece uppermost, baste horizontally across the center to hold the two layers together. Work rows of diagonal basting (p. 73) up and down the piece through both layers (left). Remove the pins around the outer edges. If required, trim the edge of the underlining so that it aligns with the edge of the garment fabric.

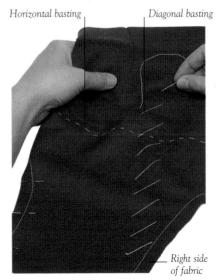

Horizontal basting

Diagonal basting

Right side of fabric

INTERFACINGS

INTERFACINGS ARE SPECIAL FABRICS used to strengthen or stiffen specific parts of a garment, such as a collar, cuffs, facings, and pocket tops. They are made in light-, medium-, and heavyweights to match fabric weights, and can be either fusible or sew-in. The latter type is preferable on sheer and fine fabrics where fusible adhesive might show through the fabric. For general use, nonwoven interfacings are ideal. For more advanced work and for tailoring, woven interfacings are available. On sheer fabric, matching organza or lawn can be used instead of interfacing.

RELATED TECHNIQUES

Hand sewing stitches, p. 74
Working hemming stitches, p. 76
Reducing seam bulk, p. 84
Attaching a shaped facing, p. 129
Attaching interfacing to
a collar, p. 143
Reinforcing a waistband, p. 167
Making a tie belt, p. 172

ATTACHING WOVEN CANVAS INTERFACING

PADDING STITCHES ARE USED mainly in tailoring to fasten canvas interfacing firmly to the fabric on lapels and collars (p. 290). When the stitches are made short and close together, they shape the fabric three-dimensionally. When they are made long and spaced apart, the stitches simply hold the woven interfacing permanently to the fabric.

CHEVRON PADDING STITCHES

Make small, even stitches

WORKING from top to bottom, make small, evenly spaced, horizontal stitches, forming a row of diagonal stitches on the right side. Work the next row back up without turning the fabric (left), forming chevrons. Continue working rows downward and upward.

PARALLEL PADDING STITCHES

Work each row downward

WORK THIS STITCH as for chevron padstitch, but work each row downward (left), restarting each row at the top. Parallel padstitch is usually larger than chevron padstitch, and its purpose is to hold the interfacing to the fabric, rather than to shape it.

SEWING SEAMS IN INTERFACING

IT IS SOMETIMES NECESSARY to join pieces of nonwoven interfacing together, either to make up the length required for a long front facing or to use the interfacing economically. To keep the seam as flat as possible so that it does not show on the finished garment, the fabric is butted together or overlapped and trimmed as shown below.

EDGE-TO-EDGE SEAM

TRIM THE ALLOWANCE from the edges to be joined, and place them together over an underlay strip of lightweight fabric or interfacing. Machine stitch close to the edge of each piece (above).

EDGE-TO-EDGE ZIGZAG SEAM

TRIM any seam allowances, place the edges together over an underlay, and zigzag stitch, catching both edges (above). It is possible to omit the underlay on an edge-to-edge seam to form a flatter join.

LAPPED SEAM

OVERLAP THE EDGES, aligning the seamlines. Machine stitch two rows of straight stitch ⅟₁₆ i n (2 mm) apart along the center of the overlapped edges. Then trim the seam allowances (above).

LAPPED ZIGZAG SEAM

OVERLAP THE EDGES, so that the seamlines are aligned. Zigzag stitch along the center of the overlapped edges (above). Trim the seam allowances on both sides of the zigzagged stitching line.

ATTACHING LIGHT- AND MEDIUMWEIGHT SEW-IN INTERFACING

LIGHT- TO MEDIUMWEIGHT INTERFACINGS are usually stitched to facings. However, on some garment pieces, such as collars, interfacings work most effectively if they are stitched directly behind the garment fabric and on top of the seam allowances. In these cases, it is preferable to interface the garment itself rather than the facing.

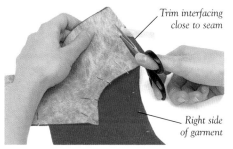

Trim interfacing close to seam

Right side of garment

1 PIN THE INTERFACING to the wrong side of the fabric pieces. Pin and stitch the interfaced pieces together through all layers, and trim the interfacing (above).

2 BASTE THE INTERFACED PIECE to the non-interfaced piece, with right sides together and raw edges even. Remove the pins. Then machine stitch (above).

3 REMOVE THE BASTING, and trim the interfacing as close as possible to the stitching (above). Trim the seam allowances, finishing as required (p. 85).

ATTACHING HEAVYWEIGHT SEW-IN INTERFACING

SINCE HEAVYWEIGHT INTERFACINGS are very bulky, they are not stitched into the seams like lighter-weight interfacings. Instead, the seam allowances are trimmed away before the interfacing is handstitched in place. Heavyweight interfacing is stitched either to the garment or to the facing, according to the pattern instructions.

Align edges of interfacing with seamlines

Basting stitches

1 CUT the heavyweight interfacing pieces. Trim the seam and hem allowances from the interfacing. Pin, then baste the interfacing to the facing or to the garment as required, keeping the trimmed edges aligned with the seamlines. Catchstitch (p. 76) the trimmed edges of the interfacing to the seamlines (left).

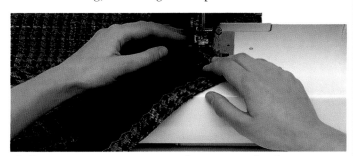

2 PIN THE INTERFACED PIECE to the non-interfaced piece. Machine stitch along the seamline close to the trimmed edge (above). Finish the seam as required (p. 85).

APPLYING FUSIBLE INTERFACING

FUSIBLE INTERFACING has one side coated with a heat-fusible adhesive. It is available in woven and nonwoven forms and in a range of weights from superfine to medium. Fusible stretch interfacing is available for use on jersey. All types of fusible interfacing should be tested on a fabric scrap, following the manufacturer's directions.

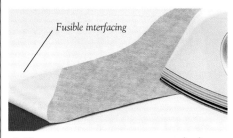

Fusible interfacing

1 CUT THE INTERFACING to match the fabric shape. (If cutting a double layer, place the adhesive sides together.) Lay the adhesive side face down on the wrong side of the fabric. Begin pressing (above).

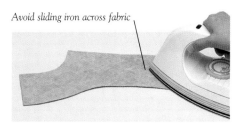

Avoid sliding iron across fabric

2 WHEN PRESSING the interfacing in position, place the iron firmly on it for a few seconds at a time. Do not slide the iron across the fabric. (If desired, use a pressing cloth to protect the iron.)

Fused interfacing and fabric are trimmed as one layer

3 ALLOW THE INTERFACING to cool. Check that it has fused all over, and re-press loose areas. Stitch the interfaced pieces to the other garment pieces. Trim the interfacing and fabric as one (above).

MAKING A DART IN INTERFACING

I N TAILORED JACKETS AND COATS, the interfacing often covers large sections of the bodice, and in such cases the pattern is likely to include darts. It is important to the appearance of the garment to make these darts as flat as possible. Make edge-to-edge, catchstitched, or lapped darts in the interfacing in order to reduce the bulk.

EDGE-TO-EDGE DART

Tailor's tacks

Dart center

1 THIS DART IS VERY FLAT and is used mainly on nonfraying interfacings and interlinings. Mark the dart with tailor's tacks joined up using a dressmaker's pencil, or use a tracing wheel and dressmaker's carbon (p. 13). Cut out the triangular dart center along the marked lines (above).

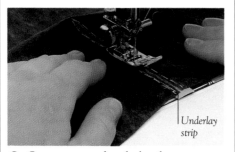

Underlay strip

2 CUT A STRIP of underlay from seam tape or fabric. Place the strip under the cut edges of the dart, positioning the cut edges together at the center of the strip. Baste in place, then machine stitch around the dart ⅛ in (3 mm) from the edges (above). Remove the basting.

CATCHSTITCHED DART

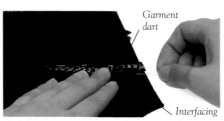

Garment dart

Interfacing

1 MARK THE DART, and cut out the center (see Step 1, Edge-to-Edge Dart, left). Place the interfacing on the garment piece and pull up the garment dart between the cut edges. Pin the interfacing dart edges close to the garment dart on both sides (above).

Garment dart

2 CATCHSTITCH the two edges of the interfacing dart to the garment dart over the line of dart stitching (above), working from the raw edge of the garment up to the point of the dart and back down the other side. Remove the pins as the work progresses.

LAPPED DART

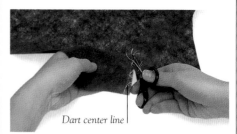

Dart center line

1 NOT AS FLAT as an edge-to-edge dart (see far left), the lapped dart is much sturdier and is therefore often used with frayable fabrics. Mark the dart stitching lines (see Step 1, Edge-to-Edge Dart, far left). Then cut a slit along the center line of the dart (above).

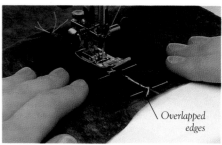

Overlapped edges

2 OVERLAP THE CUT EDGES so that the dart stitching lines are on top of each other, and pin. Stitch along the dart stitching line using a close, wide, three-step zigzag stitch if possible (above), or an ordinary zigzag stitch. Trim the interfacing on both sides of the seam.

APPLYING INTERFACING UP TO A FOLDLINE

T HE EDGE OF FUSIBLE or sew-in interfacing is often applied up to a foldline rather than a fabric edge. In these cases, the foldline must be marked accurately. Short foldlines, such as those on one-piece collars and cuffs, can be marked by a pressed crease. A long, integrated center front facing foldline should be marked with tailor's tacks.

FUSIBLE INTERFACING ON A ONE-PIECE COLLAR

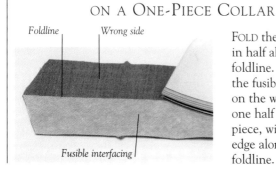

Foldline   *Wrong side*

Fusible interfacing

FOLD the collar piece in half along the foldline. Press. Place the fusible interfacing on the wrong side of one half of the collar piece, with its straight edge along the creased foldline. Press (left).

FUSIBLE INTERFACING ON AN INTEGRATED FRONT FACING

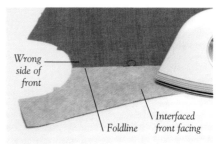

Wrong side of front

Foldline   *Interfaced front facing*

MARK the foldline on the front piece with tailor's tacks along the length and a clip at each end. Then place the fusible interfacing on the wrong side of the integrated facing and press (left).

SEW-IN INTERFACING ON A ONE-PIECE COLLAR

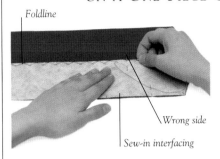

Foldline

Wrong side

Sew-in interfacing

PRESS A CREASE in the collar piece to mark the foldline. Place the sew-in interfacing on the wrong side with its straight edge aligned with the crease, and pin. Catchstitch loosely along the foldline (left).

SEW-IN INTERFACING ON AN INTEGRATED FRONT FACING

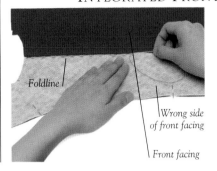

Foldline

Wrong side of front facing

Front facing

MARK the foldline with clips and tailor's tacks. Pin the sew-in interfacing along the wrong side of the front facing. Catchstitch the interfacing loosely in position along the foldline of the facing (left).

INTERFACING BY THE STRIP METHOD

IN ORDER TO REDUCE BULK at seamlines, the interfacing seam allowance can be replaced with a strip of organdy. This avoids the need to handstitch heavyweight sew-in interfacings that are too thick to be stitched into the facing seam. If organdy is not available, a very lightweight interfacing or another fine fabric can be used instead.

Border

Inner edge

1 CUT OUT the interfacing piece using the facing pattern piece. Then mark a borderline around the pattern piece 1¼ in (3 cm) in from the inner edge of the facing. Mark the inner edges of the facing pattern pieces in the same way, and cut out all of the border pattern pieces.

Shoulder seam

Chalk line

2 USING the 1¼-in (3-cm) wide border as a pattern, cut out the border pieces in organdy. Then join the border pieces together at the seams. The seams should overlap slightly. Using tailor's chalk, draw a line ⅝ in (1.5 cm) in from the inner edge along the length of the organdy border.

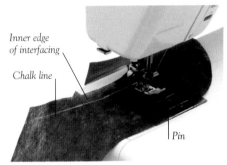

Inner edge of interfacing

Chalk line

Pin

3 USING TAILOR'S CHALK, draw a line ⅝ in (1.5 cm) in from the inner edge on all of the interfacing pieces. Then, where required, join the interfacing pieces by overlapping the edges by 1¼ in (3 cm) at the seamlines, and pinning and zigzag stitching them together (above).

Zigzagged seam

Chalk line

Inner edge

4 ON THE RIGHT SIDE, trim the interfacing seam allowances close to the zigzag stitching. Turn the interfacing to the wrong side and trim the other seam allowances. Trim away the interfacing along the line marked ⅝ in (1.5 cm) from the inner edge (above).

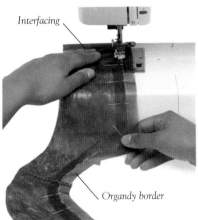

Interfacing

Organdy border

5 LAP THE INNER EDGE of the interfacing over the outer edge of the organdy border, so that the interfacing edge aligns with the chalk line on the organdy border. Pin. Zigzag stitch the interfacing to the organdy (above).

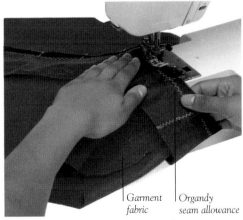

Garment fabric

Organdy seam allowance

6 PLACE THE INTERFACING on the garment or the facing piece as required, and pin in place. Stitch the interfacing to the garment fabric along the chalk line on the organdy border (above). Trim and layer all the seam allowances. Carefully cut away the organdy seam allowance close to the seamline.

LININGS

A LINING GIVES A GARMENT an attractive and luxurious finish as well as serving more practical purposes. A lining helps a woolen garment to slip on and off easily, and also makes the garment more comfortable to wear. A lining adds weight to the drape of a garment and hides all the internal construction details. On lighter fabrics, a lining prevents the shadows of the seams from showing through. It also supports loosely woven fabrics and stops them from bagging around the seat of a skirt or pants.

RELATED TECHNIQUES

Hand sewing stitches, p. 74
Working hemming stitches, p. 76
Reducing seam bulk, p. 84
Making a plain dart, p. 109
Reinforcing a waistband, p. 167
Stitching a lapped zipper, p. 252
Making a jacket lining, p. 295
Attaching a lining, p. 296

MAKING A FREE-HANGING LINING

THIS METHOD OF INSERTING A LINING involves stitching the garment and lining together at the top and sometimes the front edges, with the lining left free at the hem, so that both the garment and the lining are hemmed separately. Free-hanging linings are used mainly for skirts, as illustrated here, and for jackets and coats.

Zipper opening slightly longer than on garment

1 SEW THE SKIRT, omitting the waistband. Cut out the lining. Stitch the lining darts or make tucks instead, as shown in Making Darts for Linings (see below right). Stitch the lining seams, and press them open (above). Press the zipper seam allowances to the wrong side.

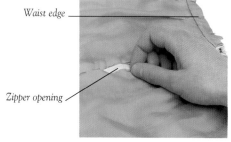

Waist edge

Zipper opening

2 PLACE THE LINING on the garment with wrong sides together, matching the seams and darts. Pin the lining to the skirt around the waist edge, and machine stitch inside the seamline. Then pin the lining around the entire length of the zipper opening (above).

Zipper tape

3 MAKE SURE that the zipper opens and closes without catching the lining. Treating the lining and the fabric as one, stitch on and finish the waistband (p. 166–171). Handstitch the lining to the zipper tape, taking care that the stitches do not go through to the right side (above).

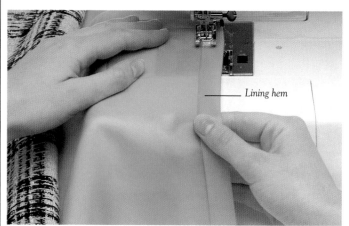

Lining hem

4 STITCH THE GARMENT HEM, then the lining hem, which should be the same width or narrower. The finished hemmed lining should be about ⅝ in (1.5 cm) shorter than the garment. Trim if necessary. Press ⅜ in (1 cm) to the wrong side along the hem edge of the lining, then press the hem to the wrong side. If desired, pin or baste, then machine stitch the hem (above).

MAKING DARTS FOR LININGS

To allow the lining room for movement, it is often best not to stitch ordinary, single-pointed darts along their length. Instead, mark the wide end of the dart with small clips into the fabric edge, and fold a tuck so that the clips match. Pin across the tuck (above), and either baste or machine stitch straight across the tuck, just inside the seamline of the dart.

ATTACHING A LINING BY MACHINE

THIS METHOD IS USED for jackets, vests, and coats with facings. (For vests, omit sleeve linings.) The lining pieces are joined, then attached to the garment facings.

Here, the lining hem is stitched by hand to the garment hem, but it could be machine stitched and left to hang, as in Making a Free-Hanging Lining (opposite).

Sleeve seam on lining

1 MAKE and fit the garment. On the lining pieces, stitch the darts as tucks, and join the side and shoulder seams. Stitch the lining sleeve seams. Insert the lining sleeves into the armholes (left).

2 PIN, then stitch the lining to the front and back neck garment facings, right sides together. Finish the stitching at twice the hem depth up from the edges. Trim and notch the seams (left).

3 PRESS. Turn the lining inside the garment. Pin the lining to the garment at the side seams. Handstitch the seam allowances together along the side seams, finishing 6 in (15 cm) above the garment hem (right).

4 FOLD ⅝ in (1.5 cm) to the wrong side at the lower edge of the lining, just below the top edge of the hem. Handstitch the lining to the hem (right), and the rest of the front edge to the facing. Hem the sleeves.

Pin holds layers in place

MAKING AN EDGE-TO-EDGE LINING

THE EDGE-TO-EDGE LINING METHOD is used for jackets and vests without facings. The lining covers the whole inside of the garment and is seamed at the edges.

The side seams are left unstitched until the lining has been stitched to the garment, which is then turned right side out. The side seams are stitched last.

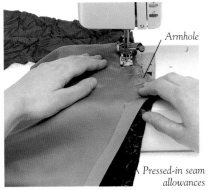

Armhole

Pressed-in seam allowances

1 MACHINE stitch the lining and garment shoulder seams. Press the seam allowances of the lining side seams to the wrong side. With right sides together, stitch the lining in position at the lower edges, the armholes, and the front and neck edges (left).

Notch to within a few threads of stitching

2 TRIM and clip the seams (left). Turn right side out by threading each front piece up through the open shoulder seam between the lining and the fabric, down through the back, and out of the side seam. Roll the seams to the lining edge, and press.

3 WITH right sides together and raw edges even, place the garment side seam edges together. Next, pin, being careful to keep the lining clear of the seamline on both sides. Stitch the garment side seams (right), removing the pins as you go.

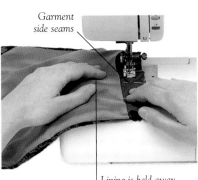

Garment side seams

Lining is held away from machine foot

4 PRESS the garment side seams open, using the point of the iron to avoid creasing. Tuck the edges of the pressed seam inside the lining, and slipstitch the lining edges together over the garment seam so that all raw edges are enclosed (right).

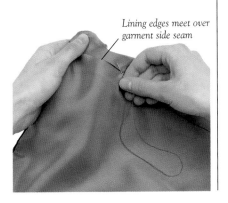

Lining edges meet over garment side seam

MAKING PANTS AND SKIRT LININGS

ADDING A LINING TO PANTS or skirts will prevent coarse fabrics from irritating the skin, give a depth of color to thin, lightweight fabrics, and reduce the risk of bagging at knees and seat. If a lining is attached to pants as they are made, the lining should be caught in the waistband as for Making a Free-Hanging Lining (p. 102).

ADDING A LINING TO PANTS

1 CUT OUT the lining to the same shape as the pants, including the allowances for the hems and seams. Mark the dart positions with clips into the edge of the lining. Fold a pleat at each dart, matching the clips, and pin before stitching across the pleat just inside the seamline of the pants (left).

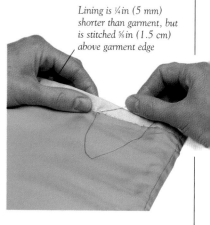

2 JOIN the lining pieces by stitching along the outside and inside leg seams, then stitch the legs together around the lining crotch seam. Leave a zipper opening that is ⅝ in (1.5 cm) longer than the zipper opening on the garment. Press the seam allowance around the waist edge to the wrong side of the lining (left).

3 PLACE the lining inside the pants, wrong sides together. Match at the seams, and pin the lining to the lower edge of the garment waistband on the inside. Tuck in the raw edge of the lining around the zipper, well clear of the zipper teeth, and pin in place. Handstitch around the waist and zipper (right).

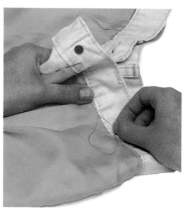

4 TRIM the lining ⅜ in (1 cm) longer than the finished pants length, and press a ⅝-in (1.5-cm) seam allowance to the wrong side. Turn the garment inside out. Pin and handstitch the folded edge of the lining ⅝ in (1.5 cm) above the garment edge (right). Remove the pins. The lining will form a pleat over the stitching.

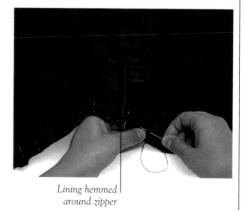

Lining is ¼ in (5 mm) shorter than garment, but is stitched ⅝ in (1.5 cm) above garment edge

LINING A FULL-GATHERED SKIRT

Right side of lining

Stitch the lining seams, leaving an opening for the zipper. Gather first the waist edge, then the lining edge. With wrong sides together, pin (above) and stitch the lining to the waist edge of the skirt. Attach the waistband. Finally, hem the garment and the lining (p. 205) separately.

HALF-LINING A SKIRT

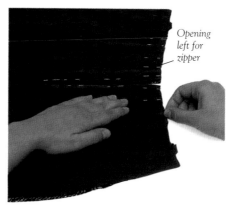

Opening left for zipper

1 MAKE THE SKIRT BACK, inserting the zipper in the center back seam. Cut out the lining, and stitch the darts and the center back seam, leaving a zipper opening. Machine hem the lining so that it is at least 2 in (5 cm) shorter than the desired skirt length. Pin the lining to the fabric, with wrong sides together and raw edges even (above).

Lining hemmed around zipper

2 SLIPSTITCH THE LINING in place around the zipper, and baste the lining around the waist edge to the skirt fabric (above). Stitch the skirt side seams, catching the edges of the lining in the seam. Edge finish the lining and skirt fabric together. Machine stitch the waistband (p. 169), treating the lining and the fabric as one. Finish the hem (p. 205).

INTERLININGS

INTERLINING IS A SEPARATE LAYER of fabric inserted between the garment and the lining to make the garment thicker and warmer. It is made from fluffy, lightweight fabrics such as brushed cotton and flannelette, which trap air to increase insulation, making the finished garment warm but not too cumbersome. If a very thick interlining is necessary, the garment may need to be made in a larger size. Sleeves are not often interlined, since they become bulky. Interlining is usually handstitched to the garment, but some fabrics may be stitched by machine to the lining.

RELATED TECHNIQUES

Taking and comparing
measurements, p. 24
Working basting stitches, p. 73
Working hemming stitches, p. 76
Reducing seam bulk, p. 84
Attaching a lining
by machine, p. 103
Making a jacket lining, p. 295

ATTACHING INTERLINING TO A GARMENT

THE INTERLINING is handstitched to the wrong side of the garment after it is sewn, and before attaching the lining. Only the front and back of the garment are interlined to avoid excess bulk. The interlining pieces are stitched together at the side and shoulder seams, and are then stitched to the garment facings or to a seamline.

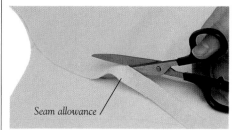

Seam allowance

1 MAKE THE INTERLINING, using lapped darts (p. 100) and lapped seams (p. 98). Trim away the seam allowance around the front and neck edges of the interlining to reduce bulk (above). Trim the lower edge of the interlining to ensure that it is level with the top of the garment hem.

2 PLACE THE INTERLINING to the wrong side of the garment, threading the sleeves through the interlining armholes. Match and pin the seams. Baste the interlining to the garment seam allowances around the armholes and the side seams, using a long diagonal basting stitch (above).

Stitch loosely

3 OVERLAP THE FACINGS with the edge of the interlining. Pin, then stitch the interlining to the facings (above), using a blind hemstitch (p. 76). Take care not to allow the stitches to show through the garment fabric. Complete the garment, covering the interlining with the lining.

ATTACHING INTERLINING TO A LINING

THE INTERLINING is machine stitched to the lining pieces before they are stitched together, and the two layers of fabric are treated as one. If a back lining pattern piece with a pleat is used when cutting out the interlining, the pleat should be omitted. The lower interlining edge is trimmed level with the foldline of the lining hem.

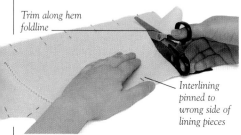

Trim along hem
foldline

Interlining
pinned to
wrong side of
lining pieces

1 SEW THE DARTS and the back lining pleat. Make lapped darts (p. 100) on the interlining, and pin all the pieces to the lining. Trim the interlining level with the fold of the lining hem (above).

Pins

2 SEW THE LINING, treating the attached interlining and lining as one piece of fabric (above). Trim the interlining next to the seam stitching to eliminate bulk in the finished garment.

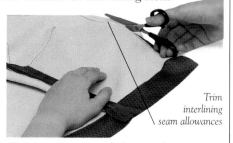

Trim
interlining
seam allowances

3 MACHINE STITCH the interlining to the lining on the front, neck, and armhole edges, just inside the seamline. Trim the interlining seam allowances (above). Complete the garment.

DARTS, TUCKS, PLEATS, & GATHERS

FORMING DARTS

A DART IS USED TO SHAPE FABRIC around the contours of the body. The wide base of a dart takes in fabric fullness so that a garment fits the narrower parts of the body. The dart stitching lines are matched, then stitched together. These stitching lines can be straight or gently curved for a close fit around the shape of the body. Darts are used mainly on women's clothes to allow fullness at the bust and hips, while shaping the fabric in at the waist. Small darts are also used to shape the back shoulder and elbow on tailored garments.

RELATED TECHNIQUES

Making bust alterations, p. 28
Working basting stitches, p. 73
Working tailor's tacks, p. 73
Hand sewing stitches, p. 74
Working machine stitches, p. 77
Joining a skirt to a bodice, p. 159
Making a basic waistband, p. 168

DIRECTORY OF DARTS

Waist darts

Bust darts

French darts

Elbow darts

Dart tucks

Contour darts

Waist darts
Used on skirts, pants, and dresses, these plain darts (see opposite) shape the fabric in at the waist to allow fullness at the hips. There are usually two waist darts at the garment front and two or four at the back of the garment.

Bust darts
These plain darts add fullness at the bust (see opposite). Single bust darts begin at the underarm side seams. Fitted garments may require two sets of bust darts, one at each underarm and the others running up either side of the waist seam.

French darts
To give a semifitted shape, these combine the underarm bust dart and waist dart into one long dart running from the bust down at an angle toward the side seam (p. 110). Since it is a wide dart, it is usually cut away for part of its length.

Elbow darts
These plain darts (see opposite) run from the sleeve underarm seam toward the elbow to shape the sleeves on tailored jackets and coats, or to allow room for movement on tight sleeves. Dart shaping at the elbow can be formed by one small dart, or by two or three very small darts or tucks.

Dart tucks
Often used at waistlines, these are made in the same way as plain darts but stitched from the wide end for part of their length (p. 112). Instead of forming a point, fabric is released from a tuck.

Contour darts
Used on semifitted and fitted styles without waist seams, these darts have two pointed ends, one providing fullness at the bust and the other fullness at the hips (p. 110). The wide central part of the dart shapes the fabric in at the waist.

PLAIN DARTS

Plain darts are folds of fabric stitched with a tapering seam to form a point. The dart is often shown on the pattern as a triangle with a central foldline and two stitching lines. Slight alterations to the garment fit may be made by redrawing dart stitching lines. If the dart size is altered, corresponding pattern pieces must be altered too.

MAKING A PLAIN DART

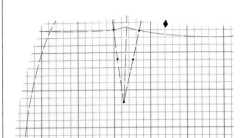

1 CHECK that the dart markings are clearly visible on the pattern (above). Pin the pattern to the fabric. Transfer the dart markings to the fabric using tailor's tacks. Remove the pattern from the fabric.

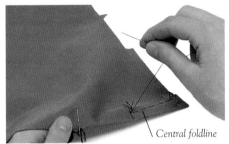

Central foldline

2 WORKING from the wrong side, fold the fabric right sides together, matching the markings. Pin, and baste (above). Be sure to check the fit before removing the tailor's tacks.

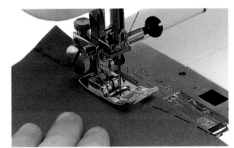

3 STARTING from the fullest part of the dart (the outer edges), stitch along the dart line, tapering gently toward the point (above). Finish with a knot or a few backstitches on or just inside the stitching.

Press dart to one side

4 PRESS the dart as it was stitched with both layers on top of each other to embed the stitching in the garment fabric. Open out the fabric, and press the dart to one side (left). Press horizontal darts downward and vertical darts toward the center, and press out any puckering at the dart point on the underside of the dart.

MAKING A DART ON THICK FABRICS

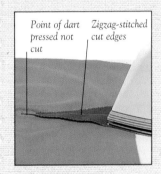

Point of dart pressed not cut *Zigzag-stitched cut edges*

Cut straight along the fold of the dart to ⅝ in (1.5 cm) from the dart point. Open out the fabric, and press the dart open as far as possible toward the dart point (left). Press the last ⅝ in (1.5 cm) of the dart point, flattening this over the stitching.

FINISHING A DART ON FINE FABRICS

Draw loop through fabric to wrong side

1 ON FINE OR SLIPPERY FABRICS, leave long thread ends attached and finish by hand. Pull one thread end to draw a loop through the fabric. Pick up the loop with a pin, and pull the loop so that the thread end emerges on the same side (above).

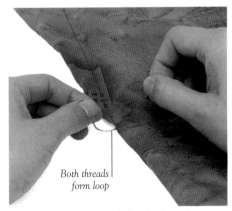

Both threads form loop

2 FORM A LOOP with both threads (above). Push the loop down onto the fabric, and pull both the threads through the loop to form a knot that lies flat on the fabric. Tie the single thread ends together twice to form a double knot.

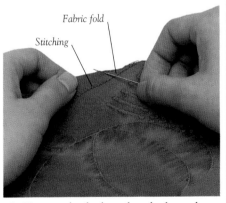

Fabric fold *Stitching*

3 THREAD both thread ends through a needle and handstitch them securely over the fabric fold (above), or through the machine stitches for about ⅝ in (1.5 cm) from the dart point. Take a stitch through the fabric layers, and trim.

MAKING A FRENCH DART

A FRENCH DART APPEARS only on the front of a garment and extends from the side seam at the hip- or waistline up to the bust. Since it is much wider than a plain dart, a French dart must be cut, or "slashed," to open up the center before it is stitched so that the stitching lines will align perfectly. Sometimes the central part is cut away.

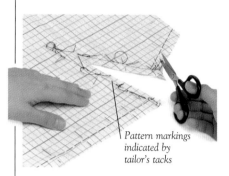

Pattern markings indicated by tailor's tacks

1 TRANSFER pattern markings, stitching lines, and any central slash line to the fabric, using tailor's tacks (left). On the pattern shown here, the center of the French dart has been cut away so that there is no slash line. Remove the pattern.

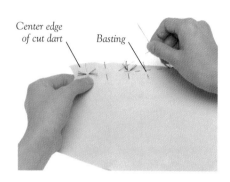

Center edge of cut dart   *Basting*

2 WITH RIGHT sides together, match the stitching lines. If necessary, gently ease or stretch one side to match the opposite markings exactly. Pin, and baste just inside the stitching line (left). Check fit, and remove the tailor's tacks.

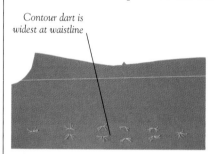

3 STITCH along the dart from the outer edge of the fabric to the end of the tapered point (left). Finish off the dart by knotting the thread ends at each end to secure the stitching firmly.

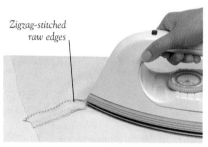

Zigzag-stitched raw edges

4 REMOVE the basting stitches. Then finish by zigzag stitching the raw edge on each side of the dart. Press the dart as stitched, then open out the fabric, and press again (left).

MAKING A CONTOUR DART

T HIS DART HAS A POINT AT EACH END, with the widest part at the center. A contour dart is often long and makes the fabric shape in at the waist on garments without waist seams. It is generally used on fitted dresses. The upper point of the dart provides fullness at the bust while the lower point allows for fullness at the hipline.

Contour dart is widest at waistline

1 PIN the paper pattern to the fabric and transfer all dart markings to the fabric using tailor's tacks. After clipping the tailor's tacks, carefully remove the paper pattern.

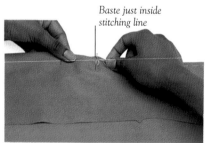

Baste just inside stitching line

2 WITH right sides together, fold the dart along the central foldline. Match the markings at the waist, the points, and the stitching lines. Pin, and baste (left). Check for fit. Remove the pins.

Upper dart point

3 THE CONTOUR DART is stitched in two halves. Starting a few stitches below the waistline, stitch to the waistline, then stitch in a tapering line to the upper dart point (above). Knot and thread ends at the point to secure.

Lower dart point

4 TURN THE GARMENT. Starting just above the waistline, stitch to the waistline, overlapping the stitching lines. Then stitch in a tapering line to the lower dart point (above). Knot thread at the point as before. Remove the basting.

Press dart on wrong side

5 AT THE WAIST, clip the dart fabric to within ⅛ in (3 mm) of the stitching line to ease the fit. Press the dart as stitched to crease the center fold. On the wrong side, open out the fabric piece, and press the dart to one side (above).

MAKING TUCKS

DECORATIVE TUCKS, whether simple or elaborate, are easy to make. They can be used to add detail on a wide range of garments, such as delicate baby's or toddler's clothes, summer tops and skirts, and sophisticated wedding dresses. Tucks are stitched folds of fabric that are formed along the straight grain. The width of a tuck and the spacing between tucks depend on the fabric thickness and on the desired design effect. Most tucks are purely decorative, but they can also be used to shape a garment, at a waistline, for instance.

RELATED TECHNIQUES

Working basting stitches, p. 73
Working tailor's tacks, p. 73
Hand sewing stitches, p. 74
Working machine stitches, p. 77
Making piping, p. 91
Joining a skirt to a bodice, p. 159
Preparing to make
a waistband, p. 166

DIRECTORY OF TUCKS

Dart tucks have open ends

Dart tucks

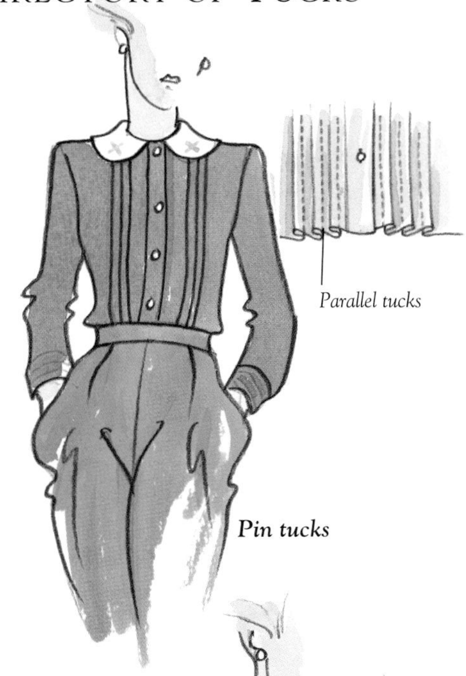

Parallel tucks

Pin tucks

Scalloped edge

No space between tucks

Cross tucks   **Shell tucks**   **Blind tucks**

Dart tucks
Used for garment shaping, dart tucks – sometimes referred to as released tucks – are generally at the waists of bodices or skirts to take in the waist (p. 112).

Pin tucks
Very narrow tucks are called pin tucks and are usually 1/8 in (3 mm) wide. These tucks can be blind (see below), or they can be spaced (p. 112). Different visual effects can be created by varying the tuck and space widths.

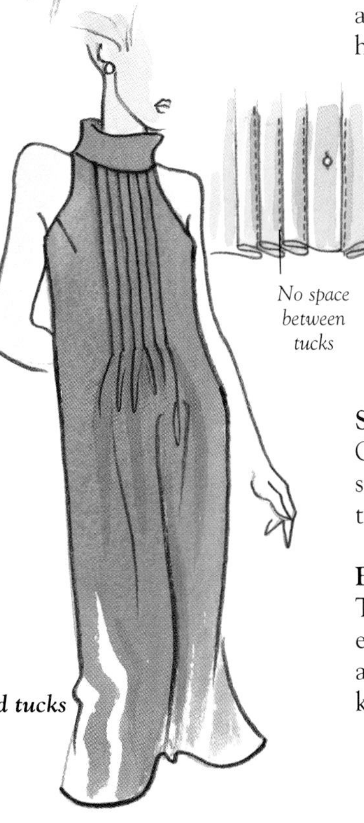

Cross tucks
Lines of neat, vertical tucks that are crossed by lines of neat, horizontal tucks create a fabric grid design, and these are commonly known as cross tucks (p. 113). Since these tucks are of a double thickness where they cross over one another, they tend to create bulk and so are suitable only for lightweight fabrics.

Shell tucks
On fine fabrics, tucks can be scalloped by hand or machine to create a ruffled effect (p. 113).

Blind tucks
Tucks that are placed close enough together so that they meet and there are no visible spaces are known as blind tucks (p. 112).

MAKING BASIC TUCKS

SPACED, BLIND, AND PIN TUCKS are all formed in the same way, but the width of each tuck and the distances between the tucks vary. Each tuck has two stitching lines that are stitched together to create a fold. Tucks used for decoration are formed on the right side, while those used only for shaping may be formed on the wrong side.

Tailor's tack

1 MARK the stitching lines of the first tuck, using rows of tailor's tacks. Mark on the right side of the fabric for decorative tucks and on the wrong side of the fabric for shaping tucks that have no decorative purpose. Clip the tailor's tacks, and carefully remove the paper pattern.

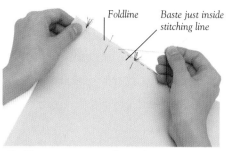

Foldline *Baste just inside stitching line*

2 FOLD THE TUCK along the center to bring the stitching lines together; the distance between the stitching lines is twice the finished tuck width. Pin, and baste (above). Remove the tailor's tacks.

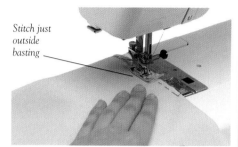

Stitch just outside basting

3 MACHINE STITCH the tuck (above), and remove the basting. To create even, parallel tucks, it is best to make one tuck at a time and use a gauge (see below) to create each subsequent tuck.

GAUGING

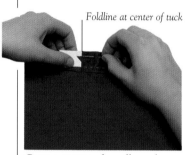

Foldline at center of tuck

CUT A STRIP of cardboard to the tuck width (marked with a notch), plus the distance between tucks. Use this strip to mark each tuck position.

STITCHING

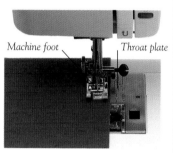

Machine foot *Throat plate*

TO CREATE NEAT, parallel tucks, use the machine foot or markings on the throat plate as a guide. Use a seam gauge or quilter guide for wide tucks.

PRESSING

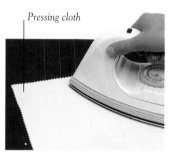

Pressing cloth

AS EACH TUCK is stitched, press it using a pressing cloth. Then open out the fabric, and press all the tucks flat in the required direction (above).

STAYSTITCHING

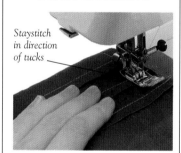

Staystitch in direction of tucks

STAYSTITCH across the ends of the finished tucks (above). This staystitching will keep the tucks in place while the garment is being worked on.

MAKING DART TUCKS

USED FOR SHAPING, dart tucks also serve a decorative purpose when they are made on the right side of the garment fabric. Because they release fullness at the ends of the tucks, they are also called release tucks. When pressing a dart tuck, take extra care to press the tuck only, not the fabric folds released at the end of the tuck.

OPEN DART TUCKS

MARK and make open dart tucks in the same way as basic tucks (see above), beginning and ending the tucks at the required positions. Keep the tucks open ended. Ensure that the stitching at both ends of each tuck is securely finished with a few reverse stitches.

CLOSED DART TUCKS

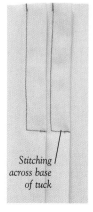

Stitching across base of tuck

CLOSED dart tucks produce a more controlled release of fabric than the softer open dart tucks. Make closed dart tucks in the same way as open dart tucks, but finish closed tucks by stitching across the base of each tuck, and securing with a few reverse stitches.

SHAPED DART TUCKS

FOR precise fitting on a fitted garment, shaped dart tucks can be used. Mark and make the tucks in the same way as basic tucks (above), placing as required. Since the stitching lines are on the cross grain, be very careful to match them exactly while pinning and basting.

STITCHING SHELL, PIPED, AND CROSS TUCKS

N ARROW TUCKS CAN BE GIVEN added interest by making them into shell tucks. Since a shell tuck has a scalloped edge, it can be used singly to form a simple edging, as well as in rows like basic tucks. Alternatively, narrow tucks can be piped to give a decorative, raised effect, or worked across one another for cross tucks.

PREPARING SHELL TUCKS

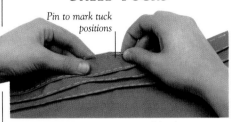

Pin to mark tuck positions

SHELL TUCKS are most suitable for narrow tucks about ⅛ in (3 mm) wide with scallops ¼–⅜ in (5 mm – 1 cm) apart. Before stitching, pin mark the positions of the narrow tucks, and baste them in place along each length (above).

HANDSTITCHED SHELL TUCKS

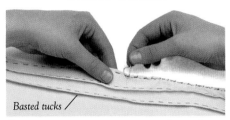

Basted tucks

ONCE THE NARROW TUCKS are basted, they can be stitched by hand or machine. For handstitching, use a small running stitch along the stitching line, and make a couple of overstitches (above) over the tuck fold at intervals to make scallops.

MACHINE-STITCHED SHELL TUCKS

Follow basting stitches

AFTER BASTING THE TUCKS, set the machine for blind hemming, and test the stitch on spare fabric. Stitch the tuck on the machine (above), with the fold to the left of the needle (the catching stitch will cross the fold and form scallops).

PIPED TUCKS

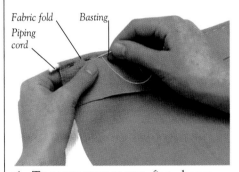

Fabric fold
Piping cord
Basting

1 TO MAKE PIPED TUCKS, first choose a piping cord suitable for the width of the tuck. Fold the tuck, matching the stitching lines. Lay the piping cord inside the fold, and baste through the two layers of fabric to enclose the cord (above).

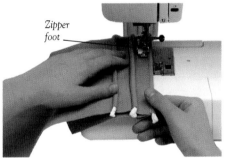

Zipper foot

2 USING A ZIPPER FOOT, machine stitch close to the cord along the basting line (above), ensuring that the needle does not catch the cord. Remove the basting stitches. Trim the ends of the cord only after the garment is completed.

ADDING TUCKS TO A PLAIN PATTERN

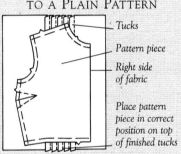

Tucks
Pattern piece
Right side of fabric
Place pattern piece in correct position on top of finished tucks

To accommodate tucks on a plain pattern piece, simply stitch the tucks in place on the fabric, and press, before the piece is cut out.

USING TUCKS TO CONCEAL ADDED FABRIC WIDTHS

Joins are easily concealed in tucks. Leave a seam allowance after the final tuck on each piece. Lap one piece over the other, and baste together along the tuck stitching line (right). Stitch, completing the tuck and joining together both the widths.

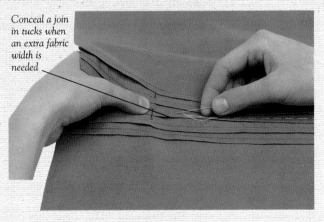

Conceal a join in tucks when an extra fabric width is needed

CROSS TUCKS

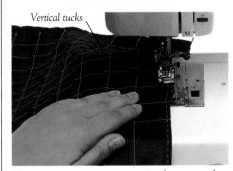

Vertical tucks

TO MAKE CROSS TUCKS, pin, baste, and stitch all the vertical tucks. Remove the basting. Press the tucks. Pin and baste the horizontal tucks, checking that the vertical tucks are lying correctly. Stitch in the direction of the vertical tucks (above).

FORMING PLEATS

PLEATS ARE FOLDS OF FABRIC that are made to take in fullness. They can be used as decorative features on sleeves and blouses but are most commonly used on skirts and dresses to take in a full skirt to fit at the waist. There are various types of pleats, which are formed using different methods. They can be pressed crisply or left unpressed to hang as soft folds. For pressed pleats, garment fabrics that crease easily are the most suitable. Pleats can either be edgestitched to hold the creases in position, or they can be topstitched from waist to hip.

RELATED TECHNIQUES

Working basting stitches, p. 73
Working tailor's tacks, p. 73
Working hemming stitches, p. 76
Reducing seam bulk, p. 84
Making topstitched seams, p. 87
Preparing to make a
waistband, p. 166
Hemming pleats, p. 212

DIRECTORY OF PLEATS

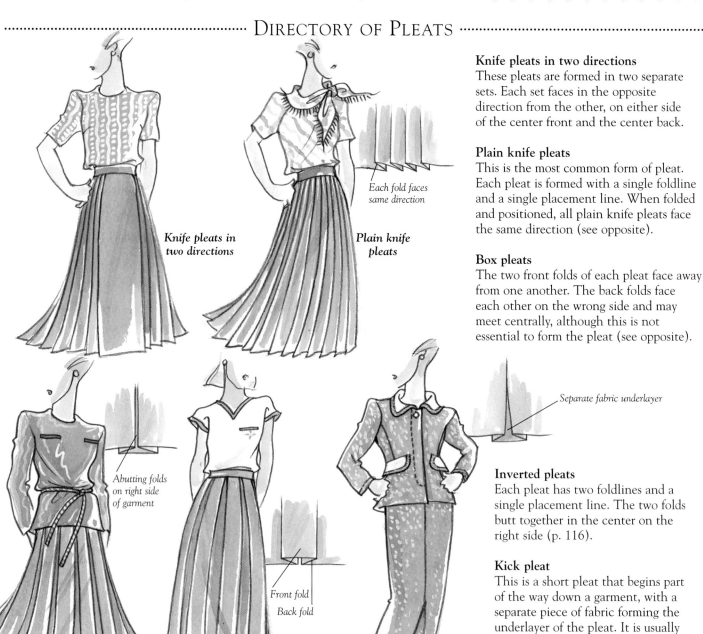

Knife pleats in two directions

Each fold faces same direction

Plain knife pleats

Abutting folds on right side of garment

Front fold

Back fold

Separate fabric underlayer

Box pleats

Inverted pleats

Kick pleat

Knife pleats in two directions
These pleats are formed in two separate sets. Each set faces in the opposite direction from the other, on either side of the center front and the center back.

Plain knife pleats
This is the most common form of pleat. Each pleat is formed with a single foldline and a single placement line. When folded and positioned, all plain knife pleats face the same direction (see opposite).

Box pleats
The two front folds of each pleat face away from one another. The back folds face each other on the wrong side and may meet centrally, although this is not essential to form the pleat (see opposite).

Inverted pleats
Each pleat has two foldlines and a single placement line. The two folds butt together in the center on the right side (p. 116).

Kick pleat
This is a short pleat that begins part of the way down a garment, with a separate piece of fabric forming the underlayer of the pleat. It is usually used on a straight skirt to allow for leg movement and can be the main feature of a garment's design.

FORMING PLEATS FROM THE RIGHT SIDE

IN GENERAL, it is best to form knife pleats and box pleats from the right side, particularly if using a patterned or plaid fabric that needs careful pleating to position motifs. The basted pleats are secured at the top by a seam or waistband. They may also be topstitched flat (often from waist- to hipline) or given an edgestitched finish.

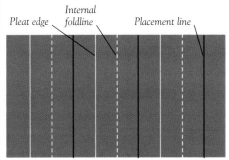

Pleat edge Internal foldline Placement line

1 PIN THE PAPER PATTERN in position on the right side of the fabric. Using tailor's tacks and two colors of thread, mark front foldlines with one color and placement lines with another. Cut the tailor's tacks, and remove the pattern.

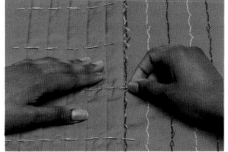

2 WITH THE RIGHT SIDE facing, fold the fabric along a foldline, and place the folded edge on the placement line, pinning at regular intervals through all thicknesses (above). Check the garment for fit, and remove the tailor's tacks.

DIAGONAL BASTING

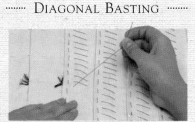

Use diagonal basting (p. 73) on springy or slippery fabrics to hold all layers of the pleats in place (above). To set the pleats, leave the basting in place until the garment is finished.

3 BASTE EACH PLEAT through all thicknesses close to the foldline, removing the pins after basting (above). To ensure sharp pleats, leave the basting in place until the garment is finished.

Iron lightly with dry cloth for soft pleats

4 WITH RIGHT SIDES facing, carefully press the pleats (above). If sharp pleats are required, use a damp pressing cloth, and leave the garment on the ironing board until it is completely dry.

Strips of thin cardboard

5 TURN THE FABRIC OVER, and press from the wrong side using a pressing cloth (see Step 4). To prevent ridges on the right side, lay strips of thin cardboard under the pleats before pressing (above).

PLEAT FINISHES

Right side

Knife pleats
After finishing the pleats, topstitch ¼ in (6 mm) in from each pleat fold from waist- to hipline (above), stitching diagonally out to the pleat fold at hip level.

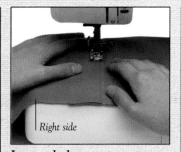

Right side

Inverted pleats
Topstitch ¼ in (6 mm) away from the center fold of each pleat down one side from waist to hip level. Pivot, stitch across the base, then pivot again, and topstitch up to the waist (above).

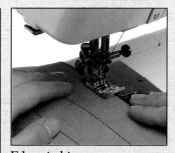

Edgestitching
This finish holds the creases of the pleats in place. Press the pleat folds and, before basting, edgestitch each pleat close to the outer fold (above). The inner fold can also be edgestitched.

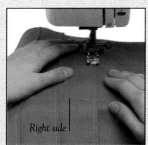

Right side

Edge- and topstitching
Edgestitch along the fold of each pleat from the hem up to hip level. Topstitch on the right side through all layers from the waistline to the edgestitching (above).

FORMING PLEATS ON THE WRONG SIDE

INVERTED PLEATS AND PLEATS that require stitching on the wrong side are formed on the wrong side. Pleats that need matching with other pattern pieces, such as those with a separate underlay (see opposite), are also formed on the wrong side. The steps below show inverted pleats; for other pleats, foldlines are matched to placement lines.

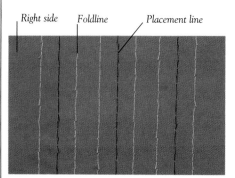

Right side   Foldline   Placement line

1 WITH THE PAPER PATTERN on the right side of the fabric, mark all foldlines and placement lines for the pleats with tailor's tacks, using a different color for each. Then cut the tailor's tacks, and remove the pattern.

Wrong side   Basting along foldline

2 FOR INVERTED PLEATS, with the wrong side up, fold along each placement line, matching each set of foldlines. Pin and baste every pleat. Machine stitch between the hip and the waist if necessary (above).

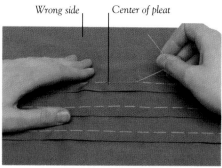

Wrong side   Center of pleat

3 UNFOLD THE PLEATS, and lay the central placement line over the joined foldlines. Then pin and baste along the center of each pleat (above). At each stage check the positions of the pleats on the right side of the garment.

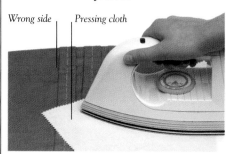

Wrong side   Pressing cloth

4 PRESS THE PLEATS on the wrong side. For sharp pleats, use a damp cloth, and allow the pleats to dry before moving. For soft pleats, iron lightly over a dry cloth.

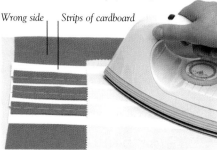

Wrong side   Strips of cardboard

5 ON LIGHT FABRICS, it may help to lay strips of thin cardboard under the pleats before pressing on the wrong side (above) to avoid ridges forming on the right side.

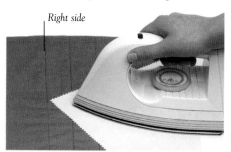

Right side

6 TURN TO THE RIGHT SIDE, and press again. Check that the pleats are still in position. Leave the basting stitches in place until the garment is finished.

STAYING PLEATS

PLEATS CAN CREATE BULK, especially around the hips. To reduce the quantity of fabric in pleats stitched to the hipline, the underfolds are cut away, and a stay cut from lining fabric is inserted to hide all the cut edges. This is called staying pleats and is shown here worked on knife pleats. Stays can be formed on the front and back.

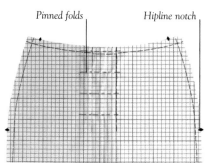

Pinned folds   Hipline notch

1 IF THERE IS NO PATTERN PIECE for a lining or stay, use the pleated pieces with the folds pinned in place (above). Cut front and back stays about 1 in (2.5 cm) longer than the marked hipline.

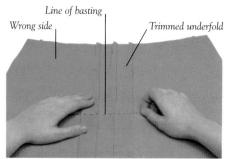

Line of basting   Wrong side   Trimmed underfold

2 TAPERING toward the hipline, trim away the unnecessary bulk from the underfolds of the pleats on the wrong side. Pin the pleats just below the hipline. Baste, and remove the pins (above).

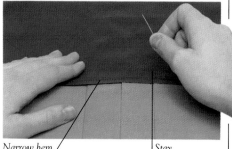

Narrow hem   Stay

3 STITCH A HEM around the lower edges of the stays. Baste the stays to the skirt along the waist and side edges. Slipstitch the lower edges of the stays to the underlayer of pleats (above).

MAKING A SEPARATE UNDERLAY

CUTTING A SEPARATE UNDERLAY for an inverted pleat allows exact positioning of motifs or plaids on the right side of the garment, and also allows a pleated skirt to be cut from a narrow fabric width. The underlay can be made from the same fabric as the rest of the skirt, or another fabric can be used for a contrasting detail.

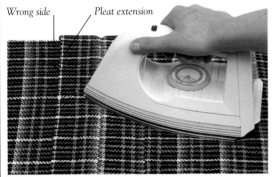

Wrong side

Pleat extension

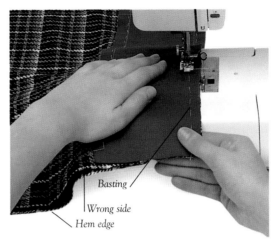

Basting

Wrong side

Hem edge

1 WITH RIGHT SIDES TOGETHER, baste along the full length of the foldlines, and stitch between the hip and the waist if necessary. Press the pleat extensions open along the foldlines (above).

2 WITH right sides together, lay the pleat underlay over the pleat extensions, match the pattern markings, and baste together. Machine stitch from the waist to the lower edge (left), leaving 6 in (15 cm) unstitched at the lower edge of each seam. Remove the basting holding the underlay and the extensions together, and press the seam flat.

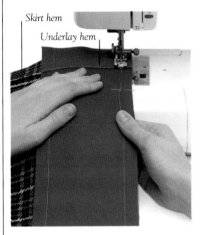

Skirt hem

Underlay hem

3 COMPLETE the skirt, and remove the basting holding the foldlines together (see Step 1). Hem the skirt and the pleat extensions separately from the underlay, ensuring that they are exactly the same length. Match, baste, and stitch the underlay to the pleat extensions, stitching from the hem upward (left).

Wrong side

Trimmed lower corner

Hem edge

4 PRESS the seams together as stitched. Trim away the lower corner of each seam allowance so that the edges do not protrude beyond the hem edge, and whipstitch through all layers to edge-finish them (left).

MAKING A SELF STAY ON AN INVERTED PLEAT

ON STITCHED-DOWN, INVERTED PLEATS, a self stay can help reduce the bulk of the fabric in the hip area. Before the self stay is made from the pleat underlay, the foldlines of the inverted pleat should be stitched together to the required depth, the placement line matched to the foldlines, and the pleat carefully pressed.

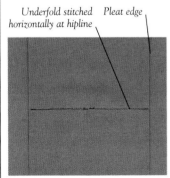

Underfold stitched horizontally at hipline

Pleat edge

1 BASTE the pleat underfolds together just below the hipline in two stages from the center outward, and stitch. Remove the basting.

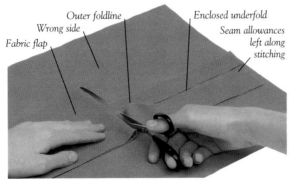

Outer foldline

Wrong side

Fabric flap

Enclosed underfold

Seam allowances left along stitching

2 CUT DOWNWARD along the outer foldlines of the pleats to ⅝ in (1.5 cm) above the horizontal lines of stitching. Fold back the fabric flap, and cut away the enclosed underfold (above), leaving ⅝-in (1.5-cm) seam allowances along the stitching.

Waist edge

3 ZIGZAG STITCH along the side edges of the flap. Fold up the flap so that the waist edges of the garment and the flap come together to form a self stay. Baste the waist edges together (above).

ADJUSTING PLEAT FIT

To alter pleat fit, divide the total adjustment by the number of pleats it will spread across. Increasing a pleat size decreases a garment's size. Decreasing a pleat size increases a garment's size. Below, a foldline is represented by a solid line, and a placement line by a dashed line. A pleat is formed by a foldline meeting a placement line.

INCREASING A KNIFE PLEAT

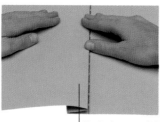

Knife pleats run left to right on women's garments

1 A KNIFE PLEAT has only one foldline and one placement line, and the pleat folds in one direction. Fold knife pleats from left to right (above), as worn.

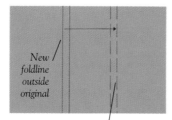

New foldline outside original

New placement line outside original

2 HALVE the amount to be increased. Redraw the foldline and the placement line, positioning them outside the original lines by this halved amount.

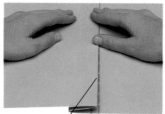

Fold to match new lines

3 FOLD THE PLEAT along the new foldline, then fold this line over to meet the new placement line (above). The new foldline increases the size of the pleat.

DECREASING A KNIFE PLEAT

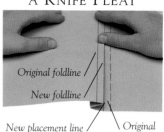

Original foldline

New foldline

New placement line

Original placement line

HALVE the decrease. Redraw the foldline and placement line inside the original lines by this halved amount. Fold the pleats so that the new lines match (above).

INCREASING AN INVERTED PLEAT

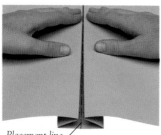

Placement line

1 INVERTED PLEATS have two foldlines, one on each side of the central placement line. Fold over both foldlines to meet at the central placement line (above).

Original foldline

New foldline

2 TO INCREASE the pleat, divide the amount of the increase in half. Draw two new foldlines, each outside the original foldlines by this halved amount.

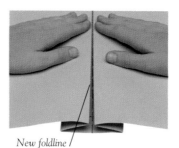

New foldline

3 FOLD THE PLEAT on both new foldlines, and bring each line over to meet at the original central placement line (above). This increases the size of the inverted pleat.

DECREASING AN INVERTED PLEAT

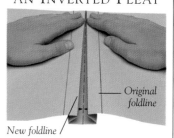

Original foldline

New foldline

DRAW TWO new foldlines, each inside the original lines by half the decrease. Fold both new foldlines to meet at the original central placement lines (above).

INCREASING A BOX PLEAT

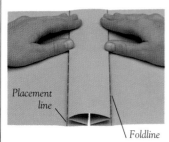

Placement line

Foldline

1 BOX PLEATS are formed using two foldlines and two placement lines. Fold the fabric away from the center of the pleat along each foldline, folding it down onto its own placement line (above).

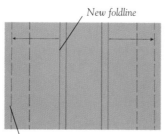

New foldline

New placement line

2 TO INCREASE the size of the box pleat, draw two new foldlines outside the original foldlines. Then draw two new placement lines on the outside of the original placement lines.

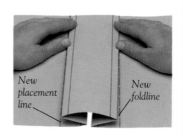

New placement line

New foldline

3 FOLD THE PLEAT along the new foldlines, and fold the foldlines outward and away from the center of the pleat, aligned with the new placement lines (above). This will make the pleat bigger.

DECREASING A BOX PLEAT

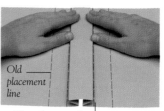

Old placement line

New placement line

DRAW TWO new foldlines and two new placement lines, both lines inside the original lines. Fold the pleat along the new foldlines, then fold outward, aligned with the new placement lines (above).

TAKING IN MULTIPLE PLEATS

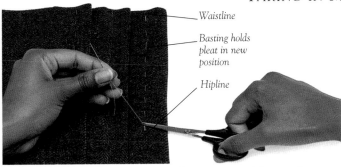

Waistline

Basting holds pleat in new position

Hipline

1 REMOVE THE WAISTBAND from the garment. Select a pleat from the center of the area needing alteration. Remove the stitching from the pleat. Unfold and refold the pleat, wrong sides together and pleatlines matching, so that the pleat projects. Baste the pleat from the waist to the hipline (above).

Pin along reduction line

2 TRY ON the garment to check the fit once the pleat has been adjusted. With the pleat wrong sides together and projecting out from the waist, adjust the garment until it fits. Mark with a pin or a dressmaker's pencil. Take off the garment, and pin in the amount of the reduction along the basted pleat (left).

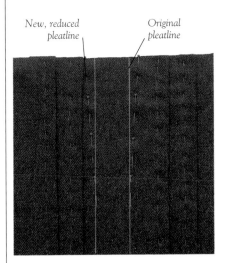

New, reduced pleatline

Original pleatline

3 REMOVE the basting and open the pleat out flat. Divide the reduction in half, and pin in the adjustments onto both sides of the pleatline. Taper the reduction line into the hipline to give a smooth seam (left). (Here the reduction is pinned ⅝in [1.5 cm] outside the waist pleatlines, taking in a total of 1¼in [3 cm].)

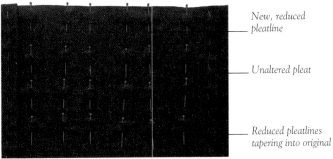

New, reduced pleatline

Unaltered pleat

Reduced pleatlines tapering into original

4 DIVIDE THE TOTAL AMOUNT of the reduction by the number of pleats the reduction is to be spread across. Mark the new pleatlines with pins, tapering smoothly into the original lines at the hip (above). Reform the pleats, matching the new lines. In this picture a 1¼in (3 cm) reduction is taken in over three pleats, ⅜in (1 cm) per pleat, ¼in (5 mm) either side.

LETTING OUT A STITCHED PLEAT

New pleatline

Original pleatline

1 TRY ON the garment, and pin in the amount that needs to be let out. Working on the wrong side, baste the new pleatline inside the original, and remove the pins (above). Remove the original stitching down to the hip.

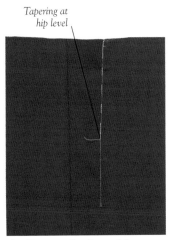

Tapering at hip level

2 STITCH the basted line. Taper the new stitching line smoothly into the original line at the hip. (Decreasing the size of the pleat by stitching inside the original pleatline will make the garment larger.)

TAKING IN A STITCHED PLEAT

Original pleatline

New pleatline

1 TRY ON the garment, and pin in the amount of fabric that needs to be taken in. Working on the wrong side, baste the new pleat stitching line outside the original pleatline, and then remove all the pins.

Tapering at hip level

2 STITCH the basted line. Taper the new pleatline smoothly into the original line at the hip. Remove the original stitching down to hip level. (Increasing the size of the pleat will make the finished garment smaller.)

Forming Gathers

SIMPLE GATHERS ARE USED to draw in fabric for fit or for a decorative effect. For soft gathers the fabric should be twice the desired finished length, and for full gathers three times the length or more, depending on the fabric weight. The piece to be gathered is seamed and pressed before gathering is begun. Gathering stitches are longer than ordinary stitches, and two rows are stitched to help the gathers to form evenly and hang well. Fabric hangs better with the straight grain, so gathering stitches should be made across the grain.

RELATED TECHNIQUES

Reducing seam bulk, p. 84
Seam finishes, p. 85
Joining a skirt to a
bodice, p. 159
Hemming a single-layer
ruffle, p. 228
Stitching a plain ruffle
into a seam, p. 229

Making and Fitting Gathers

FOR GATHERING, the machine stitch is adjusted to its longest length, and the upper tension is loosened. Both rows of gathering are stitched on the same side of the fabric, within the seam allowance, and the threads on the wrong side are pulled. If the piece to be gathered is long, the gathering stitches may be worked in sections.

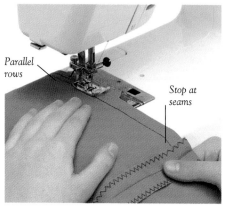

Parallel rows

Stop at seams

1 WORK TWO PARALLEL ROWS of stitches ¼ in (6 mm) apart, leaving long thread ends (above). Interrupt the stitching at each vertical seam so that the seam allowances are not gathered.

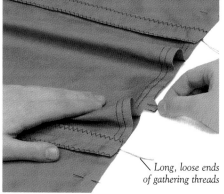

Long, loose ends of gathering threads

2 WITH RIGHT SIDES TOGETHER and raw edges even, lay the edge with the gathering stitches on the corresponding fabric piece. Pin the pieces together at the seams and notches (above).

If gathering pulls unevenly, pull one end separately to realign gathers before continuing

3 AT ONE END, wind the two gathering threads in a figure eight around a pin. At the other end, pull both gathering threads together, and gently slide the gathers along the threads (above).

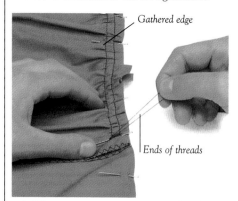

Gathered edge

Ends of threads

4 WHEN THE GATHERED EDGE fits the piece to which it is pinned, wind the ends of the threads around a pin (above). (On long edges, gather from each end toward the center, rather than across the entire length from one end.)

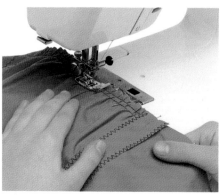

5 ARRANGE THE GATHERS EVENLY, and pin. Reset the machine stitch length and tension to the normal settings. Machine stitch carefully along the seamline over the gathers (above), removing the pins while stitching.

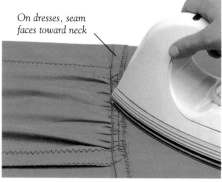

On dresses, seam faces toward neck

6 TRIM THE SEAM ALLOWANCES, and zigzag stitch to edge finish. Open out the two sections, and press the seam flat as it should lie in the finished garment (above). The gathered seam is usually pressed to lie away from the gathers.

STAYING A GATHERED SEAM

A STAY IS STITCHED to a gathered seam to strengthen it and prevent it from stretching or breaking on loosely woven and jersey fabrics. A firm, narrow stay tape, such as seam binding, twill tape, or narrow grosgrain ribbon, can be used for the stay. The stay is stitched to the seam allowance with its lower edge just above the seam stitching.

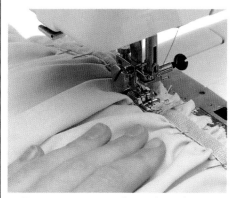

1 BEFORE TRIMMING the gathered seam allowance, pin a length of stay tape to it with one edge along the stitching line. Stitch the stay in place just above the original stitching line (above).

2 TRIM THE SEAM ALLOWANCE even with the top of the stay. Zigzag stitch along the top edge of the stay through all the layers (above). Press the seam as it should lie in the finished garment.

PRESSING GATHERS

When pressing gathers, work the tip of the iron into the opened-out gathers rather than over the folds, ironing on the wrong side of the fabric.

JOINING TWO GATHERED EDGES

W HEN ONE GATHERED EDGE on a garment is joined to another gathered edge, a stay is essential; otherwise, some gathers may move during machine stitching, which will result in uneven or puckered fabric. Since the two joined pieces will be quite thick, it is best to use a thin yet strong stay tape (see Staying a Gathered Seam, above).

CORDED GATHERS

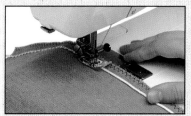

1 *For gathering bulky fabrics, or for areas where a gathering thread may break, zigzag stitch over a thin, strong cord just above the stitching line (above). Be careful not to catch the cord in the stitching.*

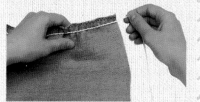

2 *Knot one end of the cord, and pull the other end to form the gathers (above). The cord may be removed after the gathered edge is stitched.*

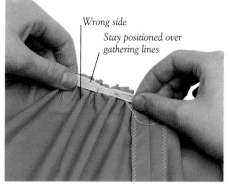

Wrong side
Stay positioned over gathering lines

1 CUT A STAY to the length of the seam, and transfer all markings to it. Pin the stay to the wrong side of one fabric piece, matching all markings. Gather the fabric. Hand baste the stay in place (above).

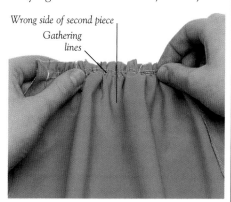

Wrong side of second piece
Gathering lines

2 WITH RIGHT SIDES together and matching all pattern markings and seams, pin the ungathered piece to the gathered one, gather it to fit, and baste it in place through all layers (above).

3 MACHINE STITCH the stay to the two gathered layers along the seamline, holding the fabric in place on both sides of the needle. Work a second, reinforcing line of stitching along the other edge of the stay and about ¼ in (6 mm) from the seamline just stitched (left). If desired, finish the seam as for Staying a Gathered Seam (see above). With the stay facing upward and avoiding flattening the gathers, press.

SHIRRING

SHIRRING IS A FORM OF MACHINE GATHERING worked in rows across fabric. It is usually worked with a cotton top thread and narrow round elastic on the bobbin to make the shirred area stretch and retract. Shirring may also be worked with ordinary thread on the bobbin so that, when the thread is pulled up, the gathered area is permanent.

ELASTIC SHIRRING

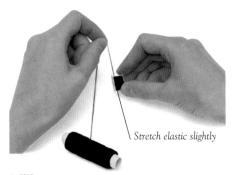

Stretch elastic slightly

1 WIND THE NARROW ROUND ELASTIC onto the bobbin by hand, until the bobbin is nearly full (above). Stretch the elastic slightly while it is being wound. The elastic then pulls the garment fabric tightly as the stitching is being worked, which in turn makes the shirring firm on the finished garment.

2 THE NORMAL STITCH TENSION will usually gather the fabric. (Test the stitching on a piece of spare garment fabric.) As more rows are worked, the shirring becomes firmer. If the shirring is too loose, tighten the screw on the bobbin tension. Stitch the first row, leaving the thread ends loose (above).

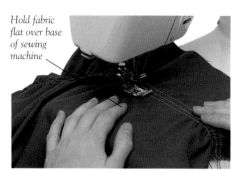

Hold fabric flat over base of sewing machine

3 STRETCH THE FABRIC out flat when stitching all the subsequent rows (above). Use the edge of the presser foot or the quilting guide to space the rows of shirring stitches evenly. The rows can be ¼–1 in (5 mm–2.5 cm) apart. The more space between the rows of stitching, the looser the shirring will be.

Knot long thread ends together to secure

4 IF THE SHIRRING IS TOO LOOSE, pull the shirring elastic from the wrong side to tighten it. Pull the thread ends through to the wrong side, and knot the thread and elastic together securely (above). Where possible, secure the thread ends within the seam allowance so that the seam stitching reinforces it.

WAFFLE SHIRRING

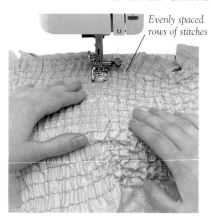

Evenly spaced rows of stitches

THIS IS FORMED by stitching a series of parallel rows of elastic shirring (see above). Turn the fabric around, and stitch a second series of rows at right angles to the first rows (left) to create squares of gathered fabric. When stitching, stretch the fabric flat for a successful result.

CORD ELASTIC SHIRRING

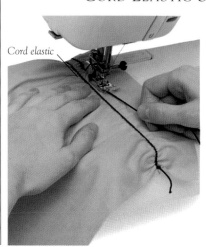

Cord elastic

WHEN only one or two rows of shirring are required, for example around a sleeve, then shirring elastic is often not firm enough. Use a stronger cord elastic instead. Zigzag stitch over the elastic on the wrong side, stretching the elastic while stitching (left). For more elasticity, pull up the elastic to gather the fabric. Knot securely.

GATHERED SHIRRING

Edges turned under before stay is handstitched

Stitch two rows as for Elastic Shirring (see above), but using ordinary thread on both the spool and bobbin. Pull up the threads, and knot securely. To stay the gathering, handstitch a fabric strip on the wrong side over the shirring (left).

GATHERING FOR SMOCKING

SMOCKING STITCHES ARE USED to gather in fullness and shape squares of fabric into garments. Smocking is worked before the garment is assembled and is best suited to fairly soft fabrics, such as crepe, that gather and fold well. Checked and striped fabrics can be smocked easily because the fabric pattern can be used as a guide for the gathering.

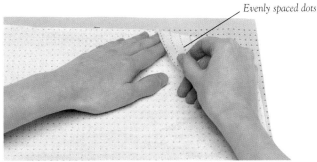

Evenly spaced dots

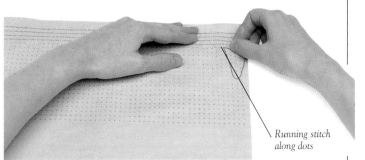

Running stitch along dots

1 WHEN ESTIMATING THE TOTAL AMOUNT of fabric that will be needed, allow about three times the required finished fabric width (more on fine fabric; a little less on thick fabrics). Press iron-on smocking dots to the wrong side of the fabric, and remove the transfer (above). Dot transfers can be indelible, so choose a similar color or, on lightweight fabrics, baste the dots.

2 USE A STRONG THREAD that is long enough to stitch the entire row. Make a firm knot at the end. Stitch across one row of dots using running stitches (p. 74), picking up a few threads of the garment fabric at each dot. Leave the thread ends hanging at the ends of the lines. Stitch all the rows in this way so that the stitches are in line, one beneath the other (above).

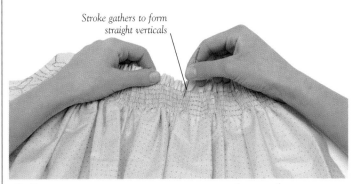

Stroke gathers to form straight verticals

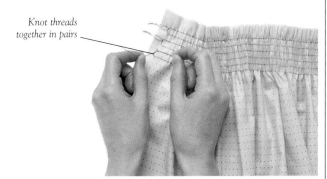

Knot threads together in pairs

3 PULL THE HANGING THREAD ENDS to gather up the garment fabric reasonably tightly until it reaches the required width. (Always check that the finished width is accurate.) Wind the long thread ends around a pin to fasten. Slide down the gathers with the blunt end of a needle (above). Smooth the gathers into very small, evenly spaced, parallel pleats.

4 KNOT THE LONG THREAD ENDS from the top two rows together securely. Repeat with the next two rows down until all the rows are secured (above). The gathering threads are removed when all the smocking is complete, although the gathering threads along the top two rows are often retained until the edge of the garment has been stitched into a seam.

SMOCKING USING A PLEATER

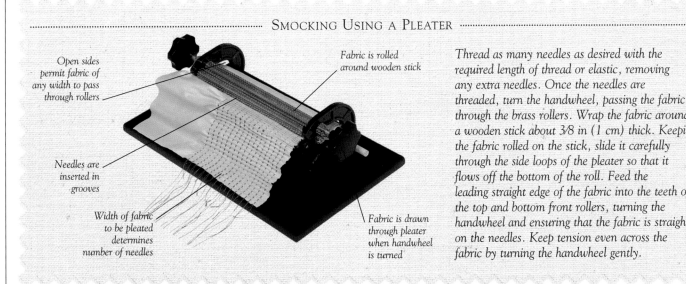

Open sides permit fabric of any width to pass through rollers

Fabric is rolled around wooden stick

Needles are inserted in grooves

Width of fabric to be pleated determines number of needles

Fabric is drawn through pleater when handwheel is turned

Thread as many needles as desired with the required length of thread or elastic, removing any extra needles. Once the needles are threaded, turn the handwheel, passing the fabric through the brass rollers. Wrap the fabric around a wooden stick about 3/8 in (1 cm) thick. Keeping the fabric rolled on the stick, slide it carefully through the side loops of the pleater so that it flows off the bottom of the roll. Feed the leading straight edge of the fabric into the teeth of the top and bottom front rollers, turning the handwheel and ensuring that the fabric is straight on the needles. Keep tension even across the fabric by turning the handwheel gently.

NECKLINES

MAKING AND ATTACHING NECKLINES

NECKLINES FRAME THE NECK AND FACE, and are one of the most conspicuous parts of a garment. Neckline styles vary from the simplest plain faced neckline, to the more complex bound neckline, to the tailored front placket opening which must be stitched with great accuracy. It is best to work on the neckline when only the garment shoulder seams are joined, so that the neckline can be opened out flat. Although the necklines shown below are mostly round, the same methods can be applied to V-shaped and square necklines.

RELATED TECHNIQUES

Hand sewing stitches, p. 74
Working machine stitches, p. 77
Reducing seam bulk, p. 84
Making piping, p. 91
Attaching interfacings, p. 98
Making and attaching collars, p. 142
Attaching zippers, p. 250

DIRECTORY OF NECKLINES

Front placket opening
This is a tailored neckline that requires precise stitching around the lower corners to allow the two layers of the opening to line up exactly (p. 138–139). This neckline is often used on jersey T-shirts, but it is easier to put on firmer fabrics, such as cotton poplin, shirting, or lawn.

Piped neckline
On a piped neckline (p. 132–133), piping is inserted between the garment edge and a facing. The facing is then folded over to the inside of the garment. Piping in a contrasting color or piping cut on the bias grain can be used to give a decorative effect.

Double-layer bound neckline
This is an ideal neckline finish for fine and sheer fabrics because the double layer of fabric conceals the raw edges within the binding (p. 135). On heavier fabrics, such as challis or crepe, however, the double-layer binding produces a slightly padded effect around the neckline.

Front placket opening

Piped neckline

Double-layer bound neckline

Single-layer bound neckline

Plain faced neckline

Shaped band neckline

Single-layer bound neckline
A neckline that is simple to make, the single-layer bound neckline (p. 134) can be used with most light- to mediumweight fabrics. This binding is suitable for use on sheer and fine fabrics where the facing would show through without it. It can be used on V-shaped, round, or square necklines.

Plain faced neckline
This is the most simple neckline and is plain on the right side of the garment with no visible facing or stitching. It is finished with a shaped facing attached to the right side of the garment neck edge, then folded to the inside to conceal the raw edges (p. 127).

Shaped band neckline
Consisting of a shaped band (round or square), cut to fit around the neckline, this type of finish has a facing, cut to the same shape, on the inside (p. 137). Contrasting fabric, checks cut on the bias grain, and stripes cut crosswise can be used to add a design feature to this neckline.

FACING A NECKLINE

A FACING IS USED TO FINISH the raw edges of a garment. When the garment edge is straight, the facing may be cut as part of the garment, then simply folded to the wrong side. This is called an integrated facing. When the garment edge is shaped, the facing is cut to the same shape, stitched on, and folded to the wrong side.

TYPES OF NECK FACING

SHAPED FACINGS ARE CUT to the shape of the edge being faced. Front and back neck facings are cut as separate pieces. A front facing combines the front edge facing with the front neck facing. A bias facing is a straight strip cut on the bias to fit a curve.

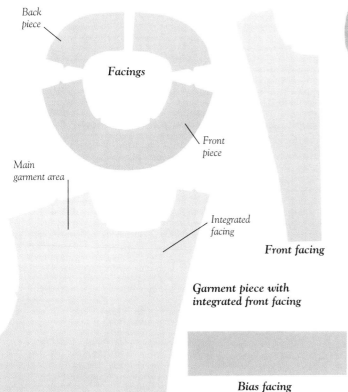

Back piece

Facings

Front piece

Main garment area

Integrated facing

Front facing

Garment piece with integrated front facing

Bias facing

APPLYING INTERFACING TO A FACING

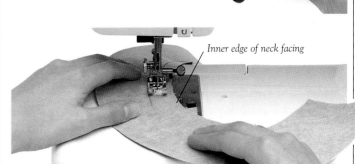

Interfacing

1 APPLY INTERFACING to the front and back neck facings. Stitch both facings at the shoulder seams. Trim the seam allowances (left). Press the seams open. If inserting a zipper, leave the facing back edges open.

Trim seam allowances to half original width

Inner edge of neck facing

2 IF THE FABRIC HAS STRETCH, staystitch around the inner edge of the facing using long machine stitch inside the seamline. Replace the pattern. Check the size of the inner edge, adjusting it by pulling up or loosening the staystitching.

FINISHING THE OUTER EDGE OF A NECK FACING

THE OUTER EDGE OF A NECK FACING is usually clean finished to prevent fraying. Machine zigzag stitching gives the quickest, flattest, and strongest finish. Ordinary zigzag stitch or three-step zigzag stitch can also be used. Alternatively, light- to mediumweight fabric can be edgestitched, and thicker fabric stitched and pinked.

ZIGZAG STITCHING

MACHINE ZIGZAG STITCHING over the raw edge is the best way to create a strong, neat finish on the raw edges of most fabrics. Set the stitch to a medium length and width.

Zigzag-stitched outer edge

EDGESTITCHING

AS AN ALTERNATIVE to zigzag stitching the raw edge of light- to mediumweight fabric, turn about ⅛ in (3 mm) to the wrong side along the outer edge, and machine stitch close to the fold.

Edgestitching

STITCHING AND PINKING

HEAVYWEIGHT, nonfraying fabrics can be finished in this way. First, machine stitch about ¼ in (6 mm) in from the raw edge, then trim the stitched edge with a pair of pinking shears.

Stitched and pinked edge

MAKING A DOUBLE-BIAS FACING

A DOUBLE-BIAS FACING can be used to provide a neat, narrow finish for curved necklines on fine or delicate fabrics where the shadow of a wider facing would show through to the right side. The finished facing can be handstitched to the garment or, alternatively, topstitched in place around the neckline on the right side.

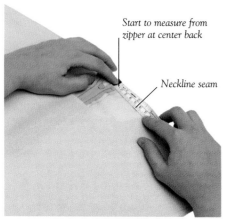

Start to measure from zipper at center back

Neckline seam

1 MEASURE around the neck at the seamline (above). Cut a bias strip as long as the neckline plus 2 in (5 cm), and twice as wide as the desired finished width plus twice the neckline seam allowance.

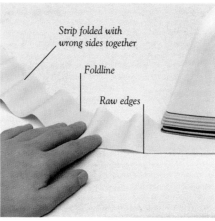

Strip folded with wrong sides together

Foldline

Raw edges

2 FOLD THE STRIP in half lengthwise, wrong sides together. Press flat. Using a steam iron, shape the strip to match the neckline curve by stretching the folded edge and easing in the raw edges (above).

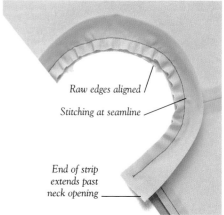

Raw edges aligned

Stitching at seamline

End of strip extends past neck opening

3 TREATING THE DOUBLE LAYER of the folded strip as one, pin the strip to the neck edge, allowing the strip ends to extend slightly past the edge of the neck opening. Stitch along the seamline.

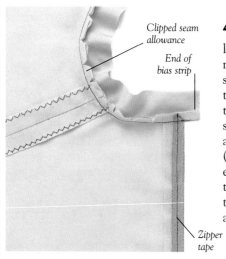

Clipped seam allowance

End of bias strip

Zipper tape

4 TRIM the seam allowances, and layer if required, making the garment seam allowance the widest. After trimming, clip the seam allowances around the curve (left). Then fold the ends of the bias strip to the wrong side at the neck opening, and pin in place.

APPLYING INTERFACING TO A NECKLINE

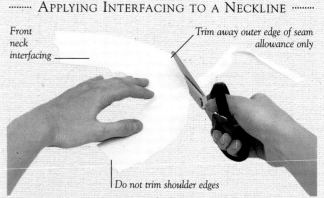

Front neck interfacing

Trim away outer edge of seam allowance only

Do not trim shoulder edges

1 To hide seam allowances behind the interfacing on fine fabrics, interface the neckline rather than the facing. Cut out the interfacing using the facing pattern pieces, and trim the seam allowance away from the outer edge (above).

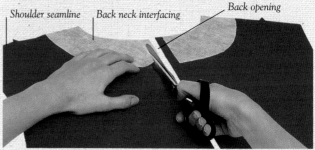

Shoulder seamline   Back neck interfacing   Back opening

2 Where there is a center back opening, trim away the seam allowances on the interfacing at either side of the neck opening (above). Baste the interfacing in place around the neckline before the garment shoulder seams are stitched.

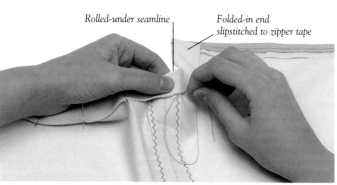

Rolled-under seamline

Folded-in end slipstitched to zipper tape

5 FOLD THE BIAS STRIP to the inside of the garment, rolling the seamline inward slightly so that it does not show on the right side. Pin the strip in place. Slipstitch the lengthwise edge of the strip to the garment (above) and the folded-in ends of the strip to the zipper tape, removing the pins as you work.

····· ATTACHING A SHAPED FACING ·····

THIS SIMPLE AND WIDELY USED TYPE OF FACING can be applied to most fabrics and is cut to the same shape as the neckline. The facing is made by applying the interfacing, stitching the shoulder seams, and finishing the outer edge by one of the methods on p. 127. The neck edge of the facing is staystitched to prevent stretching.

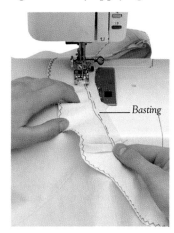

Facing ends pinned to wrong side

Staystitching

Wrong side

1 APPLY INTERFACING to the facing. Stitch the shoulder seams. Staystitch the neck edge of the facing. Pin the facing to the neck edge.

Basting

2 BASTE the shaped facing in place around the neck edge. With the facing uppermost, machine stitch the facing to the garment along the neck seamline (left), being careful to keep the shoulder seam allowances lying flat on both the shaped facing and the garment.

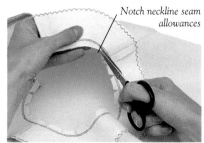

Notch neckline seam allowances

3 TRIM AND NOTCH the seam allowances all the way around the neckline (above). Trim both the center back and the shoulder seam allowances diagonally.

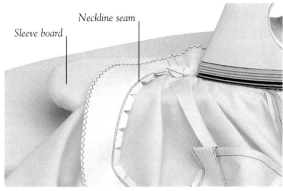

Sleeve board

Neckline seam

4 PLACE THE SEAM WRONG SIDE UP, either on a sleeve board or on the curved edge of an ironing board. Press the neckline seam open, using the point of the iron to avoid pressing in unwanted creases on the facing or on the garment (above). Then press all the seam allowances toward the facing.

Understitch facing next to seam

Right side of facing

5 PRESS the facing and seam allowances away from the garment. With the right side of the facing uppermost, understitch (p. 84) the facing by stitching just next to the neckline seam through the facing and all the seam allowances (left). Understitching in this way will hide the facing at the finished neck edge on the right side of the garment, where it might otherwise ruin the appearance of the garment neckline.

····· SHAPED FACING FINISHES ·····

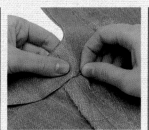

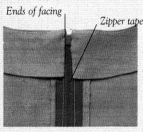

Ends of facing

Zipper tape

Whipstitching
Turn the facing to the inside, and complete Step 6 (far right). Whipstitch the facing to the garment at the shoulder seams (above).

Cross stitching
Join the facing to the garment at each shoulder seam with a cross stitch (above). Stitch through the edge of the facing and the seam allowance only.

At a zipper opening
Slipstitch the ends of the facing to the zipper tape. If required, a hook-and-eye fastening may be stitched inside the facing, above the top of the zipper.

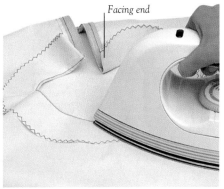

Facing end

6 TURN THE FACING to the inside of the garment, allowing the neckline seam to roll over slightly to the inside. Align the facing shoulder seam with the garment shoulder seam, and press the facing around the neck edge (above). Then fold under the ends of the facing at either side of the neck opening, and press.

ATTACHING A COMBINED FRONT AND FRONT NECK FACING

ON THIS TYPE OF FACING, the center front facing and the front neck facing are each cut in one piece. These two combined facings are stitched to the back neck facing, across the shoulder seams, to make a piece to finish the complete center front and neck edges. After the facing pieces have been joined, they are stitched to the garment.

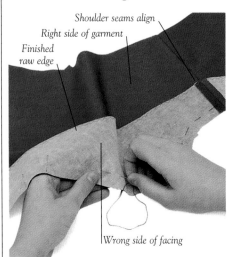

Shoulder seams align
Right side of garment
Finished raw edge
Wrong side of facing

1 STITCH the interfaced facing pieces. With right sides together, pin the facing to the garment along the front edges and around the neck, making sure to match the shoulder seams. Baste facing in place (above).

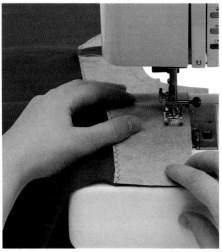

2 STITCH THE FACING around the neck and front edges (above). Remove the basting. Trim the seam allowances. Clip the curves, and trim the seam allowances diagonally across both the front corners and the shoulder seams.

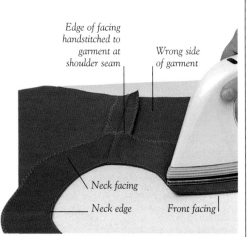

Edge of facing handstitched to garment at shoulder seam
Wrong side of garment
Neck facing
Neck edge
Front facing

3 PRESS THE FACING and the seam allowances away from the garment. Understitch through the facing and seam allowances next to the seam around the front and neck edges. Turn the facing to the wrong side; press (above).

STITCHING A FRONT AND FRONT NECK INTEGRATED FACING

WHEN THE FRONT FACING and the front neck facing are cut in one piece with the front of the garment, they are called an integrated facing. The shoulder edges of this type of integrated facing are stitched to the shoulder edges of a separate back neck facing. The joined facing is stitched to the garment around the neck edge.

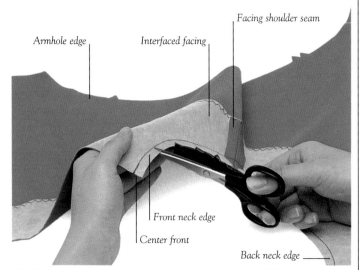

Front and front neck integrated facing
Neck edge

1 APPLY interfacing to the front and back neck facing, and the front neck integrated facing. Stitch the shoulder edges of the back neck facing to the shoulder edges of the integrated facing, and press the seams open. Fold the integrated facing to the right side of the garment front along the marked center front foldline. Pin the facing to the garment around the neck (left), making sure that the raw edges are even and that the notches and the shoulder seams are matching. Baste in place.

Armhole edge
Interfaced facing
Facing shoulder seam
Front neck edge
Center front
Back neck edge

2 STITCH THE FACING TO THE GARMENT around the neck edge. Remove the basting. Trim the seams, and layer if required, making the garment seam allowance the widest. Clip the seam allowances around the curved neck edge (above). Then trim the seam allowances diagonally across the shoulder seams and the front corners. Understitch (see Step 3, above) around the neckline. Turn the facing right side out, and press.

MAKING A COMBINED NECK AND ARMHOLE FACING

A COMBINED NECK AND ARMHOLE FACING is used on garments with narrow shoulders where, if cut separately, the two facings would overlap at the shoulders. In this method, one combined facing is cut for the front and two for the back. The shoulder seams on both garment and facing are left unstitched while the facing is attached.

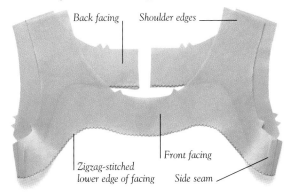

Back facing *Shoulder edges*
Zigzag-stitched lower edge of facing *Front facing* *Side seam*

1 APPLY INTERFACING to the front and back facing pieces. Pin facing side seams together, and machine stitch. Then press the side seams open. Leave the facing shoulder seams unstitched. Zigzag stitch along the lower edge of the joined facing to finish the raw edge.

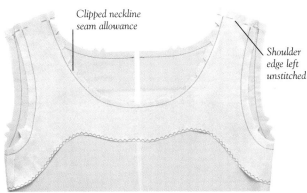

Clipped neckline seam allowance
Shoulder edge left unstitched

3 STITCH AROUND the armholes and the front and back necklines, starting and finishing securely at the shoulder seamlines ⅝ in (1.5 cm) in from the shoulder edges. Leave these edges open, and remove the basting stitches. Trim the seam allowances, and layer if required, making the garment seam the widest. Clip the allowances around the curves.

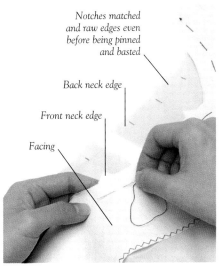

Notches matched and raw edges even before being pinned and basted
Back neck edge
Front neck edge
Facing

2 PIN a small tuck at the front and back shoulders, only on the garment pieces (see Achieving a Perfect Finish, below). With right sides together, pin the facing to the garment around the neck and armholes. Baste (left), leaving the shoulder edges open. Remove the pins around the front neck, back neck, and armholes, leaving the pins in the tucks.

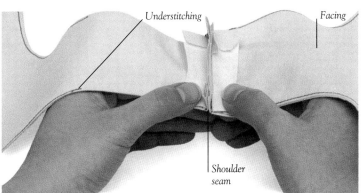

Understitching *Facing*
Shoulder seam

4 REMOVE THE PINS from the shoulder tucks. Press the facing seam, and understitch along the neckline and armhole edges as far as possible. Turn the facing to the wrong side, and press. With right sides together, fold back the facing shoulder edges (above), and pin the garment shoulder edges together. Machine stitch the garment shoulder seams. Trim the seam allowances.

ACHIEVING A PERFECT FINISH

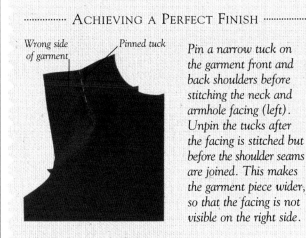

Wrong side of garment *Pinned tuck*

Pin a narrow tuck on the garment front and back shoulders before stitching the neck and armhole facing (left). Unpin the tucks after the facing is stitched but before the shoulder seams are joined. This makes the garment piece wider, so that the facing is not visible on the right side.

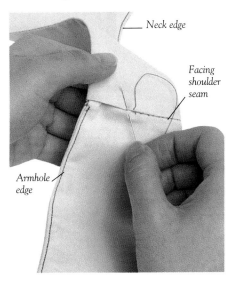

Neck edge
Facing shoulder seam
Armhole edge

5 TRIM ¼ in (6 mm) from the edges of the shoulder facing. Using the point of an iron, carefully press the garment shoulder seams open. Tuck the garment shoulder seam allowances inside the facing. Tuck the shoulder edges of the facing to the wrong side so that all the raw edges are enclosed. Whipstitch the folded edges together to close the opening (left).

PIPING A FACED NECKLINE

PIPING CAN BE PURCHASED READY MADE, or it can be made using the method on page 91. Ready-made piping tends to be fine in diameter. For a thicker trim, a length of piping cord should be covered with fabric (see opposite). The piping is sandwiched between the edges of the facing and the garment before the neckline is stitched.

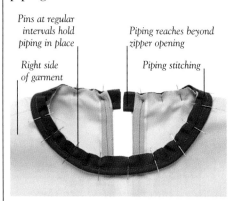

Pins at regular intervals hold piping in place

Piping reaches beyond zipper opening

Right side of garment

Piping stitching

1 PIN THE PIPING around the right side of the neck edge. The cord part of the piping should be just outside the neck seamline, and the piping stitching just inside the seamline. Allow the ends of the piping to extend past the zipper opening.

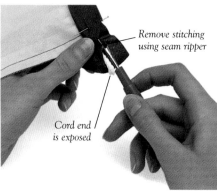

Remove stitching using seam ripper

Cord end is exposed

2 WITH THE PIPING still pinned around the neck edge of the garment, use a seam ripper to remove the seam stitching up to the edge of the zipper opening so that each end of the piping cord is released from the encasing fabric (above).

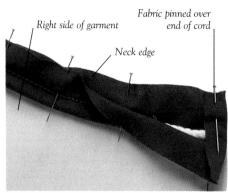

Fabric pinned over end of cord

Right side of garment

Neck edge

3 TRIM THE CORD ENDS even with the zipper opening. Trim the piping fabric ¼ in (6 mm) beyond the cord ends. Fold in the piping fabric so that it is even with the ends of the cord (above). Refold the fabric so that the edges are even, and pin.

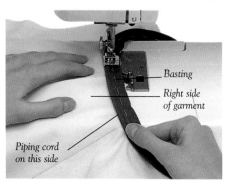

Basting

Right side of garment

Piping cord on this side

4 BASTE THE PIPING to the neckline near the piping stitching, and remove the pins. Using either a piping foot or zipper foot, stitch the piping to the neckline to the left of the stitching that encases the piping (above). Remove the basting.

Neck facing

5 PIN THE NECK FACING around the neckline over the piping, with right sides together and neck edges even. The facing should extend ⅝ in (1.5 cm) past the zipper opening. Fold these edges to the wrong side of the garment. Baste (above).

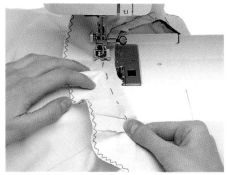

6 WORKING with the wrong side of the facing uppermost, stitch the facing to the garment (above). Make sure that the stitching line runs between the previous row of stitching and the cord part of the piping. Remove the basting.

Trim seam allowance corners at shoulder seams

7 TRIM AND LAYER THE SEAM ALLOWANCES, making the garment seam allowance the widest. Trim the corners diagonally at the back and at the shoulder seams. Clip into the seam allowances on the curves (above). Open out the facing. Press the seam allowances and facing away from the garment.

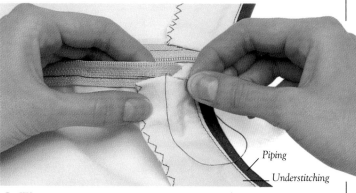

Piping

Understitching

8 WITH THE FACING STILL OPENED OUT and using a zipper foot, understitch from the right side through the facing and the seam allowances close to the piping. Turn the facing over to the inside, and press. Tuck under the raw edges at the center back, and handstitch to the zipper tape on the inside (above).

MAKING A COMBINED PIPING AND FACING

IN THIS METHOD, PIPING CORD IS COVERED and the facing is formed using a single strip of fabric. The facing and piping strip is cut across the width of jersey fabric or on the bias of woven fabric. It measures the length of the neckline seamline plus 1¼ in (3 cm), by the amount that is needed to encase the cord plus 1½ in (4 cm).

Piping cord inside fabric

1 PLACE THE CORD on the wrong side of the fabric strip. Wrap the fabric around the cord, with one seam allowance ⅝ in (1.5 cm) wide and the other 1 in (2.5 cm) wide. Using a zipper foot, stitch close to the cord. Zigzag stitch at the wider edge.

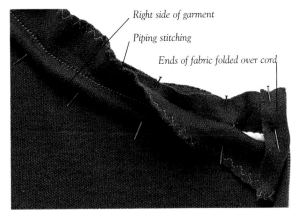

Right side of garment

Piping stitching

Ends of fabric folded over cord

2 PIN the narrower, unfinished edge of the piping to the right side of the garment, placing the edges together so that the piping stitching is aligned with the garment seamline. Allow the ends of the piping to extend past the opening edges. Release the ends of the cord and finish the ends of the piping fabric (left), as shown in Steps 2 and 3, opposite.

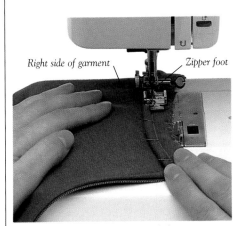

Right side of garment

Zipper foot

3 WITH THE RIGHT SIDE of the garment and the wider piping edge uppermost and using a zipper foot, stitch the piping to the garment on top of the piping stitching (above). Remove the pins as you stitch. Trim the garment and the narrower, unfinished piping edge seam allowances to ¼ in (6 mm).

Zigzagged facing covers seam on inside

Wrong side of garment

Back zipper opening

4 TURN THE PIPING FACING over to the wrong side of the garment, and press. Handstitch the edge of the facing to the garment shoulder seams, and the back edges of the piping facing to the zipper tape on the inside. (If required, stitch a hook and eye fastening to the piping on the inside of the garment.)

PIPING A NECKLINE WITHOUT A PLACKET

Overlap piping ends

1 *Allow sufficient length for the ends of the piping to overlap by 1¼ in (3 cm). Pin the piping around the neckline, overlapping the ends at one shoulder seam. Stitch the piping to the neckline (above), beginning and ending ¾ in (2 cm) on either side of the overlapping piping join.*

Cross over ends

2 *Release the cord by removing the stitching at the ends of the piping. Trim the cord ends even with the shoulder seam. Cross the empty casing ends (above). Complete the stitching across the shoulder seam. Then stitch on the neckline facing to cover the piping seam allowances.*

APPLYING A SNAP TO HEAVY CORD PIPING

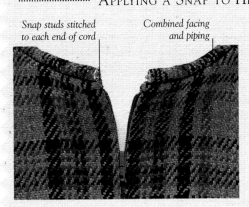

Snap studs stitched to each end of cord

Combined facing and piping

Where thick piping cord has been used in a combined piping and facing neckline, a snap fastening will provide a neater finish than the more usual hook and eye fastening. Select a snap that is the same size as the diameter of the piping cord. Using a thread that matches the fabric, stitch one half of the snap to each end of the piping on the finished neckline of the garment, making sure that the ends of the cord align neatly.

MAKING A BOUND NECKLINE

A BOUND NECKLINE GIVES A NEAT, narrow finish that is particularly suitable for fine fabrics where a facing would show through. When a pattern not intended for binding is being used, the neckline seam allowance should be trimmed away. On a bound neckline, the finished edge of the binding is aligned with the cut edge of the garment.

ATTACHING A SINGLE-LAYER BINDING

A NECKLINE WITH A SINGLE-LAYER BINDING has four layers of binding fabric and one layer of garment fabric. The seam allowance is equal to the finished width of the binding. This finish is suitable for medium- to fairly lightweight fabrics, such as crepe and fine cotton jersey. For thicker jerseys, follow the method shown in Making a Jersey Binding, opposite.

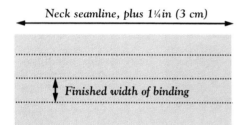

Neck seamline, plus 1¼ in (3 cm)

Finished width of binding

1 MARK AND CUT a rectangle of binding on the bias of a woven fabric or across the width of a jersey fabric. For a single-layer binding, the width of the binding rectangle should be four times the required finished width of the binding, and the length should be equal to the length of the neck seamline, plus 1¼ in (3 cm).

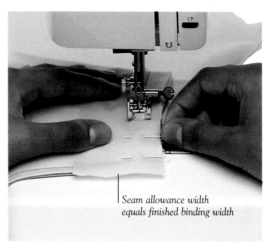

Seam allowance width equals finished binding width

2 WITH right sides together and raw edges even, pin the binding around the neckline edge. Stretch the binding slightly where necessary to fit around the curve, and allow ⅝ in (1.5 cm) to extend at each edge of the zipper opening. Stitch the binding in place, the finished binding width in from the raw edge (left).

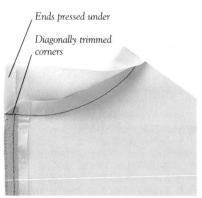

Ends pressed under

Diagonally trimmed corners

3 AT EACH END of the neckline, diagonally trim the corners of the seam allowance. Press the binding and the seam allowance away from the garment. Press the ends of the binding to the wrong side, and fold the binding over the raw edges.

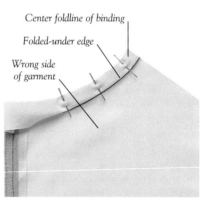

Center foldline of binding

Folded-under edge

Wrong side of garment

4 TUCK UNDER the raw edge of the binding so that it is aligned with the raw edge of the garment. Pin the binding flat on the wrong side of the neckline. The folded-under edge should be even with the previous line of stitching (left).

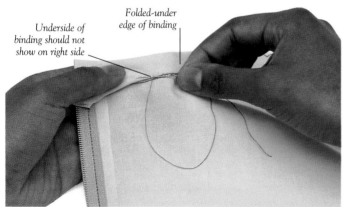

Underside of binding should not show on right side

Folded-under edge of binding

5 SLIPSTITCH THE FOLDED-UNDER EDGE of the binding to the neckline on the inside of the garment (above), following the previous line of stitching. Use small, neat stitches, and take care that the stitches do not show on the right side of the neckline. When nearing the end, unpin and realign the end of the binding if necessary. Slipstitch across the ends of the binding to secure.

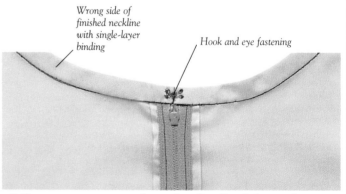

Wrong side of finished neckline with single-layer binding

Hook and eye fastening

6 PRESS THE BINDING so that it lies flat. Finish by stitching a hook and eye fastening (p. 262–263) to the ends of the binding on the inside, above the top of the zipper. This forms an invisible fastening that will hold the ends of the neckline closed and keep the zipper from slipping down. (Alternatively, a thread eye could be stitched to one edge, instead of a metal eye.)

ATTACHING A DOUBLE-LAYER BINDING

WITH A DOUBLE-LAYER BINDING, the binding strip is folded in half and used doubled throughout so that the finished neck edge has six layers of binding, plus one layer of garment fabric. This binding method is suitable for fine fabrics such as georgette and lawn, where the raw edge of the neckline would show through a single-layer binding.

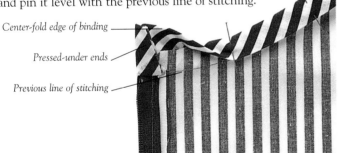

Finished width of binding

Foldline

Neck seamline, plus 1¼ in (3 cm)

1 MARK and cut a rectangle of binding on the bias of a woven fabric or across the width of a jersey fabric. The width of the rectangle should be six times the required finished width of the binding, and the length should be the length of the neck seamline, plus 1¼ in (3 cm).

Seam allowance width equals finished binding width

2 FOLD the binding in half lengthwise. Press. With right sides together, pin the doubled binding to the neck edge. Stretch the binding slightly to fit around the curve, and allow ⅝ in (1.5 cm) to extend at each edge of the zipper opening. Stitch in place, the finished binding width in from the edge (left).

3 AT EACH END, trim the corner of the seam allowance diagonally. Press the binding away from the garment, and press the ends of the binding over to the wrong side. Then turn the center-fold edge of the binding over to the wrong side, and pin it level with the previous line of stitching.

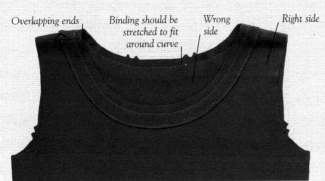

Center-fold edge of binding

Pressed-under ends

Previous line of stitching

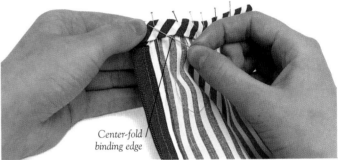

Center-fold binding edge

4 SLIPSTITCH the center-fold binding edge to the neckline on the inside and across the ends, as shown in Step 5 of Attaching a Single-Layer Binding (see opposite). Press the neckline so that the binding lies flat. Attach a hook and eye fastening to the binding ends on the inside to give a neat finish.

MAKING A JERSEY BINDING

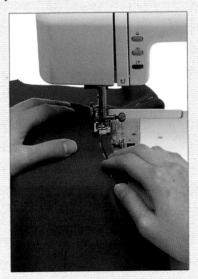

Overlapping ends

Binding should be stretched to fit around curve

Wrong side

Right side

1 *Across the width of the fabric, cut a strip three times the finished binding width plus ⅜ in (1 cm), by the neckline length plus ¾ in (2 cm). Zigzag stitch one long edge. Pin the other edge to the neckline, right sides together. Overlap the ends at a shoulder seam (p. 138–139). Stitch the strip in places, the finished binding width in from the raw edge.*

2 *Press the binding away from the garment, and fold the zigzag-stitched edge over to the wrong side so that it covers the previous stitching. Working from the right side, pin or baste near the seamline through all thicknesses of the fabric. Stitch-in-the-ditch by stitching from the right side, following the indentation made by the previous stitched seam (left). If the binding was pinned to the neckline, remove the pins as you go. Remove any basting.*

JOINING THE ENDS OF BINDING BY THE STRAIGHT METHOD

ON NECKLINES WITHOUT OPENINGS, the ends of the binding can be joined by the straight method, which is the quickest way, or by the diagonal method, which is less bulky and gives a smoother finish. Place the join at the shoulder seam or, on thick fabric, position the join next to the shoulder seam, where it is least noticeable.

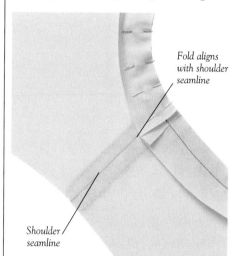

Fold aligns with shoulder seamline

Shoulder seamline

1 USING EITHER A SINGLE- or a double-layer binding (p. 134–135), fold ⅜in (1 cm) over to the wrong side at one end of the binding. With right sides together, align the folded binding with the shoulder seamline, and pin the binding to the neck edge. Stitch in place, stopping about 2 in (5 cm) from the start.

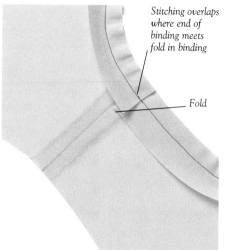

Stitching overlaps where end of binding meets fold in binding

Fold

2 MAKE SURE THAT THE END OF the binding overlaps the fold at the beginning of the binding. If necessary, trim the end of the binding so that it aligns with the raw edge of the other end. Repin in place. Complete the stitching across the binding join, overlapping the two ends of the stitching.

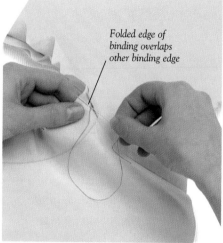

Folded edge of binding overlaps other binding edge

3 PRESS THE BINDING AWAY from the garment, using the point of the iron to avoid pressing in unwanted creases. On the right side of the garment, slipstitch the folded edge of the binding to the binding underneath, ensuring that it lies flat (above). Finish the binding according to the method being used.

USING READY-MADE BINDING

Sandwiching method
Ready-made binding comes with the raw edges pressed to the wrong side. Fold the binding in two lengthwise, ensuring that one side is wider than the other. Press. Sandwich the neckline between the two sides of the folded binding, positioning the narrower edge of the binding on the right side of the garment. Stitch (above).

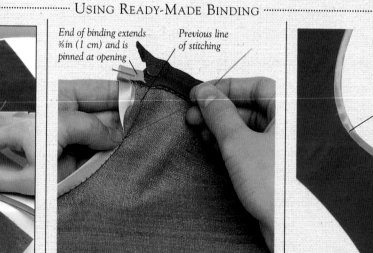

End of binding extends ⅜in (1 cm) and is pinned at opening *Previous line of stitching*

Hand-finished method
Unfold one edge of the binding. With right sides together, pin the unfolded binding edge to the neck edge with the ends extending past the neck opening. Stitch the binding along the crease on the right side, then pin the ends of the binding to the wrong side. Turn the free edge of the binding to the wrong side, and slipstitch to the previous stitching (above).

Overlapping binding aligned with shoulder seam

Binding a neckline without an opening
If there is no opening, start the binding ⅜in (1 cm) over the shoulder seamline. Stitch the binding in place, using the sandwiching method (see far left). Stop about 2 in (5 cm) from the start. Fold ⅜in (1 cm) to the wrong side at the end of the binding, aligning the fold with the shoulder seam. Complete the stitching.

MAKING A SHAPED BAND NECKLINE

A SEPARATE PIECE OF FABRIC cut to match the neckline is used to make a shaped band. The band may be made in the same or contrasting fabric. It is also possible to cut striped fabric in the opposite direction to the garment fabric as a design feature. The band can be stitched to a round, square, or decorative shaped neckline.

Staystitching around neckline

Back band pieces

Staystitching

Front band piece

1 IF THERE IS to be a center back zipper opening, a shaped neckline band is formed from one front piece and two back pieces of fabric. The band facing is then formed from three more pieces of fabric shaped in the same way. Cut out the outer band pieces, then the facing pieces, and staystitch the neck edges of all the band pieces.

2 STITCH the garment shoulder seams, but do not insert the zipper. Then staystitch around the curved neckline of the garment inside the seam allowance (left). (If the neckline is V-shaped or square, reinforce the corners with staystitching for 1 in [2.5 cm] on either side, and clip carefully into the corners.)

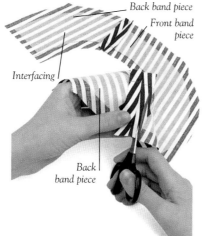

Back band piece

Front band piece

Interfacing

Back band piece

3 APPLY interfacing to the wrong side of each band piece. If using fusible interfacing, trim away the seam allowances before attaching the interfacing. If using sew-in interfacing, trim the seam allowances close to the stitching, after the pieces have been joined. Stitch the back band and front band pieces together across the shoulder seams. Trim the seams (right), and press them open.

4 WITH right sides together and raw edges even, pin the outer edge of the band to the neck edge of the garment, matching both the notches and the shoulder seams. Baste in place, and remove the pins. Clip the garment seam allowance if necessary for a smooth fit around the neckline curve. Stitch the basted seamline (right).

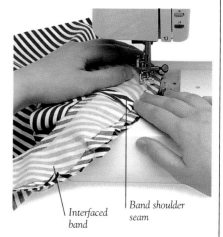

Interfaced band

Band shoulder seam

Notched seam allowances

Facing

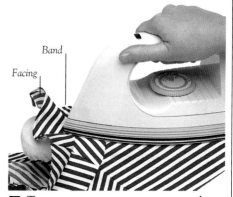

Band

Facing

5 REMOVE THE BASTING. Trim and layer the seam allowances, ensuring that the seam allowance on the band is the widest. Press the seam allowances towards the band. Notch around the curves (above) so that the completed neckline lies flat when worn.

6 INSERT THE CENTER BACK ZIPPER into the garment, making sure that the band seams are aligned when the zipper is closed. Stitch the facing pieces together, press under the outer edge, and stitch. Pin the facing to the neck edge of the band, and stitch in place (above).

7 TRIM THE SEAM ALLOWANCES, and layer if required, making the band seam allowance the widest. Clip the curves, and press the seam open. Press the facing and all the seam allowances away from the band (above). Turn the facing to the inside, and handstitch in place.

137

MAKING PLACKET BANDS

PLACKET BANDS ARE USED TO FINISH the two sides of a front neck opening. Unlike front bands, which finish the entire length of the front edges of the garment, placket bands stop partway down the garment bodice. They are usually formed from two separate fabric strips, but may sometimes be cut as one piece, with the two halves of the band joined together at the base. The two separate bands of a two-piece placket band overlap at the center of the garment when the placket is fastened. The base of the placket may have decorative topstitching.

RELATED TECHNIQUES

Working hemming stitches, p. 76
Working machine stitches, p. 77
Reducing seam bulk, p. 84
Making top stitched seams, p. 87
Applying interfacing
up to a foldline, p. 100
Making a flat collar, p. 144
Marking buttonhole position, p. 239

MAKING TWO-PIECE PLACKET BANDS

TWO-PIECE PLACKET BANDS can be used on a garment with a collar or a faced neckline. Make the placket before attaching the collar and before joining the garment front and back. If the garment neckline is finished with a facing (as here), the shoulder seams should be joined and the facing attached before the placket is made.

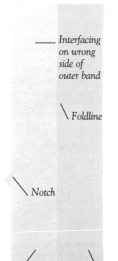

1 STAYSTITCH around the lower corners at the base of the placket opening. Clip each corner diagonally to within a thread or two of the staystitching.

Staystitching

Interfacing on wrong side of outer band

Foldline

Notch

Outer band

Band facing

2 EACH of the two band pieces has two sections: the outer band (which will be on the right side of the finished garment), and the band facing (which will be on the wrong side of the finished garment). Match the outer band edge to the one on the placket opening on the garment front. Apply interfacing up to the foldline on the wrong side of the outer band section of each of the band pieces.

Stitching across top of placket

Foldline

3 TO FINISH the top edge of one of the placket band pieces, first fold the band in half along the foldline, with right sides together, then stitch across the top, finishing the stitching ⅝ in (1.5 cm) from the long raw edges. (If the neck edge is to be finished later with a collar, leave the top edge of the placket band unfinished.)

Press along foldline

4 TRIM the seam allowances at the top of the band, and trim the corner diagonally at the fold. Press the seam open, and turn the band right side out. With wrong sides together, fold the band in half along the foldline, then press (left).

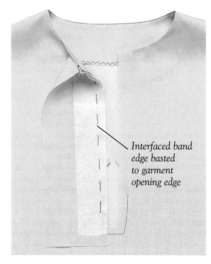

Interfaced band edge basted to garment opening edge

5 WITH right sides together and pattern markings matching, pin and baste the interfaced edge of the prepared band to one side of the garment opening, between the garment neck edge and the corner marking at the base of the opening. Pin the other band in the same way, and baste it to the other side of the opening.

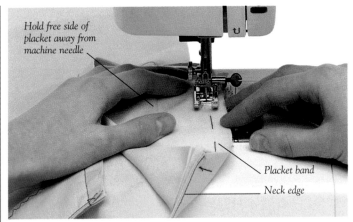

Hold free side of placket away from machine needle

Placket band

Neck edge

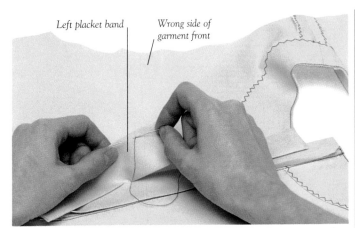

Left placket band

Wrong side of garment front

6 WITH THE INTERFACED OUTER BAND UPPERMOST, machine stitch each band to the garment between the corner marking at the base of the placket opening and the neck edge, stitching close to the line of basting (above). Remove the basting. Trim the seam allowances, and layer if necessary (p. 84).

7 PRESS THE SEAMS OPEN to give a crisp edge. Press the bands and the allowances away from the garment. On the left band, press the allowance of the long edge of the band facing to the wrong side, and trim. Pin this folded edge to the wrong side, and slipstitch to the previous stitching line (above).

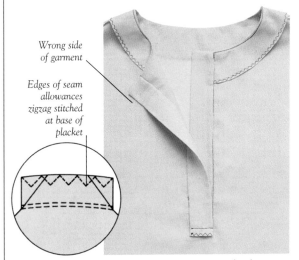

Wrong side of garment

Edges of seam allowances zigzag stitched at base of placket

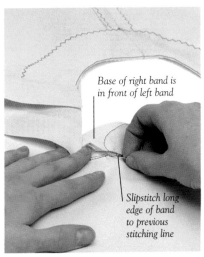

Base of right band is in front of left band

Slipstitch long edge of band to previous stitching line

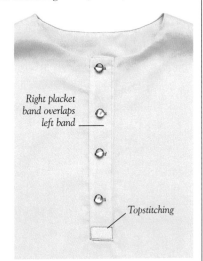

Right placket band overlaps left band

Topstitching

8 PIN THE LEFT BAND to the garment at the base of the placket, with right sides together and markings matching. Baste in position. Check from the right side to make sure that the seam is neat and even. With the garment side uppermost, machine stitch. Remove the basting. Zigzag stitch the edges together, and press downward.

9 PRESS AND TRIM the seam allowance of the right band as for the left band. Trim the seam allowance at the base of the band, and press this to the wrong side. Slipstitch the band in place (above) and the lower edges to one another.

10 MAKE the buttonholes (p. 238–247) on the right placket band, if required. Pin, and topstitch (p. 87) across the lower edge of the placket, stitching through all the layers, and using a decorative finish (see below).

TOPSTITCHING FINISHES FOR PLACKETS

Rectangle finish
A rectangle or a square gives a sporty look. Starting at the lower right corner and pivoting at the corners, stitch across the base, up the left side, then across the top, and back down to the base again.

Triangle finish
For this unusual finish, first mark the triangle apex with a pin. Starting at the lower right corner and pivoting at the corners, stitch across the base, up to the apex, and back down to the base.

Cross finish
This finish adds strength. Starting at the lower right corner and pivoting at the corners, stitch across the base, up to the top right corner, across the top, and back down to the base.

COLLARS

MAKING AND APPLYING COLLARS

COLLARS FRAME THE NECK AND FACE and, because they are close to eye level, form one of the most noticeable parts of a garment. While there are a number of different styles, all collars fall into one of three main types: standing, flat, and rolled. Plain stand collars are the simplest ones to make and are frequently used on dresses and tops. Flat collars, such as Peter Pan and sailor collars, are popular for blouses and also for children's clothes. Rolled collars and shawl collars are suitable for blouses, as well as for tailored jackets and coats.

RELATED TECHNIQUES

Reducing seam bulk, p. 84
Applying fusible interfacing, p. 99
Applying interfacing to a foldline, p. 100
Making two-piece placket bands, p. 138
Inserting a centered zipper, p. 253

DIRECTORY OF COLLARS

Front corners of Mandarin collar may be curved or squared

Mandarin collar

Shirt collar

Rolled collar

Shawl collar

Jabot collar

Stand collar

Flat collar

Mandarin collar
The pieces of this type of stand collar (see below) are often curved in shape at the front so that the collar slopes in smoothly toward the upper neck.

Shirt collar
A shirt collar (p. 150–151) has an upright stand and a collar piece that folds down over the stand. The stand may be cut out as a separate band or cut in one piece with the collar.

Rolled collar
On a rolled collar (p. 146–147), part of the collar stands up at the neck edge. The rest folds back down. The stand section may be the same depth all around, or higher at the back.

Shawl collar
A variation on the basic rolled collar, the shawl collar (p. 152) has a stand section that gradually tapers down to a thin point at the center front.

Jabot collar
In its basic form, this collar (p. 153) is a bias-cut square. The points of the square hang down in ruffles.

Stand collar
This type of collar (p. 149–150) stands up from the neckline seam. It can be made from a narrow band, or from a wider one that folds back on itself.

Flat collar
A flat collar (p. 144–145) sits almost flat at the neckline. Variations include Peter Pan and sailor collars.

PARTS OF A COLLAR

COLLARS are made from either a single section of fabric and attached so that the ends meet at the center front or the center back, or from two sections of fabric so that the ends meet at the center front and the center back. Depending on the finished shape, each collar may be cut as one piece, which is folded in half, or as two pieces, which are seamed together.

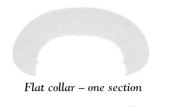

Flat collar – one section

Rolled collar – one piece

Stand collar – one piece

Flat collar – two sections

Rolled collar – two piece

Stand collar – two piece

ATTACHING INTERFACING TO A COLLAR

INTERFACING IS USUALLY APPLIED to the wrong side of the top collar piece of a rolled or flat collar, or to the outer part of a stand collar. It supports the top layer of fabric and also helps mask the indentation of the seam allowances on the right side of the garment. The exception to this rule is on a tailored collar (p. 290).

TO A VERY LIGHTWEIGHT FLAT COLLAR

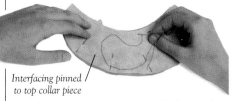

Interfacing pinned to top collar piece

USE SEW-IN INTERFACING on lightweight and fine silk fabrics, or – on very fine fabrics – use a matching organdy instead of interfacing. Pin the interfacing (p. 101) to the wrong side of the top collar piece, then baste in place (above).

TO A ONE-PIECE STAND COLLAR

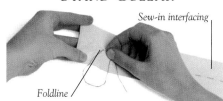

Sew-in interfacing

Foldline

APPLY A LIGHTWEIGHT sew-in interfacing to the whole collar piece. Baste the interfacing lightly to the fabric along the foldline (above). (If using fusible interfacing, interface the outer half of the collar up to the foldline only.)

TO A ROLLED COLLAR

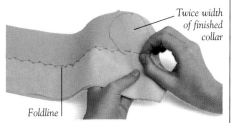

Twice width of finished collar

Foldline

APPLY SEW-IN INTERFACING to the wrong side of one half of a one-piece rolled collar up to the foldline. This half will form the top collar. Lightly catchstitch (p. 76) the interfacing to the fabric along the foldline (above).

USING DIFFERENT TYPES OF INTERFACING

LIGHT- AND MEDIUMWEIGHT SEW-IN INTERFACING is cut to fit the collar, including the seam allowances. Before applying heavyweight sew-in interfacing, the seam allowances on the interfacing are trimmed away. Fusible interfacing is steam pressed onto the whole top collar piece, including the seam allowances.

LIGHTWEIGHT SEW-IN

Trim just outside stitching line

Top collar

STITCH THE INTERFACING and top collar together just inside the seamline. With the interfaced side facing, trim away the interfacing seam allowance as close as possible to the stitching (above).

HEAVYWEIGHT SEW-IN

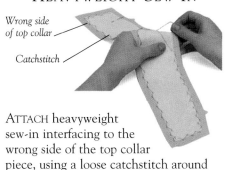

Wrong side of top collar

Catchstitch

ATTACH heavyweight sew-in interfacing to the wrong side of the top collar piece, using a loose catchstitch around the seamline (above).

FUSIBLE

Interfacing on wrong side of top collar

Machine stitching

APPLY INTERFACING to the entire top collar, and press in place. Pin the top collar to the under collar. Machine stitch around the edges. Trim the seam allowances (above).

MAKING A FLAT COLLAR

A FLAT COLLAR is easy to make and attach. If the garment has a front opening, the collar is made in one part that fits around the entire neckline with the ends meeting at the center front. If the garment has a center back zipper, the flat collar is made in two parts, as here, with the ends meeting at the center back and the center front.

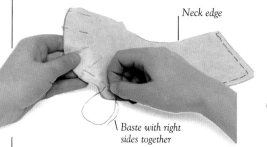
Neck edge
Baste with right sides together

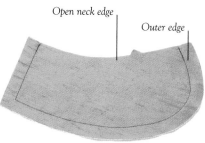
Open neck edge
Outer edge

Notched seam allowance

1 APPLY INTERFACING to the wrong side of the two top collar pieces. With right sides together and raw edges even, pin each top collar piece to a non-interfaced under collar piece. Baste in place, leaving the neck edge open (above), and remove the pins.

2 STITCH around the outer edges of each collar piece, leaving the neck edge open. On fine fabrics, use a smaller stitch to reinforce either side of the corners for about ⅝ in (1.5 cm). On thicker fabrics, stitch across the corners to blunt them. Remove the basting.

3 TRIM THE SEAM ALLOWANCES, and layer if required. Notch the seam allowances around the curves (above). Trim the corners diagonally, and taper the seam allowances on both sides of the corners. If the stitching puckers, press the collar seam flat along the line of stitching.

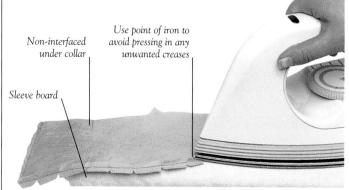
Non-interfaced under collar
Use point of iron to avoid pressing in any unwanted creases
Sleeve board

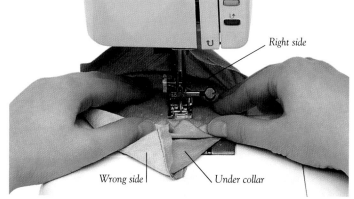
Right side
Wrong side
Under collar

4 USING A SLEEVE BOARD, work around the seam section by section, pressing the seam open (above). Use the curved part of the board for curved areas and the straight part for straighter portions of the piece. Press the seam allowances toward the under collar, again working around the collar section by section.

5 UNDERSTITCH THE COLLAR SEAM by stitching on the right side through the under collar and the seam allowances, staying next to the seamline (above). Work with the collar wrong side out. If the shape of the collar makes it difficult to understitch the whole seam, understitch as far as possible.

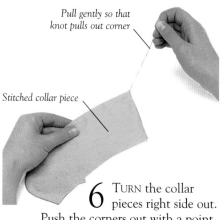
Pull gently so that knot pulls out corner
Stitched collar piece

Understitching on wrong side of collar piece
Rolled seam edge

6 TURN the collar pieces right side out. Push the corners out with a point turner, or pull them out by using a needle with a knotted double thread, passing the needle through from the inside, and then out again through the corner (above).

7 USING YOUR FINGERTIPS, roll the outer collar seam over slightly to the underside of the collar. Press the rolled seam edge, working around the collar section by section (above). Then press the collar on the right side using a pressing cloth to avoid making the fabric shiny.

⋯⋯ ROLLING A SEAM EDGE ⋯⋯

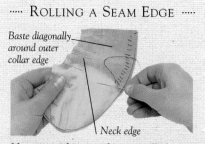
Baste diagonally around outer collar edge
Neck edge

If pressing does not keep a rolled seam from rolling back, pin the collar pieces in the correct position along the collar neck edge. Baste around the outer edge (above). Remove basting after the garment has been completed.

ATTACHING A FLAT COLLAR

THE SIMPLEST METHOD OF ATTACHING a flat collar is to sandwich the collar between the garment and the facing, so that the collar is stitched together with the facing to the garment neck edge. A one-piece flat collar and a two-piece flat collar are attached in the same way, except that the one-piece collar is left open at the center front.

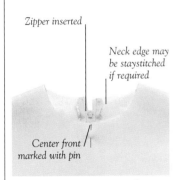

Zipper inserted

Neck edge may be staystitched if required

Center front marked with pin

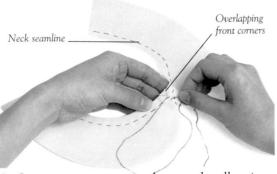

Neck seamline

Overlapping front corners

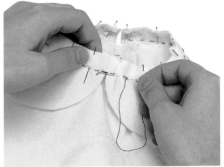

1 BEFORE ATTACHING the collar, stitch the shoulder seams, and make any darts that run into the neckline. Insert the zipper if required. Then mark the center front neck edge with a pin.

2 ON A TWO-PIECE COLLAR, baste each collar piece along the neck seamline. Overlap the front corners of the two collar pieces at the neck edge. The finished edges of the collar should intersect where the basted seamlines meet. Then baste the two overlapping front corners together securely, so that they meet across the neck seamline (above).

3 PIN THE COLLAR to the right side of the garment neck edge with the top collar uppermost, raw edges even, and the pattern markings matching. Match the point where the collar pieces intersect with the center front pin. Baste the collar in place (above), and remove the pins.

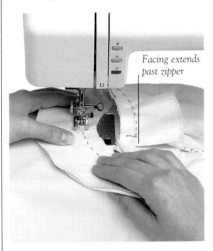

Facing extends past zipper

4 SEW the facing, and place it around the neck edge of the top collar with right sides together and neck edges even. Allow the ends of the facing to extend past the zipper at the center back. Pin the facing in place, and baste if necessary. Machine stitch along the neck seamline through all the fabric layers (left).

Back opening

Diagonally trimmed corner

5 REMOVE the basting. Trim and layer all the seam allowances, making the garment seam allowance the widest. Trim the facing seam allowance corners diagonally at the back opening and at the shoulder seams. Clip around the curves (left), cutting the clips closer together on tight curves.

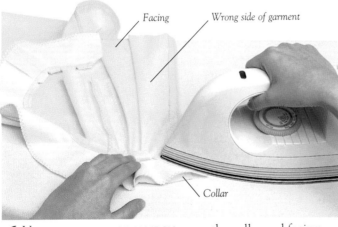

Facing   *Wrong side of garment*

Collar

6 USING THE POINT OF AN IRON, press the collar and facing seam allowances open (above). Be careful not to press in unwanted creases on either side of the seam. Then press the facing and all the seam allowances away from the garment, and understitch close to the seam (p. 84).

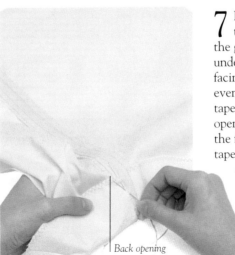

Back opening

7 PRESS the facing to the wrong side of the garment. Tuck under the ends of the facing to make them even with the zipper tape at the center back opening. Handstitch the facing to the zipper tape (left), allowing enough room for the zipper to run smoothly. If desired, stitch a hook and eye at the top of the garment opening.

MAKING A ROLLED COLLAR

THE PART OF A ROLLED COLLAR that stands upright is called the stand, and the part that folds over to lie downward is called the fall. The imaginary line dividing the stand and the fall is called the roll line. The stand may continue all around the collar or may be only at the back neck, gradually reducing in depth toward the front.

TWO-PIECE ROLLED COLLAR

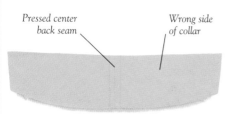

Pressed center back seam   *Wrong side of collar*

1 IF THE UNDER COLLAR is in two pieces, stitch the pieces together at the center back seam. Trim the seam allowances, and press the seam open (above). Apply interfacing to the wrong side of the top collar piece.

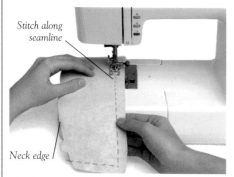

Stitch along seamline

Neck edge

3 STITCH AROUND the collar, leaving the neck edge open (above). On fine fabrics, reinforce the corners by adjusting the machine setting to a small stitch for about ⅝ in (1.5 cm) on either side of each corner. (On thick fabrics, make a diagonal stitch at each of the corners [p. 83].)

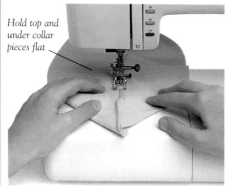

Hold top and under collar pieces flat

5 PRESS THE TOP COLLAR seam allowances toward the under collar. Understitch on the right side, by stitching through the under collar and seam allowances close to the seam (above). Understitch as far as possible toward the corners of the collar.

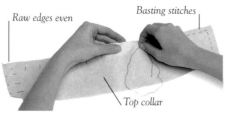

Raw edges even   *Basting stitches*

Top collar

2 PIN THE TOP COLLAR to the under collar with right sides together. Baste (above). (If the top collar and under collar have separate pattern pieces, the top collar may be slightly larger. In this case, stretch the under collar to fit.) Remove the pins.

Seam allowances notched at curves

4 REMOVE THE BASTING. Trim the seam allowances, and layer if required, making the top collar seam allowance the widest. Trim the corners diagonally, and notch the seam allowances of any curved area. Press the seam open on a sleeve board (above), section by section.

Roll seam over slightly to underside

6 TURN right side out, and pull out the corners (see Making a Flat Collar, p. 144). With your fingertips, roll the collar seam over slightly to the underside of the collar (above), and press. Press the collar section by section, allowing it to cool before attaching it to the garment (see opposite).

ONE-PIECE ROLLED COLLAR

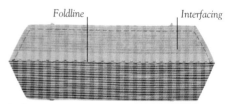

Foldline   *Interfacing*

1 APPLY INTERFACING up to the foldline on the wrong side of half the collar. For sew-in interfacing, baste around the outer edge, and catchstitch lightly along the foldline at the center.

2 FOLD THE COLLAR IN HALF along the foldline with right sides together and raw edges even. Pin. Stitch across both ends (above). Trim and layer the seam allowances. Trim the corners diagonally.

Sleeve board

End seam

3 PRESS THE END SEAMS OPEN, using a sleeve board (above). Turn the collar right side out, making sure that the corners are fully pushed out. Press, rolling the seam slightly toward the collar.

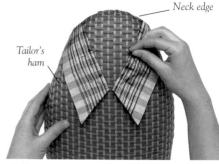

Neck edge

Tailor's ham

4 PIN AND BASTE the collar on a tailor's ham along the neck edges (above). Steam, then allow to cool. Remove the collar, and baste the neck edges together.

ATTACHING A ROLLED COLLAR

THERE ARE TWO METHODS of attaching a rolled collar. On light- to mediumweight fabrics, the collar is sandwiched between the garment and the facing, and all the layers are stitched together. On heavyweight or bulky fabrics, the top collar is stitched to the facing, and the under collar to the garment so that the seams can be pressed open.

LIGHT- TO MEDIUMWEIGHT FABRICS

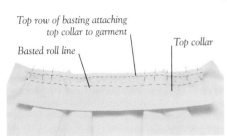

Top row of basting attaching top collar to garment

Basted roll line

Top collar

1 WITH RIGHT sides together and raw edges even, pin the prepared under collar to the neck edge of the garment, matching the notches and the matching ends of the collar to the appropriate pattern markings.

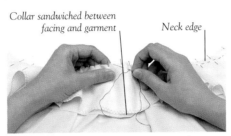

Collar sandwiched between facing and garment

Neck edge

2 STITCH THE FRONT FACING to the back facing. Press the seam open. Pin the facing to the neck edge with right sides together, sandwiching the collar between the garment and the facing. Baste (above). Remove the pins.

Center front facing

3 STITCH THE FACING around the neck and front edges, with the facing side uppermost (above). On fine fabrics, reinforce the front corners by setting the machine to a smaller stitch for about 1 in (2.5 cm) on each side of the corners.

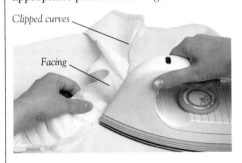

Clipped curves

Facing

4 REMOVE the basting. Trim and layer the seam allowances. Clip the curves. Press the seam allowances away from the garment and toward the facing (left).

5 ON DESIGNS that fasten to the neck, open out the facing, and understitch on the right side close to the collar seam and through the facing and seam allowances as far as possible (left). If the neck edge is to be worn open, understitch the back neck.

HEAVYWEIGHT OR BULKY FABRICS

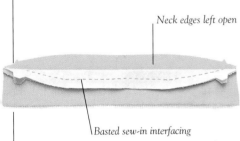

Neck edges left open

Basted sew-in interfacing

1 SEW and shape the collar (see Making a Rolled Collar, opposite). Start and finish ⅝ in (1.5 cm) in from the neck edge, and leave the neck edge open.

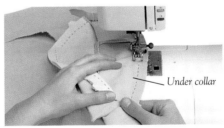

Under collar

2 WITH RIGHT SIDES TOGETHER, pin and baste the under collar to the garment neck edge, keeping the top collar out of the way. Stitch (above).

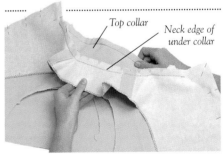

Top collar

Neck edge of under collar

3 JOIN THE FACING TOGETHER. With right sides together, pin the top collar to the facing neck edge. Stitch. Then clip the seam allowances so that they lie flat.

Center front facing

4 BASTE THE FACING to the garment between the collar ends and front edges, and stitch (above). (Pivot at the corners for a separate front facing.)

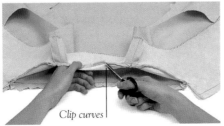

Clip curves

5 TRIM AND LAYER the neckline seam allowances. Trim the corners of the facing and the shoulder seam allowances diagonally. Clip along the curves (above).

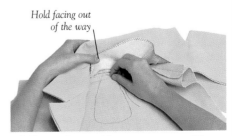

Hold facing out of the way

6 PRESS the neckline seam open. Turn the facing right side out, and pin along the neck seamline. Handstitch the seam allowances together (above).

ATTACHING A COLLAR WITHOUT A BACK NECK FACING

A COLLAR WITHOUT A BACK NECK FACING can be used on shirts and on tailored blouses where a back neck facing is unsuitable because it would be seen from the right side. The front facings are cut in one piece with the fronts, or are cut as separate pieces and stitched to the front edges. This method is not suitable for thick fabrics.

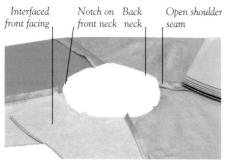

Interfaced front facing   *Notch on front neck*   *Back neck*   *Open shoulder seam*

1 MAKE THE COLLAR for the garment, but do not baste the neck edges together. If the garment has separate front facings, stitch them to the front edges. Stitch the shoulder seams, and press these seams open (above).

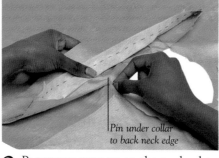

Pin under collar to back neck edge

2 PLACE THE COLLAR on the neck edge, with right sides of the garment and the under collar together. Matching the collar pattern markings to the shoulder seams, pin the under collar only to the back neck edge between the shoulder seams (above).

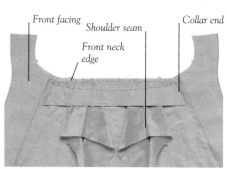

Front facing   *Shoulder seam*   *Collar end*   *Front neck edge*

3 MATCH THE ENDS of the collar to the markings on the garment fronts. Pin both the under collar and the top collar to the front neck edges between the shoulder seams and the collar ends. Clip the garment seam allowance to fit.

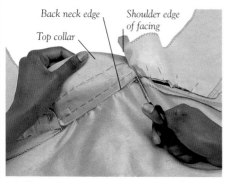

Back neck edge   *Shoulder edge of facing*   *Top collar*

4 FOLD EACH FRONT FACING to the right side on top of the collar. Press under the shoulder edge of the facing even with the shoulder seam, and pin the facing to the neck edge. At both shoulder seams, clip the seam allowance of the top collar only up to the seamline (above).

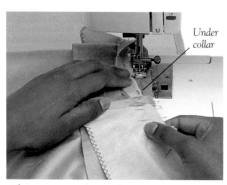

Under collar

5 IF DESIRED, baste the pinned facings and collar in place, turning back the top collar between the two clips. Machine stitch the facings and the collar to the garment. The top collar should be kept out of the way. Stitch only the under collar across the back neck edge (above).

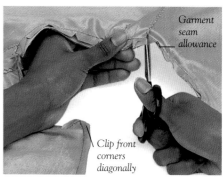

Garment seam allowance   *Clip front corners diagonally*

6 REMOVE ANY PINS or basting. Trim and layer the seam allowances. Trim the front corners and shoulder seam allowances diagonally. Clip the under collar and garment seam allowances up to the seamline at the shoulders. Clip around the curves (above).

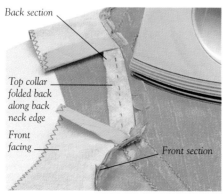

Back section   *Top collar folded back along back neck edge*   *Front facing*   *Front section*

7 CAREFULLY PRESS THE SEAM open all along the neckline (above). Then press each front section of the seam down onto the facing, and press the back section of the seam between the shoulder seams up into the collar.

8 TURN EACH FACING right side out, and pin the shoulder edge to the shoulder seam. Let the collar fall into place along its roll line. Turn under the free edge of the top collar even with the neckline stitching. Pin, and slipstitch (above).

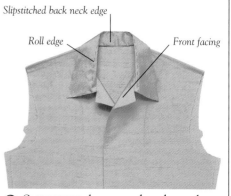

Slipstitched back neck edge   *Roll edge*   *Front facing*

9 SLIPSTITCH the pressed-under and pinned shoulder edge of each front facing to the garment shoulder seam on the inside. Remove the pins. Finally, remove any remaining basting stitches on the top collar, and press.

MAKING A ONE-PIECE STAND COLLAR

A ONE-PIECE STAND COLLAR is made from a rectangle of fabric, sometimes cut on the bias. It extends upward from the neck seamline. There are two types: the plain stand collar (below) and the turn-down stand collar (right).

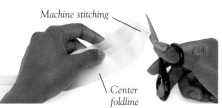

Outer collar | *Facing* | *Facing edge* | *Center foldline*

1 CUT THE INTERFACING to fit the collar piece. Trim the seam allowance from the facing edge of the interfacing, and apply the interfacing. (If the fabric is bulky, interface only half the depth of the collar piece, leaving the facing half free.)

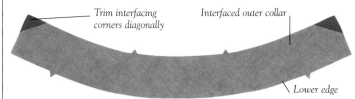

Machine stitching

Center foldline

3 FOLD THE COLLAR along the center foldline, right sides together. Pin and machine stitch the collar ends. Carefully trim the seam allowances, layering them to make the outer collar seam allowance the widest. Trim the corners at the foldline edge diagonally (above).

Pin | *Pressed-up seam allowance* | *Center foldline*

2 PRESS THE SEAM ALLOWANCE to the wrong side along the facing edge of the collar. Trim the seam allowance to ¼ in (6 mm), and pin it at each end (above). If the interfacing is sew-in, baste it in place along the center foldline.

Outer collar edge | *Rolled seam*

4 PRESS THE SEAMS OPEN, then toward the underside of the collar. Turn the collar right side out. Arrange the two end seams so that they are rolled slightly to the underside (above). Press the collar. (The outer collar edge will be stitched to the right side of the garment neckline.)

TURN-DOWN STAND COLLAR

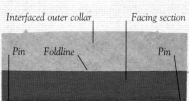

Interfaced outer collar | *Facing section*

Pin | *Foldline* | *Pin*

1 *This collar is twice as deep as the ordinary stand collar piece. Cut the interfacing to half the depth of the fabric piece, and apply it to the outer collar section. Then press the seam allowance of the facing section to the wrong side, trim, and pin the ends.*

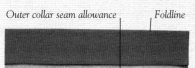

Outer collar seam allowance | *Foldline*

2 *Fold the collar in half along the foldline, with right sides together. Stitch the collar ends, remove the pins, and trim the corners (see Step 3, left). Press the seam, then turn the collar right side out (see Step 4, left).*

MAKING A TWO-PIECE STAND COLLAR

A TWO-PIECE STAND COLLAR is a plain stand collar cut in two pieces, and is either curved or rectangular. The ends of the collar can meet at either the front or the back, and the corners are rounded or pointed. Usually, only the outer collar piece is interfaced, but – if a very stiff finish is required – both pieces can be interfaced.

Trim interfacing corners diagonally | *Interfaced outer collar*

Lower edge

1 CUT THE INTERFACING TO THE SAME SIZE as the collar pieces. At the top edge of the interfacing, trim away the two corners of the seam allowances diagonally, to reduce the bulk. Apply the interfacing to the wrong side of the outer collar piece.

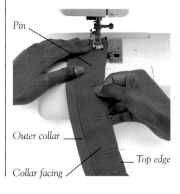

Pin

Outer collar

Collar facing | *Top edge*

3 WITH right sides together and the top edges and ends even, pin and stitch the collar pieces together around the top edge and ends (left). Trim and layer the seam, making the outer collar seam allowance the widest. Clip the seam along the curved edge, and trim the corners diagonally.

Lower edge of collar facing piece

Seam allowance | *Fold edge*

2 PRESS THE SEAM ALLOWANCE to the wrong side along the lower edge of the collar facing piece. Then trim the seam allowance to 1/4 in (6 mm). Pin along the fold edge (above). Baste the fold edge in place, and remove the pins.

4 PRESS THE SEAM OPEN WHERE POSSIBLE, then press it toward the collar facing. Understitch the seam along the top edge. Turn right side out. Arrange the seam to roll slightly toward the inner collar, and press (below).

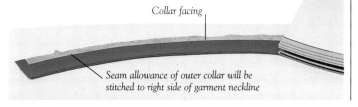

Collar facing

Seam allowance of outer collar will be stitched to right side of garment neckline

ATTACHING A STAND COLLAR

THIS METHOD IS A QUICK AND NEAT WAY of attaching a stand collar without a neck facing. The outer edge of the collar is stitched to the right side of the garment. The seam allowances are tucked into the collar, and the inner edge of the collar is handstitched to the inside of the garment. The collar fabric can be matching or contrasting.

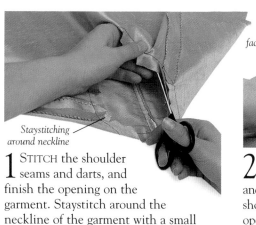

Staystitching around neckline

1 STITCH the shoulder seams and darts, and finish the opening on the garment. Staystitch around the neckline of the garment with a small machine stitch. Clip into the neckline seam allowances at intervals (above).

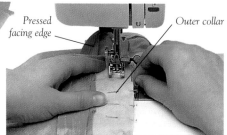

Pressed facing edge   *Outer collar*

2 PIN THE OUTER COLLAR EDGE to the neck edge with right sides together and raw edges even. The ends of the collar should be even with the edges of the opening. Baste if required. Stitch (above), taking care not to catch the pressed facing edge of the collar in the stitching.

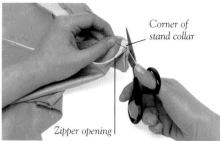

Corner of stand collar

Zipper opening

3 TRIM THE SEAM ALLOWANCES, and layer if required, making the collar seam allowance the widest. To ensure a neat finish for the collar, trim diagonally across the corners of both the collar (above) and the shoulder seam allowances, close to the stitching.

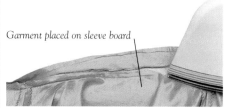

Garment placed on sleeve board

4 PRESS THE SEAM OPEN (above), then press it away from the garment. Work on the edge of a sleeve board to make it easy to press the neckline seam neatly. Tuck the raw edges of the seam allowances inside the collar.

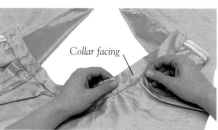

Collar facing

5 ALIGN the pressed facing edge of the collar with the stitching to enclose the raw edges inside the collar. Pin, then slipstitch along the neckline seam (above); the stitches should not show through on the right side. Remove the pins.

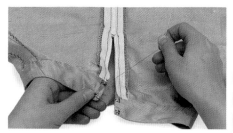

6 STITCH hook-and-eye fastenings to the wrong side of the collar ends (above), so that the edges just meet when fastened. On a plain stand collar, attach two hooks. If the collar has a turn-down piece, attach a third hook to it.

MAKING A SHIRT COLLAR WITH A STAND

A SHIRT COLLAR IS FORMED from two parts: the stand (sometimes called the band), which rises upward from the neckline, and the collar, which folds down from the top of the stand. In the traditional method shown here, the collar and stand parts are cut separately, although sometimes the collar and stand are cut as one piece.

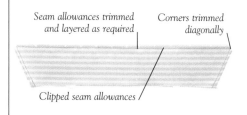

Seam allowances trimmed and layered as required   *Corners trimmed diagonally*

Clipped seam allowances

1 APPLY INTERFACING to the wrong side of the top collar. With right sides together and raw edges even, pin and stitch the top collar and under collar, leaving the neck edges open. Strengthen the corners with a small stitch, and stitch across to blunt them. Trim.

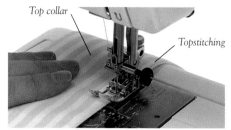

Top collar

Topstitching

2 PRESS THE SEAM OPEN. Turn the collar right side out, and pull out the corners. Press the collar, rolling the seam slightly to the underside so that it does not show on the right side. If desired, topstitch around the outer edge of the collar to give it a neat finish (above).

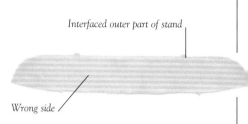

Interfaced outer part of stand

Wrong side

3 APPLY INTERFACING to the wrong side of one collar stand piece: this interfaced piece will form the outer part of the completed collar stand. (If the stand is cut in one piece with the collar, interface it as a continuation of the top collar, as described in Step 1.)

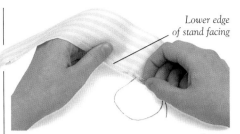

Lower edge of stand facing

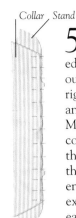

Collar Stand

4 PRESS THE SEAM ALLOWANCE to the wrong side along the lower edge of the other stand piece, and baste near the fold (above). Trim to ¼in (6 mm). This piece will form the stand facing.

5 PIN the under collar to the top edge of the interfaced outer stand piece, with right sides together and raw edges even. Match the ends of the collar to the positions that are marked on the pattern. This will ensure that the stand extends slightly past each end of the collar.

Collar

6 PLACE the stand pieces together to enclose the collar. Position the stand facing and top collar with right sides facing. Pin and baste, then remove the pins. Stitch, starting and finishing at the pressed edge of the stand facing (left).

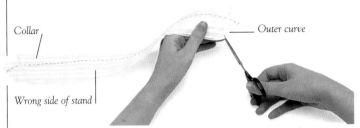

Collar

Outer curve

Wrong side of stand

7 TRIM AND LAYER THE SEAM ALLOWANCES, making the outer stand seam allowance the widest. Clip along the seam allowances, and notch the outer curves (above). Press the seam open between the stand facing and the top collar allowances.

Press top collar side first

Stand facing

8 TURN THE STAND RIGHT SIDE OUT. Pull the stand away from the collar to lie flat. Press the top collar side (above) before pressing the under collar side. Allow the finished collar to cool, leaving it flat on the ironing board before it is handled again.

ATTACHING A SHIRT COLLAR WITH A STAND

THIS COLLAR IS STITCHED to a garment with the right side of the interfaced outer stand positioned to face the right side of the shirt neckline. All raw edges are tucked inside the stand, and the stand facing edge is handstitched to the inside of the shirt. To give the collar a crisp, flat finish, the stand can be topstitched around all edges.

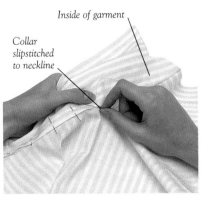

Stitching line should meet garment opening edge exactly

Neck edge

1 PIN the unpressed, interfaced edge of the stand to the neck edge of the garment, with right sides facing. The stand corners extend a little past each end, so that the stitching line meets the garment edge. Baste, then stitch. Do not catch the inner stand facing in the stitching.

Neckline seam allowance

2 TRIM BOTH the outer stand and garment neckline seam allowances (left). Layer if required, making the outer stand seam allowance the widest. Notch the seam allowances around the curve of the neckline, and trim the corners of the outer stand seam allowance diagonally.

Inside of garment

Collar slipstitched to neckline

3 PRESS the seam open, then upward inside the collar. Align the edge of the stand facing with the previous stitching line. Pin. Slipstitch the facing edge to the neckline seam (left), ensuring that the stitches do not show on the right side.

4 IF DESIRED, topstitch around the right side of the entire stand to match the stitching on the collar and to give a neat, flat finish. To make the join in the stitching appear inconspicuous when the completed garment is worn, start and finish the stitching at the top edge of the stand and at the center back.

MAKING AND ATTACHING A SHAWL COLLAR

A SHAWL COLLAR COMBINES the top and lapel of the collar in one pattern piece, eliminating the need for the seam found on a traditional jacket or revers collar.

A shawl collar is cut with a smooth curve at the outer edge, although a V-shaped notch is sometimes cut into the outer edge to imitate the tailoring of a revers collar.

Wrong side of right front

Wrong side of left front

Staystitches around neckline

Shoulder seam

Wrong side of back

1 STITCH both front pieces to the back at the shoulder seams, and zigzag stitch the seam allowances. Stitch any seams or darts that run into the neckline. Staystitch around the neckline.

Under collar *Center back seam*

2 THE COLLAR IS EASY TO MAKE if the side seams of the garment are left open. If the under collar is cut into two pieces, stitch both pieces together along the center back seam (above). Trim the seam allowances, and press the seam open.

3 WITH RIGHT SIDES TOGETHER and pattern markings matching, pin and baste the under collar to the neck edge. Clip the seam allowance if necessary for a smooth fit. With the garment uppermost, stitch the neckline seam. Remove the basting (above). Press the seam flat toward the collar.

Stitch on both sides of seam to hold seam open

Wrong side

4 TRIM THE SEAM ALLOWANCE. Trim the ends of the shoulder seam allowances diagonally. Clip the garment seam allowance, and notch the collar seam allowance. Press the seam open. On very thick fabrics, or if the seam will not stay open, machine stitch along both sides of the seam (above).

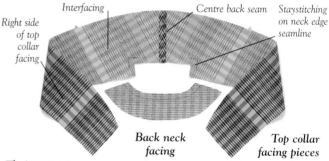

Interfacing *Centre back seam* *Staystitching on neck edge seamline*

Right side of top collar facing

Back neck facing *Top collar facing pieces*

5 APPLY INTERFACING to the wrong side of the two top collar facing pieces. Stitch together at the center back seam. Trim the seam, and press open. Staystitch the seamline for 1 in (2.5 cm) along both inner corners. Clip the neck edge. Apply interfacing to the back neck facing, and staystitch the neck seamline.

Edge to be stitched to garment

Interfaced collar facing *Back neck facing*

6 WITH RIGHT SIDES TOGETHER, pin the back neck facing to the collar facing along the neck and shoulder edges. Open out the clips on the collar to pin the neck edges together, clipping the back neck facing along the curves if necessary. Baste, and stitch with the collar uppermost, pivoting at the corners.

Zigzag-stitched outer edge *Back neck facing*

7 TRIM THE SEAM ALLOWANCES. Then trim diagonally across the corners of the back neck facing. Clip or, where the fabric is too full, notch the seam allowance if necessary so that it will lie flat (above). Press the seam open. If the garment is not being lined, trim and seam finish the outer edge of the entire facing.

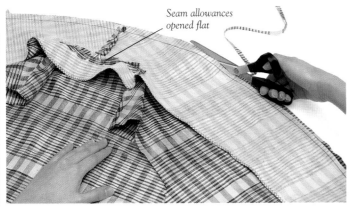

Seam allowances opened flat

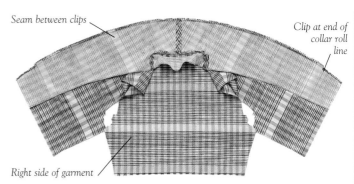

Seam between clips

Clip at end of collar roll line

Right side of garment

8 PIN THE COLLAR to the garment, with right sides together. Stitch, keeping the seam allowances of the center back and under collar open flat. Clip the seam allowances at the end of the collar roll line. Trim the collar allowance wider above the clip and the garment allowance wider below (above).

9 NOTCH THE SEAM ALLOWANCES around the curve of the collar. Press the seam allowances open by pressing the seam allowances between the clips at the roll line toward the under collar, and the seam allowances outside the clips on the outer edges of the roll line toward the collar facing.

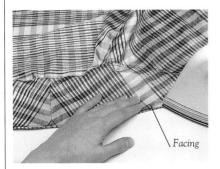

Facing

10 UNDERSTITCH the seam around the collar, underside up, then along the front edges, facing side up. Leave 1½ in (4 cm) of the seam unstitched at the roll line. Turn the facing to the wrong side, and press (left).

Top collar

Back neck facing folded back

11 PIN the top collar to the under collar around the back neck, just above the neckline seam. Blind hemstitch (p. 76) the top and the under collar seam allowances together around the back neck (left).

MAKING AND ATTACHING A JABOT COLLAR

THE BIAS-CUT JABOT COLLAR is made from a simple square of fabric. It can be stitched to a garment with a high, round neckline or to one with a V-shaped neckline with a facing. A jabot collar looks attractive when made from a sheer fabric, but light- or mediumweight fabrics that drape well, such as silk or cotton, are also suitable.

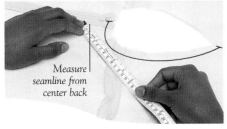

Measure seamline from center back

1 TO MAKE A JABOT COLLAR on a V-shaped neckline, measure half the neck seamline in a curve from the center back opening to the V tip at the center front (above). Double this amount to calculate the diagonal length of the jabot.

Center front tip

2 FOLD the fabric diagonally on the bias, and mark the required diagonal length along the fold. Mark a square of fabric based on this diagonal measurement, and cut. Baste along the diagonal fold from its center to one corner to mark half the length of the fabric.

Fold tacked halfway along

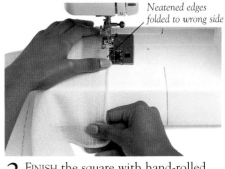

Neatened edges folded to wrong side

3 FINISH the square with hand-rolled hems (p. 206), or zigzag stitch around the edges. Fold the edges to the wrong side, and stitch them in place (above).

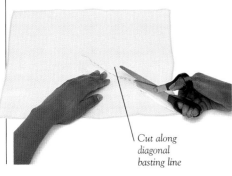

4 CUT ALONG the basted line, marking half the diagonal length of the jabot (left). (The cut edges will fit around the neckline, with the center point matched to the center of the V on the garment.)

Cut along diagonal basting line

5 WITH right sides uppermost, pin the cut collar edges to the neckline, with the end of the cut just above the seamline at the base of the V shape. Baste. Attach the neck facing in the normal way (p. 128–131), sandwiching the jabot.

STRETCH NECKBANDS

S TRETCH NECKBANDS ARE MADE from knit fabrics such as jersey and rib-knit fabric. They can be attached to jersey or woven fabric garments. On woven fabrics, the garment neckline must be large enough to fit over the head or else have an additional opening. The method used for attaching the neckband depends on the neckline shape, and on how much stretch the fabric has. A shaped stretch neckband is suitable for low necklines and for neckband fabrics with a limited amount of stretch. A straight stretch neckband is best for high necklines and stretchier fabric.

RELATED TECHNIQUES

Working basting stitches, p. 73
Reducing seam bulk, p. 84
Seam finishes, p. 85
Stitching seams on
knit fabric, p. 89
Making a bound neckline, p. 134
Making a shaped band neckline, p. 137

DIRECTORY OF STRETCH NECKBANDS

Crew neck
The crew neck is a classic round neckline with a flat band that finishes with its inner fold edge at the base of the neck. The finished band width is usually about 1¼–2 in (3–5 cm).

Polo neck
This type of neckband is a high, stand-up band that fits closely around the neck. It can be a single layer, or folded down on itself to make a double band.

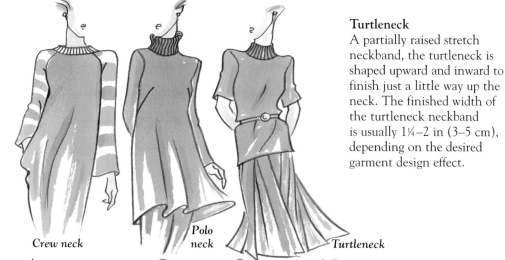

Crew neck

Polo neck

Turtleneck

Turtleneck
A partially raised stretch neckband, the turtleneck is shaped upward and inward to finish just a little way up the neck. The finished width of the turtleneck neckband is usually 1¼–2 in (3–5 cm), depending on the desired garment design effect.

MAKING AND ATTACHING A SHAPED STRETCH NECKBAND

T HIS TECHNIQUE IS USED for making neckbands from jersey fabrics that have only a limited amount of stretch, such as double jersey and fleece-backed jersey.

The neckband is pressed into the shape of the neckline curve before it is attached to the garment. A shaped stretch neckband suits flat, low, loose-fitting necklines.

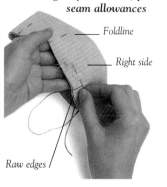

Width of neckband, plus two seam allowances

Length of neckband, plus two seam allowances

Foldline

Right side

Raw edges

1 CUT A STRIP across the width of the fabric, the length of the neckline seam plus two seam allowances, by twice the required neckband width plus two seam allowances.

3 FOLD THE NECKBAND in half lengthwise, with wrong sides together and raw edges even. Pin raw edges together, and baste loosely along the seamline (left). Remove the pins. Stitch the garment at the shoulder seams, leaving the garment side seams open.

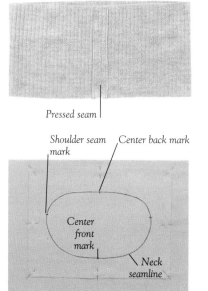

Pressed seam

Shoulder seam mark *Center back mark*

Center front mark

Neck seamline

2 STITCH the short ends of the neckband, right sides together, to form a circle. Trim the seam allowances, and press open. If using a lightweight fabric, use an overedge seam (p. 89).

4 ON a small piece of cotton fabric, draw the shape of the neck seamline, using the pattern pieces as a guide. Mark the positions of the garment shoulder seams, the center front, and center back. Pin the guide to an ironing board.

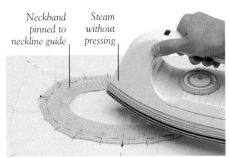

5 MATCHING THE NECKBAND SEAM to one shoulder seam and the basted seamline to the guide seamline, pin in place. Steam press to set the shape, easing in the inner folded edge (above).

Neckband pinned to neckline guide *Steam without pressing*

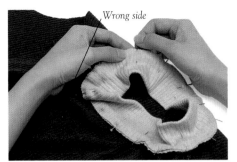

6 PIN TO MARK the center front, center back, and shoulder seams of the neckband. Then unpin the neckband from the guide. With right sides together, pin the neckband to the neckline (above).

Wrong side

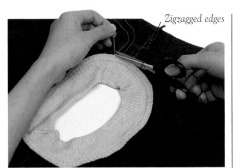

7 WORKING with the neckband uppermost, stitch the band to the neckline. Trim the seam allowances, and zigzag stitch the edges together to finish them. Trim the thread ends (above).

Zigzagged edges

ATTACHING A STRAIGHT STRETCH NECKBAND

BECAUSE THE FABRIC for a straight stretch neckband should have a fair amount of stretch, it can be used for high, close-fitting necklines. The neckband length depends on how much stretch the fabric has and how tight the neckline is to be. In general, it is cut 2–4 in (5–10 cm) shorter than the neck seamline, plus two seam allowances.

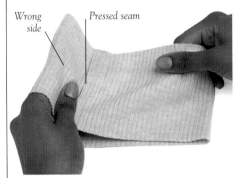

Wrong side *Pressed seam*

1 CUT A STRIP across the fabric width to the required length plus two seam allowances, by twice the finished width plus two seam allowances. With right sides facing, stitch together the short ends of the strip to form a circle. Trim the seam allowances, and press open.

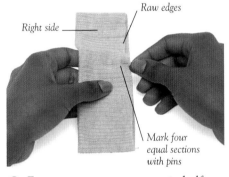

Right side *Raw edges* *Mark four equal sections with pins*

2 FOLD THE NECKBAND STRIP in half lengthwise with wrong sides together and raw edges even. Place a pin at the neckband seam, inserting it crosswise through both layers of the neckband. Divide the neckband into four equal sections, and mark with pins (above).

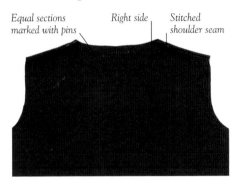

Equal sections marked with pins *Right side* *Stitched shoulder seam*

3 STITCH the garment shoulder seams together, and press the seams open. Turn the garment to the right side, and divide the neckline into four equal sections, marking the center back, the center front, and each of the shoulder seams with a pin at each point.

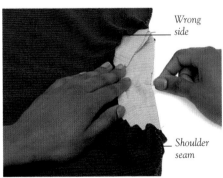

Wrong side *Shoulder seam*

4 TURN THE GARMENT inside out. With right sides together and raw edges even, place the neckband on the garment, matching the neckband seam to one shoulder seam. Pin the neckband to the neckline (above), matching the other marking pins and stretching to fit.

Wrong side of neckband

5 WITH THE NECKBAND uppermost, machine stitch around the neck seamline using a fairly short, narrow zigzag stitch (above). While stitching, stretch the neckband carefully, while holding it taut between the pins so that it fits smoothly around the garment neckline.

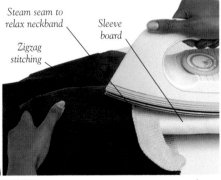

Steam seam to relax neckband *Sleeve board* *Zigzag stitching*

6 TRIM THE SEAM ALLOWANCES, and zigzag stitch the edges together. Place the neckband on a sleeve board. If the seam has stretched during stitching, hold a steam iron above the neckband, and let the steam reshape it (above). Press the seam lightly toward the garment.

155

WAISTLINES

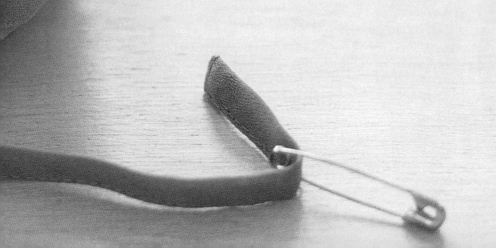

FORMING WAISTLINES

MANY TYPES OF WAISTLINES can be used on skirts, pants, and dresses. Straight waistbands are most commonly used on skirts and pants, and are suitable for all fabrics except bulky ones. For bulky fabrics, ribbon-faced waistbands are more appropriate. Faced waistlines are used mainly on skirts, and a facing can be applied to high and low waistlines. On heavy fabrics, the facing can be made from a lighter-weight fabric. Casings are quick and easy to sew, and are best suited to light- and mediumweight fabrics that gather well.

RELATED TECHNIQUES

Reducing seam bulk, p. 84
Seam finishes, p. 85
Stitching seams with
ease and bias, p. 89
Plain darts, p. 109
Making and fitting gathers, p. 120
Stitching a lapped zipper, p. 252
Inserting a centered zipper, p. 253

DIRECTORY OF WAISTLINES AND WAISTBANDS

Basic waistband
Usually 1–1½ in (2.5–4 cm) wide, the basic waistband (p. 168) is a popular style suited to a range of garment types and can be made by several methods.

Shaped waistband
This wide waistband style (p. 170) shapes outward at the side seams to accommodate both the wide part of the rib cage above the waistline, and the wide part of the hips below the waistline.

Fold-down casing
For this waistline style (p. 160), the casing is stitched to the wrong side of the garment to form a channel through which elastic or drawstring cord is threaded. A fold-down casing can also be made with a heading.

Partial casing
A waistline with a partial casing (p. 162) has a front band and an elasticized casing at the back. The casing is stitched partway around the garment waistline.

Faced waistline
The facing fabric is not visible on the right side of the garment on this simple type of waistline (p. 165). This faced style is frequently used for garments requiring a shaped waistline.

Ribbed waistband
Ready-made elasticized ribbing can be purchased to make this waistband (p. 164). It is attached to the garment waistline and forms a band. This style of waistband is suitable for both knitted and woven fabrics.

Mock casing without a seam
In this neat, narrow waistline finish (p. 163), a length of narrow elastic is stitched directly onto the wrong side of the garment fabric, using machine zigzag stitch.

Mock casing within a seam
For this type of waistline (p. 163), the waistline seam allowances are used to form two channels to hold narrow elastic.

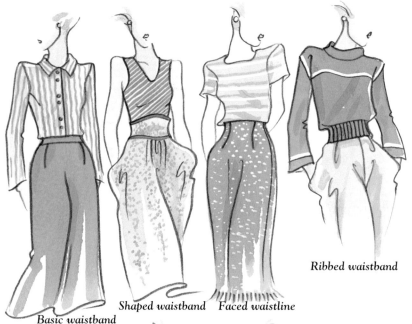

Basic waistband *Shaped waistband* *Faced waistline* *Ribbed waistband*

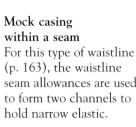

Fold-down casing *Partial casing* *Mock casing without a seam* *Mock casing within a seam*

ATTACHING A SKIRT TO A BODICE

THE TWO MOST COMMON TYPES of waistline seams join a fitted skirt to a bodice or a gathered skirt to a bodice. Although this will not be noticeable, a fitted skirt is made about 1 in (2.5 cm) larger than the bodice all around. This small amount of fullness is designed to give a comfortable fit, and is eased in to fit the bodice of the dress.

ATTACHING A FITTED SKIRT

Easestitching

Waist edge of skirt

1 EASESTITCH around the skirt waist edge. Stop and restart the stitching at the side seams, leaving long thread ends. Pin the skirt waist edge to the bodice, matching the seams (above).

2 HOLDING the thread end on the wrong side of the easestitching, ease the fabric along the thread (above), working from both ends toward the center to take in the fullness along the waist.

Skirt stitched to bodice with right sides facing

3 WITH THE SKIRT uppermost, stitch the waist edge of the skirt to the bodice. Zigzag stitch the seam allowances together to finish (left). Then trim away the raw edges that are just outside the line of the zigzag stitching.

ATTACHING A GATHERED SKIRT

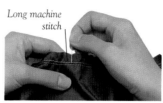
Long machine stitch

Long thread ends

1 STITCH two rows of gathering stitches (p. 120) along the waist edge of the skirt, stopping and restarting at the side seams, and leaving long thread ends. Pin the skirt to the bodice (above).

2 ON THE WRONG SIDE of the gathering, pull the two thread ends and ease the fabric along the threads (above). Arrange the gathers evenly and repin. Fasten the thread on a pin in a figure eight.

Avoid pressing in unwanted creases on gathers

3 WITH THE SKIRT side uppermost, stitch the waistline seam just outside the lower row of gathering stitches (above), removing the pins one by one as they are reached.

4 ZIGZAG STITCH the seam allowances together. (On fine fabrics, trim the seam allowances before zigzag stitching.) Press the seam allowances flat, then away from the gathers (above).

TAPING A WAISTLINE

A TAPE SEWN AROUND THE WAIST SEAMLINE prevents a soft fabric, such as jersey, from stretching, or a heavy fabric, such as velvet, from dropping. If the tape is being machine stitched in place, seam tape or narrow grosgrain ribbon should be used. If the tape is being handstitched at intervals, a firmer, stronger grosgrain ribbon is required.

BEFORE INSERTING A ZIPPER

Right sides together

1 STITCH THE SKIRT to the bodice. Baste the tape to the skirt side of the waistline seam, with the lower edge just above the seam. Stitch close to the lower edge (above).

2 TRIM the skirt and bodice seam allowances (above). Zigzag stitch the edges together. Press the seam toward the bodice. Insert the zipper.

AFTER INSERTING A ZIPPER

Machine stitching at end

1 CUT A PIECE of grosgrain 2¼ in (6 cm) longer than required. Press under ¼ in (5 mm) at each end, then 1 in (2.5 cm). Stitch. Sew hooks and eyes to the ends (above).

2 WITH the grosgrain positioned so that the ends fasten behind the zipper, handstitch the tape to the waistline seam at the side seams and darts (above).

MAKING CASINGS

T HE TUNNEL OF FABRIC that is threaded with a piece of elastic or with a drawstring cord forms a casing. A casing can be at the waist edge of a garment or around its middle. It should be ¼in (6 mm) wider than the elastic or drawstring, and a gap should be left at the ends so that the elastic can be threaded through. When a drawstring casing is made on the wrong side of a garment, the cord is brought to the right side through a gap in the seam or through buttonholes that are made at the ends of the casing before it is stitched on.

RELATED TECHNIQUES

Elastics, p. 66
Hand sewing stitches, p. 74
Working hemming stitches, p. 76
Making a faced hem, p. 214
Making automatic machine buttonholes, p. 240
Inserting a centered zipper, p. 253

MAKING A FOLD-DOWN CASING

A FOLD-DOWN CASING is a fabric allowance added to the waistline, then folded to form a fabric tunnel. This is an excellent waistband for pull-on garments.

Usually made on a straight edge, a casing can be used on a slightly curved edge if it is narrow enough. A casing with a heading has a folded ruffle that projects above the casing.

PLAIN FOLD-DOWN CASING

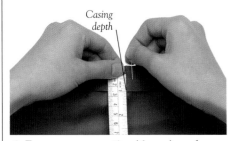
Casing depth

Wrong side
Gap for elastic

1 FOLD AND PRESS ¼in (6 mm) to the wrong side around the waist edge. Fold a turning equal to the casing depth to the wrong side. Pin (above).

2 STITCH around the lower edge of the casing, leaving a gap for the elastic to be inserted. Stitch around the top edge of the casing close to the fold (above).

FOLD-DOWN CASING WITH A HEADING

Heading at garment edge

FOLD DOWN THE WAIST EDGE (see Step 1, left), but add the heading depth. Stitch around the top and bottom of the casing. Thread the elastic (above).

ATTACHING A SEPARATE CASING

A SEPARATE CASING CAN BE STITCHED to the inside or the outside of a long garment so that the waistline can be drawn in. This casing is made with a fabric strip

that may be cut on the bias if the casing is to be curved. If the casing is stitched to a waist edge on pants or a skirt, it will serve as both a facing and a casing.

SEPARATE CASING ON A ONE-PIECE GARMENT

Stitch across both end turnings
Wrong side

1 CUT A STRIP to the elastic width, plus ¾in (2 cm). Press under ¼in (6 mm) on the short, then long edges. Stitch the short ends (above).

2 REFOLD THE LONG EDGES to the wrong side. Place the facing, right side up, on the right or wrong side of the garment. Pin in place (above).

3 STITCH the casing in place along the right side of each long edge close to the fold (above). Press, then finish (see Finishing a Full Casing, opposite).

SEPARATE CASING AT A WAIST EDGE

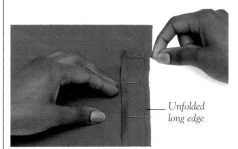

Unfolded long edge

1 CUT AND PRESS the strip (see Step 1, Separate Casing, opposite). Unfold one of the long edges, and pin this edge to the waist edge of the garment with right sides together (above).

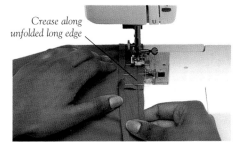

Crease along unfolded long edge

2 ENSURE THAT THE ENDS of the casing meet at a garment seam so that the garment and casing seams align. Stitch along the crease on the casing (above), and press the casing to the wrong side.

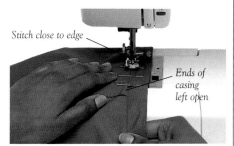

Stitch close to edge

Ends of casing left open

3 MACHINE STITCH around the lower edge of the casing (above), and stitch a second row just below the top edge of the casing. Both ends of the casing are left open for inserting the elastic.

FINISHING A FULL CASING

A FULL CASING IS STITCHED around a whole garment, so that the short ends of the casing join together neatly. The casing may be gathered using either a strip of elastic or a drawstring cord. If the casing is positioned on the wrong side of the garment, the drawstring passes to the right side through a gap in a seam, or through buttonholes.

INSERTING ELASTIC INTO A FOLD-DOWN CASING

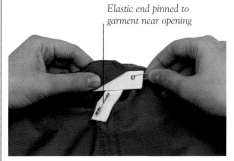

Elastic end pinned to garment near opening

1 PIN ONE END OF THE ELASTIC to the garment. Then fasten a safety pin to the other end of the elastic. Insert this end into the opening, and thread the elastic through the casing (above).

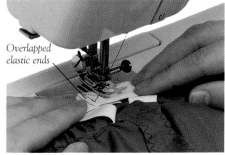

Overlapped elastic ends

2 PULL BOTH ENDS of the elastic out of the casing as far as possible. Overlap the ends by 1 in (2.5 cm). Pin. Machine stitch the ends together (above). (Or the ends can be whipstitched by hand.)

Opening

3 PULL THE CASING on either side of the opening so that the elastic slips inside. Push the gathers away from the opening, then pin it in place. Stitch the opening closed (above).

ELASTIC OPENING

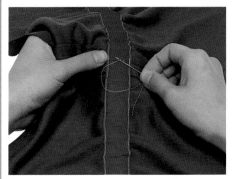

ON A SEPARATE CASING, insert the elastic, and stitch the ends of the elastic together (see Inserting Elastic into a Fold-Down Casing, above). Slipstitch the short ends of the casing together (above).

DRAWSTRING OPENING

LEAVE AN OPENING in the garment seam for the drawstring cord. Catchstitch the seam allowances flat (above). Then stitch on the casing between basted position lines, and insert the drawstring.

BUTTONHOLE OPENING

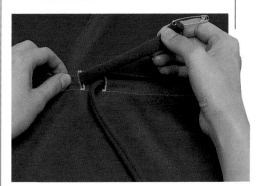

STITCH THE BUTTONHOLES in the middle of the casing position on the garment, leaving space for the drawstring cord. Stitch the casing to the garment, and thread the drawstring through (above).

MAKING A PARTIAL CASING

PARTIAL CASING WAISTBANDS are formed when the casing does not encircle the garment in one continuous strip but is required only part of the way around. A skirt or a pair of pants can have a plain waistband at the front and a casing at the back. Alternatively, the ends of the casing can be divided by an opening in the garment.

WAISTBAND WITH AN ELASTICATED BACK CASING

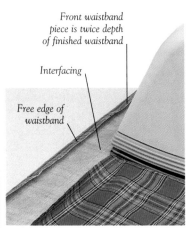

Front waistband piece is twice depth of finished waistband

Interfacing

Free edge of waistband

1 CUT a basic waistband (p. 168) long enough to fit across the garment front and seam allowances. Interface the waistband. With right sides together, stitch the waistband to the garment front. Press the seam allowance to the wrong side along the free edge of the waistband. Press the seam and waistband away from the garment (left).

End of casing

Back casing

2 ON THE BACK of the garment, make a plain fold-down casing (p. 160) to the same depth as the front waistband. Stitch the casing along its top and bottom edges. Thread through a length of elastic to fit the back waist. Align the ends of the elastic with the raw edges of the casing ends. Pin across the ends, and baste through the layers (left).

3 WITH right sides together and side edges even, pin together the garment back and front, aligning the bottom edge of the casing with the waistband seam and the top of the casing with the center foldline of the waistband. Stitch the side seams and the ends of the waistband. Press the side seams open, and clip the back seam allowance at the casing bottom (right).

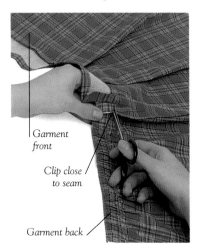

Garment front

Clip close to seam

Garment back

4 PRESS the casing side seam allowance toward the front waistband. Press the free edge of the front waistband over to the inside of the garment, so that it is level with the waistband stitching. Slipstitch the ends of the waistband to the casing. Slipstitch the inner waistband edge along the previous stitching line inside the waistband (right).

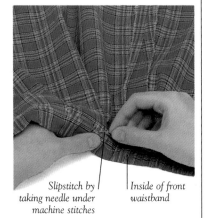

Slipstitch by taking needle under machine stitches

Inside of front waistband

WAIST CASING WITH A ZIPPER OPENING

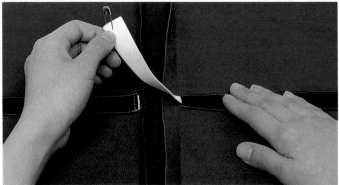

1 MAKE A SEPARATE CASING with the casing ends finishing at the zipper seamline (p. 160). Thread the waistband elastic through the casing. The beginning of the elastic should align with the end of the casing. Baste securely across the end, stitching through all the thicknesses. Gently pull the unattached elastic end, gathering up the casing to fit the waist (above). Trim the elastic. Baste this end in place in the same way as the other end.

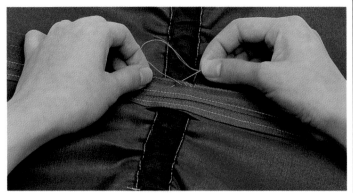

2 PRESS THE SEAM ALLOWANCES to the wrong side along the center zipper opening. Stitch in the zipper, using the centered zipper method (p. 253) so that the stitching catches in both the ends of the elastic and the casing. On the inside of the garment, whipstitch the edges of the zipper tape to the casing (above).

MAKING A MOCK CASING

MOCK CASINGS do not require a casing strip. Instead, they utilize waistline seam allowances, or the elastic is stitched directly to the garment around the waist. The seamed method has two rows of elastic, or – if both seam allowances are stitched to the same side – a single row. These casings are especially suitable for children's dresses.

MOCK CASING WITHIN A WAISTLINE SEAM

Stitch each seam allowance through both fabric layers

1 STITCH the side seams of the skirt and the bodice, leaving the back seam open. Stitch the skirt to the bodice. Zigzag stitch the raw edge of the waist seam. Press open the seam. Pin both seam allowances to the garment. Stitch the allowances ⅜in (1 cm) from the seam (left).

Elastic threaded through two channels

Center back edge

2 KNOT A LENGTH of narrow, round elastic onto a loop turner or a safety pin. Insert the loop turner or pin into the opening of one of the seam allowance channels at the center back of the garment, and thread the elastic through. Thread a length of elastic through the other channel in the same way (above).

3 PULL UP both lengths of elastic until they fit comfortably around the waistline. At one end of the mock casing, knot the ends of the elastic firmly together (right). Trim away any excess elastic. Knot the two lengths of elastic together in the same way at the other end of the mock casing.

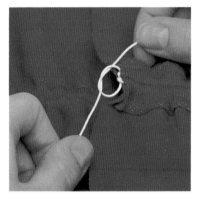

4 FINISH STITCHING the open garment center back seam, catching the ends of the knotted elastic into the seam. (Alternatively, if the garment is designed with a zipper opening, insert the zipper, using the appropriate method [p. 250–251], so that the ends of the elastic are caught into the zipper stitching.)

MOCK CASING ON A GARMENT WITHOUT A WAISTLINE SEAM

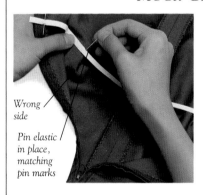

Wrong side

Pin elastic in place, matching pin marks

1 CUT THE ELASTIC to waist length, plus ¾in (2 cm). Pin mark the elastic (and waistline on the completed garment) into eight sections. With ⅜in (1 cm) of the elastic extending past the zipper opening, pin the elastic to the wrong side of the garment (left).

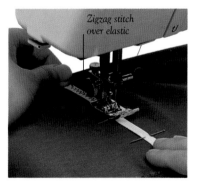

Zigzag stitch over elastic

2 STARTING at the edge of the zipper tape, reverse stitch to secure the elastic. Keep the elastic stretched, and zigzag stitch to the first pin (left). Then remove the pin. Continue, stretching the elastic before stitching. Reverse stitch to finish at the edge of the zipper tape.

3 TURN UNDER the ends of the elastic so that the folds are on the zipper tape. Make sure that the elastic is not so close to the zipper teeth that it might obstruct the slide. Then pin both the turned-under ends of the elastic in place, and overcast them securely to the zipper tape (right).

Overcast securely

4 TURN THE GARMENT right side out. On the finished garment, the zigzag stitches will have gathered the fabric at the waistline, making the waistline the same length as the unstretched elastic. When the garment is worn, the row of zigzag stitches will be partially hidden by the gathered fabric.

ATTACHING A RIBBED WAISTBAND

THIS TYPE OF WAISTBAND is used most commonly at the lower edge of sportswear tops. It may also be used on the waist of a skirt or casual pants. The elasticized ribbing is bought ready made. It usually has one ruffled edge, and this is the edge that is machine stitched along the appropriate edge of the garment.

Garment

Pins mark equal sections of garment

Ribbed waistband

Ribbing cut to fit comfortably when slightly stretched

1 DIVIDE THE GARMENT EDGE into four or eight equal sections, marking the divisions with pins. Divide the ruffled edge of the elasticized ribbing into the same number of sections, but making them smaller, and again mark the edge with pins.

Right side of garment

Stretched ribbing

3 WITH the garment positioned on the sewing machine so that the ribbing side is uppermost, stitch the ribbing to the garment along the ruffled edge of the ribbing (left). While stitching, stretch out the ribbing between the pins to ease in the fabric fullness. Hold the ribbing taut until each section between two pins is complete.

Ensure ribbing is not stretched out of shape when pressing

5 PRESS THE GARMENT seam allowances lightly, away from the length of ribbing and toward the garment (above). Avoid using too much pressure when pressing the seam allowances in place, or the ribbing may stretch and lose its shape.

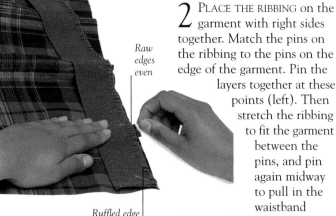

2 PLACE THE RIBBING on the garment with right sides together. Match the pins on the ribbing to the pins on the edge of the garment. Pin the layers together at these points (left). Then stretch the ribbing to fit the garment between the pins, and pin again midway to pull in the waistband fullness. Continue repinning until all of the fullness is controlled by the pins.

Raw edges even

Ruffled edge of waistband aligned with raw edge of garment

Wrong side of ribbing

Zigzag stitching

4 IF THE FABRIC IS FRAYABLE, zigzag stitch the edges of the ribbing and the fabric together, gently stretching the ribbing to fit. If the stitching has distorted the ribbing, hold a steam iron over the seam (above). The steam will relax the seam.

RESHAPING RIBBING

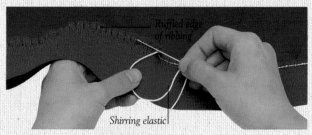

Ruffled edge of ribbing

Shirring elastic

If a seam has stretched the edge of the elasticized ribbing, thread a length of shirring elastic through the zigzag stitches on the inside of the garment (above). Pull the ends of the elastic to ease in the ribbing edge so that it is gradually reduced to the original size, then secure the shirring elastic ends.

FACING A WAISTLINE

WAIST FACINGS ARE NOT VISIBLE from the right side. On a thick fabric, a taped ribbon facing may be used to replace a waistband and reduce bulk. Otherwise, faced waistlines are used on garments simply as design features. An integrated facing is cut in one piece with the skirt or pants, and a shaped facing is cut separately.

GROSGRAIN RIBBON FACING

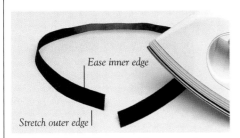

Ease inner edge

Stretch outer edge

1 CUT 1-in (2.5-cm) wide grosgrain ribbon (p. 65) to the length of the garment waistline, plus 1½ in (4 cm). Steam the grosgrain ribbon, stretching one edge and easing in the other until the ribbon takes on a slightly curved shape (above). Allow to cool.

Right side

2 STAYSTITCH the waist seamline. Place the grosgrain ribbon over the right side of the garment seam allowance so that the inner edge covers the staystitching and each end extends ¾ in (2 cm) past the zipper opening. Baste (above), and stitch the inner edge of the ribbon to the garment.

End handstitched to zipper tape

3 FOLD THE GROSGRAIN RIBBON over to the wrong side and press. Tuck the ends of the ribbon in order to avoid catching them in the zipper, and handstitch to the zipper tape. Handstitch the loose edge of ribbon to the darts and the seam allowances inside the garment (above).

INTEGRATED WAIST FACING

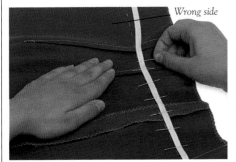

Wrong side

1 STITCH ALL SEAMS and any darts that extend into the facing. Zigzag stitch the integrated facing edge. Pin a section of twill tape to the facing (above) with the lower edge aligned with the waistline. Stitch the tape on the edge near the waistline.

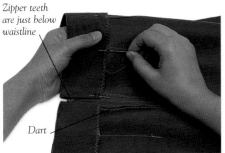

Zipper teeth are just below waistline

Dart

2 INSERT THE ZIPPER. Fold the integrated facing and twill tape to the wrong side. Press. Tuck under the facing ends and pin to the zipper tape. Handstitch the facing edge to the darts, the seams, and the zipper tape on the inside (above).

SHAPED WAIST FACING

Zigzag stitch outer edge

Front and back pieces joined to make one piece

1 APPLY THE INTERFACING to the wrong side of the front and back facing pieces. Machine stitch the facing pieces together down the side seams. Press the seams open and zigzag stitch around the outer edge of the facing to seam finish (above).

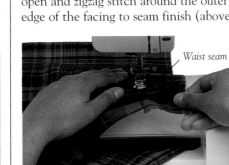

Waist seam

3 TRIM THE FACING SEAM. Press the facing and the seam allowances away from the garment. Working on the right side, understitch the facing seam, stitching through both the facing and the seam allowances close to the seam (above).

Facing should project ⅝ in (1.5 cm) at zipper edges

2 PLACE THE FACING around the waist edge of the garment, with right sides together and raw edges even. Pin the facing in place (above). Then stitch the facing to the garment, removing the pins as they are reached.

Tuck ends under where they overlap zipper

4 PRESS THE FACING to the wrong side (above). Tuck the ends of the facing under, away from the zipper, and handstitch them to the zipper tape. Then handstitch the loose edge of the facing to the inside darts and seam allowances of the garment.

MAKING AND APPLYING WAISTBANDS

WAISTBANDS GIVE NEAT, STABLE FINISHES to garments. They usually define the waistline, and can be designed in a number of ways to suit different garments. Narrow, straight waistbands are the most common and are generally about 1–1½in (2.5–4 cm) wide. Other styles include shaped waistbands, which are wider than straight waistbands and may have a decoratively shaped upper or lower edge. Stretch waistbands are elastic and are used on woven fabrics or knits, such as jersey. Ribbon-faced waistbands can reduce bulk.

RELATED TECHNIQUES

Reducing seam bulk, p. 84
Making topstitched seams, p. 87
Attaching heavyweight
sew-in interfacing, p. 99
Making a free-hanging
lining, p. 102
Stitching a lapped zipper, p. 252
Inserting a centered zipper, p. 253

PREPARING TO MAKE A WAISTBAND

MOST DRESSMAKING PATTERNS include a waistband piece that fits the garment. If you want to alter the waistband to fit your body, the waistline must be altered by the same amount. For a good fit, the position of the waistband must be checked on the garment, and the garment tried on before being finished.

POSITIONING A WAISTBAND

Pins mark waistline

1 PUT ON the finished garment, with the zipper already inserted. Tie a narrow cord around the waist. Make sure that the cord is sitting smoothly around the waistline, and that the garment fits well. Pin, or mark a chalk line on the garment, just beneath the cord line (left).

Position tape above cord

2 MEASURE the waist size by positioning one edge of a tape measure exactly along the edge of the cord (left). Do not pull the tape tight. Remove the garment. If required, pin or mark a new cutting line ⅝in (1.5 cm) above the pinned or chalked waistline.

DETERMINING STRAIGHT WAISTBAND DIMENSIONS

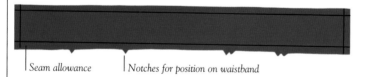

Seam allowance   *Notches for position on waistband*

TAKE THE WAIST MEASUREMENT (see Step 2, above). For the waistband length, add 1 in (2.5 cm) for ease, plus 1¼in (3 cm) for seam allowances, and at least 1¼in (3 cm) for an overlap or underlap (see below). For the waistband width, double the required finished width and add 1¼in (3 cm) for seam allowances.

SELECTING A WAISTBAND FINISH

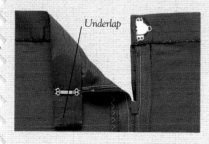

Underlap

Projecting underlap
An underlap finishing on a waistband allows room for attaching the fastening. If the underlap projects, the overlap is finished flush with the zipper edge.

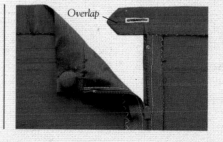

Overlap

Projecting overlap
This type of overlap can be straight across its end or shaped to a point that is suitable for a button fastening. The underlap is finished flush with the zipper edge.

REINFORCING A WAISTBAND

A WAISTBAND MAY REQUIRE STIFFENING in order to prevent stretching and to give a strong, neat finish that will not buckle. A mediumweight or a heavyweight interfacing can be used. A special fusible waistband stiffening is available; it produces a set-width waistband and has slots marking the stitching lines and the foldline.

USING MEDIUMWEIGHT INTERFACING

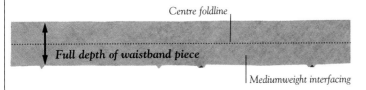

Centre foldline

Full depth of waistband piece

Mediumweight interfacing

MEASURE, CUT OUT, AND APPLY a mediumweight interfacing to the whole waistband piece, including the seam allowances (left). This will provide the waistband with extra stiffness. Topstitching may be worked around the finished waistband to give a permanently crisp edge along the foldline.

USING MEDIUM- TO HEAVYWEIGHT INTERFACING

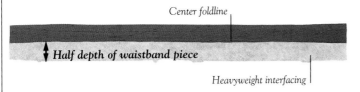

Center foldline

Half depth of waistband piece

Heavyweight interfacing

A HEAVYWEIGHT INTERFACING may be too bulky to stitch into the seam, so apply medium- to heavyweight interfacing to half of the waistband piece, up to the center foldline and including seam allowances. When using a heavyweight interfacing, trim the interfacing from the seam allowances before applying.

PINNING A WAISTBAND IN PLACE TO A WAIST EDGE

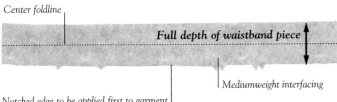

Center foldline

Full depth of waistband piece

Mediumweight interfacing

Notched edge to be applied first to garment

1 CUT OUT THE WAISTBAND PIECE to the required size (see Determining Straight Waistband Dimensions, opposite). If a pattern is being used, the notches and any other pattern markings are along the edge that will be stitched to the garment first (above). Apply the interfacing or stiffening to the wrong side of the waistband piece. With right sides together and raw edges even, place the waistband piece on the waist edge.

Matched notches

2 MATCH the waistband notches to the garment waist edge, and pin the waistband piece to the waist edge (left). Each end of the waistband piece will extend past the zipper edges to allow for the seam allowances at each end and the projecting underlap or the overlap at one end.

USING TRIPLE-SLOT FUSIBLE WAISTBANDING

1 TRIPLE-SLOT FUSIBLE WAISTBANDING forms a set-width waistband. The two outer rows of slots are stitching lines. Trim the short ends of the stiffening ⅝in (1.5 cm) in from the short ends of the waistband. If the waistband has ⅝in (1.5 cm) seam allowances, the fabric will project ¼in (5 mm) along the long edges. Place the stiffening centrally on the wrong side of the waistband, and iron on (below).

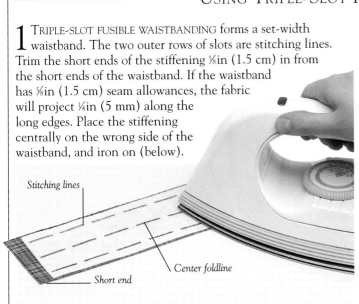

Stitching lines

Center foldline

Short end

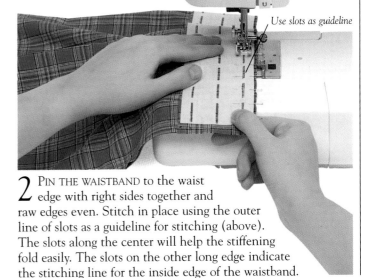

Use slots as guideline

2 PIN THE WAISTBAND to the waist edge with right sides together and raw edges even. Stitch in place using the outer line of slots as a guideline for stitching (above). The slots along the center will help the stiffening fold easily. The slots on the other long edge indicate the stitching line for the inside edge of the waistband.

167

MAKING A BASIC WAISTBAND

IN THIS STANDARD METHOD, the waistband is stitched partly by machine and partly by hand. One long edge of the waistband is stitched to the right side of the garment by machine. The other long edge is pressed under, then the waistband is folded in half, and this edge is handstitched to the wrong side of the garment.

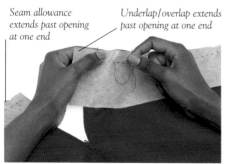

Seam allowance extends past opening at one end
Underlap/overlap extends past opening at one end

1 APPLY THE INTERFACING to the wrong side of the waistband. With right sides together and pattern markings matching, pin the waistband to the waist edge of the garment. Baste in p.lace (above). Stitch, then remove the basting.

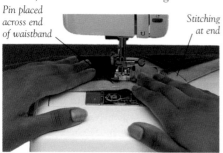

Pin placed across end of waistband
Stitching at end

3 FOLD THE ENDS of the waistband in half with right sides together. Pin across the ends of the waistband, and machine stitch (above). Trim the seam allowances. Trim the top corners of the seam allowances diagonally.

Seam allowance
Underlap/overlap

2 TRIM THE SEAM ALLOWANCES, and layer them if necessary (p. 84). Press the waistband and seam allowances away from the garment. Press the seam allowance to the wrong side on the other long edge of the waistband (above). Trim.

Wrong side
Pressed edge

4 TURN THE WAISTBAND right side out. Align the pressed edge with the inside stitching, pin, and press. Slipstitch the lower edges of the underlap/overlap together. Slipstitch the pressed edge to the machine stitching (above).

MAKING A TOPSTITCHED WAISTBAND

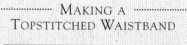
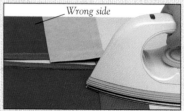

Wrong side

1 Pin the right side of the interfaced waistband to the wrong side of the waist edge, allowing the ends to extend past the opening. Stitch, then press (above), as in Step 2, left.

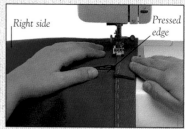

Right side
Pressed edge

2 Fold and stitch the ends, as in Step 3, left. Turn the band right side out, and pin the pressed edge, just covering the stitching. Baste, and topstitch close to this edge (above).

MAKING A TWO-PIECE WAISTBAND

THIS METHOD IS FOLLOWED when the top edge of a waistband is shaped, or when the ends of belt carriers are enclosed in the seam (p. 176–177). A two-piece waistband is made from two strips of fabric that are joined with a seam at the top edge of the waistband. Interfacing is applied to the outer waistband section.

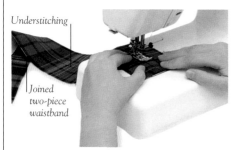

Understitching
Joined two-piece waistband

1 PIN THE WAISTBAND PIECES together along the top of the waistband, with right sides facing. Stitch, and trim. Press the facing and the seam allowances away from the outer piece. Understitch (above).

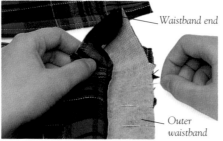

Waistband end
Outer waistband

2 FOLD THE ENDS of the waistband in half, with right sides together, and pin. Stitch, ending ⅝in (1.5 cm) from the lower edge. Trim. Pin (above) and stitch the outer piece to the waist edge.

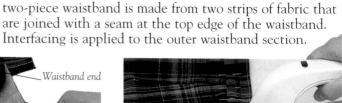

3 TRIM THE SEAM allowance. Press the waistband away from the garment. Tuck the raw edge under, align it with the stitching, pin, and press (above). Finally, slipstitch as shown in Step 4, above.

MAKING A MACHINE-FINISHED WAISTBAND

FOR THIS QUICK TECHNIQUE, all the stitching on the waistband is done by machine. The outer edge of the waistband is stitched to the right side as for the Basic Waistband, opposite. The inner long edge is pressed flat over the seam on the inside. It is then stitched-in-the-ditch from the right side along the waistband seam.

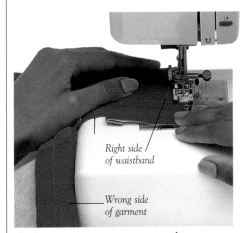

Right side of waistband

Wrong side of garment

1 APPLY THE INTERFACING to the wrong side of the waistband. Pin and stitch the waistband to the waist edge with right sides together. Press the waistband away from the garment. Trim ¼in (6 mm) from the remaining long edge, and zigzag stitch along the trimmed edge (above).

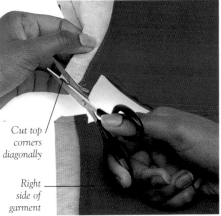

Cut top corners diagonally

Right side of garment

2 AT EACH END of the zigzagged edge, press ⅜in (1 cm) to the wrong side of the waistband. Fold both ends in half with right sides together, and stitch as for the Basic Waistband, Step 3, opposite. Trim the ends and the top corners (above). Then turn the waistband right side out.

3 PRESS THE BAND so that the zigzagged edge overlaps the seamline inside. On the right side, align and pin the lower edges of the underlap. Pin both layers of the waistband along the seamline. Stitch across the underlap edges, and stitch-in-the-ditch around the waistband (above).

MAKING A RIBBON-FACED WAISTBAND

REPLACING THE INSIDE HALF OF A WAISTBAND with grosgrain ribbon (p. 65) reduces bulk on thick fabrics. Some grosgrain ribbons have woven, rubberized strips that prevent blouses from coming untucked. If an ordinary waistband pattern is being adapted, the waistband is folded, and the facing section is trimmed to ⅝in (1.5 cm).

Foldline and ribbon edge

1 APPLY interfacing to the wrong side of the waistband. With right sides uppermost, pin the grosgrain ribbon over the trimmed edge of the waistband, aligning it with the waistband foldline. Stitch close to the ribbon edge (left).

Right side of garment

Grosgrain ribbon

Waistband interfacing

2 WITH right sides together and the pattern markings matching, pin and stitch the waistband to the garment as for the Basic Waistband, Step 1, opposite. Trim the seam (left), and layer this if required, making the interfacing the narrowest.

3 PRESS the waistband away from the garment. Press the seam allowance along the lower edge of the underlap/overlap, on the wrong side. Then fold the waistband in half at both ends, with right sides together. Pin and stitch across the ends (left). Trim.

Stitch across end of waistband

Wrong side

4 TURN the waistband right side out. Press the waistband so that the ribbon seam rolls to the inside. Pin the lower edge of the ribbon, and slipstitch it first to the lower edge of the underlap/overlap, then to the stitching on the inside of the waistband (left).

ATTACHING A SHAPED WAISTBAND

A SHAPED WAISTBAND IS CURVED to accommodate the body shape. It is usually wider than a straight waistband and the top edge is often decoratively shaped.

Depending on the width and shape of the waistband, two layers of stiff interfacing are sometimes required so that the band will not lose its shape and become limp and creased.

Joined, interfaced outer waistband pieces

Joined waistband facing pieces

1 APPLY interfacing to the wrong side of one set of waistband pieces and stitch the side seams. Trim the seams and press open. Stitch the non-interfaced waistband sections in the same way.

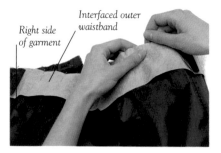

Interfaced outer waistband

Right side of garment

2 WITH right sides together, pin the lower edge of the interfaced outer waistband to the waist edge (left). Baste if required. Stitch. Press the waistband away from the garment.

3 PRESS the seam allowance on the lower edge of the waistband facing to the wrong side. With right sides together, pin the facing to the outer waistband along the ends and the top edge. Stitch, then trim and clip (right).

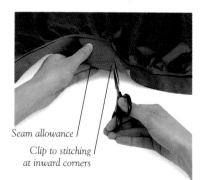

Seam allowance

Clip to stitching at inward corners

4 TURN the waistband right side out, and press, rolling the seam at the top of the waistband slightly over to the inside. Align the pressed edge of the waistband facing with the stitching on the inside, pin, and slipstitch the facing in place (right).

Wrong side

Facing

MAKING AN ELASTIC WAISTBAND

THERE ARE TWO METHODS for sewing elastic to a separate waistband, and both are suitable for knit fabrics and for garments with or without waist darts.

The two self-faced elastic waistbands can be used on knit or woven fabrics. The pants or skirt should be sewn but not hemmed before the elastic waistband is attached.

ADDING ELASTIC TO A SEPARATE WAISTBAND

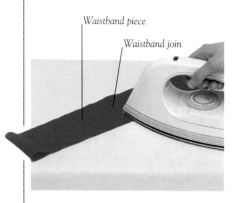

Waistband piece

Waistband join

1 CUT the waistband piece on the straight grain of the fabric. With right sides together, join the waistband ends. Press the seam open (left). Cut a length of elastic to fit the waist, plus 1 in (2.5 cm). Overlap the elastic ends and stitch.

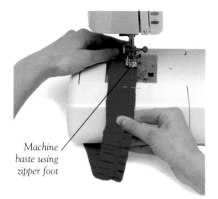

Machine baste using zipper foot

2 DIVIDE the garment edges and waistband into quarters and mark with pins. Fold the waistband in half lengthwise, wrong sides together, around the elastic loop. Machine baste just outside the seamline (left), moving the gathers out of the way while stitching.

3 WITH raw edges even and quarters matching, pin the waistband to the right side of the garment. Stitch just inside the machine basting (right), stretching the waistband between the pins. Trim and seam finish the seam allowances.

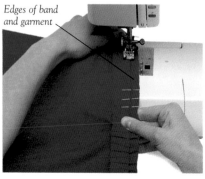

Edges of band and garment

4 DISTRIBUTE the gathers evenly around the waistband. Stitch-in-the-ditch down the side seams and center back of the waistband (right) to hold the elastic and to stop it from rolling. Topstitch if required (see opposite).

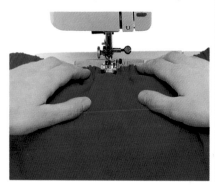

ADDING ELASTIC AND A WAISTBAND TO A GARMENT

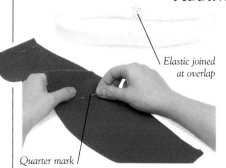

Elastic joined at overlap

Quarter mark

1 CUT the waistband piece on the cross grain and join the ends. Cut a piece of elastic to fit the waist, plus 1 in (2.5 cm). Overlap and stitch the ends. Divide the elastic, waistband, and the garment waist edge into quarters and mark with pins (left).

Waistband

2 PIN the waistband to the garment with right sides together and pins matching. Stitch. Press. Place the elastic over the waistband seam allowance close to the stitching, match the quarters, and pin. Zigzag stitch, stretching the elastic to fit (left).

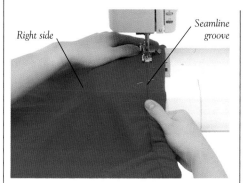

Right side *Seamline groove*

3 FOLD THE WAISTBAND over the zigzag-stitched elastic to the wrong side of the garment. Then pin in place, pinning on the right side. Stitch along the seamline groove, working from the right side (above), stretching the elastic flat inside the waistband.

FINISHING AN ELASTIC WAISTBAND

Wrong side

Adding rows of topstitching
This gives a stylish finish and stops the elastic from rolling. Using straight stitch and holding the elastic flat, stitch evenly spaced rows around the casing (above).

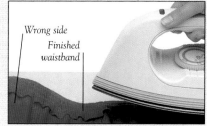

Wrong side
Finished waistband

Steaming stretched elastic
If stitching has stretched the elastic, steam the waistband by holding a steam iron over the fabric (above). This quickly restores the elasticity to the elastic.

MAKING A SELF-FACED ELASTIC WAISTBAND

Raw edge *Pin elastic to wrong side of self facing, below turn-under allowance*

1 CUT AND JOIN THE ELASTIC (see Step 1, above). Mark the elastic and garment in quarters with pins. Matching the pin marking, pin the elastic in place (above).

Lower edge of elastic

2 ZIGZAG STITCH the lower edge of the elastic to the waistband self facing, stretching it between the pins (above). Turn the elastic over to the inside.

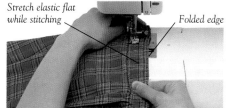

Stretch elastic flat while stitching *Folded edge*

3 ON NONFRAY FABRICS, the raw edge may be left. Otherwise, turn it under and pin. Stitch the elastic and waistband in place using a straight stitch (above).

MAKING A SELF-FACED ELASTIC WAISTBAND WITH A CASING

Wrong side

1 ZIGZAG STITCH around the raw edge of the waistline self facing. Fold the zigzagged edge to the inside, folding to the elastic width, plus ⅝ in (1.5 cm). Pin. Edgestitch close to the fold (above).

2 JOIN THE ENDS of the elastic and tuck it between the garment and the folded casing. Stitch the casing just below the edge of the elastic (above) using straight stitch and a zipper foot.

Vertical seamline

3 DISTRIBUTE the gathered fabric around the elastic waistband. At each vertical seamline, stitch-in-the-ditch down the seam (above) to hold the elastic in place and to stop it from rolling.

BELTS AND CARRIERS

A WELL-MADE BELT adds a professional finish to a garment. All belts require some form of stiffening. Tie belts are the simplest and softest type of belt, and ordinary interfacing is used to give them body. Shaped belts require greater stiffness, and this is supplied by either firm, heavyweight interfacing or buckram. Straight belts look their best if special belt stiffening is used. The fabric should fit tautly across the stiffening to give a firm finish. Most belts are held in place by carriers at the side seams of the garment.

RELATED TECHNIQUES

Reducing seam bulk, p. 84
Making topstitched seams, p. 87
Attaching light- and mediumweight
sew-in interfacing, p. 99
Applying fusible interfacing, p. 99
Making narrow tubing, p. 248
Making decorative bows, p. 303

DIRECTORY OF BELTS AND CARRIERS

BELTS

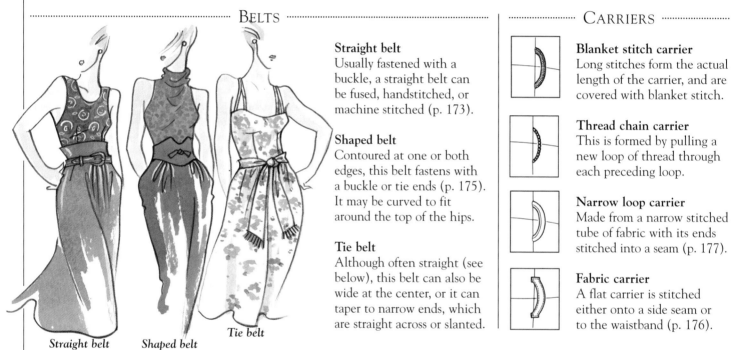

Straight belt   *Shaped belt*   *Tie belt*

Straight belt
Usually fastened with a buckle, a straight belt can be fused, handstitched, or machine stitched (p. 173).

Shaped belt
Contoured at one or both edges, this belt fastens with a buckle or tie ends (p. 175). It may be curved to fit around the top of the hips.

Tie belt
Although often straight (see below), this belt can also be wide at the center, or it can taper to narrow ends, which are straight across or slanted.

CARRIERS

Blanket stitch carrier
Long stitches form the actual length of the carrier, and are covered with blanket stitch.

Thread chain carrier
This is formed by pulling a new loop of thread through each preceding loop.

Narrow loop carrier
Made from a narrow stitched tube of fabric with its ends stitched into a seam (p. 177).

Fabric carrier
A flat carrier is stitched either onto a side seam or to the waistband (p. 176).

MAKING A TIE BELT

LIGHTWEIGHT INTERFACING IS USED on a tie belt to give body, rather than to stiffen the belt. It is usually applied to half the belt, up to the foldline, although the whole belt may be interfaced if a stiffer finish is required. Alternatively, two layers of interfacing may be used on the waistline only, leaving the tie ends with a single layer.

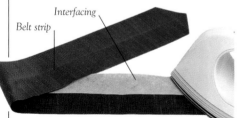

Belt strip   Interfacing

1 CUT THE FABRIC to twice the required finished width plus 1¼ in (3 cm), by the required finished length plus 1¼ in (3 cm). Apply interfacing lengthwise to half the belt strip, and press flat (above).

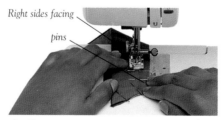

Right sides facing   pins

2 FOLD THE STRIP IN HALF. Pin, and stitch around the long and short ends ⅝ in (1.5 cm) in from the edges (above). Leave a 2¼-in (6-cm) opening in the center of the long edge for turning.

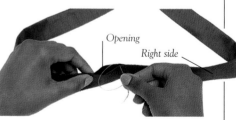

Opening   Right side

3 TRIM THE SEAM and corners. Press the seam open, and turn the strip right side out through the opening. Press flat, and tuck in the seam allowance at the opening. Handstitch the opening closed (above).

MAKING A MACHINE-STITCHED STRAIGHT BELT

IN THIS METHOD for making a straight belt, belt stiffening is inserted into a strip of fabric that has been sewn into a tube. The fabric strip is cut to the length of the stiffening plus ¾ in (2 cm), by twice the width of the stiffening plus an extra 1¼ in (3 cm).

Stiffening
Trimmed point
Seam pressed open

1 FOLD THE FABRIC STRIP IN HALF, with right sides together. Stitch the long edges together ⅝ in (1.5 cm) from the edge, and trim the seam allowances. Press the seam open, placing it centrally along the strip (above). Then trim the end of the stiffening into a point.

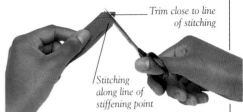

Trim close to line of stitching
Stitching along line of stiffening point

2 PLACE THE STIFFENING on the strip, with the point ⅜ in (1 cm) from the fabric edge. Mark a stitching line around the point of the stiffening. Stitch the fabric along the line. Trim (above).

DETERMINING STIFFENING LENGTH FOR A STRAIGHT BELT

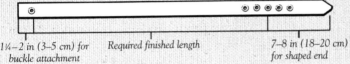

1¼–2 in (3–5 cm) for buckle attachment   Required finished length   7–8 in (18–20 cm) for shaped end

Measure the length that the belt should be when fastened. Add 1¼–2 in (3–5 cm) for the buckle and 7–8 in (18–20 cm) for the shaped end. Cut the stiffening to this length. Set the center eyelet with two on either side and a 1-in (2.5-cm) space between each.

Right side   *Stiffening point*

3 TURN RIGHT SIDE OUT. Press, with the seam centrally along the tube. Slide the stiffening into the tube (above), and press. The fabric extends ⅜ in (1 cm) beyond the stiffening at the buckle end. Attach eyelets (p. 175) and the buckle.

MAKING A HANDSTITCHED STRAIGHT BELT

A FABRIC SELVAGE IS USED for one edge of a belt strip to give the belt a neat, flat finish. The fabric is cut to twice the width of the stiffening plus ⅜ in (1 cm), by the length plus ¾ in (2 cm). Paper clips are used to hold the stiffening and the belt strip in place, instead of pins, which are difficult to insert through the bulky stiffening.

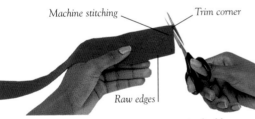

Machine stitching   *Trim corner*
Raw edges

1 FOLD ONE END OF THE BELT STRIP in half lengthwise with right sides together. Stitch across the end ⅜ in (1 cm) in from the edge. Then trim across the corner (above), and press the seam open. Turn the belt strip right side out, and press the seam flat centrally to form a point.

Raw edge of pointed end
Stiffening

2 PLACE THE STIFFENING strip centrally under the shaped fabric point. Mark the stiffening around the fabric point (above), and cut it to match this shape so that it fits inside the fabric point.

Seamline at shaped point
Stiffening

3 POSITION THE STIFFENING along the center of the fabric belt strip, making sure that it is placed centrally under the seamline on the wrong side of the shaped point (above). Push it firmly into position to fit inside the point.

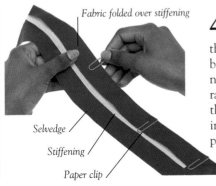

Fabric folded over stiffening
Selvedge
Stiffening
Paper clip

4 TRIM the stiffening to ⅜ in (1 cm) shorter than the length of the fabric at the buckle end of the belt, if necessary. Then fold the long, raw edge of the fabric over the stiffening, securing it in place with paper clips positioned at regular intervals along the entire length of the belt strip (left).

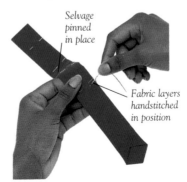

Selvage pinned in place
Fabric layers handstitched in position

5 FOLD the selvage of the fabric over the stiffening so that it covers the raw edge of the fabric belt strip. Pin the layers in place to ensure that they cover the stiffening tautly. Remove the paper clips. Handstitch the edges in place (left).

MAKING A BELT WITH A SEPARATE BACKING

A BELT with a separate backing is particularly suitable for thick fabrics where a lightweight lining or fine cotton fabric can be used for the backing to reduce bulk. The backing can be topstitched or handstitched to the stiffened belt front. Once the stitching is complete, the buckle is attached (p. 177) and eyelets inserted.

Pin holds belt and backing fabric strips together

1 CUT BELT STIFFENING to the required finished belt size and shape, including the overlap. Using the stiffening as a guide, cut the belt fabric and the backing to the correct size and shape, including a ⅜-in (1-cm) seam allowance (above).

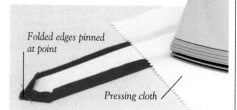

Folded edges pinned at point

Pressing cloth

2 PLACE THE STIFFENING centrally on the wrong side of the belt fabric, and fuse it in place. Fold the fabric edges over the stiffening along both the long edges and the shaped ends, and press into position (above). Baste if required.

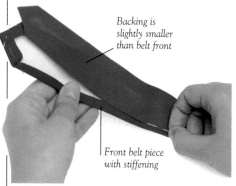

Backing is slightly smaller than belt front

Front belt piece with stiffening

3 PRESS THE RAW EDGES of the backing strip to the wrong side, making the strip slightly smaller than the belt front. With wrong sides together, pin the backing strip to the belt front (above).

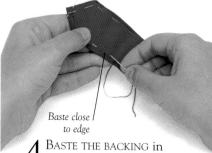

Baste close to edge

4 BASTE THE BACKING in place along the long edges and the shaped end, stitching close to the edge and through the backing and the belt fabric seam allowance only (above).

5 TOPSTITCH ¼ in (6 mm) in from the edge (right). (Or handstitch the backing to the belt fabric.) Remove the basting.

Topstitching

MAKING A FUSED BELT

THIS METHOD FOR MAKING A FUSED BELT eliminates the need for handstitching. The fusible stiffening is fused to the belt fabric, and a separate backing is also fused in place. The stiffening should be cut to the size and shape of the required finished belt. The belt fabric should be twice as wide as the stiffening and ¾ in (2 cm) longer.

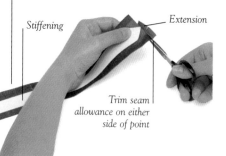

Stiffening

Extension

Trim seam allowance on either side of point

1 PLACE the belt stiffening centrally on the wrong side of the belt fabric. Fuse it in place. Trim the excess belt fabric at the shaped end, leaving a ⅜-in (1-cm) square extension at the point (left).

Fusible web

2 CUT a small piece of fusible web to fit the point, and place it over the stiffening. Fold the belt fabric over the point (left). Trim any webbing that is not covered by the belt fabric. Press to fuse the layers.

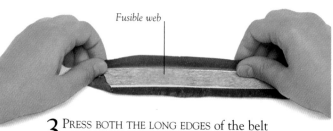

Fusible web

3 PRESS BOTH THE LONG EDGES of the belt fabric to the wrong side on top of the stiffening. Unfold the fabric edges, and place a strip of fusible web along the length of the stiffening. Refold the fabric edges over the fusible web (above), and fuse them in place.

Fusible mending tape

Pressing cloth

4 CUT A STRIP of iron-on mending tape to make a belt backing that is a little smaller than the prepared belt front. Fuse the backing in place using a hot iron and damp cloth (left). If required, topstitch along the edges of the belt on the right side.

MAKING A SHAPED BELT

BELTS THAT ARE SHAPED along the long edges cannot be stiffened with ready-made straight belt stiffening. Instead, two layers of firm interfacing are used to build up the required stiffness. Alternatively, one layer of firm cornice stiffening can be used.

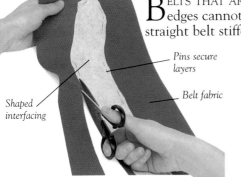

Shaped interfacing

Pins secure layers

Belt fabric

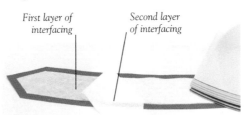

First layer of interfacing

Second layer of interfacing

Seam allowance may be clipped to lie flat

1 CUT TWO PIECES of fusible interfacing to the finished belt shape. Cut the belt fabric (above) and the backing fabric to the same shape, each with a ⅜-in (1-cm) seam allowance.

2 MAKE SURE THAT THE INTERFACING is centered on the wrong side of the belt fabric piece, and fuse it in place. Position the second layer of interfacing on top of the first layer, and fuse it in place (above).

3 FOLD THE EDGES of the belt fabric over the interfacing along the long edges and the shaped end. Clip the fabric where required. Pin, and baste in place (above).

4 PRESS THE BACKING seam allowance to the wrong side along the long edges and the shaped end (below), making it slightly smaller than the belt front so that it will not show around the edge of the finished belt.

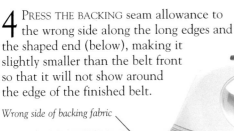

Wrong side of backing fabric

Seam allowance may be clipped on curves if necessary

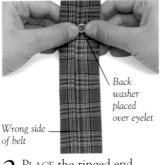

Backing fabric

Basting stitches

5 PIN AND BASTE THE BACKING FABRIC to the wrong side of the belt front. Handstitch the backing to the belt front along the long edges and the shaped end (above). (Alternatively, topstitch [see Step 5, opposite].) After stitching on the backing, remove all the basting stitches.

INSERTING EYELETS ON A BELT

A BUCKLE WITH A PRONG will require an eyelet about ¾–1¼ in (2–3 cm) from the straight end, so that the buckle can be stitched on. At the belt's shaped end, one eyelet is placed at the required fit position, then two more are added on each side. Eyelets can be made with a metal eyelet kit, or by hand using buttonhole stitches.

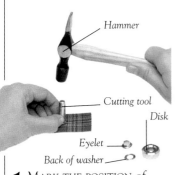

Hammer

Cutting tool

Disk

Eyelet

Back of washer

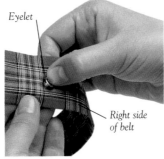

Eyelet

Right side of belt

Back washer placed over eyelet

Wrong side of belt

1 MARK THE POSITION of the eyelet by making a small cross on the right side of the belt. Place the belt face up onto the groove in the disk. Place the end of the cutting tool over the mark, and tap it gently with a hammer to cut a small hole through the belt (above).

2 HOLDING THE BELT right side up, push the cylinder end of the metal eyelet from the right side of the belt through the prepared eyelet hole in the belt (above). Make sure that the ringed end of the metal eyelet is flush with the belt fabric on the right side.

3 PLACE the ringed end face down into the groove on the disk. Put the back washer over the end of the eyelet (above). Insert the point of the cutting tool into the eyelet, and tap with a hammer two or three times to open out the eyelet edges into the washer to secure in place.

HANDSTITCHED EYELETS

Buttonhole stitching

Mark the position for the eyelet. Pierce a hole with an awl, then reinforce the edges of the hole with tiny, neat running stitches. Buttonhole stitch around the hole to finish.

MAKING BELT CARRIERS

BELT CARRIERS ARE MADE in one continuous strip. The length for each carrier is the width of the waistband or belt, plus two seam allowances, plus ⅜ in (1 cm). To obtain the total strip length, this is multiplied by the number of the carriers needed. Less bulky than basic carriers, selvage-made carriers are better for thick fabrics.

BASIC FABRIC CARRIERS FOR A GARMENT

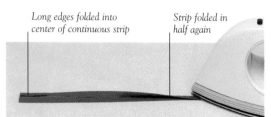

Long edges folded into center of continuous strip

Strip folded in half again

Continuous strip

Carrier

1 FOR ALL THE CARRIERS, cut one long strip on the straight grain four times as wide as the required finished width. Fold in each long edge to the center of the strip, and press. Fold the strip in half lengthwise, and press again (above). Baste the turned-under edges together if desired.

2 TOPSTITCH along one long side of the strip, close to the turned-under edges (above). Then topstitch along the opposite side of the strip, keeping close to the folded edge. Remove any basting if this has been used.

3 CUT THE STRIP into equal lengths for the individual carriers (above). Allow for the width of the belt, plus two seam allowances, plus ⅜ in (1 cm) for each of the carriers. (Add a little extra on thick fabric.)

SELVAGE-MADE CARRIERS

Carrier strip

FOR THE CARRIERS, cut one long strip three times the required finished width, with the selvage on one long edge. Fold the strip in three, and keep the selvage on the outside. Press. Topstitch along both long sides of the strip (right).

Strip folded in three

Topstitch with selvage on underside

CARRIER LOOP ON A BELT

WRAP THE CARRIER strip around two layers of the belt. Overlap the ends, and pin together (right), ensuring that the belt will slide smoothly. Trim the ends if required. Remove the carrier from the belt. Finish the ends, by hand or by machine, then stitch them together by hand. Slide in place on the belt.

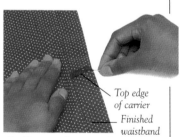

Two layers of belt

Carrier

ATTACHING A CARRIER TO A GARMENT

IN THE FIRST METHOD (below left), the carrier is stitched to the top of the waistband first. This has the advantage of concealing the stitching that attaches the carrier. In the second method, the top edge of the carrier is stitched onto the waistband last. This has the advantage of allowing the carrier to be adjusted in size before the final stitching.

STITCHING TO A WAISTBAND

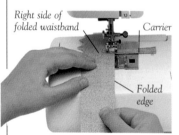

Right side of folded waistband

Carrier

Folded edge

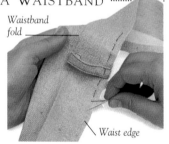

Waistband fold

Waist edge

1 PRESS the interfaced waistband in half. Overlap one carrier end over the folded edge of the waistband, and pin. Machine stitch just below the fold (above).

2 FOLD the carrier down over the stitching. Baste the other end of the carrier even with the waist edge (above). It will be enclosed in the waistband seam.

TOPSTITCHING TO A WAISTBAND

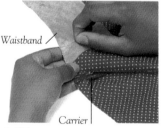

Waistband

Carrier

Top edge of carrier

Finished waistband

1 WITH RIGHT SIDES together, pin one end of the carrier at the waist edge. Pin (above) and stitch on the waistband, enclosing the carrier end in the seam.

2 FINISH the waistband. Fold under the raw edges of the carrier at the free end. Align with the top edge of the waistband, and pin (above). Stitch the top edge.

ADDING TO A TWO-PIECE WAISTBAND

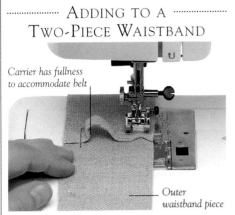

Carrier has fullness to accommodate belt

Outer waistband piece

WITH RIGHT SIDES UPPERMOST and raw edges even, pin the carrier to the outer waistband. Machine baste across the top and bottom edges, just inside the seam allowance (above). The carrier ends will be enclosed in the waistband seams.

INSERTING A TUBING CARRIER IN A SEAM

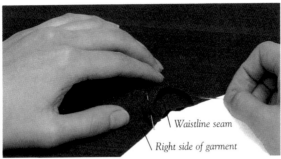

Waistline seam

Right side of garment

Finished tubing carrier

Waistline seam

1 CUT A STRIP OF THE REQUIRED WIDTH that is long enough for all the loops (see Making Belt Carriers, opposite). Make the tubing strip (p. 248). Cut the loops to the required length. Pin each loop in position on the right side of one garment piece at the waistline, the end even with the raw edge. If there is a waist seam, straddle the loop across it (above).

2 PIN the two garment pieces right sides together, with the loop sandwiched between them. Stitch the seam, enclosing the ends of the loop at the same time. Press the seam open.

ATTACHING AND COVERING A BUCKLE

BUCKLES CAN BE STITCHED on either by hand or by machine. For machine stitching, the folded-back buckle allowance must be long enough for the machine foot to be clear of the buckle. The projecting fabric at the end of the stiffening is folded back before stitching. On thick fabric, it could be trimmed away and the edge zigzag stitched.

POSITIONING A BUCKLE EYELET

Slight force punches eyelet

Buckle end of belt

POSITION THE EYELET centrally 1¼–2 in (3–5 cm) in from the end of the belt, depending on the amount allowed in the cutting out. The fabric should extend ⅜ in (1 cm) past the end of the stiffening.

HANDSTITCHING A BUCKLE IN PLACE

Wrong side of belt

Prong   *Buckle*

THREAD THE BUCKLE PRONG onto the eyelet so that it faces away from the belt. On the wrong side, tuck under the fabric end, align it with the stiffening, and pin. Handstitch it in place (above).

ATTACHING A BUCKLE BY MACHINE

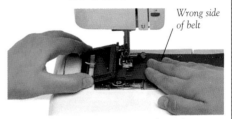

Wrong side of belt

THREAD ON THE BUCKLE, tuck under the fabric end to align with the belt stiffening, and pin. Machine stitch the fabric close to the end when it extends far enough past the buckle (above).

COVERING A BUCKLE

Peel away backing paper

1 CAREFULLY REMOVE the paper from one side of the double-sided adhesive backing provided in the buckle kit (above). Place the backing on the wrong side of the fabric. Trim the fabric to the same shape.

Fabric with adhesive backing

Buckle mold

2 PEEL THE PAPER away from half of the prepared fabric, and place the buckle centrally on the adhesive side. Then fold over the edges of the fabric to fit inside the mold, peeling off the rest of the paper as work progresses (above).

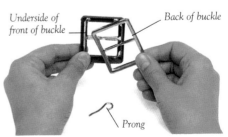

Underside of front of buckle

Back of buckle

Prong

3 FINISH COVERING THE FRONT of the buckle with the fabric. Snap on the back of the buckle to secure the fabric (above). Finally, attach the buckle prong to the front, and squeeze the looped end together using a pair of pliers.

SLEEVES AND CUFFS

MAKING SLEEVES

THE SHAPE AND STYLE OF THE SLEEVES form an important part of a garment's overall design. Set-in sleeves give a crisp, tailored look, while shirt sleeves are more casual. Raglan sleeves have characteristically deep, loose armholes; they are ideal for coats and raincoats, which require room for other garments to be worn underneath. Kimono sleeves are particularly suited to jersey fabrics, which will stretch and not restrict arm movement. Gathered sleeves with full sleeve caps are used on both women's casual dresses and bridal and evening wear.

RELATED TECHNIQUES

Working machine stitches, p. 77
Reducing seam bulk, p. 84
Taping seams, p. 89
Stitching seams with ease
and bias, p. 89
Attaching light- and mediumweight
sew-in interfacing, p. 99
Plain darts, p. 109

DIRECTORY OF SLEEVES

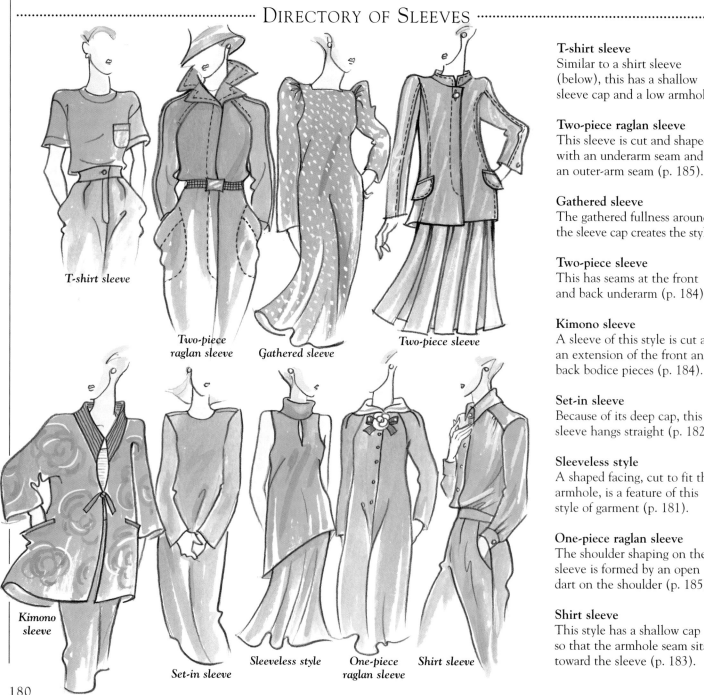

T-shirt sleeve

Two-piece raglan sleeve

Gathered sleeve

Two-piece sleeve

Kimono sleeve

Set-in sleeve

Sleeveless style

One-piece raglan sleeve

Shirt sleeve

T-shirt sleeve
Similar to a shirt sleeve (below), this has a shallow sleeve cap and a low armhole.

Two-piece raglan sleeve
This sleeve is cut and shaped with an underarm seam and an outer-arm seam (p. 185).

Gathered sleeve
The gathered fullness around the sleeve cap creates the style.

Two-piece sleeve
This has seams at the front and back underarm (p. 184).

Kimono sleeve
A sleeve of this style is cut as an extension of the front and back bodice pieces (p. 184).

Set-in sleeve
Because of its deep cap, this sleeve hangs straight (p. 182).

Sleeveless style
A shaped facing, cut to fit the armhole, is a feature of this style of garment (p. 181).

One-piece raglan sleeve
The shoulder shaping on the sleeve is formed by an open dart on the shoulder (p. 185).

Shirt sleeve
This style has a shallow cap so that the armhole seam sits toward the sleeve (p. 183).

FACING THE ARMHOLE ON A SLEEVELESS GARMENT

A PLAIN ARMHOLE WITHOUT A SLEEVE is finished with a facing. The facing may be cut in one piece with one seam joining it at the underarm. However, it is more commonly cut in two pieces, the front and back armhole facings, which are joined together at the shoulder and underarm. A very lightweight interfacing adds stability.

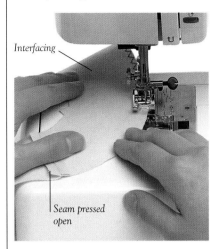

Interfacing

Seam pressed open

1 APPLY a lightweight interfacing to both the front and the back armhole facings. Then pin and stitch the front armhole facing to the back armhole facing at the underarm and shoulder seams. Trim the seam allowances, and press the seams open. Zigzag stitch around the outer edge of the facing to finish (left).

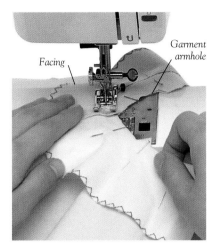

Facing

Garment armhole

2 WITH right sides together and raw edges even, pin the facing to the armhole, beginning at the shoulder seam, and pinning the side seam and notches, then pinning again in between. Stitch around the armhole (left), beginning and finishing at the underarm. Overlap the ends of the stitching.

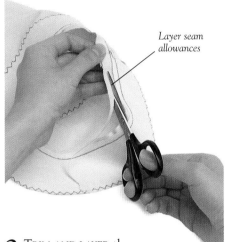

Layer seam allowances

3 TRIM AND LAYER the seam allowances, making the garment seam allowance the widest (above). (On thick fabrics, trim the corners of the seam allowances diagonally at the underarm and shoulder seams.)

Clips farther apart on straighter section of seam

Clips closer together on most curved part of seam

4 CLIP into the armhole seam allowances at approximately ¾-in (2-cm) intervals on the less curved parts of the seam, then decreasing to approximately ⅜-in (1-cm) intervals at the most curved part. In this way, the seam around the armhole will lie flat and in a smooth curve when it is turned to the inside of the garment.

Wrong side of garment

Facing

Sleeve board

5 PRESS THE FACING and the seam allowances away from the garment. Use the point of the iron to avoid pressing any unwanted creases into the armhole facing (above).

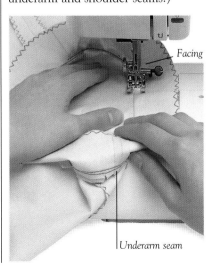

Facing

Underarm seam

6 UNDERSTITCH the facing by machine stitching through the facing and the seam allowances only, close to the seam allowances (left). Press the facing to the wrong side so that the armhole seam and understitching roll very slightly over to the wrong side. Then handstitch the facing to the garment at the shoulder seam and underarm seam.

QUICK METHOD FOR ATTACHING A FACING

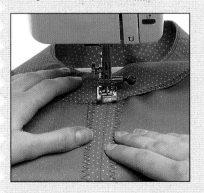

Match the facing underarm seam to the garment side seam. Pin the seam indentation through both layers. Stitch-in-the-ditch for about 1 in (2.5 cm) (left), removing the pin before the machine needle reaches it.

ATTACHING A SET-IN SLEEVE

THE SEAMLINE LENGTH along the top curve of a set-in sleeve is usually a little longer than the corresponding armhole seamline. The fullness must be eased in to form a smooth cap. Most sleeve patterns will have a single notch at the front of the armhole, a double one at the back, and a circle at the center top to match the shoulder seam.

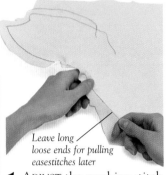

Leave long loose ends for pulling easestitches later

1 ADJUST the machine stitch to the longest length and easestitch the top of the sleeve between the notches, just inside the seamline. Leave long threads attached to both ends. Cut the threads and untangle them (above).

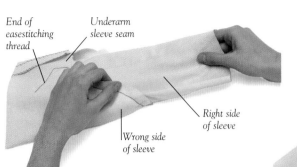

End of easestitching thread   *Underarm sleeve seam*

Right side of sleeve

Wrong side of sleeve

2 WITH RIGHT SIDES TOGETHER and raw edges even, pin the underarm sleeve seam together. Machine stitch the pinned seam, making sure that the ends of the easestitching thread do not get caught in the seam. Press the seam open and seam finish the raw edges as required. Carefully turn the seamed sleeve right side out (above).

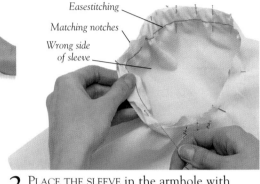

Easestitching

Matching notches

Wrong side of sleeve

3 PLACE THE SLEEVE in the armhole with right sides together. Match the notches, the sleeve seam to the underarm seam, and the center of the sleeve cap to the shoulder seam. Pin these points. Pin in between, arranging the fullness evenly. Gently pull the loose ends of the easestitching thread, easing the fullness without forming tucks or gathers (above).

4 BASTE the sleeve in place with small stitches alongside the easestitching. Working on the wrong side of the sleeve, stitch the sleeve to the armhole along the basting (left), beginning and ending at the underarm seam and overlapping the ends of the stitching. Remove the basting.

ATTACHING SET-IN SHOULDER PADS

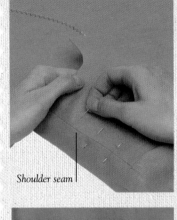

Shoulder seam

Neckline facing

Use running stitches to sew pad to armhole seam

1 *Try on the garment and insert the pads between the facing and the garment, positioning them so that they are centered on the shoulder seam and extend about ½ in (12 mm) beyond the armhole seamline. Working from the right side of the garment, pin the pads along the shoulder seam (left).*

2 *Check each shoulder pad from the inside, ensuring that it is straight and positioned under the neckline facing on the inside edge. Handstitch the armhole edge of each pad to the armhole seam (left). Secure the center of each shoulder pad to the shoulder seam under the facing, handstitching loosely so that the pads can move slightly.*

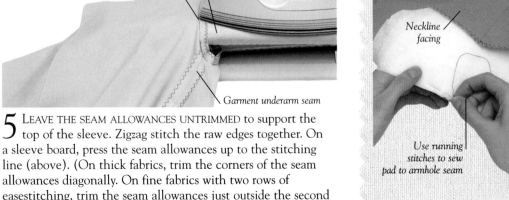

Sleeve board

Press seam allowances only

Garment underarm seam

5 LEAVE THE SEAM ALLOWANCES UNTRIMMED to support the top of the sleeve. Zigzag stitch the raw edges together. On a sleeve board, press the seam allowances up to the stitching line (above). (On thick fabrics, trim the corners of the seam allowances diagonally. On fine fabrics with two rows of easestitching, trim the seam allowances just outside the second row of easestitching and zigzag stitch the raw edges together.)

SHAPING AN ELBOW

CLOSELY FITTED and semifitted long sleeves require shaping at the elbow, on the back edge of the sleeve. This is to provide room for the elbow to bend without straining or tearing the fabric. The necessary extra fullness produced at the back of the sleeve is gathered in with darts or with easestitching to fit the front of the sleeve.

DART SHAPING

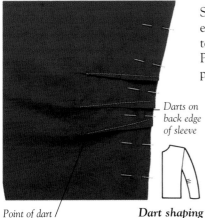

Darts on back edge of sleeve

Point of dart

Dart shaping

STITCH THE DARTS at the elbow, from the raw edges to the points (p. 109). Press each dart flat, then press it toward the bottom of the sleeve. Avoid pressing creases at the dart points. With right sides together and raw edges even, pin the back edge of the sleeve to the front edge of the sleeve (left) and stitch.

EASESTITCHING

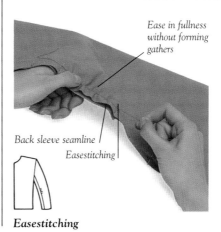

Ease in fullness without forming gathers

Back sleeve seamline

Easestitching

Easestitching

USING a long machine stitch, easestitch (p. 89) between the pattern markings, just inside the seamline. Match the seam edges, and then pin them together at the pattern markings. Pull the thread ends to ease in the fullness (left) and add pins between the markings. Then stitch the sleeve seam.

ATTACHING A SHIRT SLEEVE

A SHIRT SLEEVE IS CUT with a much shallower sleeve cap (the section where the top of the sleeve meets the garment shoulder seam) than that on a set-in sleeve. This gives the garment a looser, more casual fit. A shirt sleeve is usually attached to the armhole before both the garment side seam and underarm sleeve seam are stitched.

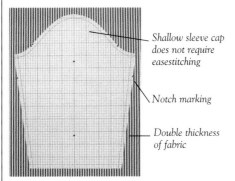

Shallow sleeve cap does not require easestitching

Notch marking

Double thickness of fabric

1 LAY the shirt sleeve pattern on a double thickness of fabric (left). Pin the pattern in place and cut out the sleeves, being sure to include all the notches and other pattern markings.

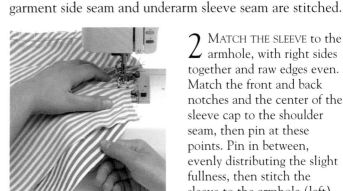

2 MATCH THE SLEEVE to the armhole, with right sides together and raw edges even. Match the front and back notches and the center of the sleeve cap to the shoulder seam, then pin at these points. Pin in between, evenly distributing the slight fullness, then stitch the sleeve to the armhole (left).

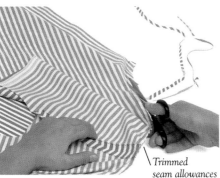

Trimmed seam allowances

3 PRESS THE SEAM and trim the seam allowances to half the original width (above). Zigzag stitch the edges together and press the seam toward the sleeve. (The seam can also be finished with a single row of topstitching near the seam, or with two rows ¼ in [6 mm] apart.)

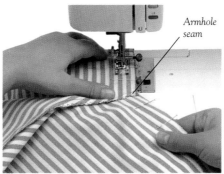

Armhole seam

4 LINE UP the garment side edges and the underarm sleeve edges, with right sides together. Pin at each end, at the armhole seam, and at the notches. Pin in between. Beginning at the lower edge of the garment side seam, stitch in one continuous seam (above).

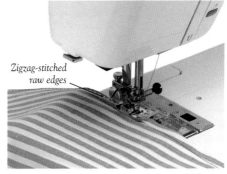

Zigzag-stitched raw edges

5 PRESS THE SEAM and trim to half the original width. Zigzag stitch the raw edges together (above) and press the seam to the back. (If there is a slit at the side seam, taper off the trimming 1¼ in [3 cm] above the top of the slit. Seam finish the slit, then zigzag stitch the seam.)

CONSTRUCTING A TWO-PIECE SLEEVE

A TWO-PIECE SLEEVE is used mainly on tailored jackets and coats. It is designed and cut in two separate pieces that are curved to follow the shape of the arm.

The seams joining the pieces are positioned toward the underside of the sleeve. The top and under sleeve pieces are joined before the sleeve is set into the garment armhole.

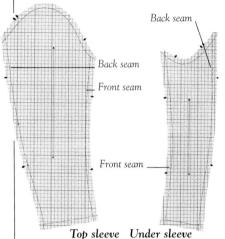

Back seam

Back seam

Front seam

Front seam

Top sleeve   Under sleeve

1 USING the pattern pieces provided, cut out a top sleeve piece and an undersleeve piece. Be sure to transfer the pattern markings accurately. Easestitch along the back edge of the top sleeve at the elbow just inside the seamline (p. 89). With right sides facing and pattern markings matching, pin the front edges of the top sleeve and under sleeve together, stretching the top sleeve to fit if necessary. Stitch.

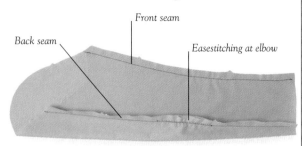

Front seam

Back seam

Easestitching at elbow

2 WITH RIGHT SIDES FACING and pattern markings matching, pin the back edges of the top sleeve and under sleeve together, using the easestitching to draw in the top sleeve at the elbow. Stitch.

MAKING A KIMONO SLEEVE

THE FRONT SECTION OF A KIMONO SLEEVE is cut out in one with the bodice front, and the back section is cut with the bodice back. A close-fitting kimono sleeve may need a gusset for comfort (p. 186–187). If it does not have a gusset, the underarm should be reinforced with a bias strip either before or after the seam is stitched.

REINFORCING THE UNDERARM SEAMLINE

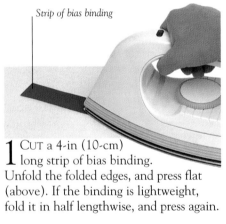

Strip of bias binding

1 CUT a 4-in (10-cm) long strip of bias binding. Unfold the folded edges, and press flat (above). If the binding is lightweight, fold it in half lengthwise, and press again.

Wrong side of back bodice

Bias strip

2 PIN THE BACK to the front along the shoulder and top sleeve seam, and the underarm and side seam. Place the bias binding over the curved part of the back underarm seamline, and baste (above).

3 STITCH BOTH SEAMS, catching in the bias strip in the underarm seam. Stitch over the bias strip again to reinforce it (above). Remove the basting. Clip along the underarm curve. Press the seams open.

REINFORCING THE FINISHED UNDERARM SEAM

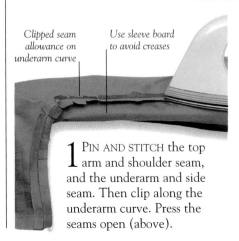

Clipped seam allowance on underarm curve

Use sleeve board to avoid creases

1 PIN AND STITCH the top arm and shoulder seam, and the underarm and side seam. Then clip along the underarm curve. Press the seams open (above).

Baste along center of strip

2 CUT A 4-IN (10-CM) STRIP of bias binding. Open out the strip, and press flat. If the binding is lightweight, fold it in half lengthwise, and press again. Place the strip over the curved part of the open back underarm seam. Baste (above).

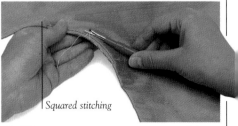

Squared stitching

3 WORKING ON THE RIGHT SIDE of the garment, machine stitch ⅛ in (3 mm) on either side of the basted seamline, squaring the stitching at the ends to make a long, narrow rectangle. Remove the basting (above), and press the seam.

MAKING A RAGLAN SLEEVE

A RAGLAN SLEEVE HAS ARMHOLE SEAMS that run from the underarm to the neckline at both the front and back of the garment. A one-piece raglan sleeve is shaped with an open dart that forms the shoulder seam, and a two-piece raglan sleeve is shaped with a seam that runs across the shoulder and down the outer arm.

ONE-PIECE RAGLAN SLEEVE

1 WITH RIGHT SIDES FACING and the edges of the dart aligned, pin the open shoulder dart together, then stitch the dart (above). With right sides facing, pin, then stitch the underarm seam. Press the shoulder dart and the seam open.

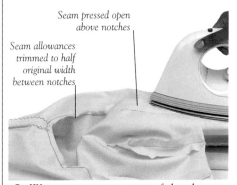

Seam pressed open above notches

Seam allowances trimmed to half original width between notches

3 WITH THE WRONG SIDE of the sleeve uppermost, stitch. Clip the seam allowances at the notches, and trim at the lower part of the armhole. Press the seam open above the notches (above).

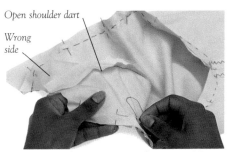

Open shoulder dart

Wrong side

2 STITCH the garment side seams. Turn the sleeve right side out, and pin it to the garment armhole, with right sides facing and neck edges, underarm seams, and pattern markings matching. Baste (above), and remove the pins.

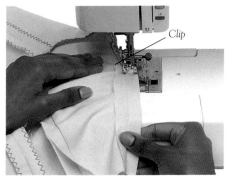

Clip

4 ZIGZAG STITCH the trimmed seam allowances together between the clips. Above the clips, zigzag stitch each seam allowance separately (above). Press the top parts of the seam open.

ATTACHING A RAGLAN SHOULDER PAD

1 *Try the garment on, and center the shoulder pad on the shoulder seam and under the shoulder curve. Pin the pad in position from the right side through the garment (above).*

2 *Check the pad position on the inside, and readjust if necessary. Loosely handstitch the pad center to the shoulder dart or seam (above).*

TWO-PIECE RAGLAN SLEEVE

WITH RIGHT SIDES facing and raw edges even, pin the front and back sleeve pieces together along the shoulder and outer seams. Stitch the outer seam, then notch the seam allowances along the shoulder curve so that the seam will lie flat when pressed open. Press the seam open. Match, pin, and stitch the underarm sleeve seam. Press the seam open, and seam finish if necessary.

FLAT CONSTRUCTION FOR A RAGLAN SLEEVE

A RAGLAN SLEEVE CAN BE SET INTO THE ARMHOLE after the sleeve seams have been stitched in the conventional way, or it can be made with a flat construction in which the garment side seam and underarm sleeve seam are stitched last.

Wrong side

Underarm seam

Garment side edge

1 STITCH the raglan sleeve, leaving the underarm seam open. Stitch the sleeve edges to the armhole, pinning together the sleeve underarm edges and garment side edges.

Wrong side

2 STITCH the raglan sleeve underarm edges and the garment side edges together in one continuous seam (above), making sure that the armhole seams match. Press the seam open.

USING SLEEVE GUSSETS

A SLEEVE GUSSET is a small diamond-shaped piece of fabric inserted into a slashed underarm opening on a kimono-type sleeve. Since such sleeves are cut in one with the front and back pieces, they have a continuous shoulder and outer arm seam and a continuous underarm and side seam. Gussets are added for free arm movement and comfort.

ONE-PIECE GUSSET

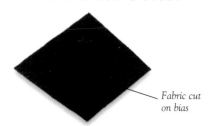

Fabric cut on bias

A ONE-PIECE SLEEVE GUSSET is made from one bias-cut, diamond-shaped piece of fabric. The piece is inserted into an opening under the arm after the continuous side and underarm seam of the garment has been stitched together.

TWO-PIECE GUSSET

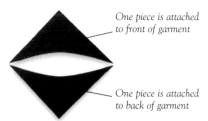

One piece is attached to front of garment

One piece is attached to back of garment

A TWO-PIECE GUSSET is made from two small, bias-cut, triangular pieces of fabric. One gusset piece is attached to the front underarm and the other is attached to the back underarm before the side and underarm seam is stitched together.

TOPSTITCHING A GUSSET

Topstitching

Topstitch around the gusset and through the seam allowances to strengthen the gusset seam, prevent fraying, and hold the seam flat.

MAKING A SLEEVE GUSSET

IF THE FABRIC IS LIGHTWEIGHT or if it frays easily, the point of the gusset opening should be reinforced before it is cut and the one- or two-piece gusset inserted. Either a square fabric patch or a piece of seam tape can be used to reinforce the point. On closely woven fabrics that do not fray easily, staystitching is sufficient reinforcement.

REINFORCING A GUSSET OPENING WITH A SQUARE PATCH

Gusset opening

1 MARK THE STITCHING LINES of the gusset opening using tailor's chalk. Cut a 2-in (5-cm) square of fabric on the bias. Place the square centrally over the point of the opening with right sides together. Pin around the edge of the square, then baste in place (above).

2 REMOVE PINS. Mark the point of the opening stitching lines on the reinforcing square using tailor's chalk. Then, using a fairly small machine stitch, staystitch just inside the opening stitching line, stitching through the reinforcing square at the point (above).

3 CUT STRAIGHT ALONG the center of the gusset opening, cutting through both the garment fabric and the reinforcing square. Be careful to finish cutting through the layers just short of the stitching at the point (above). Remove the basting.

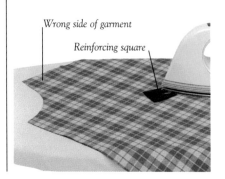

Wrong side of garment

Reinforcing square

4 TURN the square patch to the wrong side of the fabric, and roll the seam so that it is along the edge of the opening. Pull the fabric to form a point. Press the square lightly so that it lies flat (left). (A piece of seam tape can be used instead of a patch [see right].)

REINFORCING WITH SEAM TAPE

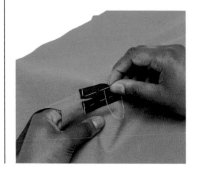

FOLD 4 in (10 cm) of tape to form a V shape. Baste the tape over the opening point on the right side (left). Staystitch the opening through the tape. Complete (see Steps 3 and 4, above and left).

INSERTING A ONE-PIECE GUSSET

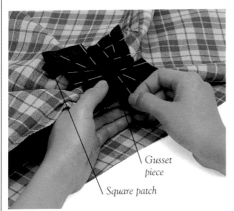

1 ATTACH SQUARE PATCHES at the underarm seams (see opposite). Stitch the side and underarm seam, leaving the slashed underarm opening unstitched. Place the gusset over the opening on the wrong side. Match the corners of the gusset to the seam ends and the opening. Align all the seamlines with right sides together. Pin the gusset in place (above).

2 WORKING ON THE WRONG SIDE of the one-piece gusset, baste the gusset to the opening around each point separately, beginning and ending at the garment seamline (above). Keeping the pins at the corners, stitch along one edge of the opening, pivot, take one stitch across the point, pivot, and stitch the other side of the opening.

3 REMOVE ALL THE PINS and the basting. Check that the corners are neat and square on the right side of the garment, then press on this side. Trim the edges of the reinforcing square and patches to about 3⁄8 in (1 cm) from the stitching. Whipstitch the gusset edges by hand (above) or machine. If required, topstitch around the gusset (see opposite).

INSERTING A TWO-PIECE GUSSET

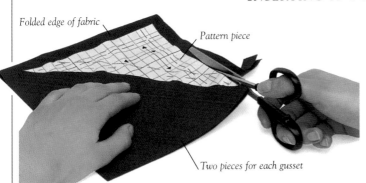

Folded edge of fabric

Pattern piece

Two pieces for each gusset

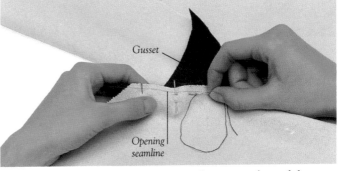

Gusset

Opening seamline

1 FOLD A PIECE OF FABRIC IN HALF. Place the two-piece gusset pattern piece on the fabric so that the long, curved center edge seam allowance of the gusset is aligned with the fabric bias. Pin the pattern piece in place, pinning through both layers. Cut out the two gusset pieces (above).

2 WITH RIGHT SIDES TOGETHER, pin the outer edges of the front gusset to the edges of the opening. Line up the opening seamline with the gusset seamline, and baste (above). Keeping the pins at the corners, stitch along one side of the opening, pivot, take one stitch across the point, pivot, and stitch the other side.

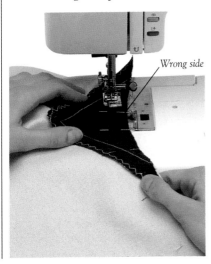

Wrong side

3 STITCH the back gusset to the garment. Zigzag stitch along the gusset edges, and press the gussets on the right side. With right sides together and the gusset seamlines matching, place the gusset and garment edges together. Pin, then stitch the underarm sleeve seam, the gusset seam, and the garment side seam (left).

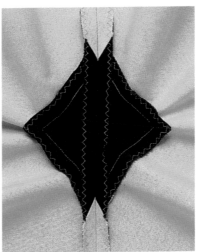

4 PRESS the new combined seam open. Zigzag stitch the raw edges of the seam allowances. (Alternatively, topstitch on the right side of the garment around the edges of the gusset, through both the garment fabric and the seam allowances [see opposite, top right].)

STRAIGHT SLEEVE FINISHES

T HE SIMPLEST STRAIGHT SLEEVE FINISH is a plain self-hem, which is frequently used on jackets and coats. There are also various types of casing, which consist of a stitched channel through which elastic is threaded to pull in a sleeve. When the channel is stitched above the edge of the sleeve, a casing with a ruffle is formed. Casings are used mainly on children's clothes and on summer dresses. A double-layer binding is an ideal finish for sheer fabrics where a hem would be visible from the right side. A faced casing is a useful finish when the sleeve is too short.

RELATED TECHNIQUES

Working hemming stitches, p. 76
Working machine stitches, p. 77
Applying fusible interfacing, p. 99
Making and attaching cuffs
with openings, p. 196
Attaching a shaped
turnback cuff, p. 201
Making a faced hem, p. 214

DIRECTORY OF STRAIGHT SLEEVE FINISHES

*Double-layer
bias binding*

Self-hem

Self-faced casing

Self-faced casing with ruffle

Double-layer bias binding
This forms a neat band around the sleeve edge and is ideal for use with sheer fabrics (p. 190).

Self-hem
This makes a plain, invisible finish (see below), which is often used on jackets, coats, and dresses.

Self-faced casing
Made from an extension of the sleeve fabric, this casing is gathered in with elastic (p. 191).

Self-faced casing with ruffle
This has an elasticated channel and a ruffle at the edge (p. 191).

FINISHING WITH A SELF-HEM

T HIS IS THE EASIEST of straight sleeve finishes and is also the method most often used. The edge of the sleeve is simply folded to the wrong side along the hemline and stitched (usually handstitched) to the inside of the sleeve. The hemming is worked a little way down from the cleaned finished edge to give an invisible, flat finish.

Wrong side

1 MARK the sleeve hemline on the right side. If necessary, remove bulk by trimming the seam allowances by half between the hemline and the raw edge (above).

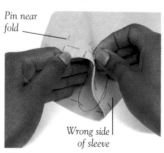

Pin near fold

Wrong side of sleeve

2 IF AN INTERFACING is required, apply it to the wrong side of the hem allowance. Turn the hem to the wrong side, and pin near the fold. Baste (above).

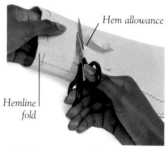

Hem allowance

Hemline fold

3 REMOVE ALL the pins. Measure the required hem depth up from the fold, and mark around the hem. Trim the hem allowance along the marked line (above).

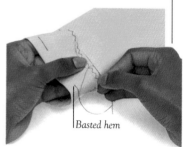

Basted hem

4 ZIGZAG STITCH the raw hem edge, and baste or pin the hem about ⅝ in (1.5 cm) below the zigzagged edge. Turn back the hem edge, and handstitch it in place (above).

FINISHING WITH A SEPARATE FACING

H ERE, THE ENDS OF A SEPARATE FACING are joined to form a circle before being attached to the sleeve. Once attached to the lower edge of the sleeve, the seam is understitched to make the facing roll naturally to the wrong side. The facing is folded to the inside of the sleeve. The hem is usually handstitched in place.

Unnotched edge of facing

Seam

Right side of sleeve *Wrong side of facing*

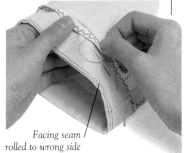

Right side of facing

Facing seam rolled to wrong side

1 IF INTERFACING is needed, apply it to the wrong side of the facing. With right sides together and raw edges even, stitch the short edges of the facing together. Trim the seam, and press open.

2 ZIGZAG STITCH the unnotched edge of the facing. With right sides together, raw edges even, and notches matching, pin the facing to the sleeve. Stitch in place (above).

3 TRIM the seam allowance and layer it, making the sleeve seam allowance the widest. Press the facing and seam allowances away from the sleeve. Understitch the facing seam (above).

4 TURN THE FACING to the wrong side of the sleeve. Roll the facing seam to the wrong side. Press. Pin ⅝ in (1.5 cm) below the zigzag-stitched edge. Handstitch (above), and remove the pins.

FINISHING WITH A BIAS FACING

I N THIS METHOD, the sleeve end is finished with a 1½-in (4-cm) wide bias-cut fabric strip. This is fitted around the lower edge of the sleeve, and the ends are pinned together to fit. The strip is then removed, and the ends are joined together to form a circle before it is stitched in place. It is hemmed to the inside of the sleeve using slipstitch.

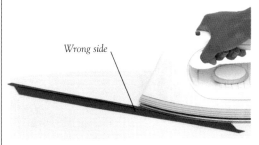

Wrong side

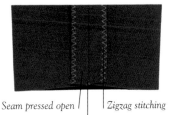

Seam pressed open *Zigzag stitching*

End of sleeve

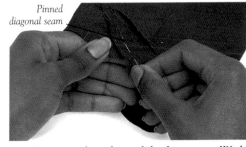

Pinned diagonal seam

1 CUT A 1½-IN (4-CM) WIDE bias strip that is long enough to fit around the sleeve lower edge, plus 2 in (5 cm). Turn ¼ in (6 mm) to the wrong side along both long edges of the bias strip. Press in the creases (above).

2 STITCH the sleeve seam. Finish the raw edges with zigzag stitching, and press the seam open. Trim the sleeve hem allowance to ¼ in (6 mm).

3 OPEN out the edges of the bias strip. With right sides together, pin the strip around the sleeve. Trim the ends of the strip so that they overlap by ½ in (12 mm), cutting on the straight grain. Pin the ends together (above).

Projecting triangle

Stitching along crease is ¼ in (6 mm) from edge

Seam rolled slightly over to wrong side

4 REMOVE the bias strip from the sleeve, keeping the ends pinned together. Then machine stitch these ends together (above).

5 PRESS THE SEAM open with the pressed edges of the bias strip still opened out (above). Then clip the projecting triangles.

6 REPIN the bias strip to the sleeve. Stitch in place along the pressed crease. Press the raw edge to the wrong side again (above).

7 FOLD THE STRIP to the wrong side of the sleeve, and press. Pin the pressed edge to the sleeve, and slipstitch in place (above).

FINISHING WITH A DOUBLE-LAYER BIAS BINDING

A DOUBLE-LAYER BIAS BINDING gives a firm but flexible sleeve finish. The binding is cut on the bias so that it will accommodate the slightly tapered shape at the lower sleeve edge. Since the bias binding forms a band around the lower sleeve edge, the binding can be made into a decorative feature if a contrasting fabric is used.

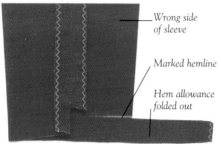

Wrong side of sleeve

Marked hemline

Hem allowance folded out

1 MARK THE HEMLINE around the sleeve. Trim away the hem allowance along the marked line (above). Cut the binding strip on the bias, making this six times the required finished width by the length around the sleeve, plus 2 in (5 cm).

Binding strip

2 PIN THE BINDING STRIP to the sleeve, right sides together. Overlap the ends of the binding, and pin them together diagonally on the straight grain. Unpin the binding from the sleeve. Machine stitch the ends as pinned (above).

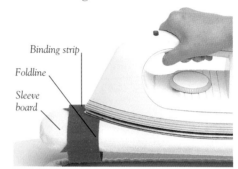

Binding strip

Foldline

Sleeve board

3 TRIM THE SEAM ALLOWANCES on the binding strip seam, and press the seam open. Fold the binding strip in half lengthwise with wrong sides together. Press a crease in the fabric along the folded edge of the strip (above).

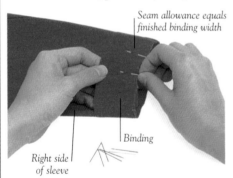

Seam allowance equals finished binding width

Binding

Right side of sleeve

4 TREATING the doubled binding as one layer, repin it to the sleeve (left), with right sides together. Stitch the seam the finished binding width in from the raw edge. Press the binding away from the sleeve.

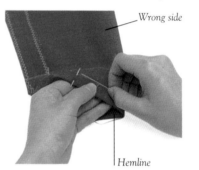

Wrong side

Hemline

5 TURN the sleeve wrong side out. Fold the binding to the wrong side of the sleeve. Pin, then slipstitch the pressed, folded edge of the binding to the back of the previous machine stitching (left).

FINISHING WITH AN APPLIED CASING

A N APPLIED CASING is a separate strip of fabric that is stitched to the lower edge of the sleeve and folded to the wrong side, like a hem. Elastic is threaded into the casing to gather the sleeve end. This type of sleeve finish is useful for adapting a sleeve that has been inadvertently cut too short for an ordinary turned-up hem.

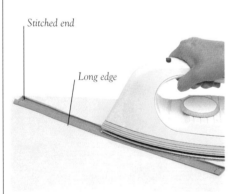

Stitched end

Long edge

1 CUT A STRIP of fabric on the straight grain, measuring the length around the sleeve, plus ¾ in (2 cm), by the width of the elastic, plus ¾ in (2 cm). Press ⅜ in (1 cm) to the wrong side at each end, and stitch. Then press ¼ in (6 mm) to the wrong side along each long edge (above).

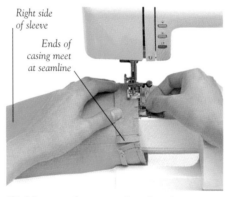

Right side of sleeve

Ends of casing meet at seamline

2 UNFOLD the pressed-under ¼-in (6-mm) seam allowance along one long edge of the strip. Pin the unfolded edge of the strip to the edge of the sleeve, with right sides together. The ends of the casing strip should meet at the sleeve seam. Stitch along the creaseline (above).

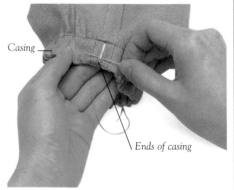

Casing

Ends of casing

3 FOLD THE CASING to the wrong side. Roll the seamline over slightly to the wrong side, and press. Pin the top edge of the casing to the sleeve, and machine stitch in place. Thread and join the elastic (see Steps 4 and 5, opposite). Whipstitch the casing closed (above).

FINISHING WITH A SELF-FACED CASING

A SELF-FACED CASING IS FORMED by folding the edge of the sleeve to the wrong side and stitching around both edges to form a channel. An opening is left in the top row of stitching to insert the elastic used to gather the sleeve edge. The stitching around the outer edge of the casing is not essential, but it gives a much neater finish.

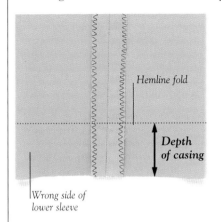

Hemline fold

Depth of casing

Wrong side of lower sleeve

1 TO DETERMINE the depth of casing required, add ⅜ in (1 cm) to the elastic width. Mark the hemline of the casing around the sleeve the required depth up from the raw edge. Mark with tailor's chalk, with pins, or by folding the casing to the wrong side and pressing in a hemline crease.

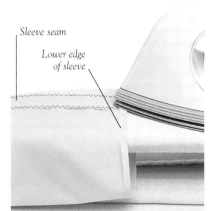

Sleeve seam

Lower edge of sleeve

2 WITH the sleeve turned to the wrong side, slip the end of the sleeve onto a sleeve board. Fold ¼ in (6 mm) to the wrong side along the raw edge of the sleeve, and press in place (left). This fold will become the casing underlap, preventing fraying and adding strength to the casing.

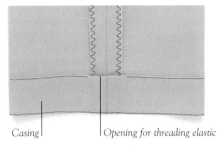

Casing | *Opening for threading elastic*

3 FOLD THE CASING to the wrong side along the marked hemline fold, and pin the casing in place. Machine stitch around the top edge of the casing, leaving a small opening at the sleeve seam. Stitch a second row around the lower edge of the casing, overlapping both ends of the stitching.

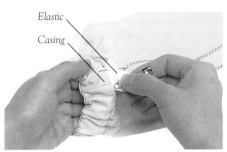

Elastic

Casing

4 CUT A STRIP OF ELASTIC to fit the wrist comfortably, plus ⅝ in (1.5 cm) for the join. Anchor one end of the elastic to the sleeve with a pin. Fasten a safety pin to the other end of the elastic, and thread it into the casing. Pull the elastic through the casing and out the opening, using the safety pin (above).

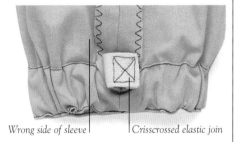

Wrong side of sleeve | *Crisscrossed elastic join*

5 REMOVE THE PINS. Pull the elastic ends out as far as possible, and overlap ⅝ in (1.5 cm). Pin. Machine stitch the ends together, either crisscrossing the center or whipstitching the ends together. Stretch the casing to pull the elastic inside. Finally, machine stitch across the opening at the top of the casing.

FINISHING WITH A SELF-FACED CASING AND RUFFLE

A RUFFLE can be added to the end of a sleeve with a self-faced casing finish by cutting the sleeve with extra length added on to the lower edge. This extra fabric can then be folded to the wrong side of the sleeve, like a very deep hem. The depth of the casing and ruffle allowance equals the depth of the ruffle, plus the depth of the casing, plus ⅜ in (1 cm). A casing for the elastic is stitched across the top part of the turned-under fabric.

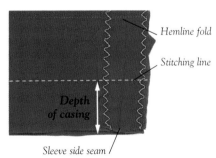

Hemline fold

Stitching line

Depth of casing

Sleeve side seam

1 MARK the sleeve hemline fold at the required finished length. Mark another line below the hemline for the depth of the ruffle. Below this line, for the depth of the casing, allow for the width of the elastic, plus ⅜ in (1 cm). Press ¼ in (6 mm) to the wrong side around the lower edge of the sleeve.

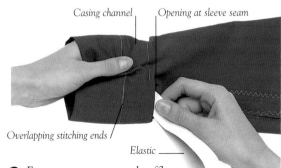

Casing channel | *Opening at sleeve seam*

Overlapping stitching ends

Elastic

2 FOLD THE CASING and ruffle allowance to the wrong side along the hemline, and press. Pin in place, and stitch around the top edge of the casing, leaving an opening at the sleeve seam. Overlapping the ends of the stitching, stitch around the second marked line to form a casing. Insert the elastic (above), and complete (see Steps 4 and 5, above).

CUFFS WITH OPENINGS

CUFFS THAT ARE INTENDED TO FASTEN snugly around the wrist require an opening at the lower edge of the sleeve in order to allow enough space for a hand to slip through. The hemmed and faced cuff-opening methods are the simplest to make. The continuous bound method gives a very neat finish to a long sleeve, with all the parts of the opening hidden and no edges visible when the cuff is closed. The shirt placket opening is the most complex to sew. This style of opening creates a tailored finish and is generally found on men's long-sleeved shirts.

RELATED TECHNIQUES

Working hemming stitches, p. 76
Applying interfacing up
to a foldline, p. 100
Forming pleats from the
right side, p. 115
Making and fitting gathers, p. 120
Attaching a shirt sleeve, p. 183
Making and attaching binding, p. 221

DIRECTORY OF CUFF OPENINGS

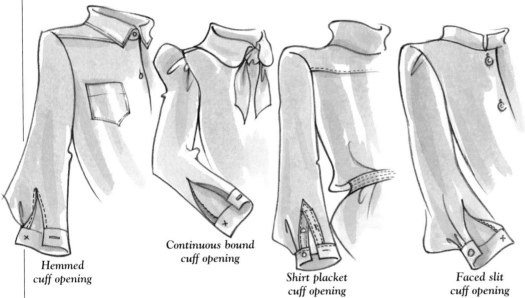

*Hemmed
cuff opening*

*Continuous bound
cuff opening*

*Shirt placket
cuff opening*

*Faced slit
cuff opening*

Hemmed cuff opening
Formed with a narrow hem, this opening (see below) can be used with a one- or two-piece lapped cuff.

Continuous bound cuff opening
Finished with a binding strip, this opening (see opposite) is used with a one- or two-piece lapped cuff.

Shirt placket cuff opening
A separate strip of fabric finishes each side of the opening. This opening (p. 194–195) is used with a shirt cuff.

Faced slit cuff opening
This opening, faced with a rectangle of fabric (see opposite), is used with all types of cuff, particularly double cuffs.

MAKING A HEMMED CUFF OPENING

THIS OPENING, where both edges are finished with narrow, tapered, machine-stitched hems, is quick to make. The front hemmed edge is folded to the wrong side before the lapped cuff (p. 197) is attached. When the cuff is buttoned, one folded-back opening edge overlaps the other edge and hides the machine stitching.

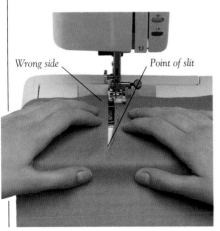

Wrong side   *Point of slit*

1 CUT the slit for the sleeve opening at the position marked on the pattern. Make a hem on one side of the slit by pressing ⅛ in (3 mm) of the fabric to the wrong side twice, tapering the turn-under to a point at the top of the slit. Pin and stitch (left). Make a hem on the other side of the slit in the same way.

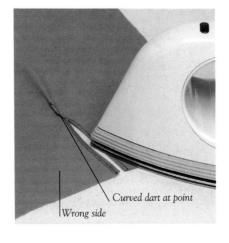

Curved dart at point

Wrong side

2 FOLD the sleeve with right sides together, so that the two hems of the opening are aligned. Stitch a short, narrow curved dart across the point of the opening to reinforce it. Then press each side of the opening on the wrong side toward the point (left). Turn the sleeve over, and press again.

MAKING A FACED SLIT CUFF OPENING

THIS IS THE EASIEST TO MAKE of all the cuff openings. The edges of the rectangular facing can be finished in two different ways. They can either be turned under and stitched to the garment, or turned under and stitched separately to avoid a stitching line on the right side of the garment. This opening can be used with any type of cuff.

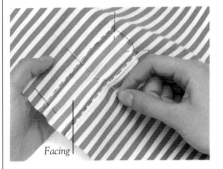

Facing

1 PRESS under ¼ in (6 mm) along both long edges and one short edge of the facing strip, and baste. Pin the facing to the sleeve with right sides together (left). Mark the position of the slit on the facing.

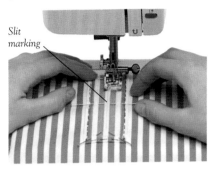

Slit marking

2 BEGINNING at the lower sleeve edge, stitch just ⅛ in (3 mm) from the slit mark (left), tapering in ¾ in (2 cm) from the point. Pivot, and take one stitch across the point. Pivot again, and stitch back up the other side.

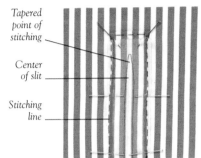

Tapered point of stitching

Center of slit

Stitching line

3 CUT the slit between the two stitching lines. Turn the facing to the wrong side. Roll the seamline slightly to the wrong side, and press. Pin the edges of the facing to the sleeve.

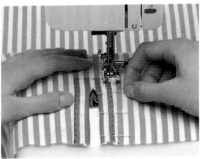

4 STITCH the facing to the sleeve, stitching close to the basted-under edges, pivoting at each of the corners, and removing the pins as they are reached. Finally, remove the basting stitches, and press.

MAKING A CONTINUOUS BOUND CUFF OPENING

THE RAW EDGES of a continuous bound opening are finished within a neat, narrow binding, making this method suitable for most fabrics, including sheer fabrics. However, this kind of opening should not be used on heavy fabrics, where the binding layers would be too bulky. It is widely used for most garments except men's shirts.

Pressed edges

1 CUT A BINDING STRIP 1¼ in (3 cm) wide by twice the length of the opening. Press under ¼ in (6 mm) along the long edges of the strip (above).

Unstitched sleeve seam

Cut between lines of staystitching

Staystitching

2 USING a small machine stitch, staystitch ¼ in (6 mm) from the slit marking, tapering in ¾ in (2 cm) from the point. Pivot, and take one stitch across the point. Pivot again, and stitch down the other side. Cut the slit to within a thread of the point (left).

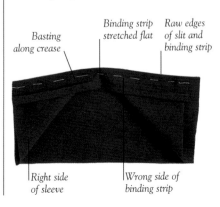

Basting along crease

Binding strip stretched flat

Raw edges of slit and binding strip

Right side of sleeve

Wrong side of binding strip

3 OPEN OUT the cut slit. Unfold one pressed edge of the binding strip, and pin this unfolded edge to the slit edge with right sides together and the staystitching aligned with the binding crease line. Baste (left). Stitch just outside the staystitching.

Binding strip opened out flat

4 REMOVE the basting. Turn the other pressed edge of the binding strip to the wrong side, and align it with the previous stitching line. Pin in place. Blind hemstitch the pressed edge to the back of the machine stitches (left). Press the finished opening.

MAKING A SHIRT-SLEEVE PLACKET OPENING

A SHIRT-SLEEVE PLACKET OPENING is constructed from two separate pieces of fabric that overlap, allowing the sleeve cuff to fit closely around the wrist. The overlap has a pointed top end, and the underlap has a straight top end. The top raw edge of the underlap is concealed beneath the overlap point, which is then topstitched in place.

MAKING A PLACKET

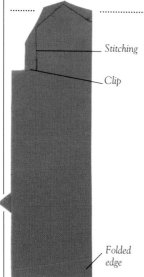

Stitching
Clip
Folded edge

1 MAKE the placket overlap by folding the cut-out fabric in half lengthwise, with right sides together. Stitch from the folded edge up, around the point, and down to the matching mark. Clip the seam allowances to within a thread of the stitching at the matching mark. Trim the seam allowances around the point. Trim the corners diagonally to reduce bulk when the overlap is turned right side out.

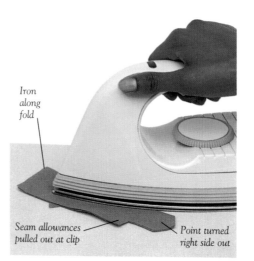

Iron along fold
Seam allowances pulled out at clip
Point turned right side out

2 TURN the placket overlap right side out. Pull out the corners around the point of the overlap so that a sharp angle is formed at each corner of the point. Pull out the seam allowances at the clip. Press the overlap points and the lengthwise center fold of the overlap (left). The point will lie flat and the corner angles will be sharp because the seams have been trimmed and tapered.

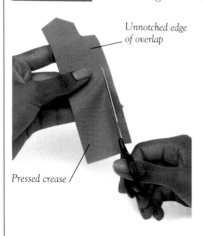

Unnotched edge of overlap
Pressed crease

3 FOLD the seam allowance to the wrong side along the long, unnotched edge of the placket overlap, and press. Unfold the seam allowance, and trim it to half its original width (left). Refold the trimmed seam allowance under along the pressed crease. The notched placket overlap edge should now project.

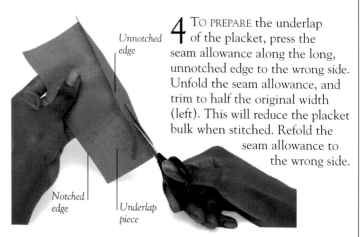

Unnotched edge
Notched edge
Underlap piece

4 TO PREPARE the underlap of the placket, press the seam allowance along the long, unnotched edge to the wrong side. Unfold the seam allowance, and trim to half the original width (left). This will reduce the placket bulk when stitched. Refold the seam allowance to the wrong side.

STITCHING A PLACKET UNDERLAP

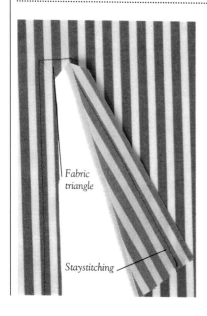

Fabric triangle
Staystitching

1 USING a small stitch length, staystitch around the placket position on the sleeve, a thread's width inside the placket stitching line. Cut along the center of the placket position. Continue cutting the placket to ⅜ in (1 cm) from the staystitching at the placket top. Cut diagonally into both corners of the placket opening. The diagonal cuts will create a triangle of fabric at the top of the placket opening.

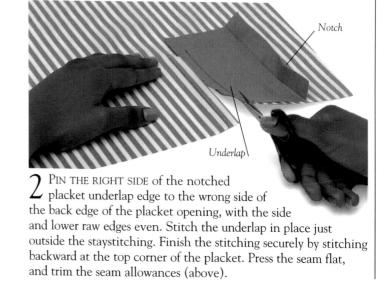

Notch
Underlap

2 PIN THE RIGHT SIDE of the notched placket underlap edge to the wrong side of the back edge of the placket opening, with the side and lower raw edges even. Stitch the underlap in place just outside the staystitching. Finish the stitching securely by stitching backward at the top corner of the placket. Press the seam flat, and trim the seam allowances (above).

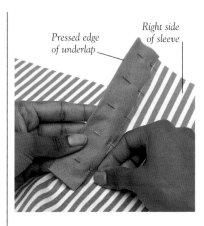

Pressed edge of underlap

Right side of sleeve

3 PRESS the seam allowances and underlap away from the sleeve. Turn the underlap to the right side of the sleeve. Pin the pressed edge of the underlap in position along the previous line of stitching (left). Stitch the pressed edge close to the fold, finishing securely at the corner of the staystitching.

Trimmed corner

Staystitching on other side of placket opening

4 AT THE TOP of the placket opening place the triangle of fabric behind the top edge of the underlap. Stitch across the base of the triangle, securing it to the underlap. Finish the thread ends securely. Then trim the corners of the seam allowance diagonally to form a point at the top (left).

STITCHING A PLACKET OVERLAP

Placket overlap

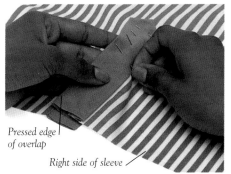

Pressed edge of overlap

Right side of sleeve

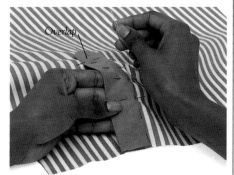

Overlap

1 PIN THE RIGHT SIDE of the unpressed, notched edge of the overlap to the wrong side of the free edge of the sleeve placket opening, with the side and bottom edges even. Stitch the placket overlap in position just outside the staystitching (above), making it secure by stitching backward a few stitches at the top corner of the placket.

2 TRIM THE SEAM ALLOWANCES to approximately half their original width, and press the seam allowances and the underlap toward the placket overlap. Fold the overlap to the right side of the sleeve, enclosing all the raw edges. Pin the pressed edge of the overlap in position along the line of previous stitching (above).

3 ARRANGE the placket overlap squarely on top of the underlap. Pin the point of the overlap to the sleeve, up to the matching mark. Keeping the underlap out of the way, baste the overlap in position up to the matching mark (above), removing the pins as they are reached. Baste around the point of the overlap. Remove any remaining pins.

TOPSTITCHING A PLACKET OVERLAP

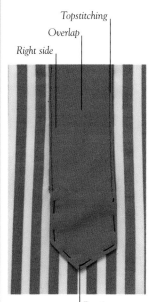

Topstitching

Overlap

Right side

Basting around point

1 ENSURING that the underlap is out of the way, topstitch (p. 87) along both long edges of the overlap. Topstitch from the bottom overlap edge up to the matching mark below the point. Leave the thread ends unsecured and long. Pull the thread ends to the wrong side. Knot and thread the ends into the topstitching. Remove the basting along the long edges of the overlap only, leaving it in place around the point.

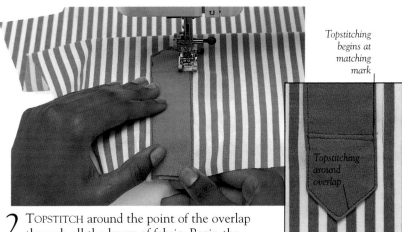

2 TOPSTITCH around the point of the overlap through all the layers of fabric. Begin the topstitching at the matching mark, and stitch across the overlap at the base of the opening (above). Pivot at the base, and stitch around the point and back up to the matching mark. Finish by working a second, reinforcing row of stitching on top of the first row. Leave the thread ends unsecured and long. Pull the thread through to the wrong side, and knot. To finish, thread the ends into the topstitching.

Topstitching begins at matching mark

Topstitching around overlap

MAKING AND ATTACHING CUFFS WITH OPENINGS

MOST TYPES OF CUFFS are made from one piece of fabric that is folded in half. Two-piece cuffs are formed from a separate outer cuff and a cuff facing, which are joined with a seam at the lower edge. Generally, only the outer section of each cuff is interfaced, although both layers may be interfaced if greater stiffness in the cuff is required.

MAKING A ONE-PIECE CUFF

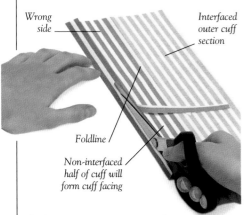

Wrong side

Interfaced outer cuff section

Foldline

Non-interfaced half of cuff will form cuff facing

1 APPLY INTERFACING to the wrong side of the outer cuff section of the cuff piece, up to the foldline. Press the seam allowance to the wrong side along the long, non-interfaced edge of the facing section, and trim (above).

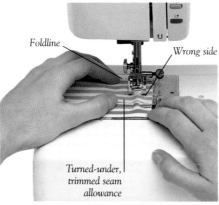

Foldline

Wrong side

Turned-under, trimmed seam allowance

2 FOLD THE CUFF IN HALF along the foldline with right sides together. Pin and stitch both ends (above). Trim the seam allowances and layer if required, making the interfaced seam the widest. Trim the corners diagonally near the fold.

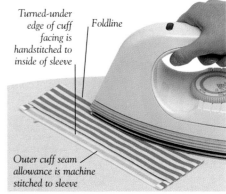

Turned-under edge of cuff facing is handstitched to inside of sleeve

Foldline

Outer cuff seam allowance is machine stitched to sleeve

3 PRESS THE SEAMS OPEN and turn the cuff right side out, pulling out and straightening the corners. Roll the seams over slightly toward the facing side of the cuff and press firmly. Press the cuff in half along the foldline (above).

MAKING A TWO-PIECE CUFF

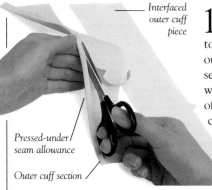

Interfaced outer cuff piece

Pressed-under seam allowance

Outer cuff section

1 CUT OUT the two cuff pieces. Apply interfacing to the wrong side of the outer cuff piece. Press the seam allowance to the wrong side along the length of the notched edge of the cuff facing piece. Trim the pressed-under seam allowance on the cuff facing piece to half its width (left).

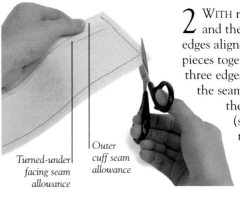

Turned-under facing seam allowance

Outer cuff seam allowance

2 WITH right sides together and the side and lower edges aligned, pin the cuff pieces together along these three edges, then stitch. Trim the seam allowances as for the one-piece cuff (see above). Trim the lower corners diagonally (left), turn right side out, and press.

ALTERNATIVE CUFF STYLES

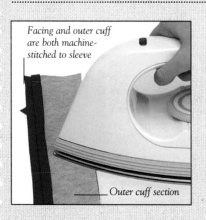

Facing and outer cuff are both machine-stitched to sleeve

Outer cuff section

Shirt cuff style
Make as for a one-piece cuff (see above), but press the lengthwise seam allowance of the outer cuff (instead of the seam allowance of the facing) to the wrong side. After stitching the ends, press the cuff (left), then turn right side out, and press again.

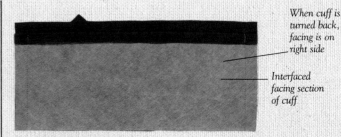

When cuff is turned back, facing is on right side

Interfaced facing section of cuff

Double cuff style
Cut out the cuff piece, which is twice as deep as a one-piece cuff. Make as for a one-piece cuff (see above), but apply interfacing to the facing section of the cuff piece, instead of to the outer section.

ATTACHING A LAPPED CUFF

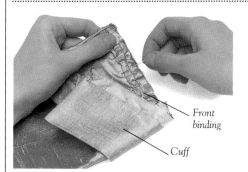

Front binding

Cuff

1 IF THE GARMENT has a continuous bound opening (p. 193), fold the front binding to the wrong side, and pin. Gather the sleeve. With right sides together and the cuff extending past the back edge of the placket for the underlap, pin the outer cuff to the sleeve (above).

Seam allowance

Cuff facing

2 BASTE the outer cuff to the sleeve, ensuring that the front cuff edge is aligned with the front placket edge. Remove the pins and machine stitch. Trim the seam allowances (above) and layer, making the cuff seam allowance the widest.

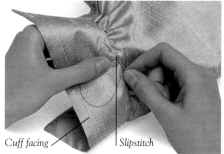

Cuff facing | *Slipstitch*

3 FOLD THE CUFF away from the sleeve. Press the seam allowances and the cuff away from the sleeve on the right side. Align the turned-under edge of the cuff facing with the cuff seam on the inside, and slipstitch in place to the back of, or below, the machine stitching (above).

ATTACHING A SHIRT CUFF

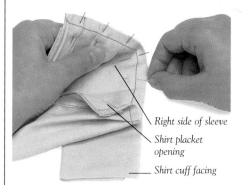

Right side of sleeve

Shirt placket opening

Shirt cuff facing

1 GATHER OR PLEAT the sleeve as desired. With raw edges even and notches matching, pin the right side of the shirt cuff facing to the wrong side of the sleeve (above), making sure that each cuff end is aligned with the edge of the shirt placket opening (p. 194–195).

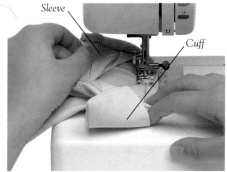

Sleeve

Cuff

2 WITH THE SLEEVE uppermost, machine stitch the cuff in place (above). Trim the seam allowances and layer if necessary, making the sleeve seam allowance the widest. Fold the cuff away from the sleeve. Then press the seam allowances and the cuff away from the sleeve.

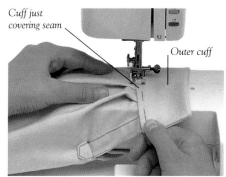

Cuff just covering seam

Outer cuff

3 PIN the turned-under edge of the outer cuff in place so that it just covers the cuff seam. Baste the turned-under edge and remove the pins. Working on the right side, machine stitch around the whole cuff (above). Remove the basting.

ATTACHING A DOUBLE CUFF

Faced slit opening

Seam allowance of outer cuff

Turned-under edge of double cuff facing

1 GATHER OR PLEAT the sleeve as desired. With raw edges even and right sides together, pin the non-interfaced edge of the outer cuff to the sleeve (above), aligning the cuff ends with the edges of the faced slit opening (p. 193).

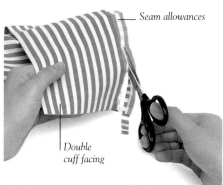

Seam allowances

Double cuff facing

2 BASTE THE CUFF to the sleeve and remove the pins. Machine stitch. Trim the seam allowances (above) and layer if necessary, making the sleeve seam allowance the widest. Fold the cuff away from the sleeve.

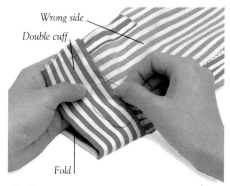

Wrong side

Double cuff

Fold

3 PRESS THE SEAM ALLOWANCES and the cuff away from the sleeve. Pin the turned-under edge of the cuff to the cuff seam on the inside, and slipstitch to the back of, or below, the machine stitching (above). Fold the cuff in half and press.

CUFFS WITHOUT OPENINGS

SIMPLER TO MAKE than cuffs with placket openings (p. 192–197), cuffs without openings must be large enough for the hand to fit through comfortably. Cuff styles in this category include straight cuff bands and straight or shaped turnback cuffs. Straight cuff bands hang down away from the sleeves, which are usually gathered into the bands. Turnback cuffs are folded back to the right side like pants cuffs. Shaped turnback cuffs are cut separately from the sleeves and in two pieces, so that the top edges can be cut into decorative shapes.

RELATED TECHNIQUES

Working tailor's tacks, p. 73
Working hemming stitches, p. 76
Working machine stitches, p. 77
Reducing seam bulk, p. 84
Applying fusible interfacing, p. 99
Making and fitting gathers, p. 120
Finishing a basic turned-up hem, p. 205

DIRECTORY OF CUFFS WITHOUT OPENINGS

Straight cuff band
A circular band attached to the lower edge of a gathered sleeve, the straight cuff band (see below) is used mainly for short sleeves, particularly on children's clothes.

Straight turnback cuff
A turnback cuff can be cut either as an extension of the sleeve (see opposite) or as a separate piece (p. 200). It is used mainly on coats and jackets made from medium- and heavyweight fabrics.

Straight cuff band   *Straight turnback cuff*   *Shaped turnback cuff*

Shaped turnback cuff
A shaped turnback cuff (p. 200–201) is cut separately from the sleeve. It can be made in a contrasting fabric, or in a different weight of fabric on the right and wrong sides to accommodate bulky or difficult fabrics. This type of cuff is used mainly for women's blouses, dresses, and coats made with sophisticated styling.

MAKING A STRAIGHT CUFF BAND

BEFORE THE CUFF BAND PIECE is stitched to the sleeve, the short ends of the piece are joined to form a tube. The lower edge of the sleeve is then gathered to fit the tube. This type of straight cuff is best used on short-sleeved garments, and when working with fairly lightweight, crisp fabrics such as lawn, gingham, poplin, and taffeta.

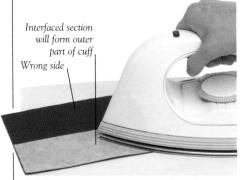

Interfaced section will form outer part of cuff
Wrong side

1 MARK THE CUFF FOLDLINE by clipping the seam allowance at each side edge. Fold the cuff in half along the foldline with wrong sides together. Press. Apply the interfacing to the wrong side of the cuff up to the creased foldline (above).

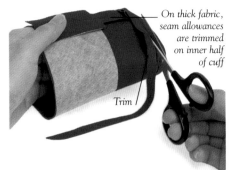

On thick fabric, seam allowances are trimmed on inner half of cuff
Trim

2 PIN AND STITCH THE ENDS of the cuff together to form a tube. Trim the seam allowances if necessary and press the seam open. Press the seam allowance to the wrong side around the non-interfaced edge of the cuff. Trim (above).

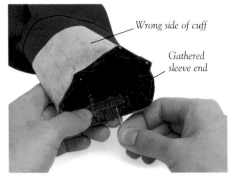

Wrong side of cuff
Gathered sleeve end

3 PIN THE RIGHT SIDE of the interfaced cuff edge to the right side of the evenly gathered sleeve end (above), with raw edges even and notches matching, and the cuff seam aligned with the garment underarm sleeve seam.

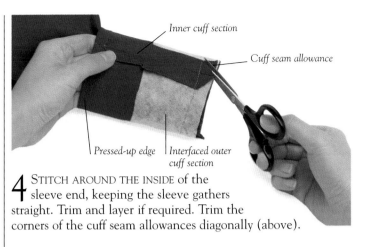

Inner cuff section

Cuff seam allowance

Pressed-up edge

Interfaced outer cuff section

Wrong side of sleeve

Inner edge of cuff is aligned with seam stitching, so that seam allowances are enclosed

4 STITCH AROUND THE INSIDE of the sleeve end, keeping the sleeve gathers straight. Trim and layer if required. Trim the corners of the cuff seam allowances diagonally (above).

5 PRESS the cuff and the seam allowances away from the sleeve. Turn the sleeve wrong side out and fold back the cuff along its center foldline. Pin and slipstitch the edge of the cuff to the line of machine stitching, or just below it (left). Press on this side using a sleeve board.

MAKING AN INTEGRATED STRAIGHT TURNBACK CUFF

AN INTEGRATED STRAIGHT TURNBACK CUFF is made in the same way as a very deep hem, then folded back to the right side of the sleeve, leaving a narrow band to form a shallow hem on the inside of the sleeve. This cuff is best made with medium- to heavyweight fabrics, which have enough body to maintain the circular cuff shape.

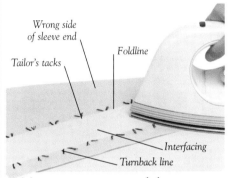

Wrong side of sleeve end

Tailor's tacks

Foldline

Interfacing

Turnback line

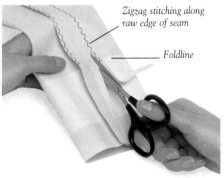

Zigzag stitching along raw edge of seam

Foldline

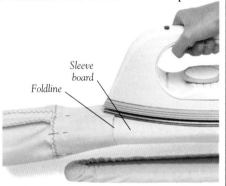

Sleeve board

Foldline

1 MARK THE FOLDLINE and the turnback line at the cuff end of the sleeve using tailor's tacks. Apply fusible interfacing to the wrong side of the cuff between the foldline and the turnback line (above). Remove the tailor's tacks.

2 STITCH THE SLEEVE SEAM, including the cuff. Zigzag stitch the raw edges of the seam above the cuff. Press the seam open. Trim the seam allowance between the raw edge and the foldline (above). Zigzag stitch the raw cuff edge.

3 FOLD THE CUFF to the wrong side along the foldline like a hem. Pin the zigzag stitched edge to the sleeve. Then press the fold around the lower edge using a sleeve board (above). Baste around the edge near the fold and remove the pins.

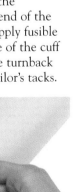

Foldline

Right side

Turnback line

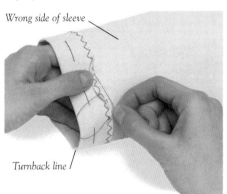

Wrong side of sleeve

Turnback line

4 TURN THE SLEEVE right side out and fold back the cuff to the right side of the sleeve, along the turnback line. Press around the fold, using a sleeve board. Baste through all the thicknesses around the edge of the cuff near the turnback line, and about ⅝ in (1.5 cm) away from the zigzagged edge on the inside (above).

5 AGAIN TURN THE SLEEVE wrong side out, and blind hemstitch the zigzag stitched cuff edge to the sleeve (above). (An alternative method is to fold down the turnback on the right side and stitch the sleeve hem; the stitching will be covered by the turnback.) Then remove the basting and press the cuff.

MOCK VENT OR PLEAT

A mock vent can be used to reduce excess fullness around a lightweight, hemmed sleeve end. Try on the sleeve and pin a small pleat on the outer arm. Press the pleat toward the back and baste along the fold. Make a buttonhole through the pleat. Finally, stitch a button to the sleeve under the pleat and fasten.

MAKING A SEPARATE STRAIGHT TURNBACK CUFF

WHEN FINISHED, A STRAIGHT FOLD forms the outer edge of this cuff. The side edges of the cuff piece are joined to form a circle before the cuff is stitched on.

If the side edges of the cuff are slightly shaped for a better fit, the stitching lines should be followed carefully. The cuff can be made in the same or in a contrasting fabric.

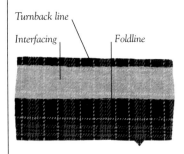

Turnback line
Interfacing
Foldline

1 ON THE WRONG SIDE of the cuff piece, mark the foldline and the turnback line. Apply the interfacing to the wrong side of the cuff between the foldline and turnback line.

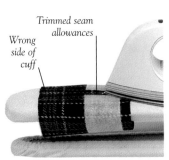

Trimmed seam allowances
Wrong side of cuff

2 STITCH the sleeve seam. Stitch together the short cuff edges, and trim, cutting closely on the interfaced section if using thick fabric. Press the seam open (above).

Stitch cuff to sleeve

3 ZIGZAG STITCH around the edge of the interfaced section of the cuff. Pin the non-interfaced cuff edge to the sleeve, right sides together, and stitch (above).

Wrong side of sleeve
Zigzagged edge of cuff
Basted foldline

4 TURN the sleeve wrong side out and press the cuff seam open. Fold the cuff back, then baste along the foldline. Baste the zigzagged edge of the cuff to the sleeve (above).

Right side of sleeve
Turnback line
Foldline

5 TURN THE SLEEVE right side out. Fold the cuff to the right side along the turnback line. Press around the turnback fold (above). Avoid pressing over the basting at the foldline because this may cause the stitching to mark the fabric.

Remove basting using seam ripper

6 BASTE AROUND the turnback edge of the cuff through all the fabric thicknesses. Blind hemstitch the zigzagged edge of the cuff on the inside (p. 76). Remove the basting around the turnback and foldline edges (above) and press.

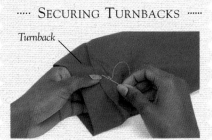

SECURING TURNBACKS

Turnback

Secure the turnback with a small cross stitch on the inside of the cuff to prevent it from falling down.

MAKING A SHAPED TURNBACK CUFF

A SHAPED TURNBACK CUFF is made from two pieces of fabric, so that the outer edge of the cuff can either be curved or cut into a decorative shape. The side edges of

the cuff may be joined to form a circle before the cuff is attached, as for the straight turnback cuff (see above), or stitched separately so that they meet edge to edge, as here.

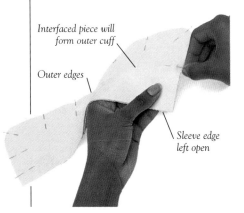

Interfaced piece will form outer cuff
Outer edges
Sleeve edge left open

1 APPLY interfacing to one of the cuff pieces. This interfaced cuff piece will form the outer side of the cuff. Then, with right sides together and raw edges even, pin the interfaced, outer cuff piece to the other, non-interfaced cuff piece around all the edges (left).

Seam allowance trimmed to half original width
Outer curves notched
Trim corners diagonally

2 STITCH THE OUTER EDGES OF THE CUFF, leaving the sleeve edge open. Trim the seam allowances. Notch along the outer curves and trim the corners diagonally (above). Using a sleeve board, press the seam open. Turn the cuff right side out. Press, rolling the seam slightly over toward the inner side.

ATTACHING A SHAPED TURNBACK CUFF

THIS TYPE OF CUFF is attached by being sandwiched between the sleeve and a facing. These layers are then stitched together around the end of the sleeve. Since this seam has many thicknesses, the seam allowances are trimmed and layered to reduce the bulk. To finish, the facing is stitched to the wrong side, like a hem.

Seam rolled slightly over to wrong side

1 STITCH THE SLEEVE SEAM and press it open. Turn the sleeve right side out, then place the cuff around the right side of the sleeve with the interfaced side outermost. With raw edges and pattern markings matching, pin the cuff to the sleeve (above). Baste. Remove the pins.

Sleeve facing

2 STITCH THE SHORT EDGES of the sleeve facing together, with right sides together and raw edges even, to form a circle. Trim the seam allowances and press the seam open. Seam finish the top, unnotched edge of the facing using a zigzag or serge finish (above).

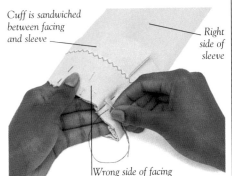

Cuff is sandwiched between facing and sleeve

Right side of sleeve

Wrong side of facing

3 PLACE THE FACING around the sleeve and over the cuff, with right sides together and raw edges even. Pin, with seams aligned and notches matching. Baste (above), then remove the pins. Machine stitch around the edge through all the fabric thicknesses.

Facing seam

4 TRIM AND LAYER the seam allowances, making the sleeve seam allowance the widest. Then trim the corners of the seam allowances diagonally, cutting close to the stitching (above). This will allow the seam to be pressed flat when the cuff is turned right side out.

5 PULL THE FACING DOWN away from the sleeve. Then press the seam allowances and the facing away from the sleeve, using a sleeve board if required. For a neat finish, understitch the seam by machine stitching the facing and the seam allowances through all the layers close to the seamline (above).

Wrong side of sleeve

Understitching

6 FOLD THE FACING UP inside the sleeve. Roll the seam over slightly towards the inside of the sleeve, and press in place. Pin the facing in position along the sleeve. Then turn the sleeve wrong side out. Blind hemstitch (p.76) the facing along the inside of the sleeve (above) and turn the sleeve right side out.

ADDING CONTRASTING CUFFS

Lining fabric

On thick fabric
When making cuffs using contrasting thick or bulky fabrics, such as a fake fur or a thick wool fabric, reduce the bulk by making the inner layer of the cuff in a lighter-weight fabric – such as lining fabric or cotton poplin – in a related color.

Garment fabric

On slippery fabric
When using fabrics such as satin or velvet, which are difficult to work with because they cannot be held in place easily, make the inner layer of the cuff in the same fabric as the rest of the garment. This will help support the contrasting, slippery fabric.

HEMS

MAKING HEMS

HEMS ARE USUALLY THE LAST THING to be stitched on a garment. Although a simple, turned-up, slipstitched hem is the one most commonly used, there are many other techniques available. For instance, a hem can be faced, or it can be finished with a binding. There are also several methods for finishing the raw edge of a turned-up hem and for securing it with hand or machine stitching. For a professional result, choose the hem that is suited to the edge being hemmed, to the thickness of the fabric, and to the design of the garment.

RELATED TECHNIQUES

Hand sewing stitches, p. 74
Working hemming stitches, p. 76
Sewing seams in interfacing, p. 98
Making a free-hanging
lining, p. 102
Hemming a jacket, p. 295
Machine-rolled hems on
fine fabrics, p. 301

DIRECTORY OF HEMS

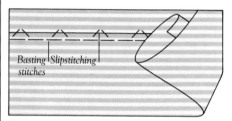

Basic turned-up hem
The most widely used hem is the turned-up hem (p. 205). It is clean finished and handstitched in place with slipstitching.

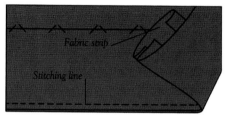

Faced hem
This type of hem (p. 214) is useful for curved edges or where fabric is short, as a separate fabric strip forms the faced hem.

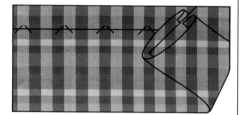

Covered hem
Ideal for reversible garments and sheer fabrics, the covered hem (p. 207) can have a matching or contrasting binding.

MARKING A HEMLINE

THE FIRST STAGE IN HEMMING is accurately marking the hemline. This is done with the fabric flat or hanging. The best way to hang a garment is to put it on, together with the underwear, belt, and shoes to be worn with the outfit. The hemlines should be pinned and checked before any excess fabric is trimmed away.

ON THE FLAT

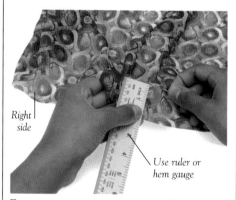

Right side

Use ruler or hem gauge

FOR STRAIGHT SKIRTS, tops, and pants, transfer the hem allowance on the pattern to the right side of the fabric with a line of pins (above). Then fold the hem to the inside, and try the garment on. Mark alterations if needed, and try on again. Repeat until correct. Use this method for other hems if no helper is available.

WITH A HELPER

Wearer should stand up straight and still

PUT ON THE GARMENT. Ask a helper to pin mark the hemline at 2-in (5-cm) intervals, measuring up from the floor with a ruler or a yardstick (above). Pin up the hem and check.

WITH HEMLINE MARKER

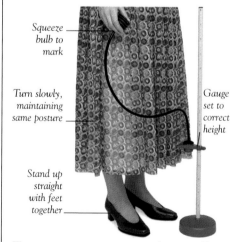

Squeeze bulb to mark

Turn slowly, maintaining same posture

Gauge set to correct height

Stand up straight with feet together

TEST THE CHALK to ensure that it will not make a permanent mark. (If in doubt, wear the garment inside out.) Standing straight, turn slowly, marking every 2 in (5 cm). Pin up the hem and try on again.

FINISHING A BASIC TURNED-UP HEM

WHEN THE HEM ALLOWANCE has been turned up and trimmed as described here, the hem edge is finished and stitched (p. 206–208). For a continuous, smooth hem, the grainline at both the center front and center back should be aligned with the seamline on the hem allowance and the garment when the hem is turned up and pinned.

TURNING UP AND TRIMMING A HEM ALLOWANCE

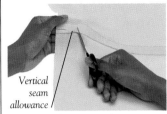

Vertical seam allowance

1 TRIM the vertical seam allowances in the hem allowance to half their width (above). This will reduce the bulk in the finished hem.

2 FOLD UP the hem along the marked hemline, and pin at 2-in (5-cm) intervals. Baste, keeping close to the folded edge (above).

Use chalk pencil or pins to mark even hem allowance

3 MARK an even width of hem allowance (above). Trim any excess. If necessary, easestitch the hem ¼ in (6 mm) in from the hem edge.

Pull to gather

4 PULL the thread ends to gather in the hem until it fits smoothly (above). Seam finish edge, press lightly, and stitch the hem (p. 206–208).

USING FUSIBLE WEB

Seams aligned

Remove pins before pressing

1 ONCE turned up, a hem can be either stitched or fused in place. To fuse, first finish the edge (p. 206). Pin the web between the hem and garment.

2 PRESS with the tip of the iron to secure the hem (left) – do not drag. Remove the pins and press with a damp cloth. Allow each section to dry before moving on.

FUSING A HEAVY FABRIC

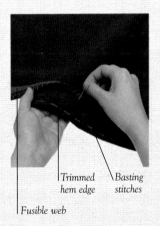

Trimmed hem edge *Basting stitches* *Fusible web*

For heavy fabrics, choose a fusible web that is nearly as wide as the hem allowance, but narrow enough to fit between the basting at the hemline and the trimmed and finished edge. Finish the edge (p. 206) and pin the fusible web in place between the hem and garment (left). Press by holding the iron in one position, and move it by lifting rather than using a gliding action.

INTERFACING A HEM

TO PREVENT A HEM EDGE from creating a line on the right side of the fabric, the hem can be interfaced. This technique adds body to hems and, because of this, it is most commonly used on tailored garments. The interfacing is cut on the bias, 2 in (5 cm) wider than the hem allowance, and attached before the hem is turned up.

Hem foldline

1 MARK hem foldline with a running stitch (above). Trim and finish the edge (p. 206). Cut interfacing strips and let the ends overlap diagonally.

2 PIN the interfacing to the wrong side, with the lower edge 1 in (2.5 cm) below the foldline (above). Catchstitch both the long edges.

3 TURN UP the hem along the hemline. Pin (above). Baste close to the fold. The interfacing should extend 1 in (2.5 cm) above the edge.

Finished hem edge

4 CATCHSTITCH around the finished hem edge, ensuring that the stitches are worked through the interfacing only (above).

SEWING HEMS BY HAND – UNCOVERED HEM EDGES

ONCE A HEM HAS BEEN TURNED UP and basted, the raw hem edge can be finished in several ways, according to the type of fabric, before being secured to the garment.

Sheer fabrics need special treatment. A double hem hides the raw edge on a sheer fabric, such as organdy. Narrow, rolled hems are better for soft sheers, such as chiffon.

TURNED AND STITCHED

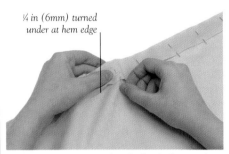

¼ in (6mm) turned under at hem edge

1 THIS is a strong finish for lightweight fabrics. Turn up the hem allowance, and baste. Fold the hem edge under ¼ in (6 mm). Press. Pin in place (above), or baste. Topstitch ⅛ in (3 mm) from the fold.

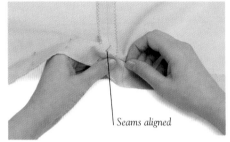

Seams aligned

2 SECURE THE HEM by using vertical hemming stitch (above) or slipstitch (p. 76). When the stitching is complete, remove the pins and the basting, and lightly press the hem allowance flat.

PINKED AND STITCHED

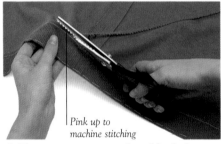

Pink up to machine stitching

1 THIS IS USED on nonfrayable, light- or mediumweight fabrics. Turn up the hem allowance, and pin or baste. Stitch ¼ in (6 mm) in from the edge, and trim close to the stitching with pinking shears (above). (If the hem is easestitched, trim to the easestitching using pinking shears.)

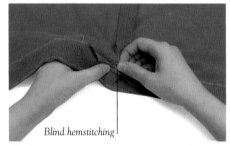

Blind hemstitching

2 TURN BACK THE HEM EDGE, and blind hemstitch (p. 76) along the line of machine stitching, securing the hem to the garment (above). Remove the pins or basting from the hem, and lightly press the seam allowance flat, pressing on the wrong side of the garment.

MACHINE STITCHED AND OVERCAST

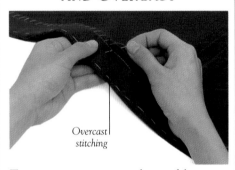

Overcast stitching

TO PREVENT FRAYING on heavy fabrics that cannot be zigzag stitched, stitch ¼ in (6 mm) in from the hem edge (if the hem is not easestitched). Overcast the edge (above), and blindstitch the hem.

ZIGZAG-STITCHED AND STITCHED

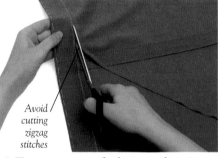

Avoid cutting zigzag stitches

1 THIS IS SUITABLE for knits, such as jersey, and light- or mediumweight fabrics with a tendency to fray. Zigzag stitch inside the hem edge using a medium-length, fairly close zigzag stitch. Trim the excess fabric up to the stitches (above).

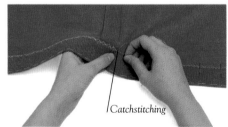

Catchstitching

2 SECURE THE HEM (above) using catchstitch (p. 76). (If there is easestitching, pull the stitching up after zigzag stitching. Always test the zigzag stitch on a piece of scrap fabric before stitching the garment. If it is too loose or tight, adjust the stitch to suit the fabric.)

HAND-ROLLED HEM ON SHEER FABRIC

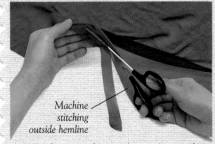

Machine stitching outside hemline

1 Machine stitch ¼ in (6 mm) outside the hemline, and trim the fabric ⅛ in (3 mm) from the stitching (above). Fold under ⅛ in (3 mm) from the hemline.

2 Quick slipstitch (p. 74) through the fold and the fabric ⅛ in (3 mm) below (above). Stitch alternately, rolling the hem in place, while pulling the thread.

Hemline basting

Hem allowance

Hem edge

1 To give added support to extra-wide hems or heavy fabrics, work a double-stitched hem. Finish the hem edge (p. 205). Baste a line halfway between the basting and the hem edge (above).

2 Fold the hem allowance back along the basting, and blind catchstitch (p. 76) the inside of the hem fold to the garment (above). When stitching, use fairly long stitches, about ⅜ in (1 cm) in length.

3 Turn the hem up and stitch again with blind catchstitch, this time along the hem edge (above). (Double stitching can be used on hems with covered or uncovered edges.)

SEWING HEMS BY HAND – COVERED HEM EDGES

On UNLINED GARMENTS where the inside seams are visible and a finished look is required, hem edges can be covered with seam or bias binding, or bound with a bias strip. Covered hem edges are also suitable for curved edges, for fabrics that stretch or unravel, such as knits, and for bulky fabrics, satin, velvet, and fabrics that fray.

SEAM BINDING

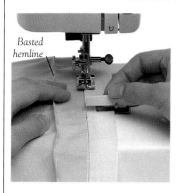

Basted hemline

USE WOVEN-EDGED seam binding for straight hems. Beginning at a seam, lap the wrong side of the seam binding ¼ in (6 mm) over the right side of the hem edge. Pin and edgestitch, turning in the second end at a seam (left). Turn up the hem, press, and slipstitch in place.

BIAS BINDING

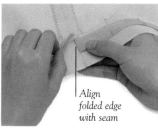

Align folded edge with seam

1 USE THIS for curved hems. Open one fold of ½-in (12-mm) wide bias binding. Place the crease just below the hem edge easestitching, on the right side. Fold in the end and align with a seam. Pin in position (left).

Stitched bias binding crease

2 OPEN the hem out flat. Stitch along the binding crease (left). Close to the end, trim the binding to overlap the ends. Stitch. Fold the binding up, pressing the hem in place. Secure the free edge to the fabric using slipstitch or blind hemstitch (p. 76).

BOUND HEM

1 THIS IS SUITABLE for heavy and silky fabrics. Pin either a ½-in (12-mm) commercial bias binding strip, or a 1-in (2.5-cm) bias strip cut from lining fabric to the hem edge. Align the edges, right sides together. Stitch ¼ in (6 mm) in from the edge, overlapping the strip ends (left).

2 PRESS the binding upwards. Wrap it over the hem edge, down to the inside of the hem, and press again. (If using bias binding, unfold along the unstitched edge.) Pin the strip in place. On the right side, stitch in the groove formed by the first row of stitching (left). Remove the pins.

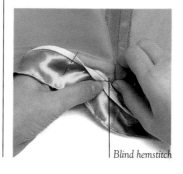

Blind hemstitch

3 TURN UP and pin the hem. Secure (left) using blind hemstitch (p. 76). Remove the pins. (When binding a satin or velvet hem edge, use a soft, woven bias strip or a jersey binding strip. Test the bias strip on a small piece of the fabric before working on the garment.)

SEWING HEMS BY MACHINE

A MACHINE-FINISHED HEM is quick to sew and forms a strong finish. Since the machine stitching will show on the right side, the hem stitching line must be neat and exactly parallel with the folded hemline. Narrow hems suit blouses, shirts, and casual flared skirts. Topstitched hems complement items with other topstitched details.

NARROW HEM

1 MARK THE HEMLINE, and trim the hem allowance to ½ in (12 mm). Press ¼ in (6 mm) of the hem edge to the wrong side twice (above).

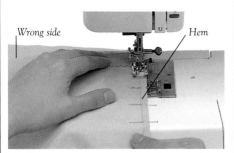

2 PIN THE HEM, matching the seamlines and aligning the grain on the hem and garment to avoid stretching and causing puckering. Stitch close to the inside fold on the wrong side (above).

TOPSTITCHED HEM

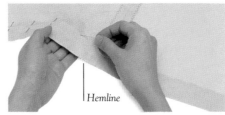

1 MARK, FOLD UP, and pin the hem. Baste near the hemline. Trim the hem allowance. Press ⅜ in (1 cm) under along the hem edge. Baste near the fold (above).

2 TOPSTITCH on the right side (above), using either straight or zigzag stitch, or any desired decorative stitch. Use the machine gauge for guidance in keeping a straight line when topstitching.

MACHINE-STITCHED BLIND HEMMING

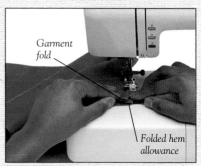

Garment fold
Folded hem allowance

This type of hem is stitched using the blind hem foot. Mark the hemline, fold, and baste the hem allowance close to the hemline. Trim the hem allowance and turn under ⅜ in (1 cm). Press. Set the machine to blind hemstitch. Lay the hem allowance down, so that the folded edge of the hem allowance is visible but the raw edge is hidden. Fold the garment back to the basting line, and stitch the folded hem allowance to the garment, catching the garment fold at intervals (above).

FINISHING A HEM

I F THERE IS A FACED OPENING on a hem edge, the facing hem can be stitched either by hand or by machine. The handstitching method is ideal for all types of light- and mediumweight fabrics, while the machine-stitching method is better for jackets and coats in medium- to heavyweight fabrics. Piped hemlines are suitable for home furnishings.

HANDSTITCHING A FACING HEM

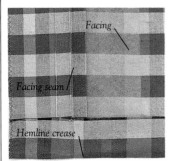

Facing
Facing seam
Hemline crease

1 UNFOLD THE FACING at the hem, and press open the facing seam. Fold up the hem, and press in a sharp crease along the hemline.

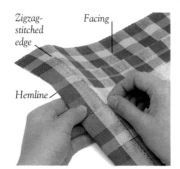

Zigzag-stitched edge
Facing
Hemline

2 UNFOLD THE HEM, and trim the hem edge if necessary. Zigzag stitch the edge. Then fold up the hem and pin it in place (above).

Catchstitch

3 HANDSTITCH (p. 76) the hem along its entire length, including the facing hem (above). Fold the facing to the inside and press.

Be sure that stitches do not go through to right side

4 SLIPSTITCH the lower edge of the facing to the hemline. Then hemstitch the inner edge of the facing to the hem allowance (above).

MACHINE STITCHING A FACING HEM

Hem allowance
Interfacing
Facing
Hemline

1 MARK the hemline on the facings and garment with a row of running stitches. On the hem allowance, mark with a pin the point that the facing reaches when it has been folded in (left). Then trim away any excess interfacing up to the hemline.

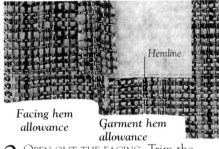

Hemline

Facing hem allowance   **Garment hem allowance**

2 OPEN OUT THE FACING. Trim the facing hem allowance to ⅝ in (1.5 cm) wide. Trim the first part of the garment hem allowance to 1 in (2.5 cm) wide, ending ½ in (12 mm) from the position marked by the pin.

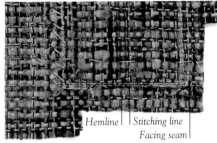

Hemline | *Stitching line*
Facing seam

3 FOLD THE FACING to the garment with right sides together. Align the marked hemlines and pin them. Stitch along the hemline from the outer edge of the facing to the facing seam, pivot, and stitch along the seam for 1 in (2.5 cm).

FINISHING A PIPED HEMLINE

Pipe the hemline (see Piping a Hemline, right). Where the ends of the piping will be caught into a seam, trim the inner cord back to the seamline. If the piping ends at a finished edge, whipstitch together the turned-under edges of the piping cord covering (below).

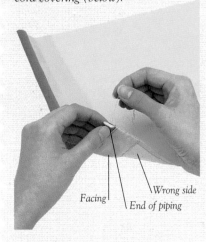

Facing | *Wrong side*
End of piping

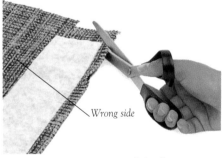

Wrong side

4 TRIM THE CORNERS of the hem allowance diagonally, close to the interfacing corners (above). Finish off the hem edge at this stage of the work if desired.

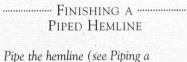

5 TURN the facing right side out. Handstitch the facing edge to the hem allowance. Complete the hem and press (above).

PIPING A HEMLINE

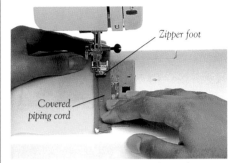

Zipper foot
Covered piping cord

1 PIN THE COVERED PIPING (p. 91) to the right side, with the hemline and the piping stitching aligned. Stitch in place using a zipper foot (above).

Wrong side

2 BASTE THE FACING TO THE HEM with right sides together and raw edges even, enclosing the piping. Stitch even closer to the cord (above).

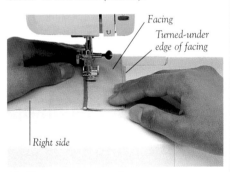

Facing
Turned-under edge of facing
Right side

3 TRIM AND LAYER the seam allowances and press them toward the facing. Understitch (p. 84) the facing, using the zipper foot (above).

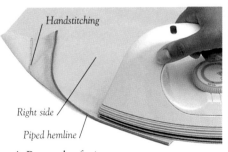

Handstitching
Right side
Piped hemline

4 PRESS the facing to the inside so that the piping forms a decorative hemline (above). Handstitch the edge of the facing in place.

HEMMING LININGS

O N JACKETS, SLEEVES, AND VESTS, and on most lined drapes, the lining hem is stitched to the main fabric; on skirts and coats, the lining is usually free-hanging (p. 102). In both methods, the lining is first attached to the garment (or drapes), leaving the last 6 in (15 cm) of each side edge unstitched. Then the hem is finished.

ATTACHED LINING

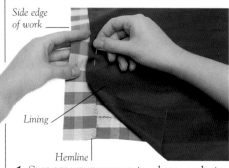

Side edge of work

Lining

Hemline

1 SMOOTH THE LINING in place, and pin, positioning the pins in a row at right angles to the hemline, and 6 in (15 cm) above it (above). If hemming a garment, try it on first to check the fit. (If possible, have a helper do the pinning.)

Row of pins above hemline

2 TRIM THE LINING to ⅝ in (1.5 cm) longer than the garment or curtain hemline (above). If the lining hem needs easestitching, machine stitch ⅜ in (1 cm) from the trimmed lining edge, using a long stitch setting (p. 89).

Side edge of work

Lining fold

3 TURN THE LINING under by 1 in (2.5 cm) so that the lining fold is ⅜ in (1 cm) above the hemline. Then pin the lining to the garment or curtain ⅜ in (1 cm) from the fold (above). Remove the pins that were inserted in Step 1.

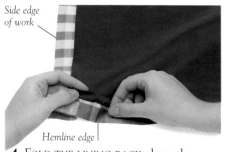

Side edge of work

Hemline edge

4 FOLD THE LINING BACK along the pinline. Slipstitch the lining and main hem allowances together (above), catching only one layer of the main fabric and one layer of lining fabric, so that the stitches do not show through onto the right side of the lining or main fabric.

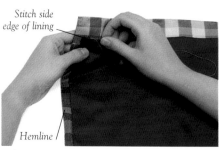

Stitch side edge of lining

Hemline

5 REMOVE ALL THE PINS holding the lining hem in place. Then lightly press the lining hemline fold, which will hang down below the line of slipstitches made in Step 4. Finally, slipstitch any remaining lining edges to the garment or to the drapery facings (above).

USING ATTACHED CURTAIN LININGS

Although linings with attached hems take longer to make up, and require more careful stitching than free-hanging linings, a slipstitched hem gives a sophisticated and professional-looking finish to curtains, especially curtains made from medium- to heavyweight fabrics. An attached lining should always be used for wide and full-length curtains.

FREE-HANGING LINING

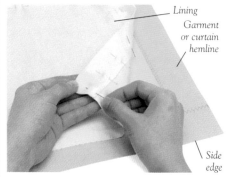

Lining

Garment or curtain hemline

Side edge

1 ATTACH THE LINING, leaving the lower side edges open, and turn it under to make a fold 1 in (2.5 cm) above the main hemline. Press, and turn under ¼ in (6 mm) of the hem edge. Pin (above).

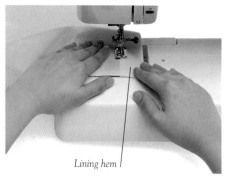

Lining hem

2 BASTE THE HEM EDGE of the lining in place, and remove the pins. Machine stitch the turned-under lining hem edge (above). Remove the basting from the lining. Then press the lining hem.

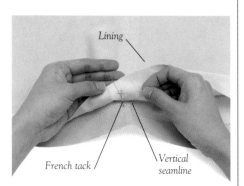

Lining

French tack

Vertical seamline

3 AT EACH VERTICAL SEAMLINE, attach the lining to the garment or curtain with a 1 in (2.5 cm) long French tack (above). The French tacks (p. 78) will keep the lining from billowing out.

MAKING CUFFS ON PANTS

CUFFS CAN EASILY BE ADDED to a pants or shorts pattern that does not have them. On straight pants the seams of the cuffs are straight, while for tapered pants the cuffs are shaped. The desired length of the finished pants can be obtained by measuring from the waistline down the side seam of existing pants.

ADDING STRAIGHT CUFFS TO A PANTS PATTERN

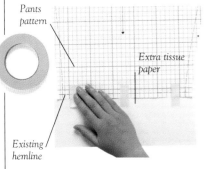

Pants pattern

Extra tissue paper

Existing hemline

1 DETERMINE the desired finished pant length. Decide on the cuff depth, double it, and add 1¼ in (3 cm). This gives the additional length needed. Tape extra tissue paper on to the pattern (left).

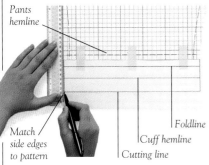

Pants hemline

Match side edges to pattern

Cuff hemline

Cutting line

Foldline

2 MARK the pants hemline, the foldline at the top of the cuff, and the cuff hemline. Add a cutting line 1¼ in (3 cm) below the bottom line. Mark the straight side edges of the cuff (left).

ADDING SHAPED CUFFS TO A PANTS PATTERN

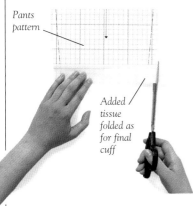

Pants pattern

Added tissue folded as for final cuff

1 TAPE extra tissue paper to the pattern piece. Then mark the hemline, the foldline, and the cuff hemline, adding 1¼ in (3 cm) on the pattern (see Step 2, above). Fold up the tissue to form the cuff, and trim it at the sides so that it is fractionally wider than the pants leg (left).

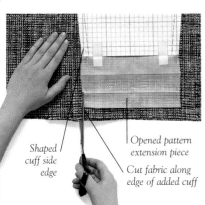

Shaped cuff side edge

Opened pattern extension piece

Cut fabric along edge of added cuff

2 OPEN OUT the pattern piece. The sides of the cuffs are now shaped to fit the pants leg, including the seam allowances. Cut out the pants pieces, taking care to shape the side edges of the cuff to match exactly the pattern for the new cuff (left).

HEMMING CUFFS ON PANTS

Baste along cuff hemline

Cuff foldline

1 BEFORE MAKING the pants, make sure that the pants hemline and the cuff foldline and hemline have all been transferred to the fabric. Sew the pants. Press the leg seams open, and finish the hem edge. Fold the fabric to the wrong side at the cuff foldline. Pin, and baste along the cuff hemline (left).

2 HANDSTITCH (left) or machine stitch the hem allowance in place along the hem edge. (If machine stitching the hem, ensure that the stitching line will be low enough to be covered by the cuff once this has been folded to the right side of the pants.) Press the hem on the wrong side of the garment.

Basted hemline

Cuff

3 TURN the pants right side out. Then fold the cuff to the right side of the pants along the basted hemline. Pin the cuff in place (left), and baste close to the fold through all thicknesses of the pants fabric. Remove the pins. Press the cuff lightly on the right side of the pants, using a sleeve board.

Vertical seam

Right side of pants leg

French tack

4 AT EACH vertical seam, sew a short French tack ⅜ in (1 cm) down from the top of the cuff to prevent the cuff from falling down (left). Remove all basting, and press the cuff again. (Alternatively, secure the cuff by machine stitching vertically down the cuff along the indentation of the pants seams. If this is stitched very precisely, it will be invisible.)

211

HEMMING PLEATS

MOST PLEATED GARMENTS and home furnishings are hemmed after pleating. Only in cases where the design of a garment allows the length to be altered by making adjustments at the waist can hemming take place before pleating. The basting on the pleat folds should be removed for 8 in (20 cm) from the hem edge before hemming.

SEAM AT FLAT PART

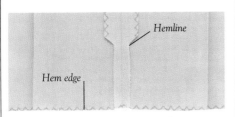

Hemline

Hem edge

1 WHERE A HEM will cover a flat, pressed-open seam, trim the seam allowance to half its width between the hemline and the hem edge.

2 FINISH THE HEM EDGE, and complete the hem (above), using the hemming method that is best for the fabric (p. 206–209). Ensure the seam aligns.

SEAM AT BACK FOLD

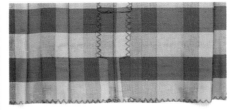

1 ON A HEM covering a back fold seam, trim the seam allowance between the hem edge and hemline (above), and trim across a hem's width above the hemline.

Hem edge stitched close to fold

2 PRESS OPEN the hem seam allowances, and sew the hem in place. Whipstitch (p. 74) together the seam allowance edges above the hem (above).

PLEATED CORNERS

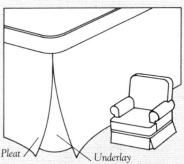

Pleat   *Underlay*

The valance hem on a bedspread or chair cover with pleated corners is stitched before the valance is sewn in place. Each pleated corner uses a separate underlay so that the pleat spreads slightly at the bottom edge. Check that the hemlines of the drop sections of the valance are level on all sides of the bed or chair before sewing the valance in place at the top edge.

FLAT SEAM STITCHED AFTER HEMMING

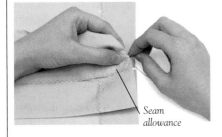

Seam allowance

ON a flat seam stitched after hemming, press the seam open, trim diagonally across both lower corners of the seam allowances, and whipstitch the corners to the hem (left).

CLOSED SEAM STITCHED AFTER HEMMING

ON a back fold seam stitched after hemming, press the seam flat to one side. Then trim the seam allowance corners diagonally, and whipstitch the trimmed corners together.

HEMMING SPECIAL FABRICS

THERE ARE SPECIAL HEMMING TECHNIQUES for lace, fur, and leather fabrics. Lace can usually have a rolled or a conventional turned-up hem, but when it has a self-edge of scallops, the scalloped edge may have to be moved to follow a curved hemline. Another alternative for edging a lace fabric is to appliqué a lace trim along the hemline.

SCALLOPED LACE ON A CURVED HEM

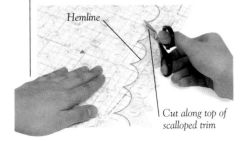

Hemline

Cut along top of scalloped trim

1 PIN THE LACE onto the pattern, with the scalloped edge along the hemline. Cut along the top of the scalloped trim where the hemline curves up (left).

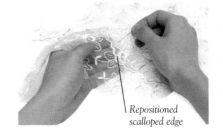

Repositioned scalloped edge

2 EASE the cut trim in place so that the tips of the scallops fall along the hemline. Pin in place (left), and baste. Cut out the garment. Whipstitch (p. 74) the cut edge of the lace onto the fabric.

APPLIQUÉD LACE EDGING

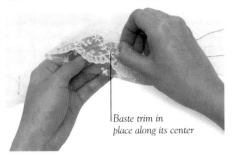

Baste trim in place along its center

1 To FINISH a lace fabric with a lace edge trim, mark the garment hemline. Place the trim on the right side of the fabric. Aligning its lower edge with the hemline, pin and baste the trim in place (above).

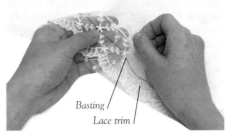

Basting
Lace trim

2 STITCH THE UPPER EDGE of the lace trim to the garment lace fabric, using whipstitch (above) or narrow zigzag stitch. (Narrow zigzag stitch is also suitable for attaching a scalloped hem [p. 216].)

3 CUT AWAY the excess garment fabric from underneath, close to the lace trim (above). (On heavy lace fabric, make a turned-up hem. Alternatively, face the hem with a suitable lining fabric.)

FUR FABRIC

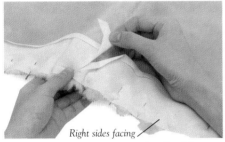

Right sides facing

1 MARK THE HEMLINE on the fur fabric, and trim the hem allowance to 1¼ in (3 cm). Pin a bias strip of lining to the hem edge, turning in and overlapping the strip ends (above). Stitch the strip and fur together ¼ in (6 mm) from the raw edges.

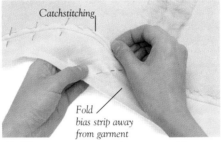

Catchstitching
Fold bias strip away from garment

2 TURN THE HEM to the wrong side along the hemline, and baste along the fold. Keeping the bias strip downward, pin the strip and the fur seam allowances to the garment. Then catchstitch the bias strip in place (above).

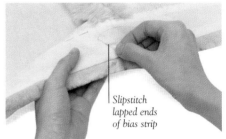

Slipstitch lapped ends of bias strip

3 PRESS THE FACING upward to cover the catchstitched edges. Pin the facing to the wrong side of the garment, and stitch. Slipstitch the lapped ends in place (above). To finish, remove the basting, and press the facing lightly.

TOPSTITCHED LEATHER HEM

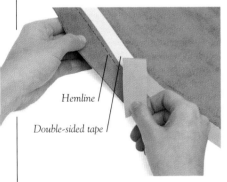

Hemline
Double-sided tape

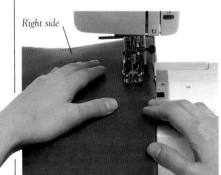

Right side

1 MARK the hemline, and trim the hem allowance to ⅝ in (1.5 cm). Stick a strip of double-sided adhesive tape to the wrong side of the garment above the hemline (left). Turn the hem to the wrong side so that it sticks to the tape.

2 WITH the right side facing up on the machine, topstitch ½ in (12 mm) from the hemline fold (left). (Paper clips can be used to secure the hem before stitching, instead of tape. For a very strong hem, use glue [see right].)

GLUED LEATHER HEM

Snip notches on curved hems to ease in fullness

Notched and glued hem

1 MARK the hemline, and trim the hem allowance to 2 in (5 cm). Mark a line 4 in (10 cm) from the edge of the hem, and turn the hem up to this line, securing it with paper clips. Notch the hem where necessary so that it lies flat (left).

2 UNCLIP the hem. Spread a suitable glue on the wrong side up to the marked line. Turn up the hem, and finger press in place. Gently pound the hem with a flat block of wood (left). Allow the glue to dry before moving the garment.

MAKING A FACED HEM

H EM FACINGS CAN BE EITHER SHAPED or made from bias strips. A shaped facing is used for asymmetrical hems, such as those on wrap skirts. Since they stretch to shape, bias strips are suitable as facings on flared skirts or other curved hems. They can also be used on bulky fabrics, or where a hem allowance is too narrow for a turned-up hem.

ATTACHING A SHAPED HEM FACING

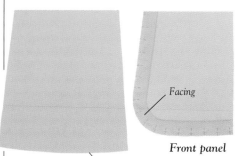

Back panel *Back panel hem edge* *Facing* **Front panel**

1 CUT a 1½-in (4-cm) wide, L-shaped facing for the curved front panel. Finish the inner edge of the facing (p. 206). With right sides together, pin the facing to the curved front panel (above). Stitch, trim, and clip the seam.

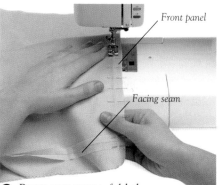

Front panel *Facing seam*

2 PRESS THE SEAM, fold the facing to the inside, and press again. Finish the hem edge of the skirt back. Open out the facing at the lower edge of the front. Pin and stitch the front to the back at the side seam (above).

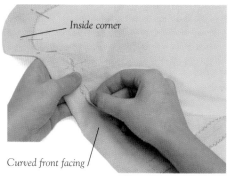

Inside corner *Curved front facing*

3 PRESS THE FACING to the inside again. Pin, then slipstitch the back hem and front facings in place (above). Continue the stitching to just around the inside corner of the facing (the vertical front edge of the facing is not stitched).

CUTTING AND JOINING BIAS STRIPS

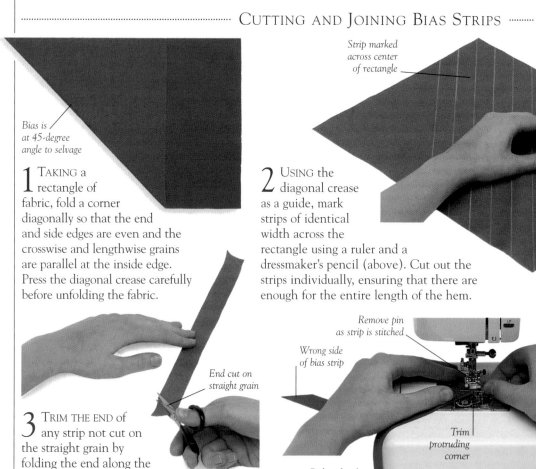

Bias is at 45-degree angle to selvage

1 TAKING a rectangle of fabric, fold a corner diagonally so that the end and side edges are even and the crosswise and lengthwise grains are parallel at the inside edge. Press the diagonal crease carefully before unfolding the fabric.

2 USING the diagonal crease as a guide, mark strips of identical width across the rectangle using a ruler and a dressmaker's pencil (above). Cut out the strips individually, ensuring that there are enough for the entire length of the hem.

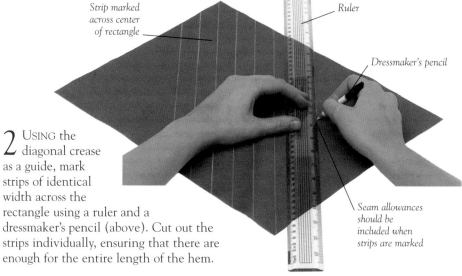

Strip marked across center of rectangle *Ruler* *Dressmaker's pencil* *Seam allowances should be included when strips are marked*

End cut on straight grain

3 TRIM THE END of any strip not cut on the straight grain by folding the end along the straight grain to form a 45-degree angle with the long edges of the bias strip. Trim along the crease (above). Mark a ¼-in (6-mm) seam allowance at each end.

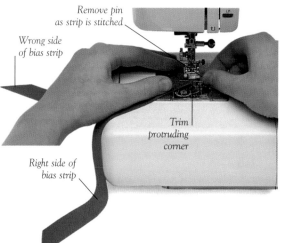

Remove pin as strip is stitched *Wrong side of bias strip* *Trim protruding corner* *Right side of bias strip*

4 TO JOIN two strips, lay them right sides together, matching the seamlines exactly so that the strips form a V shape, and pin. Stitch the strips together (left), and press the seam open. Trim the protruding corners of each seam allowance. Continue to join strips in this way until the facing is long enough to fit the hem edge.

CUTTING A CONTINUOUS BIAS STRIP

Corner cut away along bias

Lengthwise grain

1 TO JOIN SEVERAL BIAS STRIPS AT ONCE, first mark the strips across a rectangle of fabric (see opposite). Cut away the corners outside the marks at both ends of the rectangle (above). Mark ¼-in (6-mm) seam allowances, following the fabric grain across the top and bottom of the marked bias strips.

One strip end extends beyond each edge

2 WITH RIGHT SIDES together, pin the marked edges, leaving one strip out all along. Stitch. Remove the pins, and press the seam open (below).

SHAPING A BIAS STRIP

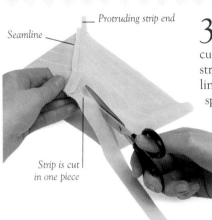

Use tip of iron to hold edge

Bias strip stretched into curve

If a bias strip is to be attached to a curved edge, first press it into the shape of the curve. Set the iron to steam. Use the tip of the iron to hold one edge, and gently stretch the opposite edge into a curve. As each section is shaped, press it under full steam to set the shape (above). Let cool before continuing.

Protruding strip end

Seamline

Strip is cut in one piece

3 BEGINNING at one end of the tube of fabric, cut a continuous bias strip along the marked lines, which now form a spiral (left). When cutting across the seam, make sure that it is kept open and that the seam allowances are flat. After cutting the strip, press the seams open again.

ATTACHING A BIAS HEM FACING

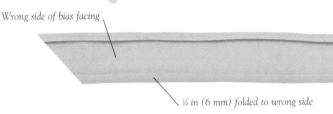

Wrong side of bias facing

¼ in (6 mm) folded to wrong side

1 MAKE A BIAS FACING from a strip 2¼ in (6 cm) wide and as long as the hem edge, plus 3 in (7.5 cm). Press ¼ in (6 mm) to the wrong side on each long edge (above). Trim the garment hem allowance to ¼ in (6 mm). Unfold one long edge of the strip, and pin it to the garment hem, right sides together.

2 TURN IN one short end, and stitch along the crease on the facing, finishing just before the end. Trim the other end of the facing so that it overlaps the first by ¼ in (6 mm). Stitch the facing in place until the stitching lines join (right).

Right side of garment

Wrong side of facing

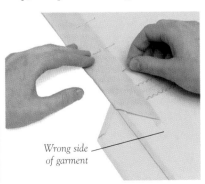

Wrong side of garment

3 PRESS the seam open. Fold the facing to the wrong side of the garment, aligning it with the seamline, and rolling the seam so that it lies toward the inside of the garment and is not visible. Pin the facing in place (left).

Facing ends

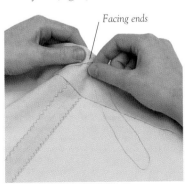

4 PRESS the facing firmly in place, and stitch the facing securely to the garment, using either slipstitch (p. 76) or hemstitch (p. 76). Slipstitch the ends of the facing together (left).

MAKING A SCALLOPED SKIRT EDGE

THE CIRCUMFERENCE OF THE SKIRT EDGE on a scalloped hem must be exactly divisible by the width of the scallop. A scallop width can be chosen and adjusted to fit the hem exactly. A scallop template should be made with the aid of a pair of compasses, a saucer, or plate. The scallop may be a half circle, or shallower, as desired.

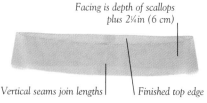

Facing is depth of scallops plus 2¼ in (6 cm)

Vertical seams join lengths | *Finished top edge*

Lower edge

1 CUT a hem facing on the bias for a flared skirt, or on the straight grain for a slim skirt. Join the lengths together.

2 PIN the facing to the hem with right sides together and lower raw edges even. Baste along the top finished edge. Then baste along the lower edge (left). Remove all the pins.

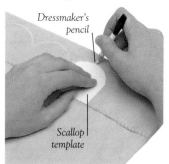

Dressmaker's pencil

Scallop template

Seam allowance should be notched at curves

3 USING the template and starting at a seam, draw the scalloped stitching line (above). Baste the hem and facing together near the stitching line and stitch.

4 TRIM (above). Clip the corners. Notch the curves and remove the basting. Turn the facing to the inside. Press. Stitch the hem in place.

MAKING A SCALLOPED CURTAIN EDGE

A SCALLOPED HEADING can be used on a flat blind or a pleated curtain. There should be at least ⅝ in (1.5 cm) between the scallops on a blind, and extra for the pleats on a pleated curtain. The width of the scallops should be designed to fit the heading length exactly. A template of the scallop is used to mark the fabric before stitching.

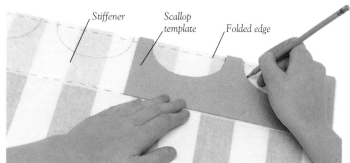

Stiffener   *Scallop template*   *Folded edge*

1 ALLOW FOR A SELF-FACING at the top that is the depth of the scallops plus 2¼ in (6 cm). Fold the facing edge ⅜ in (1 cm) under. Press. Fold the facing to the right side. Baste stiffener to the wrong side of the blind or curtain top. Mark the scalloped stitching line on the stiffener using the template (above).

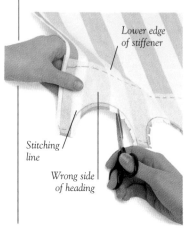

Lower edge of stiffener

Stitching line

Wrong side of heading

2 BASTE all the layers of fabric together along the marked scalloped stitching line. Then stitch the scallops, beginning and ending all the stitching with a few backstitches to secure. Remove the basting along the scallops. Trim the stiffener close to the stitches. Clip and notch the seam allowances to ease the curves (left). Remove the basting along the lower edge of the stiffener.

MAKING AN ELFIN HEM

Make a pointed elfin hem in the same way as a scalloped skirt edge (see above). For the points to be even, the circumference of the hem must be divisible by the width of the pointed template. To give the hem a floaty appearance, cut both the main fabric and the facing on the bias grain (right).

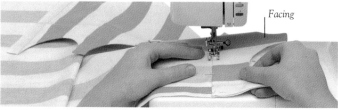

Facing

3 TURN THE FACING TO THE WRONG SIDE so that it covers the width of the stiffener. Pin in place. Stitch the facing to the curtain along the hemmed sides and along the folded-under edge at the lower edge of the self-facing (above). Press.

HEMMING CURTAINS

CURTAINS WITH THE HEMS PINNED IN PLACE should be allowed to hang unstitched for a few days so that they can drop. The curtain lining is always hemmed separately.

For a neat finish, the corners of the curtain hems should be mitered. After hemming the curtains, the hem of the lining is simply machine stitched in place for ease and speed.

MITERING A CURTAIN HEM CORNER

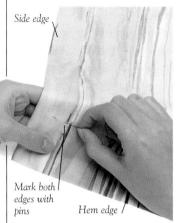

Side edge

Mark both edges with pins

Hem edge

1 FOLD ¼ in (6 mm) to the wrong side along the side edges and the hem edge. Fold the side edges and hem over to the inside. Mark with pins where the side and inner hem edges meet (above).

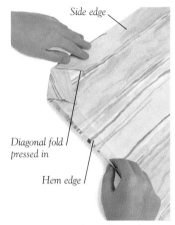

Side edge

Diagonal fold pressed in

Hem edge

2 UNFOLD the side and hem edges, then press a diagonal line through the pinned points, intersecting the corner point. Refold the side and hem turnings to miter the corner (above).

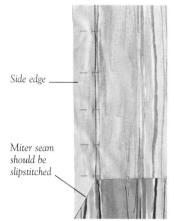

Side edge

Miter seam should be slipstitched

3 PIN THE MITER, the hem, and the side edges in place (above). Slipstitch the miter seam together. Then finish the side edges and the hem edge as appropriate and remove all the pins.

A DOUBLE HEM

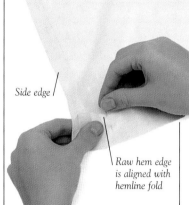

Side edge

Raw hem edge is aligned with hemline fold

TO DETERMINE the hem allowance, double the hem depth and fold over to the wrong side. Stitch the side edges. Then fold the hem in half, and pin (above). Hemstitch to finish.

WEIGHTING CURTAINS

TO PREVENT CURTAINS from billowing, put weights, either individual or in the form of a chain, at the hemline. Individual weights should be positioned at the bottom of seams and at the side edges to prevent puckering. For curtains that gap or billow at the sides, consider anchoring the lower corners to the wall or window frame.

SHEER CURTAINS

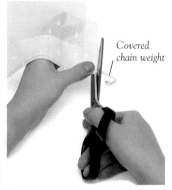

Covered chain weight

FOR SHEER or lightweight curtains, slip a covered chain weight through the hem. Anchor the weight with a few stitches at the side edges and at any vertical seam. Trim off the ends of the chain even with the side edges (above).

UNLINED CURTAINS

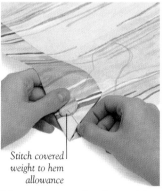

Stitch covered weight to hem allowance

MAKE POCKETS for the weights by cutting fabric to the size of each weight, plus a seam allowance. Stitch, leaving an opening. Turn right side out, insert the weight, and stitch to close. Handstitch weights along the hem at intervals (above).

LINED CURTAINS

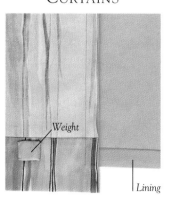

Weight

Lining

SEW THE WEIGHTS along the upper edge of the hem allowance so that they will be hidden between the curtain and the lining. The weights may be covered as for unlined curtains (see left), or stitched to the hem like buttons.

ANCHORING CURTAINS

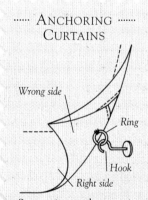

Wrong side

Ring

Hook

Right side

Sew a ring to the curtain edge within the hem. Hang the curtain. Screw a hook into the wall or the window frame. The hook should point down, level with the ring. Pull the ring over the hook.

EDGES

BINDING EDGES

BINDING IS A METHOD of finishing a raw edge by applying a strip of fabric. Banding is a variation in which a wider fabric strip is used. Both types can be made from contrasting fabric. Finished banding and binding can look very similar, but binding is generally narrower. Binding is most suitable for reversible garments and for sheer fabrics. Since banding, unlike binding, extends beyond the raw edges to which it is applied, it can be used to add length to a garment and is useful in cases where a wide contrasting band is required along an edge.

RELATED TECHNIQUES

Hand sewing stitches, p. 74
Making a plain seam, p. 82
Making topstitched seams, p. 87
Making a shaped
band neckline, p. 137
Making a continuous
bound cuff opening, p. 193
Marking a hemline, p. 204

MAKING AND ATTACHING BANDING

BANDING IS USED TO COVER AND EXTEND the raw edge of a garment. If used at the hem, no hem allowance is needed. The banding strip is cut on the straight grain for straight edges and on the bias for curved edges. On jersey fabrics, it is cut along the length of the fabric for straight edges, or across the width for curved edges.

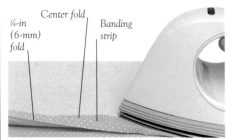

1 CUT A STRIP twice the required finished width, plus ½ in (12 mm). Press ¼ in (6 mm) to the wrong side along both long edges. Fold the strip in half lengthwise, with wrong sides together and pressed edges even. Press (above).

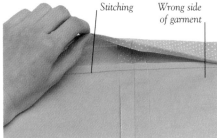

2 IF REQUIRED, join the ends of the strip together. Turn right side out. With right sides together, stitch one edge to the garment along the crease. Press the banding away from the garment, and refold along the center (above).

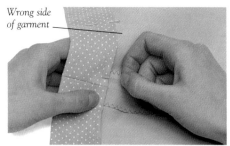

3 ALIGN the other folded edge of the banding with the previous stitching on the wrong side of the garment, enclosing the raw edges. Pin in place (above). Slipstitch, ensuring that the stitches do not show on the right side.

QUICK JERSEY BANDING

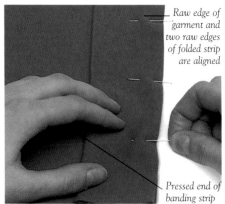

1 CUT A STRIP twice the required finished width, plus ½ in (12 mm). Press under the seam allowance of one short edge. Press in half lengthwise, wrong sides together. Pin the raw edges to the right side of the garment (above).

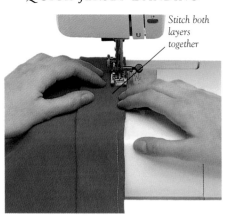

2 TUCK THE RAW EDGE of the end of the banding strip inside the pressed end so that the raw ends are completely hidden. Machine stitch both layers of the strip to the garment, leaving a ¼ in (6 mm) seam allowance (above).

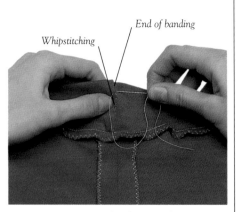

3 ZIGZAG STITCH both raw edges together. Press the banding away from the garment, and the seam allowance towards the garment. Whipstitch (p. 74) the pressed end of the banding to the end that is tucked inside (above).

MAKING AND ATTACHING BINDING

BINDING IS USED TO ENCLOSE a raw edge on a garment. It is made from a strip of fabric that is cut on the bias or the straight grain as for a banding strip (see opposite).

Unlike banding, binding does not extend the garment edge. Single binding can be used on any fabric, but double binding is advisable only on sheer fabrics.

PREPARING A STRIP FOR SINGLE BINDING

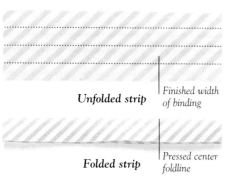

Unfolded strip | Finished width of binding

Folded strip | Pressed center foldline

1 CUT THE BINDING STRIP so that it is four times the required finished width (top). Fold the strip in half lengthwise, with the wrong sides together, and press it to form a crease (above).

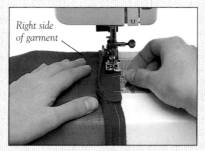

Central crease

2 OPEN OUT the binding strip. Fold both long edges over to the wrong side to meet at the center crease, and press. Refold the binding strip along its central crease (above), and press again.

SINGLE BINDING

1 PIN OR BASTE ONE EDGE of the binding to the garment, right sides together. Stitch along the binding crease. Fold the binding to the wrong side (above).

2 THE CENTER FOLD of the binding is now aligned with the encased raw edges. Align the folded-under edge with the previous stitching on the wrong side. Then pin this edge in place (above).

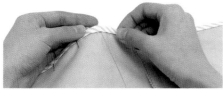

3 SLIPSTITCH THE BINDING to the line of previous stitching, or just above the previous stitching, on the inside (above). Take care that the stitches do not show on the right side of the garment. Press.

DOUBLE BINDING ON SHEER FABRICS

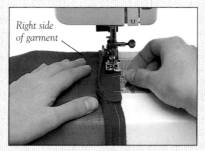

Right side of garment

1 *Cut a strip six times the finished width. Press in half, with wrong sides facing. Pin the doubled binding to the garment. Stitch the width of the binding in from the edge (above).*

Wrong side

2 *Turn the folded center edge of the binding to the wrong side, align it with the previous stitching, and pin in place (above). Slipstitch the doubled binding to the wrong side, as shown in Step 3 of Single Binding, left.*

TOPSTITCHED BINDING

Strip folded in half
Pressed center foldline

Sides of strip folded

1 CUT A STRIP as shown in Step 1, left. Fold the strip in two, with one side measuring ⅛ in (3 mm) wider than the other side (top). Press. Refold so that the edges meet at the center (above). Press.

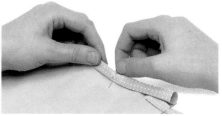

2 REFOLD THE BINDING along the center fold. With the narrower half of the binding on the right side, sandwich the raw edges of the garment inside the binding, and pin in place (above).

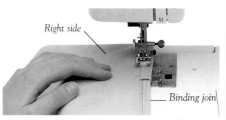

Right side

Binding join

3 AT THE BINDING JOIN, turn under the raw edge of the binding at one end, and overlap the other end. With the narrower half of the binding uppermost, topstitch close to the inner edge (above).

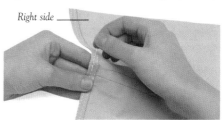

Right side

4 REMOVE any remaining pins. Then whipstitch (p. 74) the ends of the binding together at the join (above). When all the stitching has been completed, press the binding flat.

MITERING A DECORATIVE BIAS FACING

A DECORATIVE BIAS FACING is made from contrasting binding and is stitched in place to finish on the right side of the main fabric, forming a neat trim. The binding can be purchased ready-made, or it can be made using bias strips (p. 214–215) prepared by pressing ¼ in (6 mm) to the wrong side along both long edges.

INSIDE CORNER

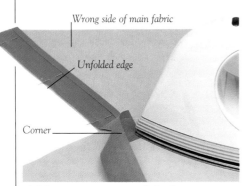

Wrong side of main fabric

Unfolded edge

Corner

1 UNFOLD ONE EDGE of the bias strip, and pin the right side of this edge to the wrong side of the main fabric up to the corner. Then fold the strip back onto itself diagonally at the corner, and press (above). Continue along the other edge.

Trim mitred seam

2 UNPIN THE STRIP from the fabric. With the strip still folded along one long edge, stitch the two layers together along the diagonal crease. Trim the corner to ¼ in (6 mm) from the stitching (above). Press the seam open.

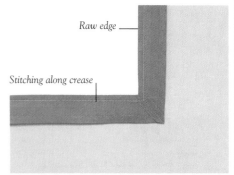

Raw edge

Stitching along crease

3 REPIN THE STRIP to the main fabric with the edges even. Then stitch the bias strip in place along the crease (above). Clip into the corner, and fold the strip to the right side. Press. Pin and stitch the other edge of the strip in place.

OUTSIDE CORNER

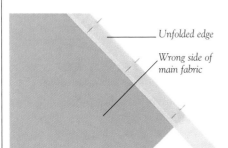

Unfolded edge

Wrong side of main fabric

1 UNFOLD one edge of the bias strip along the crease. With the right side of the strip to the wrong side of the fabric, pin up to the corner (above). Mark the strip with a pin where the corner of the stitching will be.

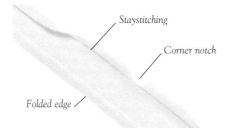

Staystitching

Corner notch

Folded edge

2 UNPIN the bias strip. Staystitch the opened crease for ⅜ in (1.5 cm) on each side of the corner mark. Cut a V-shaped notch in the unfolded edge of the strip at the mark.

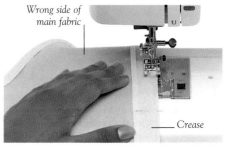

Wrong side of main fabric

Crease

3 REPIN THE BIAS STRIP to the fabric, again placing its right side to the wrong side of the fabric, and stitch it in place along the crease up to the corner. Pivot at the corner. Continue stitching along the other main fabric edge (above).

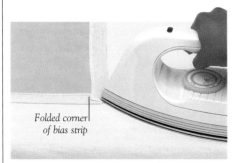

Folded corner of bias strip

4 FOLD THE BIAS STRIP at the corner so that the uppermost fold of the strip is aligned with the main fabric edge, and the underneath fold is folded diagonally across the corner. Then press in the corner folds (above).

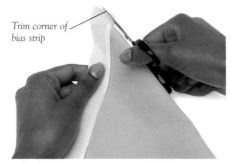

Trim corner of bias strip

5 UNFOLD THE STRIP, and – being careful to keep the main fabric out of the way – stitch the two layers of the bias strip together along the diagonal crease. Trim the corner of the strip ¼ in (6 mm) from the stitching line (above).

Push out corners

6 PRESS THE DIAGONAL seam open. Turn the bias strip to the right side of the main fabric (above). Press the strip on the right side, aligning the seam at the edge. Slipstitch the inner edge of the strip to the main fabric so that it lies flat.

MITERING A HEM

To CREATE A NEAT FINISH on a plain hem, the corners of the hem need to be mitered. Before a corner is mitered, the raw edge of the hem should be finished. This can be done with a zigzag stitch only, or by pressing ¼ in (6 mm) to the wrong side along the hem edge. A pressed-under hem edge should be kept folded while the miter is stitched.

Crease along top of hem allowance

1 PRESS THE HEM ALLOWANCE to the wrong side along both edges on each side of the corner. Unfold the hem allowance. Fold the corner to the wrong side diagonally across the point, then press in the fold (above).

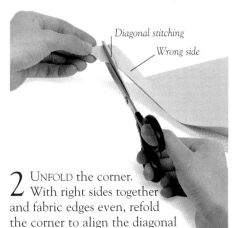

Diagonal stitching
Wrong side

2 UNFOLD the corner. With right sides together and fabric edges even, refold the corner to align the diagonal creases. Stitch along the crease. Trim the corner to ¼ in (6 mm) (above).

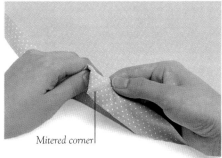

Mitered corner

3 PRESS THE DIAGONAL SEAM open. Turn the hem and the corner right side out: using a point turner or your finger, push out the corner from the inside so that it forms a sharp point (above). Press the hem, then handstitch to the wrong side.

MITERING A FLAT TRIM

BEFORE A FLAT TRIM SUCH AS BRAID or ribbon is attached along a hemline, the edge of the fabric should be finished by stitching a mitered hem to the wrong side (see above). Alternatively, ¼ in (6 mm) of the fabric can be pressed to the right side along the edge, so that the raw edge is covered and protected by the trim.

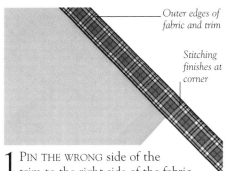

Outer edges of fabric and trim
Stitching finishes at corner

1 PIN THE WRONG side of the trim to the right side of the fabric, working along the outer edge and up to the corner. Stitch the trim to the fabric along the outer edge. Stop stitching at the corner.

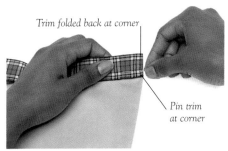

Trim folded back at corner
Pin trim at corner

2 FOLD THE TRIM back on itself at the corner of the fabric. Align the folded edge of the trim with the unstitched fabric edge. Pin the folded layers of the trim together on the unstitched edge at the corner (above).

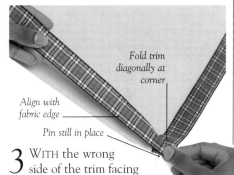

Fold trim diagonally at corner
Align with fabric edge
Pin still in place

3 WITH the wrong side of the trim facing the right side of the fabric, align the trim with the other fabric edge, folding it diagonally across the corner (above). Press.

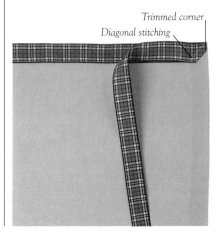

Trimmed corner
Diagonal stitching

4 FOLD the trim back on itself so that the unstitched portion of the trim is lying on top of the stitched part with right sides together. Stitch across the diagonal crease at the corner through the trim and fabric layers. Remove the pin. Trim the seam allowances at the corner to ¼ in (6 mm).

Mitred corner

5 UNFOLD the trim, and press the diagonal seam flat. Pin the trim to the other fabric edge, aligning the outer edge of the trim with the edge of the fabric. Stitch the trim in place along the outer edge, then stitch the inner edge of the trim to the fabric (left), pivoting at the inner corner of the hem.

ATTACHING MITERED BANDING

SINCE BANDING EXTENDS BEYOND the main fabric edge equally on the right and the wrong side, mitering inside and outside corners is not as easy as for simple bound edges. On woven banding, one edge is machine stitched in place and the other edge is handstitched to the wrong side. On jersey banding, both edges are machine stitched together. A banding strip is cut to twice the required finished width, plus two seam allowances.

WOVEN BANDING – INSIDE CORNER

Staystitching on main fabric

1 PRESS the seam allowances to the wrong side along both the long edges of the banding strip. Then staystitch just inside the seamline on both sides of the corner for 1 in (2.5 cm). Clip into the corner just to the staystitching (left).

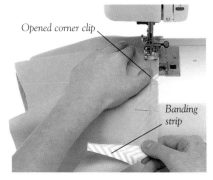

Opened corner clip

Banding strip

2 UNFOLD the pressed edge along one side of the banding strip. With right sides together and raw edges even, pin the banding edge to the main fabric, opening out the corner clip to fit the banding. Stitch in place (left).

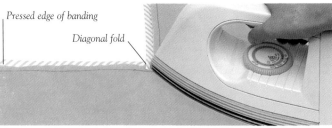

Pressed edge of banding

Diagonal fold

3 PRESS THE BANDING STRIP and the seam allowances away from the main fabric. At the inside corner, arrange the banding so that it folds diagonally across the corner on the right side. Press the diagonal fold in place (above).

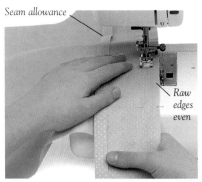

Handstitched pressed edge

4 FOLD the free edge of the banding to the wrong side. Arrange its pressed edge level with the stitching on the inside. Pin in place. At the corner, fold the banding diagonally. Handstitch in place (left). Remove the pins, and press.

WOVEN BANDING – OUTSIDE CORNER

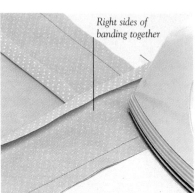

Seam allowance

Raw edges even

1 PRESS the seam allowances to the wrong side along both long edges of the banding. Unfold one pressed edge, and pin it to the fabric with right sides together. Stitch to within ⅝ in (1.5cm) from the corner.

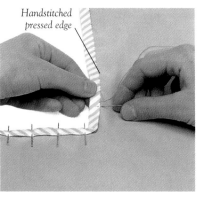

Banding folded diagonally, wrong sides together

2 FOLD the banding back on itself, with a diagonal fold even with the end of the stitching line. Press. On the unstitched edge, mark the distance of the finished width of banding away from the line of stitching with a pin (left).

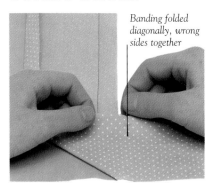

Right sides of banding together

3 FOLD the banding back on itself so that there is a straight fold across, even with the pin. Press. Align the edge of the banding with the fabric, placing it past the corner, and pin it to the fabric. Stitch along the crease from the fold to the end. Press flat (left).

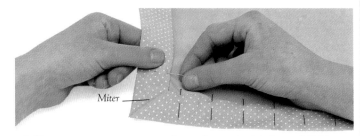

Miter

4 PRESS THE BANDING away from the main fabric, and fold the free edge of the banding to the wrong side, aligning it with the stitching on the inside. Fold the corner to form a neat miter on both sides. Pin (above), and slipstitch in place. Press.

JERSEY BANDING – INSIDE CORNER

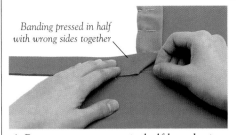

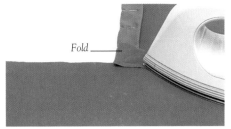

Banding pressed in half with wrong sides together

Fold

Seam allowances trimmed to ¼ in (6 mm)

Clip corner

1 PRESS THE BANDING in half lengthwise. Staystitch the corner of the main fabric, and clip into it. With right sides facing, pin banding to the main fabric, folding at the corner so remaining edges parallel (above).

2 FOLD THE BANDING back on itself so that the fold across its width is in line with the pinned raw edges of banding. Lightly press creases at the corner of the banding (above).

3 UNPIN the banding, and fold it across the corner, with right sides together. Stitch a V-shaped seam along the creases. Clip to the stitching (above).

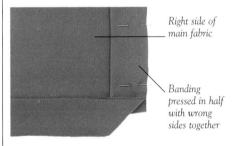

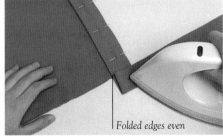

Right side

Clip opened out at fabric corner

Finished band extends beyond main fabric

4 OPEN OUT the banding, and press the V-shaped seam open. Then refold the banding in half lengthwise with wrong sides together and raw edges even. Press (above).

5 WITH RIGHT SIDES together, repin the fabric to the banding, opening out the clip in the fabric to fit around the corner on the banding. Stitch in place (above), pivoting at the corner.

6 FINISH the raw edges together, using a zigzag stitch. Press the seam allowance toward the main fabric, then press the banding away from the main fabric (above).

JERSEY BANDING – OUTSIDE CORNER

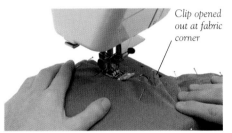

Right side of main fabric

Banding pressed in half with wrong sides together

Folded edges even

Seam stitched along pressed creases

1 PRESS THE BANDING in half lengthwise. With right sides facing, pin the banding to the main fabric up to the corner. Fold the banding back diagonally, level with the corner.

2 REFOLD THE BANDING back on itself so that its fold is aligned with the folded edge on the pinned part of the banding. Lightly press creases at the corner to mark the fold (above).

3 UNPIN THE BANDING, and open it out. Refold it across the corner, right sides together. Stitch a V-shaped seam along the diagonal creases. Trim the seam allowances to ¼ in (6 mm) (above).

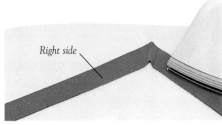

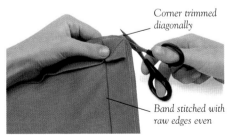

Right side

Corner trimmed diagonally

Band stitched with raw edges even

Whipstitching

4 OPEN OUT THE BANDING, and press the V-shaped seam open. Refold the banding in half lengthwise with wrong sides together and raw edges even. Then press the banding flat (above).

5 WITH RIGHT SIDES together, repin the banding to the main fabric, opening out the corner of the banding to fit. Stitch, pivoting at the corner. Trim the corner diagonally (above).

6 ZIGZAG STITCH the raw edges together. Press the banding away from the main fabric. Whipstitch the inner corner of the banding at the base of the diagonal seam (above).

MITERING BINDING

BINDING CAN BE MADE BY CUTTING a strip four times the required finished width. The seam allowance should be the same as the finished width of the binding.

On hand-finished binding, one edge is stitched by machine, and the other by hand. Topstitched binding (see opposite) is stitched in place with one row of machine stitching.

HAND-FINISHED BINDING – INSIDE CORNER

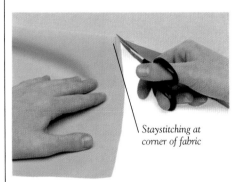

1 STAYSTITCH on each side of the corner for about 1 in (2.5 cm). Clip into the corner (left). Press the seam allowances of the binding to the wrong side along both edges of the binding strip.

Staystitching at corner of fabric

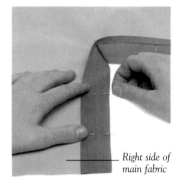

2 UNFOLD ONE EDGE of the binding strip. With right sides together and raw edges even, pin the unfolded edge of the binding strip to the main fabric. Open out the clipped corner, and stitch the binding in place along the crease. Fit the binding strip around the corner and pin in place (left).

Right side of main fabric

3 PRESS the binding away from the main fabric on the right side. Turn to the wrong side, and arrange the binding to form a diagonal fold across the corner on the right side of the fabric, and a straight fold to align with the stitching on the wrong side. Then press the folded corner (right).

Straight fold on wrong side

4 FOLD the free edge of the binding over to the wrong side. Slipstitch the pressed edge of the binding along the previous line of stitching. Arrange the binding with a neat diagonal fold across the corner. Continue slipstitching along the other edge of the binding (right).

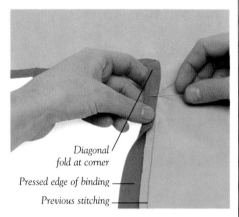

Diagonal fold at corner
Pressed edge of binding
Previous stitching

HAND-FINISHED BINDING – OUTSIDE CORNER

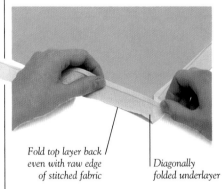

1 WITH right sides together and raw edges even, unfold and stitch one edge of the binding to the main fabric. Finish stitching a seam allowance width in from the edge. Miter the binding at the corner (left).

Fold top layer back even with raw edge of stitched fabric
Diagonally folded underlayer

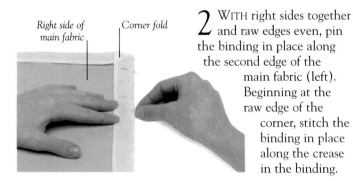

Right side of main fabric
Corner fold

2 WITH right sides together and raw edges even, pin the binding in place along the second edge of the main fabric (left). Beginning at the raw edge of the corner, stitch the binding in place along the crease in the binding.

Pressed edge *Wrong side*

3 Press the binding away from the main fabric. Fold the pressed edge of the binding to the wrong side. Arrange neat diagonal folds at the corner of the binding as before, and align the pressed edge with the previous line of stitching (above).

4 PIN the folded edges of the binding in place (right). Slipstitch the edge of the binding along the previous line of stitching. If the binding is wide, slipstitch across the diagonal corner fold on both the right and wrong sides.

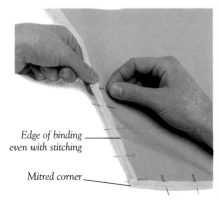

Edge of binding even with stitching

Mitred corner

TOPSTITCHED BINDING – INSIDE CORNER

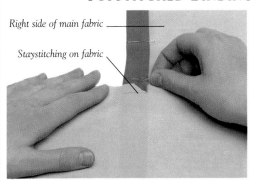

Right side of main fabric

Staystitching on fabric

1 PRESS THE SEAM ALLOWANCES of the binding strip to the wrong side. Press the binding in half lengthwise, wrong sides together. Staystitch the corner of the fabric for 1 in (2.5 cm) on each side. Clip to the stitching. With the wrong side of the binding to the right side of the fabric, overlap the binding edge over the fabric edge the width of the seam allowance. Pin up to the corner (left).

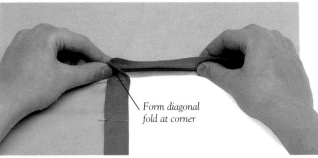

Form diagonal fold at corner

2 FOLD the binding diagonally to fit around the corner. Continue along the other edge, overlapping the edge with the binding for the width of the seam allowance, in the same way as the first edge (left).

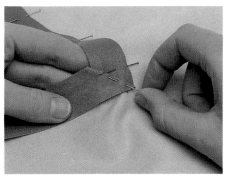

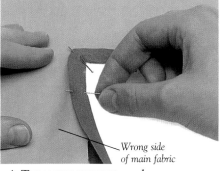

Wrong side of main fabric

3 PIN THE DIAGONAL FOLD at the corner on the edge of the binding already pinned to the fabric (above). Continue pinning the binding in place, working along the edge of the fabric from the corner to the ends of the binding.

4 TURN THE BINDING to the wrong side, and pin it in position, folding the binding diagonally across the corner. Baste the binding in place, making sure that the basting catches all layers of fabric. Then remove the pins (above).

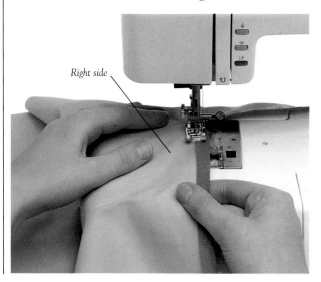

Right side

5 WORKING on the right side of the fabric, topstitch the binding in place close to the pressed edge of the binding. Make sure that the stitching passes through all the layers of fabric, paying particular attention to the edge of the binding on the wrong side. Pivot the stitching at the corner, and continue to topstitch along the other side (left). Remove all the basting stitches.

TOPSTITCHED BINDING OUTSIDE CORNER

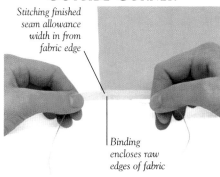

Stitching finished seam allowance width in from fabric edge

Binding encloses raw edges of fabric

1 PRESS THE SEAM ALLOWANCES of the binding to the wrong side along both long edges. Press the binding in half lengthwise. Sandwich the edge of the main fabric in between the binding. Topstitch the binding from one end up to the corner. Knot the thread ends to finish (above).

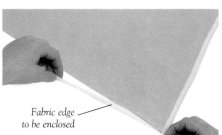

Fabric edge to be enclosed

2 TURN the binding around the corner, and arrange the binding to form a neat, diagonal fold on both sides of the main fabric. Sandwich the other edge of the fabric in between the binding (above), and pin the binding in place along the other edge.

Right side

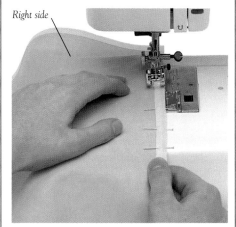

3 FROM THE RIGHT SIDE of the fabric, topstitch the binding in place (above). Be careful that the stitches pass through all the fabric layers, in particular the edge of the binding on the wrong side. Remove the pins as they are reached.

RUFFLES

RUFFLES CAN BE MADE from single or double layers of fabric. The outer edges of single-layer ruffles are finished with narrow hems. A folded or seamed edge forms the outer edge on a double-layer ruffle. Single-layer ruffles are best made from crisp fabrics such as mediumweight cotton, and they are suitable where a double fabric layer would be too bulky. Double-layer ruffles are advisable on frayable fabrics. For a softly gathered ruffle, the fabric strip should be at least twice the finished ruffle length. A slightly longer length results in extra fullness.

RELATED TECHNIQUES

Reducing seam bulk, p. 84
Seam finishes, p. 85
Forming pleats from the
right side, p. 115
Making and fitting gathers, p. 120
Facing a neckline, p. 127
Sewing hems by hand, p. 206

DIRECTORY OF RUFFLES

Ruffle with heading   *Circular ruffle*   *Double-edged ruffle*   *Plain ruffle*

Ruffle with heading
This type of ruffle is gathered a short distance from its top edge. The heading forms a decorative finish (see opposite).

Circular ruffle
A circular ruffle that forms a soft frill, this is often used at garment necklines (p. 231).

Double-edged ruffle
This ruffle is gathered along its center to form a ruffle that is equal in distance from the top and bottom edges (see opposite).

Plain ruffle
One edge of a plain ruffle is hemmed. The other is gathered to fit and stitched to a seam or unfinished edge (see opposite).

HEMMING A SINGLE-LAYER RUFFLE

ALL THE EDGES OF A SINGLE-LAYER RUFFLE that are not enclosed in seams are finished by a narrow, double hem. When handstitching a hem, a line of machine stitching is sewn ¼ in (6 mm) from the hem edge. After trimming, the stitching is used as a guide for the hem. The machine-stitched method requires a special machine foot.

BY HAND

Trim close to stitching

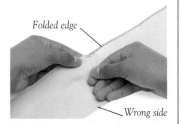
Folded edge
Wrong side

1 STITCH a line ¼ in (6 mm) in from the hem edge. Trim the hem edge to ⅛ in (3 mm) (above). Fold the raw edge to the wrong side along the stitching.

2 USING small stitches and working on the wrong side of the fabric, make a rolled hem (p. 206) and stitch in place along the folded edge of the ruffle (above).

BY MACHINE

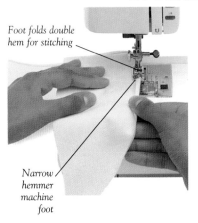
Foot folds double hem for stitching
Narrow hemmer machine foot

A NEAT and narrow hem can be made using a special narrow hemmer machine foot (p. 18). This foot is available for different hem widths. With the foot and fabric positioned, guide the raw fabric edge into the groove of the machine foot. The foot folds a double hem and stitches it in place, in one complete step (left).

MAKING A SINGLE-LAYER RUFFLE

MADE FROM A SINGLE LAYER OF FABRIC, this ruffle is used to decorate or lengthen items. The ruffle strip depth is calculated including ⅝ in (1.5 cm) for a seam allowance, such as the top of a plain ruffle, and ⅜ in (1 cm) for a narrow hem. Before the ruffle is gathered and attached, it must be hemmed (see opposite).

PLAIN RUFFLE

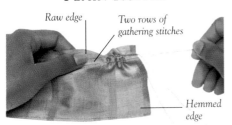

Raw edge *Two rows of gathering stitches*

Hemmed edge

HEM the short ends of the ruffle. Stitch a narrow hem along one long edge, and stitch two rows of gathering stitches ¼ in (6 mm) apart, along the other edge. Pull up the gathers (above).

RUFFLE WITH HEADING

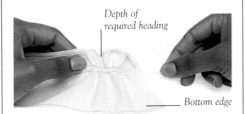

Depth of required heading

Bottom edge

HEM the short ends and both long edges. Stitch a row of gathering stitches the depth of the heading down from the top edge. Stitch a second row ¼ in (6 mm) below the first. Pull to gather (above).

DOUBLE-EDGED RUFFLE

Hemmed long edge of ruffle

HEM the short ends of the ruffle. Stitch a row of gathering stitches ⅛ in (3 mm) above the center of the ruffle. Stitch a second row ¼ in (6 mm) below the first row. Pull up the gathers (above).

MAKING A DOUBLE-LAYER RUFFLE

MADE FROM A DOUBLE LAYER OF FABRIC, this ruffle is used on lightweight fabrics where a hem would show through on the right side. It requires less stitching than a single-layer ruffle. For a plain ruffle, allow twice the ruffle depth plus two seam allowances. For a ruffle with a heading and for a double-edged ruffle, allow twice the ruffle depth.

PLAIN RUFFLE

HEM OR JOIN the short ends, and fold the fabric in half lengthwise. Stitch a row of gathering stitches, and a second row ¼ in (6 mm) above. Pull up the gathers along the seamline of the folded edge (above).

RUFFLE WITH HEADING

Heading facing *Lower facing*

PRESS THE HEADING and lower facings to the wrong side so that the raw edges meet at the heading. Stitch a row of gathering stitches close to each raw edge. Pull up the gathers evenly (above).

DOUBLE-EDGED RUFFLE

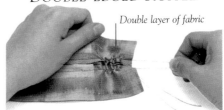

Double layer of fabric

PRESS THE LONG EDGES to the wrong side of the fabric so that the raw edges meet at the center. Stitch a row of gathering stitches close to each raw edge. Pull up the gathers evenly (above).

STITCHING A PLAIN RUFFLE INTO A SEAM

A PLAIN RUFFLE MAY BE USED at the front edge of an item between the main fabric and the facing, or around a skirt where a ruffle is inserted partway down the garment. The ruffle is gathered, then sandwiched between two fabric layers. If the top edges of the ruffle are exposed on the inside, they should be zigzag stitched together.

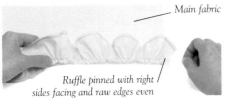

Main fabric

Ruffle pinned with right sides facing and raw edges even

1 PIN THE MAIN FABRIC edge at 6-in (15-cm) intervals. Mark the ruffle edge into the same number of sections, and attach to the garment at the pins. Pull up the gathers (above).

Gathering stitches

2 TWIST THE ENDS of the gathering threads around the pin at each end in a figure eight. Pin the ruffle to the fabric. Stitch together just below the lower row of gathering stitches (above).

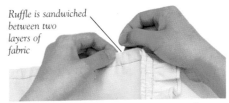

Ruffle is sandwiched between two layers of fabric

3 WITH RIGHT SIDES FACING, pin the fabric with the attached ruffle to the second fabric layer (above). Stitch the seam, sandwiching the ruffle between the two layers of fabric with raw edges even.

FINISHING A RUFFLE SEAM ON A STRAIGHT EDGE

A PLAIN RUFFLE, either single layer or double layer, is often stitched to the main fabric edge to give a decorative finish. The ruffle may be pleated, although a gathered style is more common. The trimmed seam allowances can be zigzag stitched together or serge finished to give a clean finish on both the right and the wrong sides.

1 MAKE THE RUFFLE, and stitch it to the main fabric edge. Trim the ruffle seam allowance only to ¼ in (5 mm) (above). Press ⅛ in (3 mm) toward the ruffle along the fabric seam allowance.

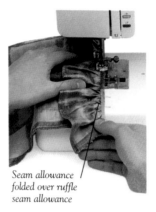

Seam allowance folded over ruffle seam allowance

2 FOLD OVER the pressed ⅛-in (3-mm) main fabric seam allowance so that the ¼-in (5-mm) ruffle seam allowance is covered, ensuring that its edge is aligned with the ruffle stitching. Pin to hold in place. Stitch close to the pressed edge (left).

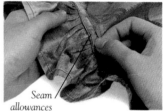

Seam allowances

3 FOLD THE RUFFLE away from the fabric edge. Press the seam allowances toward the fabric, and slipstitch in place (above).

FINISHING A RUFFLE SEAM WITH A BIAS STRIP

I N THIS METHOD, A BIAS STRIP IS USED to cover the seam allowances on a plain ruffle seam. Ready-made bias binding, 1 in (2.5 cm) wide, can be used. Alternatively, the bias strips can be cut from fabric (p. 214–215). Bias strips can be used to finish a straight ruffle seam but are particularly suitable for curved ruffle seams.

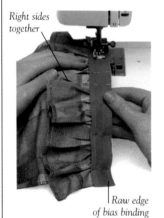

Right sides together

Raw edge of bias binding

1 MAKE the ruffle, then stitch it to the main fabric edge. Unfold one of the long edges of the bias binding, and place this edge along the ruffle seam allowance, with raw edges even. Pin in place. Stitch along the ruffle seam stitching (left).

Trim all layers

2 TRIM THE RUFFLE, the bias strip, and the fabric seam allowances to ¼ in (5 mm) (above). Fold the ruffle away from the fabric. Fold the bias binding over the seam allowances, and pin to the fabric.

3 SLIPSTITCH the edge of the bias binding in place (above). (To position cut bias strips, tuck the raw edges under before stitching.)

ATTACHING A RUFFLE WITH HEADING

A RUFFLE WITH HEADING can be used to cover a seam allowance. The ruffle is stitched to the wrong side of the main fabric, then turned to the right side so that the seam allowance is hidden behind the ruffle heading. A second row of stitching on the right side conceals the raw edge. A double ruffle can be attached in the same way.

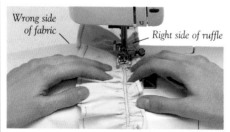

Wrong side of fabric

Right side of ruffle

1 PLACE THE NARROW, top part of the ruffle toward the main fabric edge with wrong sides together. Pin the row of gathering nearest the wider part of the ruffle level with the seamline. Stitch just outside the gathering (above).

2 TRIM the main fabric seam allowance to ¼ in (5 mm). Turn the ruffle to the right side, with the ruffle heading over the seam allowance. Pin (above). Stitch just outside the gathering nearest the ruffle heading.

····· CENTERING A DOUBLE-······ EDGED RUFFLE

When attaching a ruffle away from an edge, topstitch alongside the gathering stitches, right sides facing upward.

MAKING A CIRCULAR RUFFLE

THE OUTER EDGE of a circular ruffle is much wider than its inner edge. When the inner edge is attached flat to the main fabric, without any gathering, the outer edge becomes fluted. More than one circle may be used to make up a long ruffle. The ends of the ruffle may be left as straight edges, or tapered into the seam (see below).

CUTTING OUT AND PREPARING CIRCULAR RUFFLE PIECES

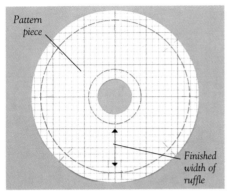

Pattern piece

Finished width of ruffle

1 PIN THE PATTERN to the fabric (above). Cut out a single or double layer as required. (The ruffle may be left as a complete circle, as for a cuff.)

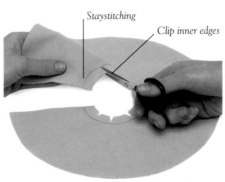

Staystitching

Clip inner edges

2 STAYSTITCH around the inner edge of the circle, just inside the seam allowance. Clip the seam allowance at close intervals all around (above).

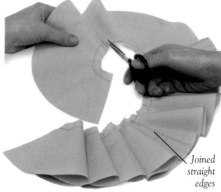

Joined straight edges

3 TO JOIN two or more circles together for extra length, stitch the straight, cut edges together. Staystitch, and clip the inner edges (above) as in Step 2.

SINGLE-LAYER RUFFLE

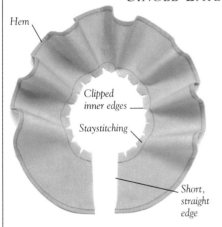

Hem

Clipped inner edges

Staystitching

Short, straight edge

STITCH a narrow hem (p. 228) around the outer edge of the single-layer ruffle (left). (Alternatively, finish the edge with zigzag stitch. Press the zigzag-stitched edge to the wrong side, then stitch from the right side along the center of the stitching.) Hem any short, straight edges. Attach the ruffle using one of the methods shown opposite, or attach using a facing.

DOUBLE-LAYER RUFFLE

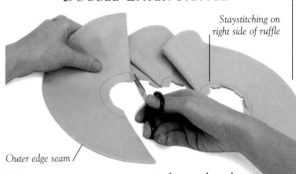

Staystitching on right side of ruffle

Outer edge seam

WITH RIGHT SIDES FACING, stitch together the outer edges of the ruffle. Trim, notch, and press. Turn through. Staystitch and clip the inner edge (above).

SPECIAL RUFFLE TREATMENTS

Top collar piece

Ruffle

Stitching a ruffle to a collar
With right sides together and raw edges even, pin the prepared plain ruffle (p. 229) to the outer edge of the top collar, arranging extra fullness at the corners or curves (left). Pin the under collar piece to the ruffled piece with right sides together. Stitch the outer edges of the collar, trimming and notching the seam allowances. Turn to the right side.

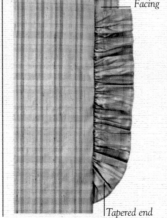

Facing

Tapered end

Tapering ruffle ends
If a straight edge at the end of a ruffle is not suitable for the design of the garment or home-furnishing item, taper the end into the seam. When pinning the ruffle to the main fabric, gradually take a wider seam allowance until the end of the ruffle is enclosed within the seam allowance. With the ruffle sandwiched between the facing and the main fabric, pin the facing in place. Stitch. Turn right side out, and press.

FASTENINGS

USING BUTTONS

BUTTONS WERE ORIGINALLY MADE from bone or horn, but today most buttons are made from plastic, glass, or metal. Flat buttons have stitching holes pierced through from the front to the back, while shank buttons have a protruding stitching hole or a metal loop at the back of the button, forming a shank. Most flat buttons require a thread shank to allow space for the fabric layers to lie smoothly when the garment is buttoned. On bulky fabrics, shank buttons can also have an additional thread shank to provide extra movement.

RELATED TECHNIQUES

Machine feet, p. 18
Threads, p. 63
Hand sewing stitches, p. 74
Preparing jacket layers, p. 287
Repairing a buttonhole, p. 307

DIRECTORY OF BUTTONS

Two-hole button
This is a flat button with two stitching holes. If the button is purely decorative, it is stitched to the garment with no shank (p. 236).

Four-hole button
Any flat button such as this requires a thread shank on thick fabrics (p. 236).

Ball button
Spherical, the ball button has a stitching hole pierced or molded across the back.

Dome button
This half-ball button has a shank at the back and is most suitable for use with thick and heavy fabrics.

Two-hole button

Four-hole button

Fabric-covered button

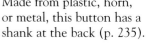
Shank button

Ball button

Dome button

Rivet button

Novelty button

Fabric-covered button
Made from a kit or made to order, this button matches the garment and has a shank (p. 236–237).

Shank button
Made from plastic, horn, or metal, this button has a shank at the back (p. 235).

Rivet button
A nonsew button, this is attached by a rivet inserted through the fabric from the wrong side.

Novelty button
This button may be an individual shape, or one of a series or set. It may be flat but often has a shank.

CHOOSING BUTTON POSITIONS

BUTTONHOLES CAN BE MADE horizontally or vertically. On a horizontal buttonhole, the button sits at the end of the buttonhole nearest the garment edge. To allow room for the shank, the button is placed ⅛ in (3 mm) in from the buttonhole end. On a vertical buttonhole, the button is stitched in the center or at the top of the buttonhole.

HORIZONTAL BUTTONHOLES

OVERLAP the edges of the garment so that the center lines match. Place a pin ⅛ in (3 mm) in from the end of the buttonhole (left). Remove the buttonholed edge, and secure the pin to mark the button position.

VERTICAL BUTTONHOLES

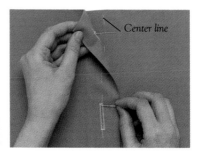

Center line

CHECK that the center lines are matching. Pin through the buttonhole ⅛ in (3 mm) down from the top end. Remove the buttonholed edge, lifting it over the pin. Secure the pin in place to mark the button position.

ATTACHING FLAT BUTTONS

O N VERY LIGHTWEIGHT FABRIC, flat buttons can be stitched directly against the fabric. However, on most medium- and heavyweight fabrics, thread shanks will be needed to accommodate the buttonholed layer of fabric so the button will lie flat underneath when it is buttoned. The thicker the fabric, the longer the shank should be.

STITCHING A FOUR-HOLE FLAT BUTTON

TO STITCH THE BUTTON, use two parallel stitches (far left), a cross with two stitches (left), a square with four stitches (right), or three stitches from the same hole (far right). Stitch until the button is secure.

STITCHING A TWO-HOLE FLAT BUTTON

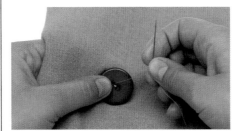

SECURE THE THREAD END at the button position on the wrong side. Stitch up through one hole in the button and down through the other. Make about six stitches in this way. Finish securely.

MAKING A THREAD SHANK

Wind thread tightly under button

HOLD THE BUTTON tilted slightly against the fabric to produce a small gap while stitching on the button. Wind the thread around the stitches to form a short shank (above), and fasten the thread to finish.

USING A SPACER TO FORM A SHANK

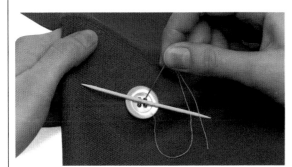

1 SECURE the thread end. With the button in position, place a toothpick, needle, or matchstick across the top of the button to form a spacer. The thicker the spacer, the longer the shank will be. Attach the button, stitching over the spacer (left). Finish with the thread between the button and the fabric.

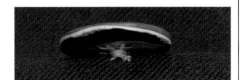

2 REMOVE THE SPACER. Wind the thread around the stitches between the button and the fabric to form a firm shank. Finish the thread ends securely on the wrong side of the fabric.

ATTACHING SHANK BUTTONS

B UTTONS WITH BUILT-IN SHANKS are stitched in place so that the wider part of the shank lies along the length of the buttonhole. The thread is secured with a few backstitches on the wrong side. On bulky fabric, or if the button has a short shank, an additional thread shank may be formed by winding the thread around the stitches.

ATTACHING SHANK BUTTONS

1 SECURE the thread end. Place the button in position with its shank parallel to the buttonhole. Pass the needle through the fabric and shank alternately (above), making six to eight stitches.

2 FASTEN THE BUTTON to check the fit (above). The shank should sit along the direction of the buttonhole, not pressed against the edges. Unbutton. Finish stitching securely on the wrong side.

MAKING AN ADDITIONAL THREAD SHANK

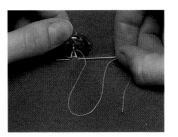

1 SECURE the thread end on the wrong side. Hold the button between the thumb and forefinger to keep a constant space between the shank and the fabric. Stitch the button in place (above).

2 FINISH STITCHING with the thread between the button and the fabric. Wind the thread around the stitches to make a firm shank. Return the needle to the wrong side, and finish securely.

SEWING ON BUTTONS BY MACHINE

MACHINE STITCHING BUTTONS onto a garment can save time, but only flat buttons can be sewn on with a machine, and not all machines are able to finish off a button. Generally, it is necessary to tie off the thread ends by hand. Buttons that are sewn onto anything other than very thin fabrics should have a thread shank to secure them.

TWO-HOLE BUTTON

PLACE THE BUTTON and fabric under the button sew-on foot. Set the stitch to zigzag, with the stitch length at zero. Adjust the stitch width so that the needle enters the center of each hole. Stitch.

FOUR-HOLE BUTTON

TO SECURE a four-hole button, stitch the first two holes (see left). Raise the needle and foot slightly. Move the button to line up the second set of holes with the needle. Lower the foot, and stitch.

MAKING A SHANK

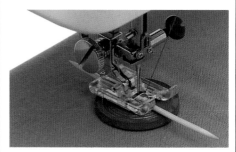

CENTER THE BUTTON, and raise the needle just above the hole. Then insert a toothpick across the button. Stitch. Bring thread ends between button and fabric and wind them around the shank. Secure.

MAKING BUTTONS

BUTTONS CAN BE MADE either to match an item, or to be a contrasting feature. Button kits are available and are relatively easy to use, with easy-to-follow instructions for making fabric-covered buttons. An important aspect of making buttons is choosing a suitable fabric; lightweight fabrics should be backed for extra strength.

MAKING A PLAIN FABRIC-COVERED BUTTON

Button shell placed on wrong side of fabric

1 USING THE PATTERN in the button kit, cut out a circle of fabric to fit the button size. If the fabric frays, add a little extra all around. Then fold the fabric over the shell, and catch it onto the hooks, pulling it evenly over the shell (left).

Rim of button back secures fabric

2 SMOOTH THE FABRIC onto the hooks all around. Position the button back onto the shell so that the shank projects through the center of the button back. Squeeze together until the back clicks onto the shell (left).

REINFORCING BUTTONHOLE FASTENINGS

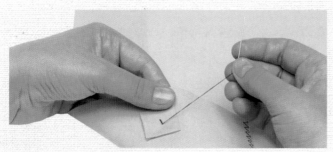

Reinforcing on a lightweight fabric
If working with a lightweight fabric or a single fabric layer, place a small square of folded fabric or seam binding behind the button on the wrong side of the garment. Stitch through the button, fabric, and folded square (above). Secure, stitching on the wrong side.

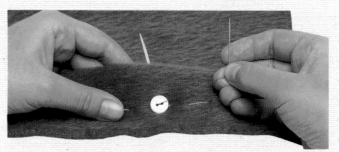

Reinforcing on a heavyweight fabric
When using heavyweight fabric, place another small button on the wrong side of the fabric. Attach the main button, stitching through the reinforcing button at the same time. Make a shank if required, using a toothpick behind the button to form the shank (above).

MAKING A FABRIC-COVERED BUTTON WITH A METAL RIM

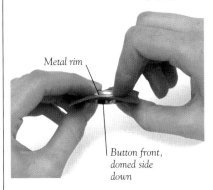

Metal rim

Button front, domed side down

1 CUT OUT the fabric a little larger than the button mold. Position the fabric, right side down, onto the wrong side of the decorated metal rim. Then place the button front, domed side down, onto the fabric (left).

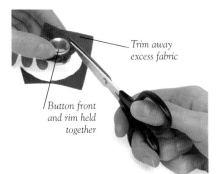

Trim away excess fabric

Button front and rim held together

2 USE the pusher to ease the button and fabric into the rim. On the right side, check that the fabric fits smoothly over the domed button front within the rim. Trim the fabric to ¼ in (5 mm) outside the edge of the rim (left).

Thick fabric notched to give smooth fit

3 TUCK THE EDGES of the fabric over to the inside of the button, on the wrong side of the domed button front. If thick fabric is being used, it may require notching to reduce the bulk and enable the covering to fit smoothly (above).

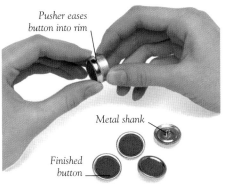

Pusher eases button into rim

Metal shank

Finished button

4 PLACE THE BUTTON BACK, shank side up, onto the fabric-covered front and rim of the button. Then use the hollow side of the pusher to push the button back into the rim (above). The back should clip in to hold the fabric.

···· "BUTTONING" A PILLOW ····

Double strand of thread

With a button on each side and using a long upholstery needle, stitch up through the pillow center and the top button. Stitch back through the pillow and the other button. Repeat, then secure the thread ends.

MAKING A CHINESE BALL BUTTON

1 PIN ONE END of a length of cord or fabric tubing to a flat surface. Then loop the cord once. If the cord begins to unravel at the end, wrap clear adhesive tape neatly around to secure.

2 MAKE a second loop of equal size on top of the first, and thread the end of the cord under the pinned end. (When using fabric tubing, take care to keep the seam pointing downward.)

3 MAKE A THIRD LOOP, weaving over and under each previous loop. Thread over the top of the second loop and under the first, then over the second half of the second loop and under the first.

4 WORKING FROM BOTH ENDS of the cord or tubing, gradually and evenly tighten all the loops. Then work the fullness from the center loop around and through the other two loops to the ends.

5 CONTINUE TO TIGHTEN the loops in the same manner until a ball forms (above). Trim the ends of the cord or tubing, and stitch flat to the underside of the ball, securing the ends out of sight.

MACHINE BUTTONHOLES

BUTTONHOLES STITCHED with a close zigzag stitch or a close satin stitch are the most common types of machine buttonholes. Bound buttonholes have edges finished with narrow pleats of fabric, either matching or contrasting, and piped bound buttonholes have edges padded with a fine cord. Both of these types are most often used on coats and jackets. Bulky fur fabrics have buttonhole edges finished with tape on the inside. Other special fabrics, such as leather and suede, also require buttonhole finishes adapted to suit their particular characteristics.

RELATED TECHNIQUES

Working machine stitches, p. 77
Making bar tacks, p. 79
Making topstitched seams, p. 87
Making piping, p. 91
Making two-piece
placket bands, p. 138
Making a faced hem, p. 214
Repairing a buttonhole, p. 307

DIRECTORY OF BUTTONHOLES

Machine-worked
This has two square ends and is stitched with a very close machine zigzag stitch (p. 240).

Corded machine
This type of buttonhole is stitched over a fine cord to give a raised effect (p. 240).

Bound
This has two tiny pleats, or lips, that meet at the center of the buttonhole (p. 241).

Piped bound
Both sides of the buttonhole are finished with fabric strips enclosing a fine cord (p. 243).

Tape-bound
The edges of the buttonhole are finished with twill tape to reduce bulk (p. 244).

Topstitched leather
The cut edges of the buttonhole are outlined by secure topstitching (p. 245).

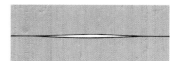

Piped leather
Folded strips are stitched behind the buttonhole in the leather or suede (p. 245).

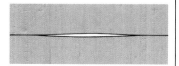

In-seam
This is formed by leaving a gap in a seam. It can be left plain or be topstitched.

MEASURING BUTTONHOLE LENGTH

ON FLAT BUTTONS, the diameter of the button should be measured, then an extra ⅛–¼ in (3–6 mm) added, depending on the thickness of the button. Buttonholes for round, domed, and novelty buttons are more difficult to measure accurately. It is often simplest to check the length required by cutting trial slits in spare pieces of fabric.

FLAT BUTTONS

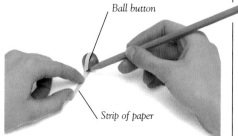

Button

Sewing gauge

MEASURE ACROSS the center of the button (above) and add ⅛ in (3 mm) for the thickness of the button. (On heavyweight fabrics, thick buttons may require an extra ¼ in [6 mm].)

ROUND BUTTONS

Ball button

Strip of paper

WRAP A STRIP OF PAPER around the button, and mark where the end of the strip meets the long strip (above). The buttonhole length is half the measurement from the end of the strip to the mark.

TESTING SIZE

MAKE A TEST BUTTONHOLE from a piece of garment fabric and the appropriate interfacing. Cut the buttonhole to the required length. Slip the button through to test the size (above). Adjust if necessary.

MARKING BUTTONHOLE POSITION

The center front line of the buttonhole is marked on both pattern pieces. When the garment edges are overlapped and fastened, the center lines should match.

Horizontal buttonholes are made so that they will overlap the center line, with the corresponding buttons stitched along the center line on the underlayer of the garment.

HORIZONTAL

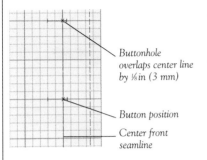

Buttonhole overlaps center line by ⅛ in (3 mm)

Button position

Center front seamline

The button sits at the end of the buttonhole nearest the garment edge. The outer horizontal ends of each buttonhole extend ⅛ in (3 mm) beyond the center line so that, when fastened, the buttons lie along the center line.

VERTICAL

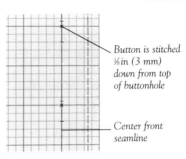

Button is stitched ⅛ in (3 mm) down from top of buttonhole

Center front seamline

Vertical buttonholes lie along the center front line. Buttons are stitched ⅛ in (3 mm) down from the top of the buttonhole, also on the center line. Vertical buttonholes are used on shirts or on garments with front bands.

MARKING BUTTONHOLES

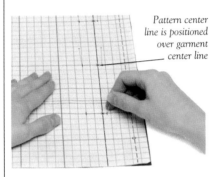

Pattern center line is positioned over garment center line

1 PLACE the pattern piece on top of the garment. The center line on the pattern should match that on the garment. Mark the buttonhole positions at each end with vertical pins through all the layers (left).

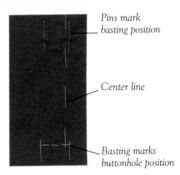

Pins mark basting position

Center line

Basting marks buttonhole position

2 REMOVE the pattern piece, but leave the marking pins in place, reattaching them so that they lie flat on the fabric. Mark a line between the pins with a line of running stitches or a dressmaker's pencil. Baste across each end to mark the buttonhole positions.

MAKING A HAND-GUIDED MACHINE BUTTONHOLE

This method involves stitching the long sides of the buttonhole with the stitch set at a fraction less than half width. A tiny gap is left between the stitching lines, and the buttonhole is cut without snipping the stitches. The stitch is set at the broadest width to stitch across each end. A close zigzag or satin stitch is used for the buttonhole.

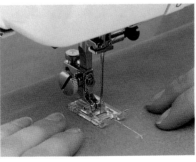

1 POSITION the buttonhole marking centrally under the machine foot. Swing the needle to the right. Line up the buttonhole center line, bring back the needle just to its left, and lower the foot. Stitch (left).

2 STITCH slowly and carefully along to the other end of the buttonhole (left), stitching just left of the center line. Finish with the needle to the right and inserted in the fabric. Raise the foot.

3 PIVOT the fabric, and lower the foot (left). Make one stitch so that the needle is to the right, and lift the needle. Adjust the stitch to the full width, then work six stitches to form a bar tack. Finish with the needle to the left.

4 RAISE the needle, then reset the stitch width. Stitch the other side of the buttonhole (left). Raise the needle. Adjust the stitch to the full width. Work six stitches to form a second bar tack. Finish the thread ends neatly.

MAKING AUTOMATIC MACHINE BUTTONHOLES

THE STITCH WIDTH and the stitch length of automatic buttonholes, although initially preset, can be varied to accommodate different fabrics, using the appropriate control buttons on the machine. Buttonholes can be worked either fully automatically or semi-automatically, depending on the type of buttonhole foot used.

FULLY AUTOMATIC BUTTONHOLE FOOT

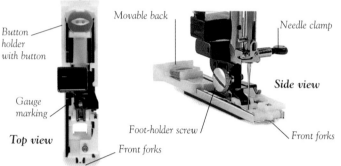

Button holder with button

Movable back

Gauge marking

Top view

Front forks

Foot-holder screw

Needle clamp

Side view

Front forks

ON A FULLY AUTOMATIC BUTTONHOLE FOOT, set the buttonhole length by placing the button in the button holder. This ensures that the buttonhole is the appropriate length for the button, allowing the button to slide through easily. If the button is very thick, add extra length to the buttonhole to accommodate the thickness, following the machine instructions.

SEMI-AUTOMATIC BUTTONHOLE FOOT

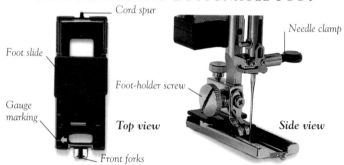

Cord spur

Foot slide

Gauge marking

Top view

Front forks

Foot-holder screw

Needle clamp

Side view

THE SEMI-AUTOMATIC SLIDING BUTTONHOLE FOOT has a measure along its left side for gauging the buttonhole length. Before stitching, mark the buttonhole length on the garment, and move the slide so that the lower mark on the slider is level with the start of the buttonhole marking on the garment. Slide both thread ends to the left of the foot before stitching.

FULLY AUTOMATIC BUTTONHOLE

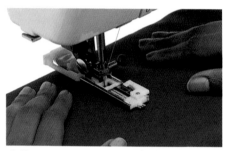

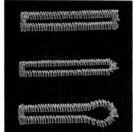

Straight bar tack

Rounded end

Keyhole end

1 PLACE THE FOOT over the buttonhole position with the needlehole on the foot level with the front end of the buttonhole marking. The machine will complete the entire buttonhole to the correct length in one operation (above).

2 FOR VERTICAL or horizontal buttonholes, stitch a straight bar tack across each end (top). For horizontal buttonholes, stitch one rounded end (center). For tailored garments, stitch one keyhole end (bottom).

SEMI-AUTOMATIC BUTTONHOLE

1 START THE MACHINE. It will make the bar tack and stitch backward up the left side of the buttonhole marking (above). Stop at the top mark. Press the memory button on the machine so that it makes the bar tack. Stitch along the other side. Stop at the end of the buttonhole.

CORDED BUTTONHOLE

1 USING a sliding buttonhole foot, thread buttonhole twist or a similar thick, twisted thread onto the foot. Lower the needle into the garment. To make the buttonhole semi-automatically (see right), stitch the sides and the bar tack stitches over the filler cord (above).

2 AFTER THE BUTTONHOLE is finished, pull the ends of the filler cord taut. Thread each cord end onto a large-eyed needle, and draw both ends through to the wrong side. Secure the cord ends underneath one of the bar tacks on the buttonhole (p. 79), and trim the ends.

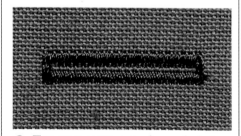

2 THE SEMI-AUTOMATIC buttonhole has a straight bar tack across each end (above). If the buttonhole stitching is not dense enough or if an extra-strong finish is required, for example on a jacket, stitch the buttonhole a second time along the top of the previous lines of stitching.

MAKING BOUND BUTTONHOLES

BOUND BUTTONHOLES have two tiny pleats, or lips, of fabric forming the edges of the buttonhole. These can be made using a rectangular fabric patch or two separate strips of fabric. Bound buttonholes are worked through the front layer of fabric before the facing is made. The back of each buttonhole is formed through the facing.

STITCHING

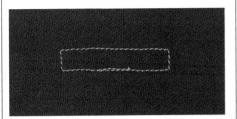

MARK THE BUTTONHOLE using a dressmaker's pencil or tailor's chalk, and stitch with each lip no wider than ⅛ in (3 mm) (except on thick fabrics, when each lip may be up to ¼ in [6 mm] wide).

CUTTING

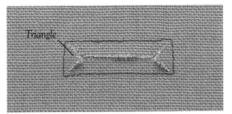

Triangle

WORKING FROM THE CENTER outward, cut along the center of the buttonhole to about ¼ in (6 mm) from each end. Clip diagonally into each corner, forming small triangles. Do not cut the stitching.

INTERFACING

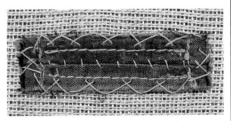

TO USE A FIRM INTERFACING, such as hair canvas, behind the buttonhole, stitch the buttonhole, and cut out an opening in the interfacing. Catchstitch around the edges of the buttonhole strips.

PATCH METHOD

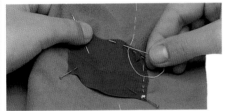

1 CUT OUT A PATCH 2 in (5 cm) longer than the buttonhole. Then press in a crease along the center. With right sides together, pin the patch in place with the crease level with the button marking. Baste around the edges (above).

2 ON THE WRONG SIDE of the garment, mark lines the required length of the buttonhole, ⅛ in (3 mm) either side of the buttonhole marking (above). (On thick fabric, the lines may each be up to ¼ in [6 mm] from the marking.)

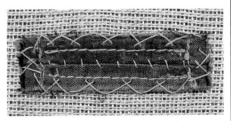

3 STITCH around the marked rectangle through both the fabric and the patch, using small machine stitch. Overlap the ends of the stitching on one long edge (above). Count the stitches across the short ends so that both are equal.

4 CUT THE CENTER of the stitched rectangle (see Cutting, above). Remove the basting, and turn the patch to the wrong side. Roll the seam to the edge of the opening (above). Press.

5 FORM the buttonhole lips by folding each long edge of the patch over the opening (above). The folded edges of the lips should meet exactly along the center of the buttonhole opening.

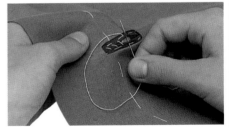

6 CHECK THAT the lips are evenly formed on the right side. Baste along the center of each lip to hold the fold in place, then diagonally baste the folds of the lips together (above).

Patch ends

7 WITH the garment right side up, fold back the garment fabric along the side of the buttonhole to expose the end of the patch and the fabric triangle (see above). Stitch across through all layers (left), and repeat at the other end of the buttonhole.

8 FOLD BACK the fabric at the top of the buttonhole to expose the patch and the long fabric edge of the buttonhole. Stitch inside the original stitching line (left). Repeat on the other long edge, turning back the fabric at the base of the buttonhole.

SIMPLIFIED PATCH METHOD

Patch centered over buttonhole marking

Horizontal basting

Right side

1 CUT A PATCH 2 in (5 cm) wide and 1 in (2.5 cm) longer than the length the buttonhole will be. Machine baste the patch along the buttonhole marking and ¼ in (6 mm) on each side (above).

Stitch parallel to fold

Long edge

2 FOLD ONE LONG EDGE toward the center along the basted line. Press. Stitch ⅛ in (3 mm) in from the fold the exact length of the buttonhole (above). Fold back the long edge.

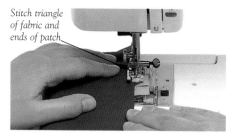

3 REPEAT STEP 2 on the remaining side of the patch. The buttonhole lips are now formed and stitched. Press the edges of the lips away from the center buttonhole marking (above).

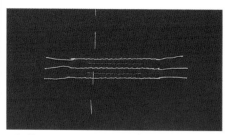

4 ON THE RIGHT SIDE, there should be five parallel rows of stitching (above). Remove the basting, and cut into the buttonhole center to within ¼ in (6 mm) of the ends. Cut triangles in the corners.

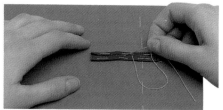

5 ON THE RIGHT SIDE, cut through the ends of the patch to form two strips. Pull the patch through the opening to the wrong side (above). The lips should be even and meet at the center. Baste.

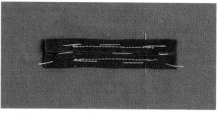

Stitch triangle of fabric and ends of patch

6 FOLD BACK THE FABRIC to expose the ends of the patch and the triangle of garment fabric. Stitch twice across the end and the base of the triangle (above). Then repeat at the other end.

ONE-PIECE FOLDED METHOD

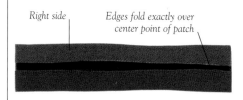

Right side

Edges fold exactly over center point of patch

1 CUT A PATCH 1 in (2.5 cm) wide by the buttonhole length, plus 1 in (2.5 cm). With right sides out, fold over the long edges so that they meet at the center (above). Press. Baste along the patch ⅛ in (3 mm) in from each fold.

2 PLACE THE PATCH centrally on the right side of the garment, with the open side upward, over the position where the buttonhole will be cut. Then baste down the center of the patch, along the buttonhole position (above).

3 USING a small machine stitch, stitch along the exact center on each half of the patch for the buttonhole length required (above). Pull the thread ends through to the wrong side, and tie them off securely. Remove the basting.

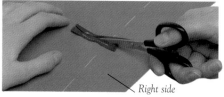

Right side

4 ON THE RIGHT SIDE, cut along the center of the patch, making two strips (above). On the wrong side, cut the fabric along the center of the buttonhole opening to within ¼ in (6 mm) from each end. Cut triangles diagonally into the corners, just short of the stitching.

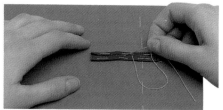

5 PULL THE STRIPS THROUGH the opening to the wrong side so that the folded edges form two even lips meeting at the buttonhole center (above). Pull out the triangular ends to square the corners, and press. Baste the lips together using diagonal stitches.

Strip ends

6 FOLD BACK THE FABRIC at the end of the buttonhole. The strip ends and buttonhole fabric triangle will now be exposed. Stitch twice across the ends of the strips and the base of the triangle to secure them together (above). Finish the ends neatly. Repeat at the other end.

ONE-PIECE TUCKED METHOD

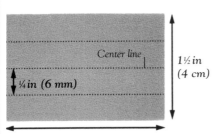

Center line

1½ in (4 cm)

¼ in (6 mm)

Length of hole, plus 1 in (2.5 cm)

1 CUT A FABRIC PATCH 1½ in (4 cm) wide by the length of the buttonhole, plus 1 in (2.5 cm). On the wrong side, mark the center line and lines ¼ in (6 mm) above and below the center line.

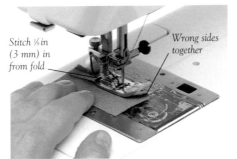

Stitch ⅛ in (3 mm) in from fold

Wrong sides together

2 FOLD THE PATCH along the top ¼ in (6 mm) line, and stitch across ⅛ in (3 mm) in from the fold. Repeat on the lower line. Complete (see One-Piece Folded Method, opposite).

ADDING PIPING

To strengthen the buttonhole lips, thread either yarn or soft cord through them, using a tapestry needle, after the lips have been made but before the triangular ends of the buttonhole have been stitched.

PIPED METHOD

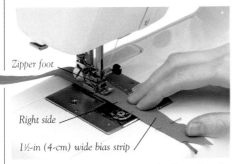

Zipper foot

Right side

1½-in (4-cm) wide bias strip

1 FOLD A BIAS STRIP around a length of narrow piping cord, and pin. Stitch near the cord (above). Cut into strips, two for each buttonhole, each the length of the buttonhole plus 1 in (2.5 cm).

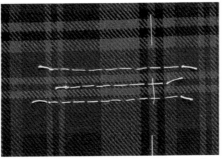

2 MARK the buttonhole position with basting on the right side of the fabric. Baste a line twice the width of the strip of corded piping above and below the stitching that marks the buttonhole.

3 ON THE RIGHT SIDE, center the strips over the buttonhole marking, with the piped edge next to the lines and the excess fabric basted in the center. Baste the strips in place. Mark the buttonhole length.

Zipper foot

4 STITCH each strip just inside the previous stitching close to the piping (left), starting and finishing at the exact points where the buttonhole ends. Finish all the thread ends securely.

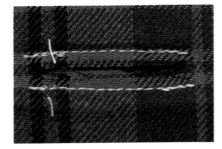

5 REMOVE the basting. On the wrong side, cut the fabric along the center of the buttonhole to ¼ in (6 mm) from each end. Cut diagonally into the corners to form two fabric triangles, up to but not over the stitching.

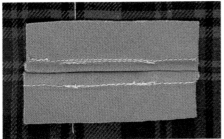

6 PULL THE STRIPS through the opening to the wrong side. The strips form the lips (above). Ensure that the triangular fabric ends are turned through the opening, and lie under the strips.

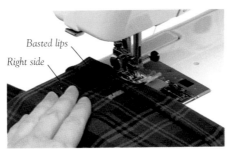

Basted lips

Right side

7 BASTE THE LIP EDGES together. Fold back the fabric to expose the strip ends and the fabric triangle. Stitch twice across the strip end and the triangle base (above). Repeat at the other end.

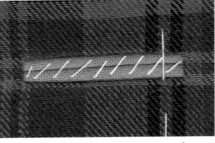

8 FINISH THE THREAD ENDS securely. Trim the edges of the piping strips ¼ in (6 mm) outside the buttonhole stitching line, and press. Finish the garment before removing the basting.

FINISHING FACINGS ON BOUND AND PIPED BUTTONHOLES

Bound and piped buttonholes are made at an early stage of a garment's construction. Since the facing is not attached until later, the buttonhole is cut through the facing when the garment is almost complete. The oval method can be used on stretch fabrics. In general, the rectangular method looks neater and more professional.

OVAL METHOD

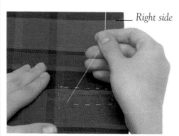

1 ALIGNING the center front markings on the garment and facing, baste around the buttonhole to join the garment and facing together (above).

2 PUSH A PIN through the right side of the fabric at each end of the buttonhole (above). Insert the pin vertically, but slightly inward.

3 TURN to the facing side of the garment. Cut along the center of the buttonhole between the pins, if possible on the straight grain (above).

4 TUCK UNDER the cut edges even with the buttonhole stitching, forming an oval shape. Pin in place. Slipstitch the edges (above).

RECTANGULAR METHOD

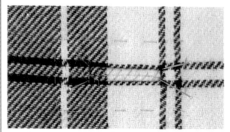

1 BASTE AROUND the buttonhole through both the facing and the garment fabric. On the garment side, push a pin vertically through each of the four corners of the buttonhole.

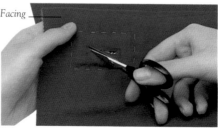

2 TURN TO THE FACING SIDE and cut along the center of the buttonhole, finishing ¼ in (6 mm) in from each end, using the four pins as a guide. Then cut diagonally into each corner (above).

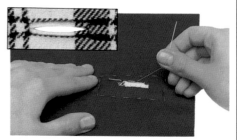

3 REMOVE THE PINS. Tuck under the raw edges of the facing, even with the buttonhole stitching, to form a rectangle. Pin in place. Slipstitch the edges to the back of the buttonhole (above).

MAKING BUTTONHOLES ON SPECIAL FABRICS

Special fabrics and real or simulated suede, leather, and fur require adaptations of buttonhole techniques to suit the fabric. The fur method uses tape to reduce bulk. Twill tape or grosgrain ribbon can be used; these are sold in different widths. The leather and suede methods take advantage of the nonfraying nature of the materials.

TAPE-BOUND BUTTONHOLES ON FUR

1 CUT along the buttonhole (above). Cut four strips of twill tape ½ in (12 mm) wide and 1 in (2.5 cm) longer than the length of the buttonhole.

2 PLACE TWO TAPES on the wrong side, so that they are exactly even with the cut buttonhole edges. Catchstitch the tapes in place.

3 PLACE the other two tapes on the right side. Oversew to join the tapes and the cut edges of the buttonhole, using small, fine stitches (above).

4 PUSH THE TAPES through to the wrong side to bind the buttonhole (above). Then slipstitch the free edges of the tape to the catchstitched tape.

TOPSTITCHED BUTTONHOLES ON LEATHER OR SUEDE

Wrong side

1 CLEARLY MARK the positions of the buttonholes on the wrong side of the fabric. Mark the buttonhole stitching lines ¼–⅜ in (6 mm–1 cm) either side of each buttonhole (left). Check that the buttonhole size is correct before pinning or stitching, since this will mark the fabric.

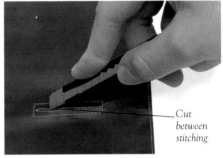

2 FOLLOWING THE BUTTONHOLE markings, take one handstitch across each end of the buttonhole to mark the right side of the fabric. Then make a third stitch along the length of the buttonhole at the center (above). The stitches form guides for stitching around the buttonhole. Leave long thread ends.

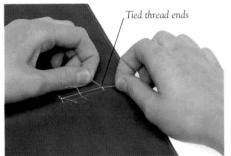

Tied thread ends

3 TIE THE LOOSE THREAD ENDS firmly together on the wrong side of the fabric, to make the stitch markings taut and straight (above). Check that the marking is correct on the right side.

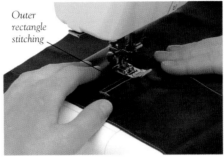

Outer rectangle stitching

4 ON THE RIGHT SIDE of the fabric, machine straight stitch an outer rectangle around the buttonhole position, using the four corners of handstitching as a guide (above). Secure the thread ends.

Cut between stitching

5 STITCH ALONG ONE SIDE of the center marking, pivot, and make five stitches backward and forward across one end. Complete the stitching. Cut between the center stitching (above).

PIPED BUTTONHOLES ON LEATHER OR SUEDE

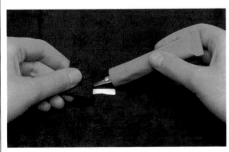

1 ON THE RIGHT side of the fabric, lightly mark the buttonhole positions. Mark lines, the required width of the piping, ⅛–¼ in (3–6 mm) above and below each buttonhole position. Cut out a rectangle along the marked lines (left).

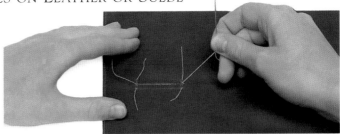

Piping lips

Adhesive tape holds pieces of piping at each end

2 CUT TWO PIECES of fabric for the piping, 1½ in (4 cm) wide by the length of the buttonhole, plus 1 in (2.5 cm). Fold each in half lengthwise, wrong sides together. Glue the long edges, and tape so that the folded edges touch (above).

3 PLACE THE LIPS behind the cut opening, with the folded edges of the lips meeting along the center of the opening. Glue the edge of the fabric around the opening of the lips (above).

4 ATTACH THE FACING. Working on the right side, stitch around the cut opening through all the layers (above). (If the fabric sticks under the machine foot, use tissue paper under the opening.)

Facing

5 TURN TO THE FACING SIDE. Clip the facing just inside the corners of the stitching (above). If the buttonhole requires pressing, place brown paper between the iron and the fabric.

HANDSTITCHED BUTTONHOLES

A HANDSTITCHED BUTTONHOLE is cut before being stitched. It is usually worked on double fabric and through any garment facing. A rectangle of straight stitching around the buttonhole marking acts as a stitching guide. Fabric that frays easily can be backed with fusible interfacing, or the cut edges can be oversewn before the buttonhole stitching is worked. A single strand of thread is normally used to stitch buttonholes; standard sewing thread is used for lightweight fabrics, buttonhole twist for medium- and heavyweight fabrics.

RELATED TECHNIQUES

Threads, p. 63
Hand sewing stitches, p. 74
Making bar tacks, p. 79
Applying fusible interfacing, p. 99
Custom tailoring, p. 282
Repairing a buttonhole, p. 307

DIRECTORY OF HANDSTITCHED BUTTONHOLES

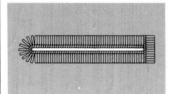

One round and one square end
This style of buttonhole is always used horizontally on a garment. When fastened, the button sits toward the round end of the buttonhole, which then supports the button and prevents the garment opening from gaping.

Two square ends
Used on vertical buttonholes where the button, when fastened, sits partway down the buttonhole, this style is not subject to stress. It is used mainly as a buttonhole on shirts, but can also be used for ribbon openings.

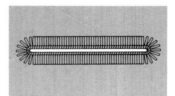

Two round ends
This is a distinctive way to finish a vertical buttonhole on a garment. It is used mainly for openings through which ribbon or cord is threaded. The width of the buttonhole is determined by the size of the ribbon or cord.

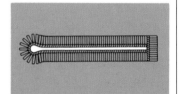

Piped keyhole
Designed as a horizontal buttonhole, this style of fastening has a small hole cut at the round end with the stitching fanned around it (p. 247). The stitching is worked over a fine cord to appear dense and rounded.

MAKING A HANDSTITCHED BUTTONHOLE

ON FRONT OPENINGS, horizontal buttonholes overlap the center line of the garment by 1/8 in (3 mm). The steps below illustrate a buttonhole with one round and one square end. The round end will support the button under stress. Vertical buttonholes are worked in a similar way, but with either two straight or two round ends.

1 MARK THE BUTTONHOLE line (p. 234), and decide on the stitch depth. Use a short, 1/16-in (2-mm) stitch on fine fabrics, and a longer stitch on thick fabrics. Stitch a rectangle just under a stitch length outside and all around the buttonhole marking (above).

2 CUT CAREFULLY along the center of the buttonhole marking. If necessary, overcast the raw edges to prevent fraying (above). Working on the right side with the round end of the buttonhole to the left, secure the thread end with small backstitches at the lower right corner.

3 BUTTONHOLE STITCH (p. 75) along one long edge. Insert the needle from the back to the front of the fabric (above). Pass the thread behind the eye end of the needle and under the point. Pull the needle through, ensuring that the knot formed covers the cut edge.

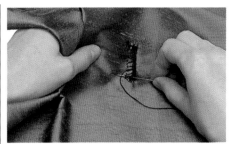

4 WORK THE STITCHES close together to cover the raw edge. Using the same stitch, fan out five or seven slightly longer stitches around the end of the buttonhole (above). The center stitch should be in line with the cut edges.

5 BUTTONHOLE STITCH along the other edge. Stitch through the knot of the first stitch, bringing the needle out just below the last stitch. Form a bar tack with three or four long stitches to make the square end of the buttonhole (above).

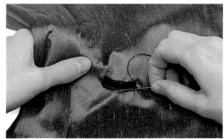

6 WITH THE NEEDLE POINT toward the buttonhole and beginning at one end, buttonhole stitch across the long stitches (above), picking up the garment fabric underneath. The stitches should form a neat row of knots along the bar tack base.

MAKING A PIPED KEYHOLE BUTTONHOLE

THIS TAILORED BUTTONHOLE is found mainly on heavy or bulky fabrics, such as those used for jackets and coats. The rounded end of the keyhole allows the button shank to sit neatly at the garment edge. Buttonhole twist is used for the stitching, and heavy-duty thread is applied as the filler cord to add strength to the stitching.

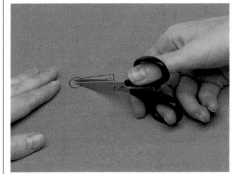

1 MARK THE BUTTONHOLE with a small circle at one end. Stitch all around, one stitch length away from the marking. Cut along the center of the buttonhole, and snip away the circle at the keyhole end (above). (An awl can also be used to pierce the keyhole end.)

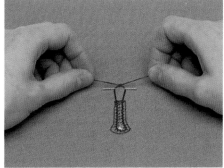

2 CUT A PIECE OF THIN CORD or a double thread of buttonhole twist to fit around the buttonhole. Overcast the cord around the edge of the buttonhole inside the previous stitching. Knot the ends of the cord around a pin beyond the square end of the buttonhole (above).

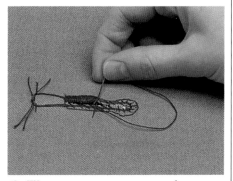

3 WITH THE KEYHOLE END on the right, begin at the square end and buttonhole stitch along the edge to cover the previous stitching. Work close stitches, and pull the knot of each stitch over the cut edges, so that all the stitches sit side by side with no gaps (above).

4 FAN OUT THE STITCHES around the eyelet, turning the fabric piece while stitching. The knots should be formed very close together so that they cover the cut edge of the buttonhole. Turn, and continue stitching along the other edge to the end (above).

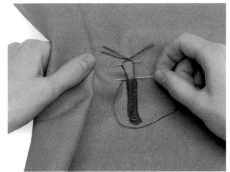

5 FINISH THE LAST STITCH by stitching through the knot of the first stitch, bringing the needle out at the lower left corner of the square edge. Make three or four long stitches across the end of the buttonhole to form the base of the bar tack that finishes the end (above).

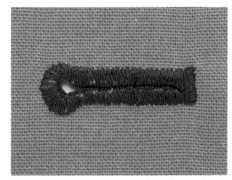

6 PULL THE CORD ENDS slightly so that the buttonhole is smooth and taut. Tie the ends at the bar tack again, and trim. Tuck the knot and ends under the bar tack. Finish with blanket stitches worked close together over the long edges, picking up the fabric underneath.

247

BUTTON LOOPS

Button loops are a decorative form of fastening and can be made in different ways. They are usually attached at the edge of a garment. Loops, formed from a very narrow, flexible tube of fabric, are usually used with round or domed buttons as decorative fastenings on bridal and evening gowns. The loops can be positioned in various places, depending on the garment style. Frog fastenings, generally used on jackets or long dress coats, can be made from tubing, corded tubing, or purchased cord.

RELATED TECHNIQUES

Working machine stitches, p. 77
Making bar tacks, p. 79
Reducing seam bulk, p. 84
Attaching a carrier to a
garment, p. 176
Making a faced hem, p. 214
Making buttons, p. 236

DIRECTORY OF BUTTON LOOPS

Spaced loops
The loops are set apart, one at each button position (see opposite). Generally, the loops are equally sized and spaced.

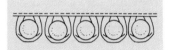

Unspaced loops
These are equal-sized loops placed close together (see opposite). They are usually used with small buttons.

Frog fastenings
These are available in pairs. One frog has a Chinese ball button (p. 237) in its center loop, and the other has a loop that projects over the garment opening onto the button.

MAKING NARROW TUBING

Soft, pliable fabrics, such as lawn, crepe de Chine, crepe, and challis, are most suitable for making narrow tubing. These strips can be cut on the straight grain of the fabric, but strips cut on the bias form much smoother, neater loops. Narrow tubing can be made with a cord in the middle if cut on the bias.

TUBING

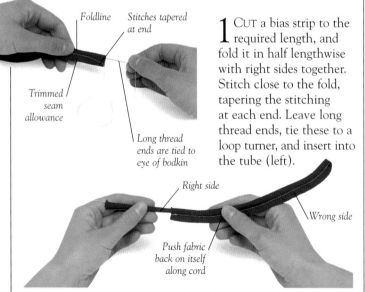

Foldline *Stitches tapered at end*

Trimmed seam allowance

Long thread ends are tied to eye of bodkin

Right side

Wrong side

Push fabric back on itself along cord

1 Cut a bias strip to the required length, and fold it in half lengthwise with right sides together. Stitch close to the fold, tapering the stitching at each end. Leave long thread ends, tie these to a loop turner, and insert into the tube (left).

2 Thread the loop turner along the tube, and start to pull the fabric right side out. Ease the tube along itself until all the tube fabric is right side out (above). Avoid pulling and stretching the tube, or splitting the stitches. Trim the tapered ends.

CORDED TUBING

Right sides together

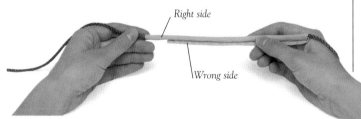

Right side

Wrong side

1 Cut a bias strip to fit around the cord. Cut the cord to slightly over twice the length of the strip. Wrap the strip over half the cord. Using a zipper foot, stitch across the end of the strip and the cord center, then along the strip (left).

2 Trim the seam allowance to about ⅛ in (3 mm). Push the fabric along the cord so that it turns back on itself to cover the other half of the cord (above). Keep the fabric seam straight, and trim the excess cord at the ends.

FORMING LOOPS

THE LOOPS CAN BE FORMED as they are stitched onto the fabric. However, on slippery fabrics it is easier to form the loops on a paper guide. Guidelines drawn on the paper ensure that all the loops are the same size and are evenly spaced. Both the loops and the paper guide are then stitched to the fabric, and the paper is torn away later.

POSITIONING BUTTON LOOPS

1 CUT A PIECE OF PAPER for the button loop guide, the length of the opening by 2½ in (6.5 cm). Draw a line for the seamline and another ¼ in (5 mm) parallel to it as a guide for the raw edges of the loops (above).

2 PLACE THE BUTTON on the marked seamline, the desired distance from the top. Pin one end of the tube on the ¼ in (5 mm) line, and form a loop around the button. Pin the end (above), and trim. Mark each loop position on guide.

UNSPACED LOOPS

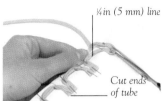

¼ in (5 mm) line

Cut ends of tube

FORM THE GUIDE with no space between the loops. Pin each loop to the guide with the ends on the ¼ in (5 mm) line, and trim (above). Fasten the raw edges with tape. Machine baste the loops through the tape.

SPACED LOOPS

Tape over ends

MARK the loop positions on the paper guide, with even spacing between loops. Cut the loops, and pin them to the paper, with the raw edges aligned with the ¼ in (5 mm) line. Tape the ends in place (above), then machine baste.

STITCHING LOOPS

Carefully tear off paper

1 PLACE THE PAPER GUIDE with the loops attached to the right side of the garment. Pin in place. Stitch just inside the seamline. Remove the tape and pins. Tear off the paper guide (above).

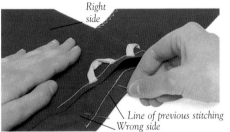

Right side

Line of previous stitching
Wrong side

2 PLACE THE FACING and the garment right sides together. Pin together on the wrong side (above). Stitch along the seamline just outside the previous line of stitching.

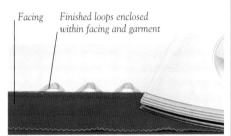

Facing   *Finished loops enclosed within facing and garment*

3 TRIM AND LAYER the facing seam allowances, pressing them away from the garment. Understitch the seam on the right side. Press the facing over to the wrong side, revealing the loops (above).

MAKING A FROG FASTENING

A FROG FASTENING IS MADE from one length of cord or tubing arranged into four loops that are stitched together at the center. If using a cord that frays, tape should be wrapped around each end and stitched through. The frog is formed right side down, so that the seam on the tubing lies centrally on the upper side.

End of cord to be stitched to back of other cord at center after trimming

1 MARK the finished size of the frog on a sheet of stiff paper, and pin the loop along this marking. Form the first loop with a short end of cord overlapping the long piece at the center. Pin (above), then handstitch in place. Trim the short end.

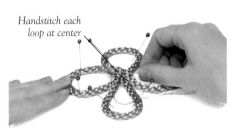

Handstitch each loop at center

2 CONTINUE FORMING and pinning the four loops in place. Handstitch each loop at the center as it is formed (above). Make sure that the stitching does not show on the right side. Stitch to secure the end loop. Turn the frog right side up.

3 MAKE REMAINING FROGS as needed. Pin and stitch the button frog in place, through the underside of the cord. Stitch a ball button to the center loop, and arrange the other frog to overlap the fabric edge and the button (above). Stitch.

ATTACHING ZIPPERS

Z IPPERS ARE AVAILABLE IN DIFFERENT TYPES, weights, and lengths. Chain and coil zippers are general-purpose zippers made in a wide range of colors and lengths. Coil zippers are usually lighter in weight than chain zippers and are useful for fine fabrics. Invisible zippers come in fewer colors, and the size range is limited to fit the average skirt or dress opening. Since they are used on jackets, separating zippers are usually long and heavy. On women's garments, fly zippers normally lap right to left, while on men's clothes they lap from left to right.

RELATED TECHNIQUES

Machine feet, p. 18
Working machine stitches, p. 77
Making bar tacks, p. 79
Stitching a corner, p. 83
Seam finishes, p. 85
Stitching curved seams, p. 88
Repairing zippers, p. 306

DIRECTORY OF ZIPPERS

Chain zipper
This is a mediumweight zipper with metal or plastic teeth.

Coil zipper
A coil zipper has synthetic coils of polyester or nylon attached to a woven tape.

Invisible zipper
A type of coil zipper, this zipper has teeth that are concealed on the underside.

Separating zipper
This chain zipper separates at the base into two halves.

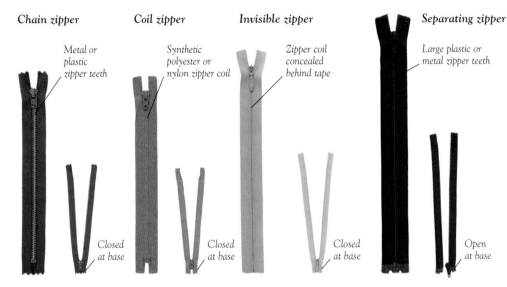

Chain zipper
Metal or plastic zipper teeth
Closed at base

Coil zipper
Synthetic polyester or nylon zipper coil
Closed at base

Invisible zipper
Zipper coil concealed behind tape
Closed at base

Separating zipper
Large plastic or metal zipper teeth
Open at base

DIRECTORY OF METHODS OF APPLICATION

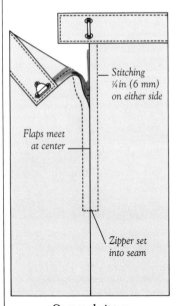

Stitching ¼ in (6 mm) on either side
Flaps meet at center
Zipper set into seam

Centered zipper

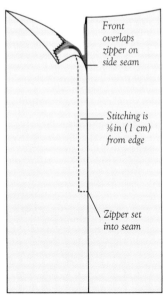

Front overlaps zipper on side seam
Stitching is ⅜ in (1 cm) from edge
Zipper set into seam

Lapped zipper

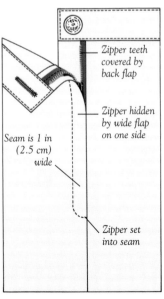

Zipper teeth covered by back flap
Zipper hidden by wide flap on one side
Seam is 1 in (2.5 cm) wide
Zipper set into seam

Fly zipper

Centered zipper
Stitched an equal distance out on both sides, this zipper is used mainly at center back dress openings. It can also used at the back of skirts (p. 253).

Lapped zipper
One side of this zipper is stitched close to the teeth; the other is spaced away from them. It is used mainly at the center front or back, or at a side seam (p. 252–253).

Fly zipper
This zipper is stitched to the underwraps of a fly fastening. Only the curved topstitching is visible (p. 254–255).

Concealed zipper

Once inserted, this zipper looks like a continuation of the seam with no stitching visible from the outside (p. 256–257).

Exposed zipper

The teeth of this zipper remain exposed. It is stitched into a part of the garment where there is no seam (p. 258).

Separating zipper

This zipper is used on jackets because it opens completely (p. 257). It is usually stitched to expose the zipper teeth, which are often a color that contrasts with the garment. The teeth can also be covered.

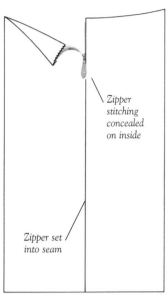

Zipper stitching concealed on inside

Zipper set into seam

Invisible zipper

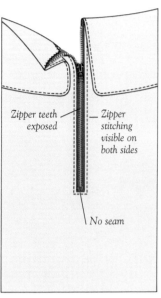

Zipper teeth exposed

Zipper stitching visible on both sides

No seam

Exposed zipper

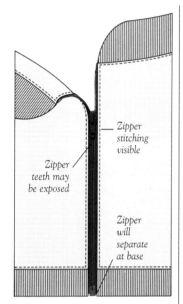

Zipper teeth may be exposed

Zipper stitching visible

Zipper will separate at base

Separating zipper

········· USING A ZIPPER FOOT ·········

A ZIPPER FOOT HAS A SINGLE TOE, rather than the two toes found on a conventional sewing foot, and it is also narrower. Most zipper feet can be adjusted to sit either to the right or the left of the needle, so that the foot does not ride over the bumpy zipper teeth, making the stitching uneven. A concealed zipper foot is used for invisible zippers.

SETTING A ZIPPER FOOT

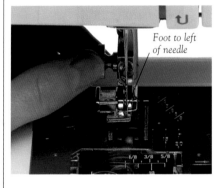

Foot to left of needle

SET the zipper foot to the left of the needle so that the stitching guidelines on the needle plate can be followed. Loosen the screw at the back of the foot. Set the foot as close to the needle as possible. Tighten the screw (left).

STITCHING WITH A ZIPPER FOOT

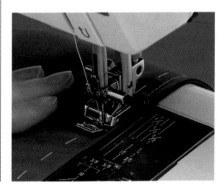

PLACE the garment under the zipper foot. The foot should be to the left of the zipper teeth, and the needle between the foot and the teeth. Using the guidelines, stitch close to the zipper (left), reversing neatly at the start and finish.

ALIGNING A ZIPPER FOOT

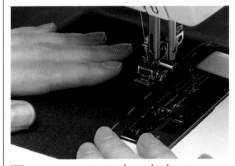

WHERE POSSIBLE, stitch with the zipper open so that the fabric edge can be aligned with the stitching guideline on the needle plate (above), to keep the stitching straight and even. Close the zipper to finish the stitching.

SHORTENING A PLASTIC ZIPPER

1 Measure the new zipper length and mark with a pin. Using a zigzag stitch with the length set at zero but wide enough to stitch across the teeth, stitch on the pin marking to make a new stop.

Cut across teeth below stop

2 Cut off the excess zipper. Tape ⅝ in (1.5 cm) below the zigzag stop (above). Insert the zipper into the garment, stitching carefully across the base of the teeth or coil. (Do not stitch across metal teeth.)

STITCHING A LAPPED ZIPPER

THIS IS THE MOST WIDELY USED method for inserting a zipper at the top of a seam, for example, at the waist of a skirt or pants. It is also used at side and center-back openings on dresses. One side of the opening is stitched close to the zipper teeth, and both this stitching and the zipper are then hidden by the overlapping opposite edge.

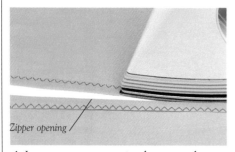

Zipper opening

1 LEAVE AN OPENING in the seam the length of the zipper plus ¾ in (2 cm). Finish the raw edges of the seam. Press the seam open, and continue pressing the seam allowances to the wrong side along both edges of the opening (above).

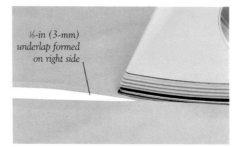

⅛-in (3-mm) underlap formed on right side

2 WORKING FROM THE RIGHT SIDE of the garment, refold the right-hand edge of the opening, reducing the seam allowance by ⅛ in (3 mm) to form a ⅛-in (3-mm) underlap. Press the underlap flat along the opening (above).

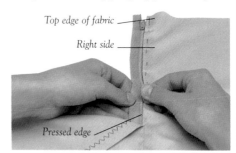

Top edge of fabric

Right side

Pressed edge

3 PIN THE ZIPPER TAPE behind the right-hand edge of the opening so that the zipper teeth lie next to the pressed edge (above). The top of the zipper teeth should be positioned ¾ in (2 cm) down from the top edge of the fabric.

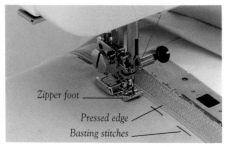

Zipper foot

Pressed edge

Basting stitches

4 BASTE THE ZIPPER TAPE in place. Remove the pins. Topstitch down the zipper, from top to base, between the basting and pressed edge (above), sliding the pull tab past the needle (see opposite). Finish stitching, and remove the basting.

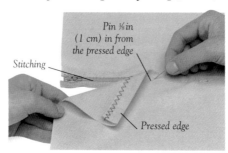

Pin ⅜ in (1 cm) in from the pressed edge

Stitching

Pressed edge

5 PLACE THE LEFT OPENING EDGE over the zipper so that the zipper is hidden and the stitching is just covered. Pin the zipper tape in place ⅜ in (1 cm) in from the pressed edge (above). Pin just below the base of the zipper teeth.

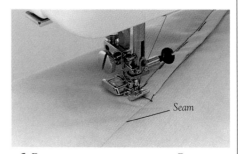

Seam

6 BASTE THE ZIPPER IN PLACE. Remove the pins. Stitch the zipper from the top edge, sliding the tab pull past the needle while stitching. Pivot the fabric at the base of the zipper, and stitch across to the seam (above). Remove the basting.

STITCHING AN ENCLOSED LAPPED ZIPPER

AN ENCLOSED ZIPPER IS ONE THAT IS INSERTED in a seam where the seam continues above and below the zipper. This type of opening is used mainly in the side seams of fitted dresses with sleeves, where the garment design makes a center-back zipper unsuitable. The overlapping edge of the opening should be in the garment front.

Top edges of zipper tape

1 STITCH THE TOP EDGES of the zipper tape together, just above the top of the zipper teeth (above). Measure the zipper from the stitching to below the bottom stop. Stitch the garment seam, leaving an opening equal to this length. Baste along the opening seam. Press the seam open.

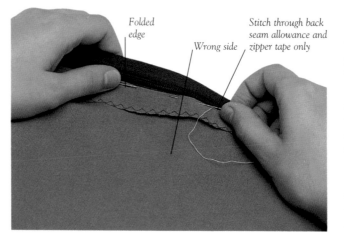

Folded edge

Wrong side

Stitch through back seam allowance and zipper tape only

2 UNFOLD the back seam allowance so that it lies under the garment front. Refold the allowance ⅛ in (3 mm) past the opening to make an underlap. Pin the zipper tape so that the folded edge is next to the zipper teeth. Baste (left), and remove the pins. Using a zipper foot, topstitch the zipper along the edge.

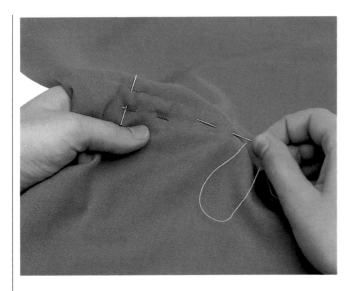

3 TURN to the right side of the fabric, and pin the zipper tape flat behind the zipper opening. Baste the front edge of the opening to the zipper tape ⅜ in (1 cm) in from the basted seam (left). Using a zipper foot, stitch across the base of the zipper ⅜ in (1 cm) in from the seam. Pivot the fabric, and continue stitching along the basted edge. Remove the basting.

······· SHAPING STITCHING ········
ON A LAPPED ZIPPER

Stop stitching just below the zipper base. Lower the needle, and lift the foot. Pivot to the correct position for stitching to the seam, either straight across or at an angle. Lower the foot, and stitch to the seam. Reverse stitch over the base stitching to finish.

········· INSERTING A CENTERED ZIPPER ·········

A CENTERED ZIPPER IS AN ALTERNATIVE to a lapped zipper. It is simpler to insert, but is used only at center openings, mostly at the center back openings of dresses.

The zipper is positioned behind the two edges of the opening, with the stitching spaced evenly down both sides. This method can be used for a centered enclosed zipper.

Basted seamline

1 STITCH THE SEAM, leaving an opening the length of the zipper teeth plus ¾ in (2 cm). Finish the raw edges of the seam. Baste the edges of the zipper opening together along the seamline (above). Press the seam allowances open, and turn the garment to the right side. Place the zipper centrally behind the basted opening.

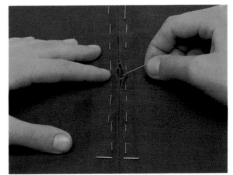

2 PLACE THE TOP of the zipper teeth on the opening ¾ in (2 cm) down from the top edge of the fabric. Pin the zipper in place ¼ in (5 mm) in from the basted zipper opening. Separate a small section of the basted opening edges, using either a pin or a needle, to check that the zipper is centered behind the opening (above).

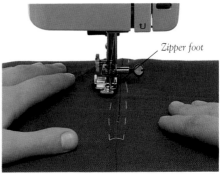

Zipper foot

3 BASTE THE ZIPPER IN PLACE, stitching the basting slightly wider at the top of the zipper to accommodate the pull tab. Remove the pins. Stitch the zipper in place, using the basting as a guide (above). Take care to stitch next to the basting, not over it. Stitch to the bottom stop of the zipper, finishing with the needle down.

············ SLIDING THE PULL TAB PAST THE NEEDLE ············

Stop stitching partway along the zipper. With the needle down, raise the zipper foot. Slide the pull tab gently past the needle so that it is behind the raised zipper foot (left). Check that the line of stitching has not moved, and realign it if it has. Lower the foot to continue, and complete the stitch.

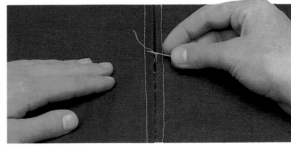

4 PIVOT THE FABRIC, and stitch across the base of the zipper, counting the stitches up to the seam. Work the same number of stitches past the seam on the other side. Pivot the fabric again, and stitch up the second side of the zipper. Finally, remove the basting by pulling out the stitches with a pin (above).

INSERTING A ZIPPER WITH A FLY

FOR MEN'S PANTS, some women's pants, and casual skirts, it is necessary to insert a zipper with a fly. The technique is easier than it seems and gives a professional finish to the zipper opening. Adding a zipper guard behind the zipper is especially useful on close-fitting garments to prevent underwear from becoming caught in the zipper.

SIMPLE ZIPPER FLY

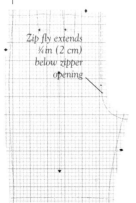

Zip fly extends ¼ in (2 cm) below zipper opening

1 TO INSERT a zipper fly where the pattern does not allow for one, a fly extension must be added when cutting (left). Follow the line of the crotch seam, and add a 1-in (2.5-cm) extension. Curve this in to meet the crotch edge about ¾ in (2 cm) below the zipper opening.

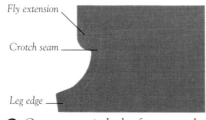

Fly extension
Crotch seam
Leg edge

2 ON PANTS, stitch the front crotch seam from the zipper opening to 2 in (5 cm) above the inside leg, so that the leg seam can be stitched before the crotch seam. (On skirts, stitch the center front seam up to the opening.)

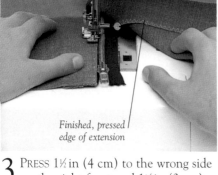

Finished, pressed edge of extension

3 PRESS 1½ in (4 cm) to the wrong side on the right front and 1¼ in (3 cm) on the left. Baste the zipper behind the left front, with the teeth aligned with the pressed edge and ¼ in (2 cm) below the top edge, then stitch this side (above).

4 ON THE LEFT FRONT, mark ⅜ in (1 cm) in from the stitched edge with pins. Lay the pressed edge of the right front over the zipper so that it is level with the pinline. Baste in place (above). Remove the pins.

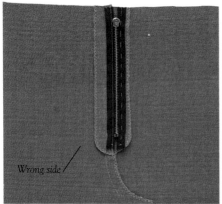

Wrong side

5 WORKING ON the wrong side of the garment, baste the unstitched zipper tape to both the extension and the garment, about ¼ in (6 mm) away from the zipper teeth (above). Baste through all the thicknesses of fabric.

Curve stitching in at zipper base

6 ON THE RIGHT SIDE, and using a zipper foot, stitch through the right front and the zipper tape using the line of basting as a guide. Stitch in a curve at the bottom to meet the seam just below the zipper stop (above). Remove the basting.

MAKING A FLY FACING

1 CUT A PIECE of fabric for the zipper facing 4 in (10 cm) wide and ¾ in (2 cm) longer than the zipper. The zipper facing should give an underlap of 1¼ in (3 cm). Check the underlap allowance on the waistband and lengthen it if necessary. (On bulky fabrics, use a firm, lightweight cotton for the zipper facing.)

Fabric for zipper facing

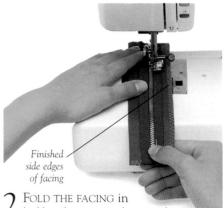

Finished side edges of facing

2 FOLD THE FACING in half with wrong sides together. Zigzag stitch the side and lower raw edges together to finish. With the zipper facing up, pin, then stitch the right-hand zipper tape to the facing about ¾ in (2 cm) in from the finished edge (above).

3 STITCH THE ZIPPER and the facing to the garment (see Simple Zipper Fly, left). Ensure that the facing is not caught in the second row of stitching. Handstitch the facing to the fly extension at the base of the zipper on the wrong side (above).

INSERTING A ZIPPER FLY BY THE ADVANCED METHOD

THIS METHOD PROVIDES a more professional finish than a simple zipper fly (see opposite) but is used in similar garments. The first edge of the zipper tape is stitched to the fly facing so that the stitching will not show. Since the fly topstitching does not attach the zipper to the garment, it can be widely spaced. A zipper facing is useful but not vital.

Right front *Left front*

Crotch seam

1 MARK with basting stitches the curved fly topstitching line on the right front of the garment. Stitch the front sections together, stitching along the crotch seam from the bottom of the zipper opening, stopping 2 in (5 cm) from the inside leg seams.

Fly facing

2 FINISH THE SEAM and the outer edge of the fly extension with zigzag stitching. With right sides together and raw edges even, place the straight edge of the fly extension on the right front. Pin (above), and stitch.

3 TRIM AND LAYER the seam allowance as required (p. 84). Open out the fly extension, and press the facing and the seam allowances flat (above), then press the seam allowances away from the garment.

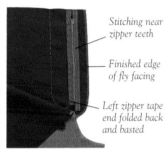

Stitching near zipper teeth

Finished edge of fly facing

Left zipper tape end folded back and basted

4 WITH THE ZIPPER right side down and the left edge of the zipper tape even with the seam, baste and stitch the left side of the zipper tape to the fly extension. Stitch the right side of the zipper tape to the fly extension twice.

Basting guideline

5 AFTER COMPLETING the stitching, fold the fly extension to the wrong side and press the seam at the edge. On the right side, pin the garment to the extension, using the line of basting as a guide (above).

Right side

6 WORKING on the right side, topstitch along the basted guideline (above), then remove all the basting. With right sides together, stitch the zipper facing pieces together, stitching along the curved edges.

7 TRIM AND LAYER the fly facing seam allowances. Notch the curve so that the zipper facing will lie flat. Turn the fly facing right side out, and press. Zigzag stitch the unstitched zipper facing edges together to finish (above).

8 FOLD UNDER and press the left edge of the opening to the wrong side ¼ in (6 mm) beyond the center front. Open the zipper. Pin the pressed left front to the zipper tape so that it is level with the zipper teeth (above).

9 WORKING ON the wrong side of the garment, position the zipper facing over the zipper. Align the long, curved edge of the facing with the previous line of topstitching. Pin the facing in position (above).

10 TURN to the right side of the garment, and baste along the left edge of the zipper through the garment, zipper tape and zipper facing. Using a zipper foot, stitch along the basted edge near the zipper teeth (above).

11 REINFORCE the base of the zipper opening with a bar tack (p. 79). The bar tack is sewn by hand (above), or by machine, stitching across the seamline several times. Catch the zipper facing in the bar tack when stitching.

INSERTING A CONCEALED ZIPPER

A CONCEALED ZIPPER MUST BE INSERTED using a special zipper foot. The machine stitching is worked on the inside of the garment so that there is no visible stitching. The finished zipper is completely hidden, and the opening looks like a continuation of the seam. Concealed zippers are available in only a limited selection of lengths.

Opened concealed zipper

1 WORKING on the wrong side, press the concealed zipper so that the tapes are smooth and the coil stands up away from the tapes (above). This helps the zipper slide smoothly through the machine foot.

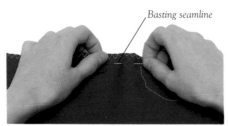

Basting seamline

2 THE ZIPPER is inserted before the seam is stitched. Zigzag stitch the raw edges. Baste the edges of the opening to mark the seamlines, continuing for about 2 in (5 cm) below the end of the zipper (above).

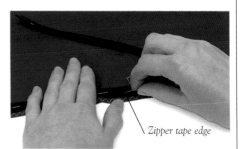

Zipper tape edge

3 WITH right sides together and the zipper open, pin and baste the right side of the zipper to the right side of the garment opening so that the zipper coil is positioned along the basted seamline (above).

4 USING a concealed zipper foot, fit the right-hand groove on the underside of the foot over the zipper coil, and stitch (above). Secure the thread ends.

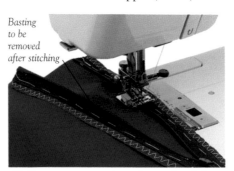

Basting to be removed after stitching

5 PIN AND BASTE the other side of the zipper along the seamline. Position the left groove on the underside of the foot over the zipper coil, and stitch (above).

Ordinary zipper foot

6 CLOSE THE ZIPPER. Pin and baste the seam below the zipper end. Using an ordinary zipper foot, stitch the seam, just overlapping the zipper stitching (above).

FINISHING A CONCEALED ZIPPER

O N MANY FABRICS, the zipper stitching described above is sufficient, but sometimes, particularly on soft fabrics, extra stitching on the inside improves the finish. Also, where the concealed zipper is inserted into an enclosed opening, the zipper must be stitched at the top. None of this stitching shows on the right side of the fabric.

REINFORCING ZIPPER TAPE

ON SOME soft and lightweight fabrics, the spring of the coil on a concealed zipper will make the garment fabric pucker. To prevent this, stitch the outer edges of the zipper to the seam allowances on both sides. Stitch through the zipper tape and seam allowance only, so that no stitching shows on the right side.

FINISHING ENCLOSED OPENINGS

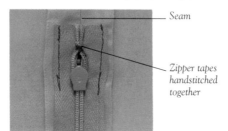

Seam

Zipper tapes handstitched together

ON ENCLOSED OPENINGS, insert the zipper (see above). Handstitch the zipper tapes together above the top of the zipper coil. Stitch the top edges of the zipper tape to the seam allowances. Stitch the seams above and below the zipper as usual.

SUPPORTING THE COIL

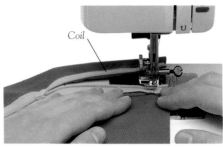

Coil

INSERT THE ZIPPER (see above). Keeping the coil upright, stitch across the tops of the zipper tape at right angles to the coil (above). This line of stitching encourages the coil stand up, which helps the pull tab glide up and down easily.

MATCHING PATTERNS ON A CONCEALED ZIPPER

I T IS NOT POSSIBLE TO CHECK the right side of a garment while stitching a concealed zipper. This may cause problems when working with checked and striped fabrics. The fabric should therefore be matched when the pattern pieces are cut (p. 38) and seamed; insert the zipper by using one of the methods shown below.

MATCHING STRIPES

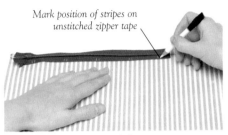

Mark position of stripes on unstitched zipper tape

1 STITCH ONE SIDE of the zipper tape to the right side of the opening (see Step 4, opposite). Close the zipper. Mark the stripes on the edge of the other zipper tape using a dressmaker's pencil (above).

Stripes match on both sides once zipper is basted in place

2 OPEN the zipper and, with the markings on the zipper tape matching the stripes on the fabric, baste the other zipper edge in place. Close the zipper. Check that the pattern matches on the right side before stitching in place.

MATCHING DIAGONALS

STITCH ONE EDGE of the zipper. Place double-sided tape over the unstitched zipper tape. Position the pressed-under seam allowance so that the stripes match (above). Stitch the other tape.

INSERTING A SEPARATING ZIPPER

T HERE ARE TWO METHODS for inserting open-ended zippers. With the centered method, the fabric edges meet at the center of the zipper to conceal the zipper teeth. With the exposed method, the zipper teeth are left visible as a decorative feature. The garment neck and hem edges can be finished before or after the zipper is inserted.

CENTERED METHOD

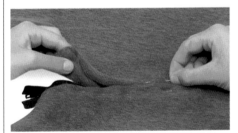

1 PRESS THE SEAM ALLOWANCES under along the zipper opening. Pin the zipper in place from the right side, with the zipper teeth centered and the pull tab ¼ in (5 mm) below the neck edge (above).

2 OPEN THE ZIPPER, and turn the garment wrong side out. Unpin the top edges of the zipper tape (above). Tuck the ends of the zipper tape under the neck facing, and repin in place. Baste if desired.

3 USING A ZIPPER FOOT, stitch the zipper in place about ⅜ in (1 cm) away from the pressed-under edge (above). Remove the basting. The pressed-under edge should almost cover the zipper teeth.

EXPOSED METHOD

1 PRESS THE SEAM ALLOWANCES under along the zipper opening. Pin the zipper in place from the right side with the edges slightly apart and the zipper teeth exposed evenly down the opening (above).

2 BASTE THE ZIPPER in position (above). Remove the pins. If the garment neck edge is already finished, fold under the ends of the zipper tape on the wrong side, and repin the ends of the zipper tape.

Zipper foot

3 OPEN THE ZIPPER. Using a zipper foot, stitch the zipper in place close to the zipper teeth (above). Stitch a second row ¼ in (6 mm) away from the first to hold the zipper tape flat. Remove the basting. Press.

INSERTING AN EXPOSED ZIPPER

AN EXPOSED ZIPPER is inserted in an area of fabric that has no seam. The opening is faced, and the zipper teeth are left visible. This type of opening is usually decorative as well as functional. Both the topstitched and concealed methods are used at the garment edge. When using the enclosed method, both ends of the zipper are enclosed.

TOPSTITCHED METHOD

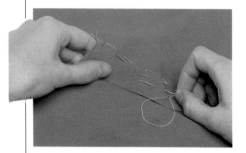

1 MARK the length of the zipper teeth plus ¾ in (2 cm) centrally on the facing. With right sides together, pin the facing centrally over the zipper position on the garment, and baste in place (left).

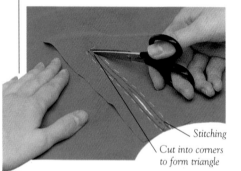

Stitching
Cut into corners to form triangle

2 STITCH ⅛–¼ in (3–6 mm) on both sides of the zipper marking and below it, across the base. The width between the stitching should expose the zipper teeth. Cut along the marking, and into the corners (left).

3 PRESS the seams open, and press the facing to the wrong side so that it does not show on the right side. Place the zipper centrally behind the opening. Baste in place. Using a zipper foot, stitch around the fabric edge (left).

CONCEALED STITCHING METHOD

1 FACE the opening (see Steps 1 and 2, left). Place the zipper centrally behind the opening, and pin. Slip baste (p. 73) the fold of the garment fabric to each side of the zipper tape (left).

Triangle of fabric

2 LIFT the fabric at the base of the zipper to expose the lower edge of the facing and the cut triangle of garment fabric at the base of the zipper (see left). Stitch across the base of the triangle to secure it to the facing.

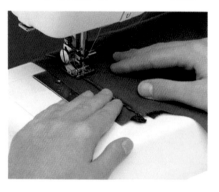

3 FOLD one side of the zipper, exposing the wrong side of the facing and the first stitching. Stitch over this stitching, through the seam allowance, zipper tape, and facing (left). Stitch the second zipper side. Remove the basting.

INSERTING AN ENCLOSED EXPOSED ZIPPER

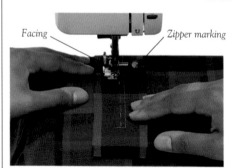

Facing *Zipper marking*

1 CUT THE FACING to 2 in (5 cm) by the zipper length, plus 2¼ in (6 cm). Mark the position of the zipper opening on the facing, and pin the facing to the garment with right sides together. Stitch a rectangle ⅛–¼ in (3–6 mm) on either side of the zipper marking (above).

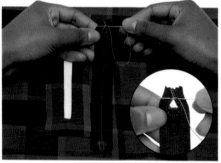

2 CUT ALONG the zipper marking to ⅜ in (1 cm) from each end, then cut diagonally into the corners. Press the facing over to the wrong side to enclose the raw edges of the seam allowances. Handstitch the top edges of the zipper tape together above the zipper teeth (above).

Stitch just inside basting

3 WITH THE RIGHT side of both fabric and zipper uppermost, place the zipper centrally behind the opening. Pin in place. Baste, and remove the pins. Using a zipper foot, stitch the zipper close to the edge of the zipper opening inside the line of basting (above). Remove the basting.

INSERTING AN ENCLOSED ZIPPER WITH PIPING

A N ENCLOSED ZIPPER is inserted in a seam that is stitched above and below the zipper. Enclosed zippers are often used on dress side seams and on removable cushion covers where the seam may also be piped. The piping is stitched on before the zipper is inserted. This method forms a lapped zipper with the overlap on the edge opposite the piping.

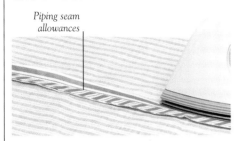
Piping seam allowances

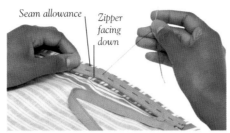
Seam allowance — *Zipper facing down*

Zipper foot

1 STITCH THE PIPING in place using a zipper foot. Baste the complete seam, with right sides together. Stitch, leaving an opening for the zipper. Press the seams open. Press the seam allowances along the opening (above). Remove the basting.

2 LIFT THE SEAM ALLOWANCE on the piped edge. Place one side of the zipper tape on the seam allowance, right sides together, with the zipper teeth against the piping. Baste the zipper in place (above). Machine stitch, using a zipper foot.

3 CLOSE THE ZIPPER. Lay the fabric out flat with right sides uppermost. Pin the unstitched zipper tape to the other side of the opening, ⅜ in (1 cm) from the edge, and baste. Remove the pins. Stitch the zipper in place (above). Remove basting.

INSERTING A ZIPPER IN PLEATS

A ZIPPER ON A PLEATED SKIRT is inserted underneath a pleat to be as inconspicuous as possible. On an inverted pleat, the zipper is stitched underneath the two meeting folds of a pleat to conceal it. On box pleats, the zipper is stitched centrally between two pleats. On knife pleats, the zipper is concealed at the underfold of a pleat.

ZIPPER IN INVERTED OR BOX PLEATS

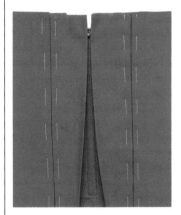

ON AN INVERTED pleat, place the seam requiring the zipper opening at the center of the pleat underfold. Insert the zipper by the centered method (p. 253). The folds of the pleat will meet over the zipper so that it is covered. (On box pleats, the zipper is inserted in a seam between two pleats and may be more visible.)

INSERTING A HANDSTITCHED ZIPPER

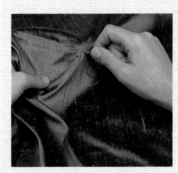

Handstitched zippers are not as strong as machined zippers, but they give a couture finish. On easily marked fabrics such as velvet, handstitching is easier than machining. Baste the zipper, following the lapped (p. 252) or centered method (p. 253). Stitch using prickstitches (left).

INSERTING A ZIPPER IN KNIFE PLEATS

Stitch with zipper closed — *Zipper foot*

1 POSITION THE SEAM requiring the zipper at the underfold of the pleat. Stitch the seam, leaving an opening. Clip the innermost seam allowance at the base of the zipper opening, and press the seam open flat above the clip (above).

2 TURN TO THE RIGHT SIDE. Pull back the garment to expose the lower pressed edge. With right sides uppermost, place the zipper behind the pressed edge, the teeth next to the edge. Pin, baste, and stitch the zipper in place using a zipper foot.

3 TURN to the wrong side. Extend the unstitched edge away from the opening, and position the free edge of the zipper along it, with the teeth ⅛ in (3 mm) from the seamline. Pin, baste, and stitch in place (above).

OTHER FASTENINGS

HOOKS ARE VERSATILE FASTENERS that can fit into both straight bars and round eyes, and are strong enough not to open under stress. They are made in different sizes and strengths, and are frequently used on waistbands and at the tops of zipper openings. Sew-on snap fasteners are available in a range of sizes, and nonsew snaps provide an alternative to buttonholes on casual garments. Hook-and-loop fasteners, usually cut from a strip, are easy to open and close and are often used for garment details such as cuffs, and in home furnishings.

RELATED TECHNIQUES

Hand sewing stitches, p. 74
Reducing seam bulk, p. 84
Making a bound neckline, p. 134
Preparing to make a
waistband, p. 166
Stitching a lapped zipper, p. 252
Inserting a centered zipper, p. 253

DIRECTORY OF FASTENINGS

Hook and looped eye

Hook and straight eye

Standard hooks and eyes
These fasteners have looped eyes for use on adjoining fabric edges, or straight eyes for use with lapped fabric edges (see opposite).

Covered hook and eye
This large set has a looped eye. It is used on coats, jackets, and garments made from deep-pile fabrics.

Skirt hook and bar
This sturdy set is used on pants and skirt waistbands (see opposite). The design stops the hook from slipping off the straight eye.

Ball stud   *Socket stud*

Snap fastener
Made from nylon or metal, this fastener is formed from a ball and socket, which simply press or snap together and are easily pulled apart (p. 263).

Stud cap   *Socket stud*

Ball stud   *Rivet*

Nonsew snap fastener
This fastener has a decorative metal cap. The fabric is held between the socket stud and the stud cap. The other edge is held between the ball stud and the rivet. The two sides then snap together (p. 263).

Pronged ring

Socket stud

Ball stud

Button back

Button mould

Nonsew covered snap
Designed to look like a covered button, this ball-and-socket fastener is available in a kit containing five pieces that snap together. It is covered by a circle of fabric (p. 263).

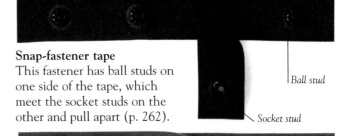

Snap-fastener tape
This fastener has ball studs on one side of the tape, which meet the socket studs on the other and pull apart (p. 262).

Ball stud

Socket stud

Hook-and-loop fastener tape
The looped nap of this fastener meets the matching hooked nap. The naps lock when pressed together, and unlock when pulled apart (p. 262).

Looped nap

Hooked nap

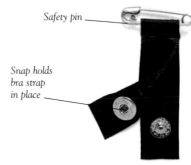

Safety pin

Snap holds bra strap in place

Lingerie strap guard
This is designed to prevent bra straps from slipping out from under narrow shoulder straps. The guard is fastened to the garment with a safety pin (p. 263). The bra strap is slipped between the two tapes and held by the snap.

HOOK-AND-EYE FASTENERS

HOOKS AND EYES ARE USED to fasten overlapping edges on fabric areas where a neat join is required. Using double thread for strength, the thread is attached to the fabric with a couple of small, close backstitches, where they will be hidden by the hook. The hook is placed toward the edge of the fabric, with its end ⅛ in (3 mm) from the edge.

HOOK AND LOOPED EYE

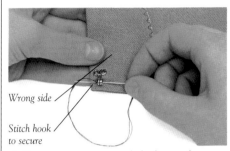

Wrong side

Stitch hook to secure

1 STITCH AROUND each hole on the hook, without stitching through to the right side. Take two or three stitches over the neck of the hook to secure it (above). Finish with backstitches near the hook.

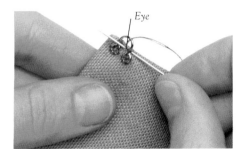

Eye

2 POSITION THE EYE so that the loop projects over the fabric edge by about ⅛ in (3 mm). Fasten the thread securely. Stitch around each hole. Stitch over each side of the eye inside the fabric (above).

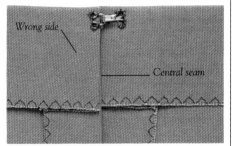

Wrong side

Central seam

3 FASTEN THE HOOK and eye. The finished edges of the two parts of the garment should just meet and lie flat, so that no part of the hook or eye is visible on the right side of the garment.

HOOK AND STRAIGHT EYE

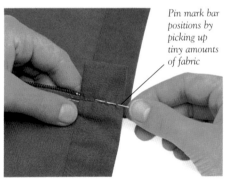

Pin mark bar positions by picking up tiny amounts of fabric

1 STITCH THE HOOKS to the wrong side of the overlapping edge, with their ends about ⅛ in (3 mm) in from the edge. Close up the opening, and mark the positions of the bars with pins on the right side of the underlap (above).

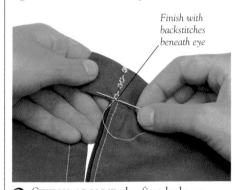

Finish with backstitches beneath eye

2 STITCH AROUND the first hole on a bar. Slip the needle between the fabric layers, along to the second hole, and stitch around it. Slip the needle to the second bar position and stitch. Finish by fastening the thread securely (above).

SKIRT HOOK AND BAR

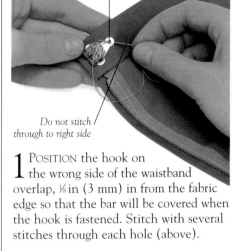

Hook

Do not stitch through to right side

1 POSITION the hook on the wrong side of the waistband overlap, ⅛ in (3 mm) in from the fabric edge so that the bar will be covered when the hook is fastened. Stitch with several stitches through each hole (above).

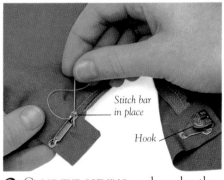

Stitch bar in place

Hook

2 CLOSE THE OPENING, and overlap the waistband ends. Position the bar on the right side of the waistband so that it corresponds with the hook. Pin through the holes to hold the bar in place, and secure it with several stitches (above).

COVERED HOOK AND EYE

COVERED HOOKS AND EYES give a neat finish and are used where they are visible on the garment. Attach the hook and eye using a matching thread, then cover with close blanket stitches (above), taking care not to catch the fabric under the bar.

BUTTONHOLE-STITCHED FINISH

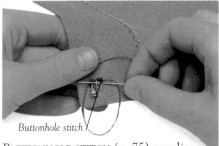

Buttonhole stitch

BUTTONHOLE STITCH (p. 75) supplies a neat finish for hooks, eyes, bars, and snap fastenings. Position the fastener as usual, and stitch around the hole with a closely spaced buttonhole stitch (above), pulling the knots onto the fabric.

HANDSTITCHED BARS, EYES, AND LOOPS

THESE FASTENING HOLDERS are formed by working long stitches, which are then covered with buttonhole or blanket stitch. Thread bars, eyes, and loops are less noticeable on a finished garment than metal eyes and, when worked in buttonhole twist, can be just as strong. Thread button loops are made at the garment edge to form a discreet fastening.

THREAD BARS

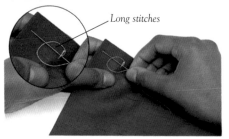

1 STITCH THE HOOK onto the garment with its end ⅛ in (3 mm) from the fabric edge. Close the opening, and mark each end of the bar position with pins (above). Fasten the thread firmly to the fabric with a couple of backstitches at one end of the marked position.

2 STITCH SEVERAL long stitches on top of one another between the bar markings. Take a small blanket stitch through the fabric at one end, and work closely spaced blanket stitch over the long stitches (above). Take the final stitches through the fabric. Finish securely.

THREAD EYES

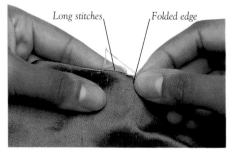

1 FASTEN THE THREAD firmly at the fabric edge. Using either single or double thread, take four long stitches at the fabric edge (above), passing the needle through the fold of the fabric. Leave the stitches slightly loose.

THREAD BUTTON LOOP

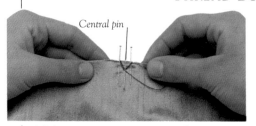

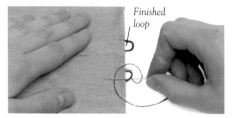

1 MARK THE LOOP WIDTH with two pins. Mark half the diameter of the button with a central pin. Fasten the thread, and loop it outside the outer pins and around the central pin. Slide the needle through the fabric (above). Repeat four times.

2 CHECK THAT THE BUTTON will fit through the loop. Cover the threads with buttonhole stitch (p. 75) to form a neat finish to the loop (above). Take the first and last stitch through the fabric at each end, and secure the thread.

2 TAKE a small blanket stitch through the fabric at the end of the loop. Cover the threads with close blanket stitch (above). Finish off with a small blanket stitch over the threads and through the edge of the fabric. Secure.

TAPE FASTENERS

STURDY HOOK-AND-LOOP FASTENER TAPE is used mainly for fastenings on sportswear and outdoor wear. One half of the tape has hooks and the other has loops. When pressed together, the hooks cling to the loops. Snap-fastener tape is lighter, and is often used on baby garments to close the leg seams. It is also used to fasten comforter-cover openings.

HOOK-AND-LOOP FASTENER TAPE

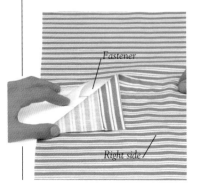

PIN ONE SIDE of the tape on the opening edge, and stitch along the tape edges. Press the second strip onto the first. Fold over the other side of the opening, and pin it to the second strip of tape (left). Separate the tapes and stitch the second strip on the wrong side.

SNAP-FASTENER TAPE

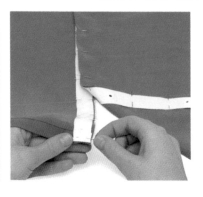

FINISH AND TRIM any seam allowances. Press them to the wrong side on the overlapping edge, and to the right side on the underlapping edge. Tuck under the tape ends, and pin the tape along the edges to cover the raw edges (left). Stitch the tape using a zipper foot.

SNAP FASTENERS

Snap Fasteners (also called press studs) are used where a lightweight fastening is needed. They are available in a black or silver metal finish in a range of sizes. Small, clear plastic snaps may be used on fine fabrics. There are many types of nonsew snap with decorative metal or colored caps, which are attached using a special tool or a hammer.

BALL-AND-SOCKET FASTENERS

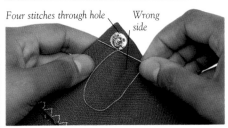

Four stitches through hole   *Wrong side*

1 FASTEN THE THREAD firmly to the wrong side of the overlapping edge. Stitch the ball stud to this edge, without stitching through to the right side. Finish with backstitches at the stud edge (above).

2 CLOSE THE OPENING. Pass a pin through the center of the ball stud to mark the position for the socket stud (above). Mark the point with another pin or a dressmaker's pencil.

Socket stud   *Right side*

3 STITCH THE SOCKET STUD firmly to the right side of the underlapping edge in the same way as the ball stud (see Step 1). Use four stitches to secure each hole and backstitches at the base (above).

NONSEW COVERED SNAPS

Assembly tool

1 CUT A FABRIC CIRCLE to the correct size. (If the fabric is thin, use a double layer.) Cover the button shell (p. 236). Place the pronged button back and the socket stud on the assembly tool (above).

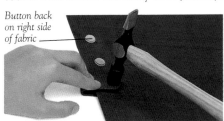

Button back on right side of fabric

2 MARK THE SNAP POSITION on both fabric edges. Fold the tool in half so that the two halves of the snap meet at the mark. Tap the tool with a hammer to lock the snap together (above).

3 WITH THE BACKING RING and the ball stud on the assembly tool, apply to the other fabric edge, with the ball stud on the right side. Press the button shell onto the button back (above).

NONSEW SNAPS

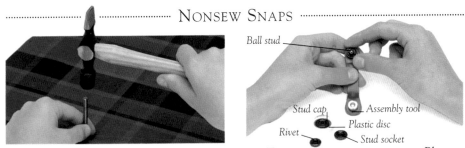

1 MARK THE STUD POSITION on the overlapping edge of the fabric. Place the plastic disk from the kit under the mark, flat side up. Make a hole, using the sharp end of the piercing tool (above).

Ball stud   *Assembly tool*   *Stud cap*   *Plastic disc*   *Rivet*   *Stud socket*

2 TURN THE PLASTIC DISK OVER. Place the stud cap in the groove. Press the ball stud firmly onto the appropriate end of the assembly tool so that it will snap in place when closed (above).

Wrong side

3 WITH RIGHT SIDE DOWN, position the stud cap underneath the hole in the fabric so that the cap projects through. Place the socket on the tool over the cap, and hammer in place (above).

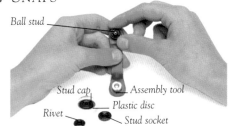

4 REPEAT THIS PROCESS for the underlapping edge. Push the backing rivet on the disk through the hole in the fabric. Place the ball stud on the other end of the tool, and hammer in place (above).

MAKING A LINGERIE STRAP GUARD

Fasten a thread firmly onto the wrong side of the garment. Make a thread chain (p. 78) to hold the lingerie strap in position. Stitch it to one hole of one half of the snap fastener (left). Stitch the other half of the snap fastener to the garment.

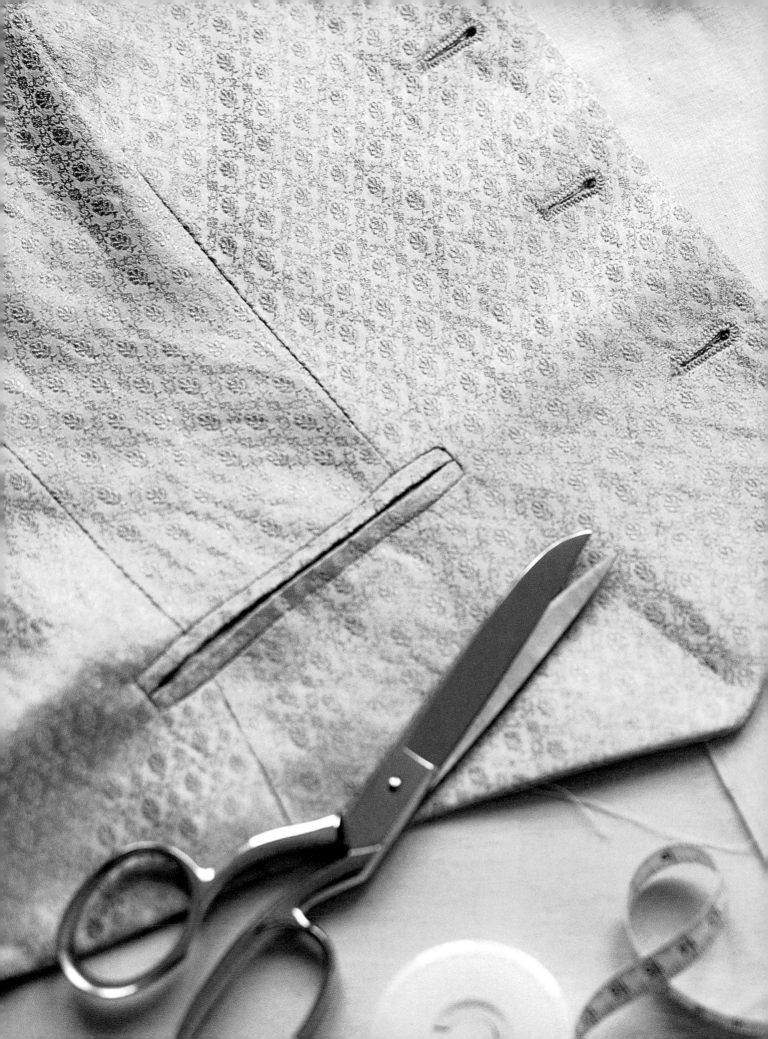

POCKETS

MAKING AND APPLYING POCKETS

ASIDE FROM BEING FUNCTIONAL, pockets are usually decorative, too, whether they are large, external patch pockets or more discreet inside pockets with bound edges. Pockets applied to the right side of a garment may be made up from a matching or a contrasting fabric. They can also be ornately topstitched or finished with flaps. Depending on their design, pockets can be used to give a garment a more tailored or a more casual appearance. There are many methods for making pockets, and most of them are fairly easy to execute.

RELATED TECHNIQUES

Working with checks
and stripes, p. 38
Working basting stitches, p. 73
Working tailor's tacks, p. 73
Working machine stitches, p. 77
Seam finishes, p. 85
Interfacings, p. 98

DIRECTORY OF POCKETS

*Patch pocket
with self-flap*

*Slashed pocket
with flap*

*Patch pocket
with separate flap*

Front hip pocket

Basic patch pocket

In-seam pocket

*Bound
slashed pocket*

*Slashed pocket
with welt*

Patch pocket with self-flap
This type of patch pocket has a self-facing at the top edge that is folded down to form the flap (p. 270).

Slashed pocket with flap
On this pocket, a flap is stitched into the upper edge of the pocket opening and hangs down (p. 277).

Patch pocket with separate flap
This patch pocket has a separate flap that is attached to the garment above the opening of the pocket (p. 270).

Front hip pocket
Only the opening of this pocket is visible, running from the waistline to the side seam (p. 273).

In-seam pocket
Attached to a seam opening, this type of pocket hangs inside the garment, often pants (p. 271).

Basic patch pocket
Placed outside the garment, this pocket is unlined, with a top facing and curved lower corners (p. 267).

Bound slashed pocket
This type of pocket looks like a bound buttonhole with two fabric pleats that meet in the center (p. 274).

Slashed pocket with welt
The slashed welt stands up, covering the pocket opening. On a self-welt (or stand) slashed pocket, the welt is part of the pocket (p. 278).

PRODUCING A NEAT FINISH ON A POCKET

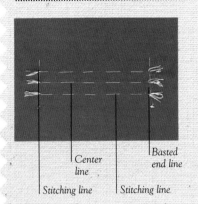

Center line

Stitching line

Basted end line

Stitching line

Marking a slashed pocket
For a neat finish, mark slashed pockets accurately. Start by marking the four corners and the center and stitching lines with tailor's tacks. To mark both sides of the fabric, baste along the stitching, center, and end lines, extending the lines beyond the tailor's tacks.

Interfaced facing

Strong patch pocket
Reinforcing the top edge of a patch pocket with interfacing gives a lasting finish. On a self-faced patch pocket, cut the interfacing to fit the facing, and press (left) or baste it to the wrong side, with the lower edge along the facing foldline.

MAKING AN UNLINED PATCH POCKET

AN UNLINED PATCH POCKET is generally used on shirts and jackets. The basic patch pocket has curved lower corners and an integrated facing. For extra body at the top of the pocket, the facing should be interfaced (see above) before the pocket is sewn. The completed pocket can then be topstitched or handstitched to the garment.

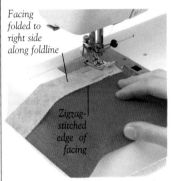

Facing folded to right side along foldline

Zigzag-stitched edge of facing

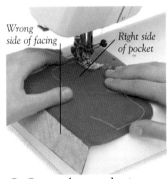

Wrong side of facing

Right side of pocket

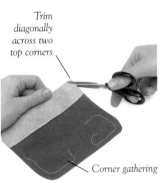

Trim diagonally across two top corners

Corner gathering

Pocket to be topstitched across just above zigzag stitching

Seam allowance notched at curves

1 INTERFACE the integrated facing up to the foldline, and zigzag stitch the top edge. Fold the facing to the right side, pin, and stitch (above).

2 STITCH long gathering stitch around each lower curved corner, just a thread's width into the seam allowance from the seamline (above).

3 TRIM the pocket seam allowances to ⅜ in (1 cm), leaving the long thread ends of the corner stitches. Trim the top corners diagonally (above).

4 TURN THE FACING right side out. Turn under the seam allowances. Press. Pull the gathering threads to form smooth curves (above).

MAKING A SQUARE PATCH POCKET

A SQUARE PATCH POCKET is used on the same type of garment as a basic patch pocket with curved lower corners, where a more angular style suits the garment. It is also made in the same way except at the lower corners. To give the pocket extra body and strength, the integral facing should be interfaced before the pocket is sewn.

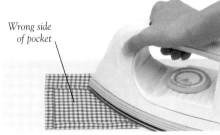

Wrong side of pocket

Trim away excess fabric

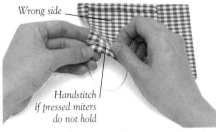

Wrong side

Handstitch if pressed miters do not hold

1 FINISH THE FACING EDGE, and stitch the sides (see Step 1, above). Press the seam allowances to the wrong side. Turn the facing right side out (above).

2 OPEN THE SEAM ALLOWANCES at the lower corners. Fold the corners diagonally to the wrong side across the pressed corners. Press, and trim (above).

3 REFOLD the seam allowances, forming a miter at the corners, and handstitch (above) or re-press to hold the miters in place until the pocket is attached.

LINING A PATCH POCKET

PATCH POCKETS ARE USUALLY LINED to prevent the raw edges of the pocket piece from fraying and to stop pockets that are made in soft fabrics from bulging. Lining can also be used to give a firm edge to loosely woven fabrics. Sheer fabrics should be self-lined to prevent the line of a facing from showing through on the right side.

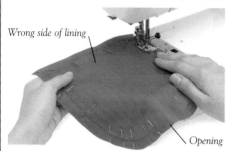

Wrong side of lining

Opening

1 CUT OUT THE POCKET PIECE from the garment fabric. Cut the lining fabric to the same size and shape. With right sides together, pin the lining to the pocket. Machine stitch, leaving a 1½-in (4-cm) opening in the stitching at the center of the lower edge (above).

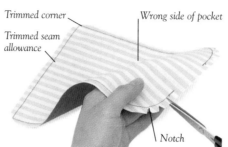

Trimmed corner

Trimmed seam allowance

Wrong side of pocket

Notch

2 TRIM THE SEAM ALLOWANCES to about ¼ in (6 mm). Trim the top corners diagonally, and taper the seam allowances on either side of the corner. (Trim the lower corners of square pockets in the same way.) On curved corners, notch the seam allowances (above).

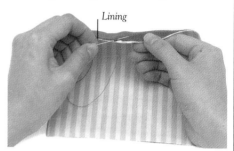

Lining

3 TURN THE POCKET right side out by pulling it through the opening at the lower edge. Pull out the corners, and roll the seam so that it lies toward the lining of the pocket and will not show on the right side. Press, then slipstitch the opening closed (above).

····· A SELF-LINED POCKET ·······

Cut the pocket piece to twice the desired depth. Fold the pocket piece in half, with right sides together. Sew the pocket, as shown in Steps 1–3 above, omitting the stitching across the top edge.

LINING A SELF-FACED PATCH POCKET

THE LINING OF A POCKET that has an integrated facing (p. 267) is attached to the top raw edge of the integrated facing. To determine the size of the lining, the pocket piece is cut first and the facing folded down.

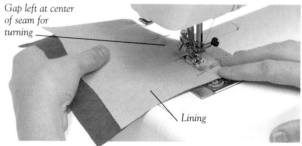

Interfacing to be applied down to foldline

Gap left at center of seam for turning

Lining

1 APPLY INTERFACING to the integrated facing down to the foldline on the wrong side. Fold the facing to the wrong side along the foldline.

2 MEASURE FROM THE LOWER EDGE of the facing to the lower edge of the pocket. Cut the lining to this length, plus a 1¼-in (3-cm) seam allowance at the top edge. Unfold the facing. With right sides together, pin the lining to the top edge of the facing. Stitch, leaving a 1½-in (4-cm) gap at the center of the seam (above).

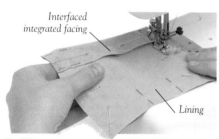

Interfaced integrated facing

Lining

3 WITH RIGHT SIDES of the fabric facing, position the lower edge of the lining so that it is even with the lower edge of the pocket piece. Align both of the raw edges. Pin, and stitch the side and the lower edges (above).

Clip top corners

Opening

4 TRIM THE SEAM ALLOWANCES. Then trim the corners of the integrated facing seam diagonally (above), and taper the seam allowances near the corners. (If the pocket has curved corners, notch the seam allowances on the corners.)

Slipstitching

5 TURN THE POCKET right side out by pulling it through the opening in the lining and facing seam. Pull out the corners, and roll the seam to the edge so that it lies toward the lining side. Press. Slipstitch the opening closed (above).

ATTACHING A LINED PATCH POCKET

A LINED PATCH POCKET can be either handstitched or machine stitched in place, although a pocket that is handstitched is not as strong as one that has been machine stitched. Before the prepared lined pocket (see opposite) is attached, any surface details, such as decorative topstitching, monograms, or trim, should be completed.

MACHINE STITCHING

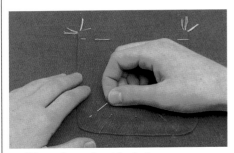

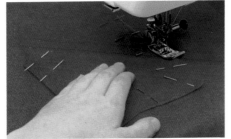

1 WITH the right side facing uppermost, place the prepared lined pocket (see opposite) in the correct position marked on the garment. Pin the pocket in place with the pins pointing outward (above). If then desired, baste around the pocket edge to hold in place and remove pins.

2 MACHINE STITCH around the edge of the pocket, using the inner edge of the machine foot as a guide (above). The stitching is usually positioned near the pocket edge, although sometimes, on bulky garments such as jackets, it can be ¼–⅜ in (6 mm–1 cm) in from the edge.

HANDSTITCHING

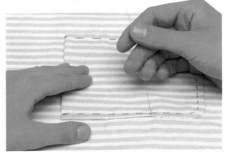

WHEN PREPARING TO HANDSTITCH a lined pocket to a garment, baste the pocket to the right side of the garment. Stitch around the three sides with small, even slipstitches. Stitch firmly, but do not pull too tightly because this will cause the pocket edge to pucker.

REINFORCING POCKET CORNERS

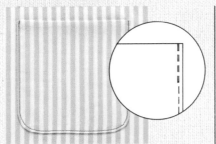

Reverse stitching method
Reverse stitch for approximately ⅝ in (1.5 cm) at the start and finish of the pocket stitching. Stitch accurately, one line over the other, so that the double reinforcement is inconspicuous.

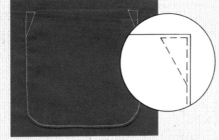

Machine-stitched triangle method
Small triangles stitched at the pocket corners will spread the strain on the sides of the pocket opening. Begin machine stitching at the top corner, then stitch down for ¾ in (2 cm), and diagonally up and across the top.

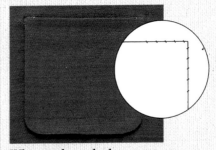

Whipstitch method
A frequently used method to reinforce the pocket corners on fine, delicate fabrics is to whipstitch the corners by hand. Using a very small whipstitch, handstitch the top corners of the pocket for ¼ in (6 mm).

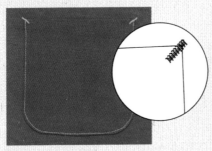

Bar tack method
Handstitch three long stitches diagonally across the pocket corner. Using a close blanket stitch, work across these long threads, catching the fabric underneath.

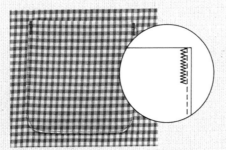

Zigzag stitch method
After finishing the pocket with reverse stitching, adjust the sewing machine to a narrow, ⅛ in (3 mm) zigzag. Stitch again at the corners for ⅝ in (1.5 cm) to reinforce.

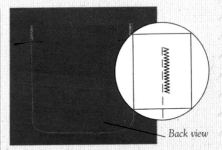

Back view

Fabric patch method
Attach a small piece of fabric to the wrong side of the garment corner before the pocket is stitched on. Combine with any other method to give added strength.

MAKING A PATCH POCKET WITH A SELF-FLAP

THIS TYPE OF POCKET is made with a combined flap and pocket piece. The flap simply folds down onto the right side of the patch pocket. To add a flap to a plain patch pocket pattern, first trim away the integrated facing along the foldline. Then add a piece of paper that is twice the depth of the required finished flap, and reattach the integrated facing piece at the top of the pocket. Cut out, and mark the top and bottom of the flap with tailor's tacks. Clip at each edge in order to mark the flap foldline along the center of the flap.

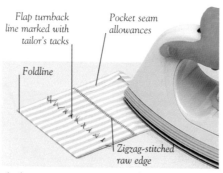

Flap turnback line marked with tailor's tacks

Foldline

Pocket seam allowances

Zigzag-stitched raw edge

1 APPLY INTERFACING to the facing and the outer part of the flap up to the foldline. Fold the interfaced section to the right side, and stitch both sides. Turn right side out. Press the pocket seam allowances to the wrong side (above).

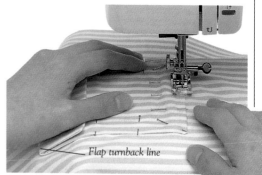

Flap turnback line

2 POSITION THE POCKET on the garment with right sides facing upward, and pin the pocket in place. Stitch the pocket to the garment (above), starting and finishing at the flap turnback line. Finally, fold the flap down, and press.

ATTACHING A SEPARATE FLAP TO A PATCH POCKET

THIS SPORTY STYLE OF POCKET is used mainly on shirts. The flap is made separately from the pocket and is stitched on above it, leaving room for easy hand access.

The patch pocket and flap can be finished with a single row of topstitching, but a double row gives a crisper finish. Use either a contrasting or a matching color thread.

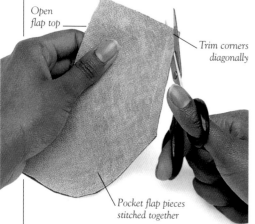

Open flap top

Trim corners diagonally

Pocket flap pieces stitched together

1 APPLY INTERFACING to the outer flap piece. With right sides facing, pin the flap pieces together. Stitch, leaving the top open. Trim the seam allowances and corners (above).

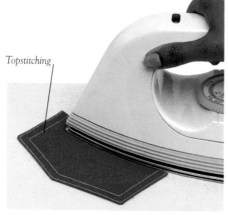

Topstitching

2 TURN THE FLAP right side out. Roll the seam slightly to the underside, and press in place. Topstitch near the edge, then topstitch again about ¼ in (6 mm) in from the edge. Press (above).

REDUCING BULK ON A FLAP

After rolling, seam allowances are basted together

With the inner flap uppermost and the seam allowance at the upper edge over your forefinger, roll the seam allowance down with your thumb in order to reduce the bulk on the outer flap (above).

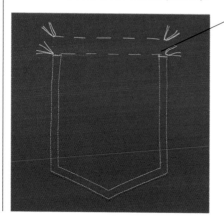

Tailor's tack on garment

3 MARK the pocket top and the flap positions with tailor's tacks at each end and lines of basting between the tailor's tacks. Pin the pocket in place. Topstitch the pocket to the garment near the edge, then about ¼ in (6 mm) in from the edge.

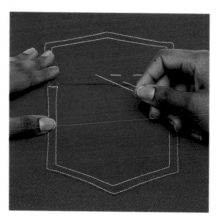

4 PLACE the flap on the garment with right sides together and the finished edge of the flap pointing upward. Place the flap between the tailor's tacks, with the raw edge overlapping the upper marked line by ⅝ in (1.5 cm). Baste in place (left), and machine stitch.

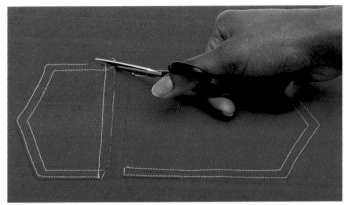

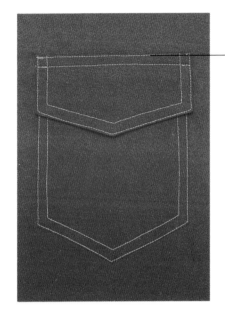

Topstitching along top of flap

5 REMOVE ALL THE BASTING STITCHES. Trim the raw edges of the pocket flap to a depth of approximately ¼ in (5 mm). Trim across the corners diagonally to neaten them, using a pair of small, sharp dressmaking scissors (above). This allows the folded-over flap to conceal the seam allowance and to lie flat over the top of the pocket, giving a neat finish.

6 WITH the flap still pointing upward, press the seam and seam allowances flat. Fold the flap down over the allowance. Press. Topstitch the flap to the garment, stitching close to the top edge of the flap. Stitch a second row of topstitching ¼ in (6 mm) below the first row. Press to finish.

MAKING AN ALL-IN-ONE IN-SEAM POCKET

THIS IS THE SIMPLEST TYPE of pocket to make and is used in the side seams of loose-fitting skirts and pants. The pocket is cut in one piece with the garment front and back, and it is stitched around at the same time as the side seams. No stitching is visible from the right side. When the pocket opening is on the bias grain of the fabric, the pocket needs to be reinforced in order to prevent it from stretching or sagging. The most effective reinforcement method is to stitch a short length of seam tape across the entire front pocket edge.

Seam tape

1 CUT A PIECE OF SEAM TAPE 2 in (5 cm) longer than the pocket opening. Pin the tape to the wrong side of the front pocket opening within the seam allowance, and with one edge along the seamline. Stitch along this edge (above).

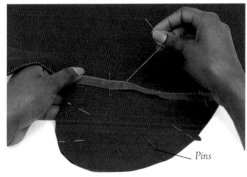

Pins

2 WITH RIGHT SIDES together and pattern markings matching, pin the front pocket to the back pocket around the edges and along both garment seams above and below it. Baste the front to the back along the opening between the pocket opening markings (above).

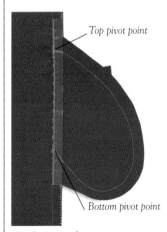

Top pivot point

Bottom pivot point

3 STITCH the entire seam (including the pocket seam), pivoting at the top and bottom of the pocket at the pocket opening markings.

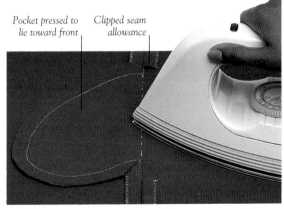

Pocket pressed to lie toward front *Clipped seam allowance*

4 WORKING ON THE BACK of the garment only, clip the seam allowance to within a few threads of the pivot points. Press the seam open, both above and below the pocket. Turn the pocket toward the garment front, and press along the basting (above).

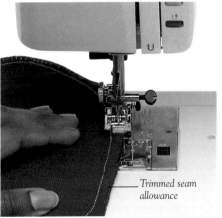

Trimmed seam allowance

5 REMOVE THE BASTING along the pocket opening, and trim back the seam allowances to ⅜ in (1 cm). Then zigzag stitch both seam allowances together to finish (above).

271

MAKING A SEPARATE IN-SEAM POCKET

FOR THIS STYLE OF POCKET, the two pocket pieces are cut separately from the garment. Normally this is done to make the pattern layout more economical in the amount of fabric used. It is advisable to make these pockets from the same fabric as the garment. If the garment has a lining, the pockets may require a facing strip (see opposite).

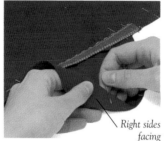

Right sides facing

1 STITCH seam tape at the front pocket opening (p. 89). Pin and stitch the front pocket piece to the garment front, then the back piece to the back. Zigzag stitch the seam edges together (above).

Right sides facing

2 PRESS the pocket pieces away from the garment. Then place the front and back pockets together, and baste along the pocket opening. Pin the pocket (above) and garment seams.

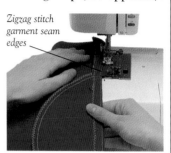

Press seams open above and below pocket

3 STITCH the garment and pocket in a continuous seam, pivoting at the pocket opening markings. Clip the back seam allowance to these markings. Press the pocket toward the front (above).

Zigzag stitch garment seam edges

4 REMOVE the basting. Trim the seam allowance around the pocket, then zigzag stitch the edges together. Finish the edges of the seams above and below the pocket (above).

MAKING AN EXTENSION IN-SEAM POCKET

THIS TYPE OF POCKET is cut separately from the garment, usually so that the pockets can be made of the lining fabric to reduce bulk. Each garment piece is cut with an extension at the pocket opening position, in order that the pocket fabric will not be visible when the pocket is pulled open.

Garment extension at pocket opening

1 STITCH seam tape onto the pocket opening on the garment front (p. 89). With right sides together, stitch the front pocket piece to the garment front at the pocket extension. Stitch the back pocket piece to the garment back. Trim each seam, and zigzag stitch the edges together (left). Then press the seam toward the pocket.

2 PLACE THE GARMENT FRONT and back pieces together, with right sides facing so that the raw edges of the pockets are even. Pin around the pocket and along the seams above and below the pocket. Baste the front to the back along the pocket opening (above).

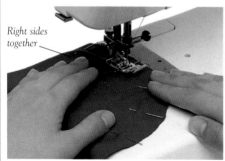

Right sides together

3 STITCH THE POCKET and the side in one continuous seam. Starting at the top of the seam, stitch to the top of the pocket and pivot at the marking. Then stitch around the pocket (above), pivoting at the bottom marking to continue along the rest of the seam.

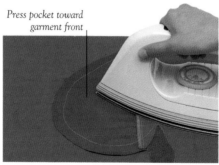

Press pocket toward garment front

4 CLIP THE BACK seam allowance to the pattern markings at the top and the bottom of the pocket. Press the garment seams open, then press the pocket toward the garment front (above). Press along the basted pocket opening on the right side of the garment.

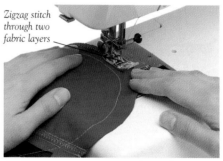

Zigzag stitch through two fabric layers

5 REMOVE THE BASTING from the pocket opening. If required, trim the seam allowances around the pocket to about ⅜ in (1 cm). Zigzag stitch the edges together for a neat finish (above). Zigzag stitch to finish the raw edges of the seams above and below the pocket.

ADDING A FACING TO AN IN-SEAM POCKET

A FACING MAY BE REQUIRED on a separate in-seam pocket when the pocket is made from lining fabric, in order to reduce bulk and thereby ensure that the garment hangs properly. The facing strip is cut from the garment fabric and masks the lining fabric of the pocket so that it does not show when the pocket is pulled open.

Length of opening + 3¼ in (8 cm)

*5 cm
(2 in)*

1 CUT A STRIP of the garment fabric 2 in (5 cm) wide by the length of the opening, plus an extra 3¼ in (8 cm). For a fitted garment, cut a facing strip for both the front and back pocket pieces. (On most other garments that have a little fullness, it is necessary to add a facing strip only to the back pocket piece.)

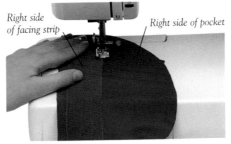

Right side of facing strip　　*Right side of pocket*

2 PIN THE WRONG SIDE of the strip to the right side of the pocket piece, with one long edge even with the straight edge of the pocket. Stitch. Zigzag stitch the opposite edge to the pocket (above).

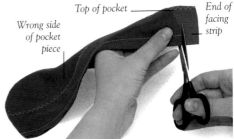

Top of pocket　　*End of facing strip*

Wrong side of pocket piece

3 TRIM THE TOP AND BOTTOM of the strip even with the pocket (above). If facing both pocket pieces, pin a facing to the other piece so that it is a mirror image of the first, and stitch as before.

MAKING A FRONT HIP POCKET

F RONT HIP POCKETS are most commonly featured on casual wear, sportswear, and jeans. On this style of pocket, part of the garment front is actually cut away in order to form the pocket opening. The pocket is attached to the garment at the side seam and at the waistline. It is made from two pieces: a facing piece and a pocket piece.

Center seam tape along stitching line of pocket opening

1 REINFORCE THE POCKET opening on the garment front if it is likely to stretch. Baste a narrow seam tape along the stitching line of the opening on the wrong side of the front (above).

Garment pocket opening

Seam allowance

2 WITH RIGHT SIDES TOGETHER and raw edges even, pin the pocket facing to the garment front, and stitch. Trim and layer the seam. Clip the seam allowances at the curves (above).

3 PRESS THE FACING and seam away from the garment. If the opening is not to be topstitched, understitch by stitching through the facing and seam allowances near the seam (above).

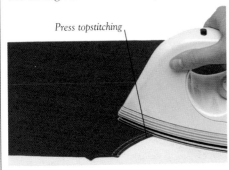

Press topstitching

4 PRESS THE POCKET FACING to the wrong side (above). Topstitch along the opening edge. If the topstitching is near the edge, omit the understitching, but if it is placed about ⅜ in (1 cm) in from the edge, understitch and topstitch.

Side edge of garment

Inner edges of pocket pieces

5 PIN THE POCKET PIECE to the pocket facing, with right sides together and inner edges even. Stitch around the inner edges. Trim the seam, then zigzag stitch to finish. Baste the pocket to the front at the side, and also at the waist edge (above).

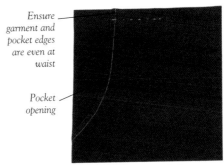

Ensure garment and pocket edges are even at waist

Pocket opening

6 PIN AND STITCH the front of the garment to the back, enclosing the side edges of the pocket in the side seam. Press the seam open. The upper edge of the pocket is treated as part of the waist edge when the waistband is stitched on.

······················· MAKING A BOUND POCKET ·······················

THIS TYPE OF SLASHED POCKET looks similar to a large bound buttonhole. One pocket piece is cut longer and is used to bind the pocket opening, forming two pleats of fabric, or lips, that meet along the center of the opening. The shorter pocket piece may be cut from lining fabric to reduce the bulk behind the pocket, allowing it to lie flat.

Large pocket piece

Stitching line

Stitching line

Small pocket piece

Finished pocket depth

Finished pocket width

Finished pocket width

1 CUT TWO POCKET PIECES, or adapt the shapes given with the pattern. Cut both pieces to the required pocket width, plus 1 in (2.5 cm). Cut the longer piece to the required finished depth of the pocket, plus 2½ in (6.5 cm). Cut the shorter piece to the required finished depth of the pocket, plus ⅜ in (1 cm).

Wrong side of pocket piece

Stitching line

2 WITH right sides together, place the large pocket piece over the pocket position marked on the garment. Arrange the pocket piece pointing downward so that the straight edge is parallel with the stitching lines. The pocket piece should overlap the lower marked stitching line by 1 in (2.5 cm). Pin in place and baste the pocket in position. Working on the wrong side of the garment, stitch the rectangle shape around the basted marking.

Clip diagonally into corners

3 STARTING AT THE CENTER and working out to each end, cut along the center line through all the fabric thicknesses to ⅜ in (1 cm) from each end. Carefully clip diagonally into each corner just short of the stitching (above).

Straight edge of pocket

4 PULL THE POCKET PIECE through the opening. Pull to square the corners at each end of the opening. Press the triangular ends and pocket piece away from the opening. Press the straight pocket edge over the opening (above).

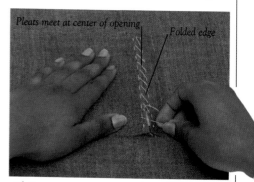

Pleats meet at center of opening

Folded edge

5 FOLD THE POCKET to form pleats that meet along the center of the opening. Pin, checking that the pleats are equal and even. Press. Baste each folded edge. Remove the pins. Hold the pocket binding in place with diagonal basting (above).

···················· PREPARING POCKET OPENINGS ····················

Final width marker

Stitching line

Center line

Marking the pocket
Draw a guide on pattern paper (above). Following the guide, baste across the final width markers. Baste three parallel lines, extending the lines about 1 in (2.5 cm) beyond the final width markers.

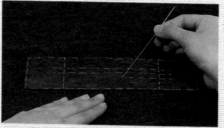

1 Reinforce lightweight or loosely woven fabric with a rectangle of interfacing. Cut the interfacing 4 in (10 cm) longer and 2 in (5 cm) wider than the opening. Baste or iron this to the wrong side of the opening. Mark the opening (see left) with basting (above).

2 Begin stitching at the center of one long edge of the opening. Follow the rectangle exactly and pivot at the corners, making right angles. Count the stitches at the short edges to ensure an equal length. Overlap the stitching to secure.

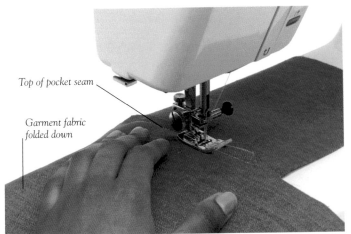

Top of pocket seam

Garment fabric
folded down

6 TURN TO THE RIGHT SIDE of the garment, and fold it back to
expose the side edge of the pocket. Stitch across the triangle
and pleat ends at each end of the opening. Fold down the
garment fabric to show the seam across the top of the pocket.
Stitch across the top seam through the seam allowances and
pocket as close as possible to the previous stitching (above).

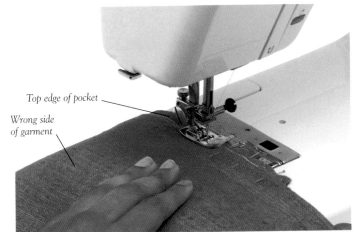

Top edge of pocket

Wrong side
of garment

7 WITH RIGHT SIDES TOGETHER and straight edges even,
place the second, smaller pocket section on top of the
one stitched to the garment, and pin them together. Fold back
the fabric to show the seam along the lower edge of the pocket
opening. Stitch along the seam allowances and both pocket
pieces (see Step 6), close to the previous stitching (above).

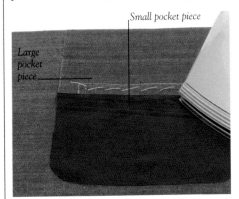

Small pocket piece

Large
pocket
piece

8 TURN BACK to the wrong side of
the garment and remove the pins
holding the two pocket pieces together.
Turn down the smaller pocket piece,
folding it at the seam that has just been
stitched. Press flat (above).

Pocket edges
are even

9 FOLD THE LARGE POCKET PIECE down
onto the small piece. The edges of
the pieces should be even when lying
flat. If they are not, trim them to the
same length. Pin the sections together
around the edges (above).

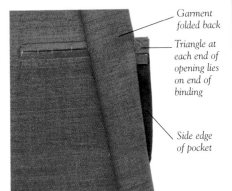

Garment
folded back

Triangle at
each end of
opening lies
on end of
binding

Side edge
of pocket

10 TURN TO THE RIGHT SIDE. Fold
back the garment fabric to expose
the side edge of the pocket. Machine
stitch across the base of the triangles
and binding ends. Check that the
binding ends are straight.

Wrong side of garment

Pocket bag

11 STITCH AROUND THE POCKET BAG, starting at the top
folded edge and continuing across the triangular ends
on top of the previous stitching. Zigzag stitch the raw edges
together to clean finish them (above), and press the zigzag-
stitched edges. Remove the basting from the opening, and press.

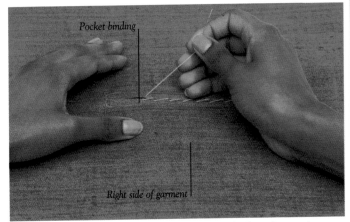

Pocket binding

Right side of garment

12 TURN TO THE RIGHT SIDE. Then check that the pocket
bindings are straight and even, and that the corners are
square and secure. Diagonally baste the edges of the binding
together with fine thread (above). Press the opening, and leave
the diagonal basting in place until the garment is complete.

MAKING A TWO-PIECE FLAP

A FLAP IS ATTACHED TO A GARMENT above a patch pocket (p. 267–271), or is integrated into the opening of a slashed pocket (see opposite). A rectangular flap can be cut in one piece, but a shaped flap is made from two separate pieces – a front flap piece and a facing piece. The simplest type of shaped flap has curved bottom corners.

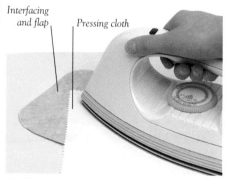

Interfacing and flap — *Pressing cloth*

1 CUT TWO IDENTICAL flap pieces, and one layer of interfacing to the same size and shape as the flap pieces. Apply the interfacing to the wrong side of one flap (above). This forms the front flap.

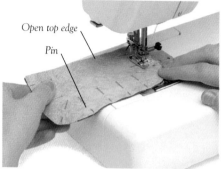

Open top edge — *Pin*

2 WITH RIGHT SIDES TOGETHER and raw edges even, pin the interfaced front flap to the facing piece. Pin or baste. Stitch around the side and lower edges only (above).

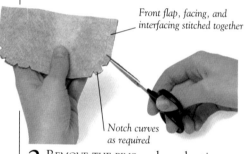

Front flap, facing, and interfacing stitched together — *Notch curves as required*

3 REMOVE THE PINS and any basting. Trim the seam allowances, and layer if required, making the interfaced seam allowance wider. Cut notches into the seam allowance at the curves (above).

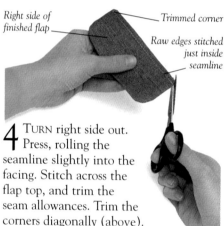

Right side of finished flap — *Trimmed corner* — *Raw edges stitched just inside seamline*

4 TURN right side out. Press, rolling the seamline slightly into the facing. Stitch across the flap top, and trim the seam allowances. Trim the corners diagonally (above).

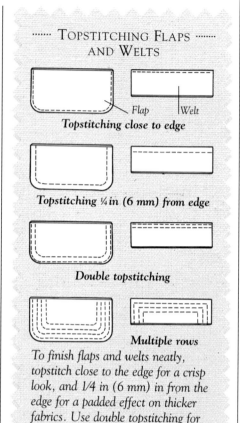

TOPSTITCHING FLAPS AND WELTS

Flap — *Welt*

Topstitching close to edge

Topstitching ¼ in (6 mm) from edge

Double topstitching

Multiple rows

To finish flaps and welts neatly, topstitch close to the edge for a crisp look, and 1/4 in (6 mm) in from the edge for a padded effect on thicker fabrics. Use double topstitching for sportswear, and multiple parallel rows for a more elaborate, detailed finish.

MAKING A ONE-PIECE WELT OR FLAP

A WELT IS USUALLY STITCHED into the lower edge of a slashed pocket. It is also sometimes used in combination with a flap, which is attached to the upper edge of the pocket opening. Welts and flaps that have straight edges can be cut in one piece. Straight-edged one-piece welts and flaps are made in the same way.

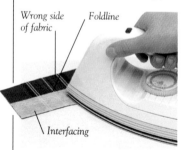

Wrong side of fabric — *Foldline* — *Interfacing*

1 APPLY INTERFACING to the wrong side of the welt or flap piece, up to the foldline (above). This interfaced half will form the outer side of the finished welt or flap.

Folded edge — *Open edge*

2 FOLD THE WELT or flap in half along the foldline, with right sides together and raw edges even. Pin across each short end of the welt or flap (above).

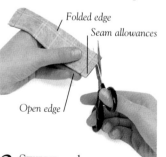

Folded edge — *Seam allowances* — *Open edge*

3 STITCH each end of the welt or flap. Remove the pins. Trim the seam allowances, then trim the corners at each end of the fold diagonally (above).

Edges stitched together just inside seamline — *Right side of folded edge*

4 TURN right side out. Press, rolling the seams slightly to the underside. Stitch the raw edges. Trim the seam allowances, and across the corners (above).

MAKING A SLASHED POCKET WITH A FLAP

A SLASHED POCKET WITH A FLAP is a concealed pocket that has a pocket bag hanging on the inside of the garment and a flap covering the pocket opening. The flap is made separately and attached to the garment before the opening is cut and the two pocket pieces are stitched on. The longer pocket piece is used to face the opening.

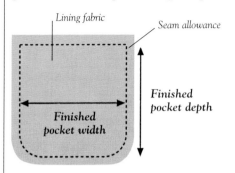

Lining fabric
Seam allowance
Finished pocket depth
Finished pocket width

1 CUT OUT the short pocket piece and transfer any pattern markings. For garments made from heavyweight fabrics, lining fabric may be used for the short pocket piece to reduce bulk. (This piece will be hidden under the longer piece on the inside of the finished garment.)

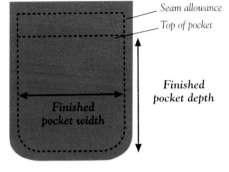

Seam allowance
Top of pocket
Finished pocket depth
Finished pocket width

2 CUT OUT the long pocket piece and transfer any pattern markings. Be sure to cut this piece from the main garment fabric, since it will be visible through the pocket opening when the flap is up. This piece is longer than the other pieces, since it is used to face the pocket opening.

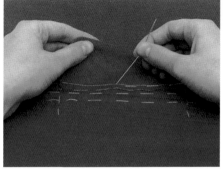

3 MARK THE POCKET POSITION with tailor's tacks, then make the flap (see opposite). With right sides together and the raw flap edges above the center line, place the flap on the garment. Align the flap seamline with the upper marked stitching line. Baste in place (above).

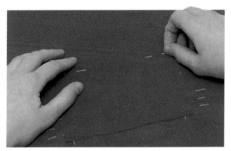

4 KEEPING THE FLAP pointing upward, pin the long pocket piece on top of the flap and over the pocket position, right sides together (above). The straight edge overlaps the lower marked stitching line by the width of the seam allowance.

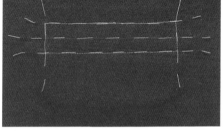

5 WORKING on the wrong side, stitch around the rectangle, following the basting. Pivot at the corners, counting the stitches across the ends to ensure that they are equal. To finish, overlap the stitching in the center of one long edge.

6 STARTING AT THE CENTER, cut along the marked center line to within ⅜ in (1 cm) of each end. Clip diagonally into each corner to a thread or two from the stitching – being careful not to cut through it – to form triangles at each end (above).

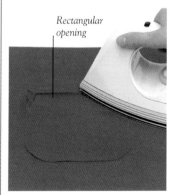

Rectangular opening

7 PULL the pocket piece through the opening to the wrong side. To make the opening rectangular, pull the fabric and the triangles gently away from the opening at each end. Press (above).

8 WITH right sides together, pin the straight edge of the short pocket piece to the single layer of the straight edge of the long pocket piece. Then stitch along the previous line of stitching.

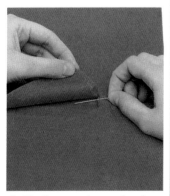

Short pocket piece

9 PRESS the short pocket piece downward, away from the opening (above). With right sides together, and making sure that the flap is facing downward, pin the long pocket piece to the short one.

10 STITCH the pocket bag pieces together, and finish the bag (p. 278). On the right side of the garment, make a bar tack (p. 79) at each corner of the flap to strengthen it (above).

FINISHING A POCKET BAG

THE PART OF A CONCEALED POCKET that hangs down inside the garment is called the pocket bag. This bag may be cut in one piece (as on the Slashed Pocket with Self-Welt, below) or in two pieces (as on the Slashed Pocket with Flap, p. 277). Both one- and two-piece bags are stitched in the same way once the pocket opening is complete.

1 FOLD the upper pocket piece down onto the lower pocket piece, with the raw edges even. If one piece is longer than the other, trim it to the same length. Then pin the pieces together around the side and lower edges (left).

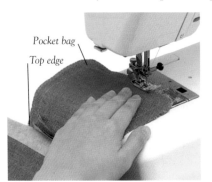

Pocket bag
Top edge

2 WITH the under pocket facing upward, stitch the bag together. Begin at the folded top edge, close to the previous stitching at the end of the opening, and catch in the triangles. Zigzag stitch the raw edges together (left).

MAKING A SLASHED POCKET WITH A WELT

A WELT IS USUALLY a slim, rectangular shape, standing upward from the garment to cover a concealed-pocket opening. A slashed pocket with a welt is made in the same way as one with a flap (p. 277), except that the welt is stitched to the lower stitching line of the pocket opening. Welts are used on vests and tailored jackets.

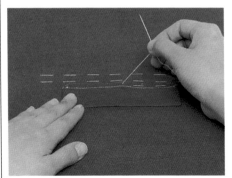

1 MAKE A WELT (p. 276), then mark the pocket position. With right sides together and the welt seamline aligned with the lower marked stitching line, baste the welt in place (above).

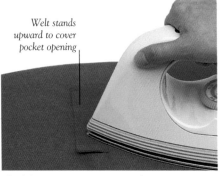

Welt stands upward to cover pocket opening

2 MAKE UP THE POCKET the same as Pocket with Flap (p. 277), following Steps 4–9, but in Step 9 make sure that the welt is pressed upward (above). Finish the pocket bag as explained above.

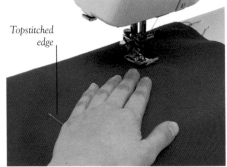

Topstitched edge

3 TOPSTITCH the ends of the welt to the garment by machine to provide a strong finish (above). (Alternatively, for a plain welt, slipstitch the ends of the welt to the garment by hand.)

MAKING A SLASHED POCKET WITH A SELF-WELT

THIS TYPE OF CONCEALED SLASHED POCKET has one pattern piece that forms both the pocket bag and the pocket welt. Because the welt in turn forms a decorative part of the pocket on the right side, it is important to match the pocket to the garment if the fabric has checks, stripes, or any other design that requires fabric matching.

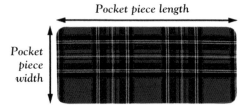

Pocket piece length
Pocket piece width

1 CUT THE POCKET PIECE on the straight grain. Transfer any pattern markings. The length of the pocket piece is twice the welt depth, plus twice the pocket depth, including seam allowances. The width includes seam allowances.

2 FOLD THE POCKET in half widthwise, and press in a crease. Unfold. With right sides together, place the pocket over the marked pocket position on the garment, aligning the pocket crease with the marked lower stitching line. Pin in place around the pocket opening (left).

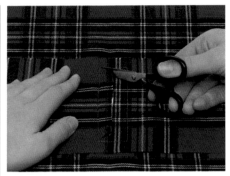

3 WORKING ON THE WRONG SIDE, stitch around the rectangular pocket opening, following the basting (p. 267). Remove the basting. Starting at the center and working toward each end, cut along the marked center line, stopping ⅜ in (1 cm) from each end. Clip diagonally into each corner to form triangles of fabric (above).

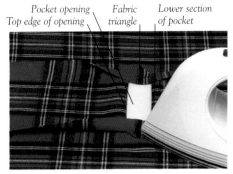

Pocket opening · Fabric triangle · Lower section of pocket
Top edge of opening

4 PULL THE POCKET through the opening to the wrong side. Gently pull the fabric and triangles at each end to make the opening into a rectangular shape, and press the triangles away from the opening (above). Then press the pocket away from the pocket opening around the seamline just stitched.

5 FOLD THE LOWER SECTION of the pocket so that it forms a pleat, with the fold edge of the pleat meeting the top edge of the opening. Press this in place. Baste along the pleat to hold it in position, then baste the fold edge of the pleat to the top edge of the pocket opening, using long, diagonal whipstitches (above).

Seam allowance
Wrong side

6 TURN THE GARMENT right side out, then fold the fabric back over itself to expose the seam allowances along the lower edge of the pocket opening. Stitch the seam allowances to the pocket, stitching as close as possible to the previous stitching (above).

·········· COMBINING A FLAP AND A WELT POCKET ··········

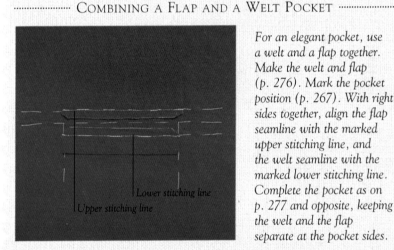

Lower stitching line
Upper stitching line

For an elegant pocket, use a welt and a flap together. Make the welt and flap (p. 276). Mark the pocket position (p. 267). With right sides together, align the flap seamline with the marked upper stitching line, and the welt seamline with the marked lower stitching line. Complete the pocket as on p. 277 and opposite, keeping the welt and the flap separate at the pocket sides.

7 ON THE WRONG SIDE of the garment, fold the upper section of the pocket onto the lower section, right sides together. The lower edges of the pocket should be even – if not, trim to the same length. Pin the sides and lower edges of the pocket bag pieces together (above).

Wrong side

8 TURN THE GARMENT right side out, and fold it back to expose the pocket. Machine stitch along the side and the lower edges of the pocket (see Finishing a Pocket Bag, Step 2, opposite). Zigzag stitch the pocket edges together (above). Remove the basting stitches.

9 CHECK THAT THE WELT is positioned straight on the right side of the garment and that the corners are square and secure. Press. Baste the welt closed, using diagonal whipstitches and a fine thread (above). Remove the basting after the garment has been completed.

PROFESSIONAL TECHNIQUES

CUSTOM TAILORING

CUSTOM TAILORING is the traditional method of tailoring that relies on a layered arrangement of reinforcing and structuring linings, interfacings, and interlinings. These fabrics are handstitched and steamed to give shape and stability to the garment. (Fusible interfacings are never used.) To achieve a perfect fit, and to avoid extensive pattern changes later, a test garment is first made, usually from muslin or inexpensive cotton. Traditionally tailored garments should follow the contours of the body while allowing enough ease for comfort and movement.

RELATED TECHNIQUES

Reducing seam bulk, p. 84
Choosing interfacings and interlinings, p. 95
Attaching a woven canvas interfacing, p. 98
Making a dart in interfacing, p. 100
Making an edge-to-edge lining, p. 103
Making bound buttonholes, p. 241

CHOOSING FABRICS

THE LAYERED ARRANGEMENT of classic tailoring uses different interlinings, interfacings, and linings that are chosen according to the weight and type of the main garment fabric. A heavyweight fabric needs stronger, thicker layering fabrics than a lightweight fabric, although the techniques used to make the garment are the same.

HEAVYWEIGHT FABRICS

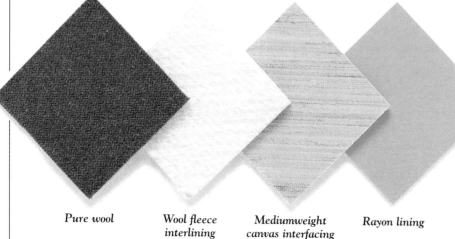

Pure wool *Wool fleece interlining* *Mediumweight canvas interfacing* *Rayon lining*

THE FINEST FABRIC for classic tailoring is pure wool, either a worsted or a woolen. Worsteds have a firm, flat face and are traditionally used for tailored suits and formal wear. Woolens are softer and more loosely woven. Both respond well to pressing and steaming, and both hold the tailored shape. An interlining, such as wool fleece, provides weight and warmth. Mediumweight canvas interfacing is used for most fabrics. Good-quality, non-synthetic interfacing should be chosen, rather than bound interfacing, which can be stiff. A mediumweight fabric, such as rayon, should be used for the lining.

LIGHTWEIGHT FABRICS

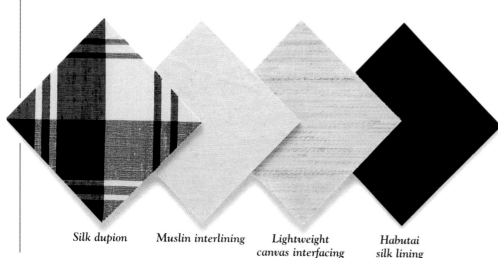

Silk dupion *Muslin interlining* *Lightweight canvas interfacing* *Habutai silk lining*

SILK AND LINEN are both suitable for making tailored garments. They should be thick enough and sufficiently tightly woven to support a jacket structure. Some blends work well with custom tailoring – these include linen blended with viscose, which reduces creasing, and silk mixed with wool, which gives the silk more body. Some cottons, such as seersucker, are also suitable. Soft mull or muslin should be used for interlining, and a lightweight canvas is the best choice for the interfacing. Cotton lawn can be used as an interlining when a stiff structure is required. A lightweight fabric, such as habutai silk, should form the lining.

CHOOSING A STYLE

WHEN SELECTING A PATTERN TO MAKE, choose a style that is within your dressmaking skills, since custom tailoring requires a relatively advanced level of sewing ability. A tailored garment is cut from a precise pattern. It should follow the contours of the body while allowing enough ease for comfort and movement. The style that best suits the custom method of tailoring is a classic jacket or blazer. This is usually fitted or semi-fitted, with a two-piece, set-in sleeve with a wrist vent, a revers (or notched) collar, and front pockets. Decide on a single- or double-breasted style, and if the lapel is to be long or short.

The pattern
Always check the back of the pattern envelope to see if a lining pattern is included. It is essential for a tailored jacket to be lined to cover and protect the inner, structural layers of interlining and interfacing. A lining also allows a garment to be put on and taken off with ease. Only some pattern envelopes include interfacing patterns and have the collar roll line already marked, for speed.

Design features
A number of distinctive features reflects the amount of time, care, and attention devoted to the construction of a custom garment. The collar has three separate layers – an under collar, a reinforcing and shaping layer of interfacing, and a top collar – which are all molded for strength and shape. The seam created when the collar is sewn to the lapel is called the gorge line and is a focal point. Care should be taken when sewing it. Tailored buttonholes provide a detailed and specialized finish on the garment. Sleeve vents are a traditional design feature; alternatively, the sleeves can be mitered, giving them a stylish angle. A tailored jacket usually has either bound or flap pockets.

A WELL-TAILORED SUIT

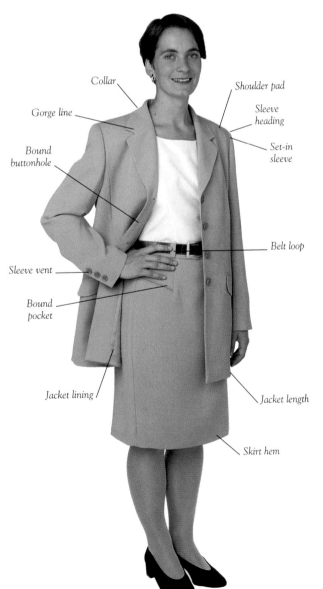

Collar
A tailored collar is structured from three pieces: two pieces of fabric and one piece of interfacing. The interfaced under collar gives support and structure to the upper collar.

Gorge line
This is the seam where the collar meets the lapel on a traditional notched-collar jacket.

Bound buttonhole
Buttonholes and buttons are finished by hand on the outside of the tailored garment. Buttons are sewn with a shank.

Sleeve vent
A vent is made from overlapping fabric. The jacket sleeve is made to fit over the hand and the buttons are not intended to be undone. Alternatively, the sleeve can have a mitered opening.

Bound pocket
This type of pocket lies flat against the fabric and does not interfere with the structured line of the garment.

Jacket lining
The lining reinforces and strengthens the garment, hides its inner construction, and takes much of the daily wear and tear.

Collar
Gorge line
Bound buttonhole
Sleeve vent
Bound pocket
Jacket lining
Shoulder pad
Sleeve heading
Set-in sleeve
Belt loop
Jacket length
Skirt hem

Shoulder pad
Pads are used to shape and build up the shoulder area of the jacket. The size and shape of the pads vary with body shape and garment style.

Sleeve heading
The heading is added to the sleeve after it has been set in. It supports and raises the sleeve cap.

Set-in sleeve
A well set-in sleeve is essential to a tailored jacket. Careful easing, basting, and stitching create a smooth curve and ensure perfect balance in the hang of the sleeve.

Belt loop
Also called carriers, these are included on the skirt if it is to be worn belted. The belt loop helps keep the waistline neat.

Skirt hem
The skirt hem is longer than the lining. A loose lining is always added to a tailored skirt to allow it to hang properly and to prevent it from riding up or bagging.

Jacket length
The length depends on the style of jacket chosen. A classic jacket ends just below the hipline. For a slimming effect, the jacket always covers the widest part of the hips and the bottom.

MAKING A TEST GARMENT AND ADJUSTING TO FIT

A TEST GARMENT, usually made from muslin or an inexpensive cotton, allows the finished tailored jacket to be a perfect fit. All markings are transferred by dressmaker's carbon or are thread traced (marked with a line of basting) onto the garment. It is then altered to fit, and sewn. The jacket pattern is adjusted from the test garment.

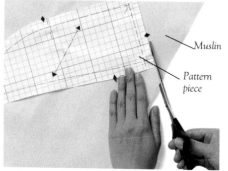

Muslin

Pattern piece

1 USING the cutting layout on the pattern guidesheet, position the muslin with a right and wrong side. Pin on the pattern. Cut out the jacket front and back, side front and side back (if any), upper and under sleeve, and the under collar (above).

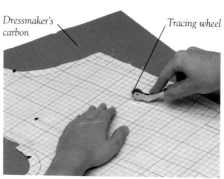

Dressmaker's carbon

Tracing wheel

2 ON THE WRONG SIDE of the muslin, transfer the inside markings from the pattern using dressmaker's carbon and a tracing wheel (above). Mark the stitching lines and the notches and dots used for matching garment pieces and seams.

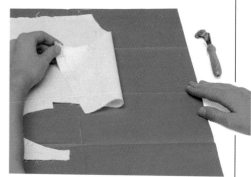

3 TRANSFER the outside markings to the right side of the fabric (see Step 2). Mark lengthwise and crosswise grainlines, center front, waistline, buttonhole and pocket positions. Remove the dressmaker's carbon from the muslin (above).

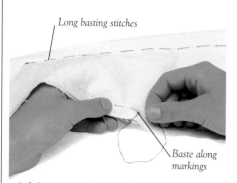

Long basting stitches

Baste along markings

4 MATCHING the notches and the dots, pin the jacket body pieces together and baste, either by hand or machine, following the markings. Baste the sleeve sections together (above). Press all the seams flat, then open.

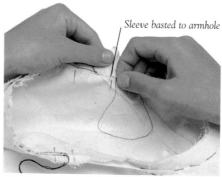

Sleeve basted to armhole

5 STITCH two rows of gathering stitches around the crown of the sleeve. Match, and pin each sleeve into its armhole. Pull up the gathering threads, distributing the ease evenly, then baste each sleeve into its armhole (above).

Neckline edge

6 BASTE THE UNDER COLLAR pieces together down the center back seam. Match the under collar to the neckline, ensuring that the seamlines match and the edges overlap. Pin and baste together along the neckline (above).

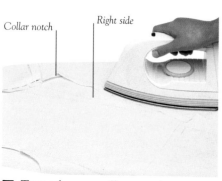

Collar notch

Right side

7 TURN the seam allowance between the collar notch and the lapel notch to the right side of the garment. Below the notch, turn the seam allowance over to the wrong side of the garment. Press the seam allowances flat (above).

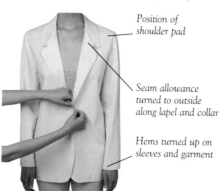

Position of shoulder pad

Seam allowance turned to outside along lapel and collar

Hems turned up on sleeves and garment

8 TURN UP THE GARMENT and sleeve hems along the marked hemlines, then pin. Pin the shoulder pads in position, and the front together at the buttonhole markings (above). Check that the vertical and horizontal grainlines are straight.

MARKING THE ROLL LINES

Roll line

If roll lines are not marked, place the garment on a dress form or on the wearer, and check the collar fit. Pin mark the roll on the under collar and lapels (above). Remove, and thread trace the pinned roll lines.

FITTING THE TEST GARMENT AND ADJUSTING THE PATTERN

Seam sits squarely

1 CHECK THE FIT on the front of the garment. Check that the shoulder seams sit squarely on the shoulders (left). All curved seams or darts should be correctly positioned over the bust. Check that the vertical center front lines are aligned, and that the buttonholes and pockets are well positioned. The garment hems should be the correct length.

Turned-up hems

Buttonhole positions

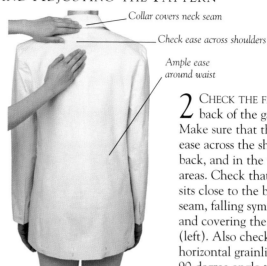

Collar covers neck seam

Check ease across shoulders

Ample ease around waist

2 CHECK THE FIT on the back of the garment. Make sure that there is ample ease across the shoulders, the back, and in the waist and hip areas. Check that the collar sits close to the back neck seam, falling symmetrically and covering the neck seam (left). Also check that the horizontal grainlines run at a 90-degree angle to the floor.

ADJUSTING THE LENGTH IF THE UPPER BACK IS TOO SHORT

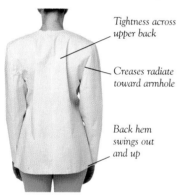

Tightness across upper back

Creases radiate toward armhole

Back hem swings out and up

1 A JACKET THAT IS TOO SHORT in the upper back feels tight and rides up over the shoulders. Creases extend from the center of the upper back out toward the armholes, and the hem swings up and out at the center back.

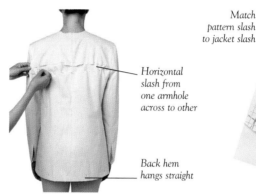

Horizontal slash from one armhole across to other

Back hem hangs straight

2 SLASH THE JACKET horizontally across the tight upper back. Insert a piece of fabric under the slash, spreading the edges farther apart until the jacket feels comfortable, the creases disappear, and the hem hangs straight. Pin (above).

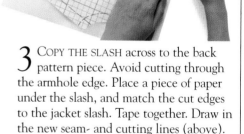

Match pattern slash to jacket slash

3 COPY THE SLASH across to the back pattern piece. Avoid cutting through the armhole edge. Place a piece of paper under the slash, and match the cut edges to the jacket slash. Tape together. Draw in the new seam- and cutting lines (above).

ADJUSTING THE LENGTH IF THE UPPER BACK IS TOO LONG

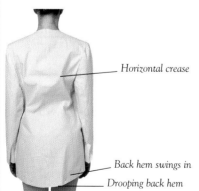

Horizontal crease

Back hem swings in

Drooping back hem

1 A JACKET THAT IS TOO LONG in the upper back will form creases that fall between the shoulders across the jacket back. The jacket back hem may droop and swing in at the center back.

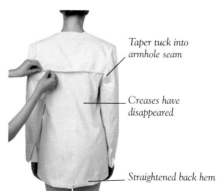

Taper tuck into armhole seam

Creases have disappeared

Straightened back hem

2 PIN THE EXCESS FABRIC into a straight horizontal tuck, beginning at the baggy area of the jacket center back (above). Taper the tuck into the armhole seam. Do not alter through the seam.

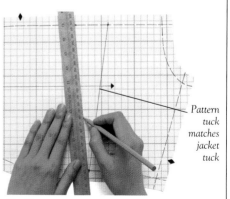

Pattern tuck matches jacket tuck

3 COPY THE GARMENT TUCK across and draw the two lines onto the back pattern piece (above). Fold the lower line up to meet the top line, and taper the tuck in to the armhole seamline. Tape.

ADJUSTING A TIGHT CENTER BACK

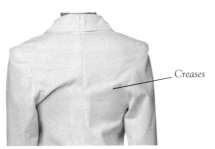

Creases

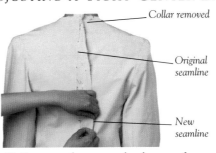

Collar removed

Original seamline

New seamline

New pinned armhole seamline

1 TIGHTNESS IN A CENTER BACK jacket seam can be felt all the way down the length of the back seam from the neckline to the waist. Creases are visible, radiating out from the center back seam toward the armholes and the side seams.

2 REMOVE the center back seam from the neckline down to the waist. Pin in the new seamline, tapering in to the original line at the waist (above). (Clip the remaining seam allowance to allow for turning out the seam if needed.)

3 REMOVE THE BACK of both armhole seams if the center back is still tight. Outside the original seam allowance, pin the sleeve cap to the jacket back (above), tapering the pinning into the original seam allowance at the underarm.

Amount of alteration

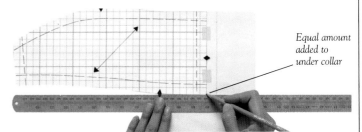

Equal amount added to under collar

4 TO TRANSFER THE NEW SEAMLINES to the pattern, attach tracing paper under the center back, back armhole, and under collar back seams. Measure the amount let out on the test garment, and transfer the new markings to the pattern (above).

5 TO COMPLETE THE ALTERATION, let out the under collar seamline the same amount as the alteration on the center back seamline. Transfer the markings to the pattern tissue (above). Alter the top collar the same amount.

CONSTRUCTING AN INTERFACING PATTERN

A ONE-PIECE INTERFACING PATTERN is made using the original pattern piece, which allows the interfacing to fit perfectly and to support a jacket. A two-piece back interfacing pattern overlaps at the center back neck and is attached only along the seamlines. The body of the interfacing is left loose, to allow for movement.

FRONT INTERFACING

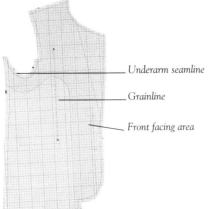

Underarm seamline

Grainline

Front facing area

USING THE ORIGINAL front pattern piece, mark a point 2 in (5 cm) below the underarm seamline. Mark the front facing area plus ⅝ in (1.5 cm). Connect both in a curve (above). The shaded area is now the interfacing pattern. Transfer the markings, including the grainline.

BACK INTERFACING

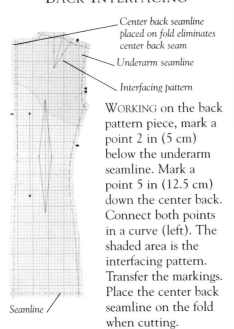

Center back seamline placed on fold eliminates center back seam

Underarm seamline

Interfacing pattern

Seamline

WORKING on the back pattern piece, mark a point 2 in (5 cm) below the underarm seamline. Mark a point 5 in (12.5 cm) down the center back. Connect both points in a curve (left). The shaded area is the interfacing pattern. Transfer the markings. Place the center back seamline on the fold when cutting.

BACK INTERFACING FOR STRETCH FABRICS

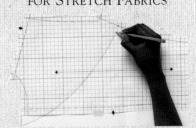

Mark a point 2 in (5 cm) below the underarm seamline, using the back pattern piece. Mark a point 1 in (2.5 cm) beyond the center back seamline at the neck. Connect both points in a curve (above). Trace and transfer all the markings. Overlap both the center back edges and stitch only along the seamline.

PREPARING JACKET LAYERS

INTERFACING IS USED TO HELP SHAPE and support the outer fabric and to prevent a jacket from stretching, wrinkling, or sagging. Interlining is cut from the same pattern as the jacket and is mounted on to the fabric pieces before the interfacing for warmth and support. The fabric and interlining, once attached, are treated as one.

TRANSFERRING PATTERN MARKINGS

USING TAILOR'S TACKS, transfer the markings on the pattern to the fabric. Mark the buttonholes, center front line, vent foldlines, pocket placement, and all the grainlines. Remove the pattern. Except for the matching dots, replace the tailor's tacks with thread tracing (left).

MARKING UP INTERLINING AND INTERFACING

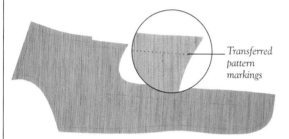

Transferred pattern markings

MARK THE INTERFACING by transferring all the pattern markings, including the seamlines, using dressmaker's carbon and a tracing wheel. Mark the collar and the lapel roll lines. Mark the interlining in the same way, including the seamlines.

ATTACHING INTERLINING

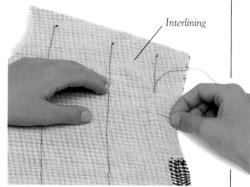

Interlining

PIN THE INTERLINING to the wrong side of the fabric. Using diagonal basting stitch, catch the two layers together (above). Keep the stitches loose, and catch only single threads from the garment fabric. Interlining is attached to all the front and back body sections, and may be attached to sleeves, as needed.

ASSEMBLING JACKET LAYERS

BEGIN ASSEMBLING the interlined jacket by sewing all the internal seams (for example, princess seams, if on the pattern.) The side seams and shoulder seams are not stitched at this stage. The internal darts must be sewn, then slashed and pressed open to reduce bulk and give a smooth appearance to the outside of the garment.

Catchstitching
Shoulder dart

1 IF USING thick interlining, cut away the dart marked on the back shoulder of the interlining to expose the fabric. Sew the fabric dart only, then slash and press open. Stitch the pressed edges down, catching only to the interlining (left).

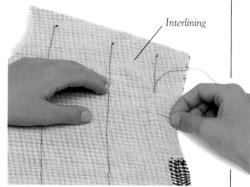

Press seam flat
Tailor's ham

2 MAKE remaining darts as in Step 1. With right sides facing, match, pin, baste, and stitch all the internal seams (not the shoulder or side seams). Clip and notch the seam allowances. Press the seams flat, then press open over a tailor's ham (left).

Seam allowance
Catchstitching

3 CATCHSTITCH the garment seam allowances to the interlining (left), so that the internal seams will lie flat. The stitches must not catch the garment fabric underneath. Press each seam and dart again, using a tailor's ham where necessary.

Attached and finished pocket
Bound buttonhole

4 MAKE any bound buttonholes required (p. 241–244). Stitch the buttonholes on the right-hand side for a woman's jacket, and on the left-hand side for a man's jacket. Construct the pockets according to the pattern guide sheet (p. 274–279), and attach them to the garment.

ATTACHING A FRONT INTERFACING

THE FUNCTION OF A FRONT INTERFACING is to support and shape a jacket front. The correct type of interfacing must be used. The interfacing should be firm enough to support the jacket without interfering with the natural hang of the outer fabric. It should also protect the jacket from wear and tear, and during the cleaning process.

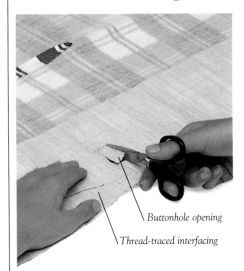

Buttonhole opening
Thread-traced interfacing

1 POSITION THE MARKED and thread-traced front interfacing piece to the wrong side of the garment front. Pin in place. Match the buttonhole markings marked on the interfacing piece over the bound buttonholes already made on the garment front. Baste in position. Cut out the rectangular buttonhole openings from the interfacing (above).

Baste through all layers of fabric

2 PULL THE RAW EDGES of the bound buttonholes through the openings to the wrong side of the interfacing. Check that the thread tracing on the jacket is aligned with the carbon lapel roll line marked on the interfacing. Baste the length of the lapel roll line, working through all the fabric layers (above). Remove all the thread tracing from the jacket front.

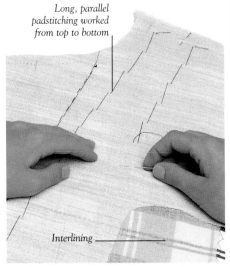

Long, parallel padstitching worked from top to bottom
Interlining

3 SECURE THE INTERFACING to the interlining, using long, parallel padstitch – rows of even, spaced stitches that are worked in one direction only, and formed as for one row of cross stitch (p. 75). Stitch about 2 in (5 cm) apart (above). Catch the interlining rather than the fabric, taking care not to stitch into the seam allowance.

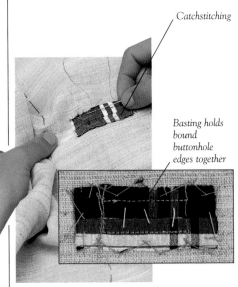

Catchstitching
Basting holds bound buttonhole edges together

4 CATCHSTITCH (p. 76) the raw edges of the bound buttonholes to the garment interfacing (above). Be careful to catch only the interfacing, so that the stitches do not show on the jacket front. Using a pressing cloth, gently press the buttonholes on the wrong side of the garment.

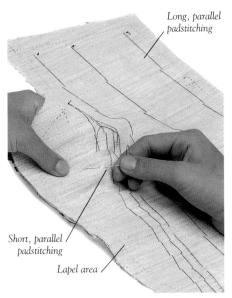

Long, parallel padstitching
Short, parallel padstitching
Lapel area

5 BEGINNING AT THE ROLL LINE, fill in the lapel area only with short, parallel padstitch (see Step 3). (Alternatively, fill the lapel area using chevron padstitch [p. 98] or diagonal padstitch.) Padstitch catching only a thread or two of the fabric (above). Do not padstitch into the seam allowance.

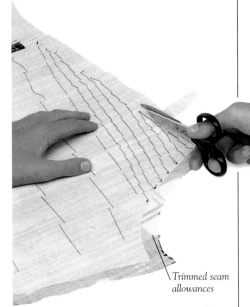

Trimmed seam allowances

6 TAKING CARE NOT TO CUT any of the padstitching, trim away the seam allowances of the interfacing from the side seams, front opening, shoulder, neck, and upper lapel (above). Leave the seam allowances in place around the armhole edges, since the interfacing helps to add support to the finished sleeves.

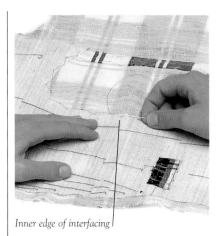

Inner edge of interfacing

7 TO ATTACH the edges of the trimmed interfacing, catchstitch the edge of the interfacing to the garment, stitching along the neck, shoulder, and side seams, catching only the interlining below. Catchstitch the shaped inner edge of the interfacing to the interlining to reduce bulk (left).

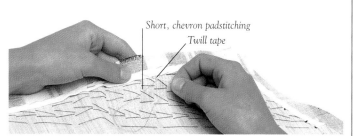

Short, chevron padstitching
Twill tape

8 TO STABILIZE THE SEAMLINES along the upper lapel edges and the front opening, pin preshrunk ¼-in (6-mm) twill tape to the length of the garment, with the outer edge against the seamline. Cut the pinned tape ends where they meet at the front opening and the upper lapel. Do not overlap the ends. Whipstitch both tape edges to the interfacing along their length (above).

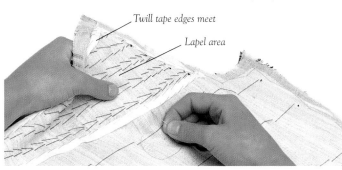

Twill tape edges meet
Lapel area

9 TO STABILIZE THE LAPEL ROLL LINE, pin the twill tape onto the garment with one edge of the tape placed along the roll line outside the lapel area. To reduce bulk, trim the tape edges so that the edges meet neatly, rather than overlap. Whipstitch both long edges of the twill tape to the interfacing (above).

10 POSITION THE LAPEL, with the wrong side facing upward, over a tailor's ham or seam roll. Hold the iron a short distance above the lapel and release a jet of steam at the fabric (right). Leave the ham in place until the area has cooled and dried. This sets in the shape of the lapel.

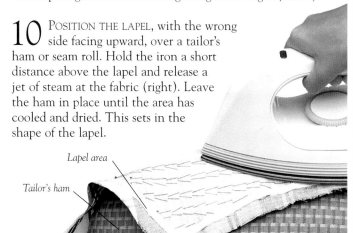

Lapel area
Tailor's ham

ATTACHING A ONE-PIECE BACK INTERFACING

INTERFACING IS APPLIED TO THE BACK only of a tailored jacket on the top section, across the back, and around the armholes. The back interfacing supports the sleeves and the collar at the back neck. It defines the shoulder line by preventing the garment from dropping between the armhole seam allowances and the shoulder blades.

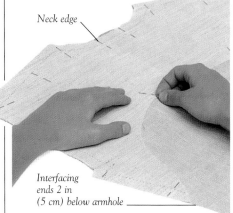

Neck edge
Interfacing ends 2 in (5 cm) below armhole

1 MAKE UP ALL THE DARTS on the back interfacing. Lay the jacket back on a flat surface, such as a table top, wrong side up. Place the interfacing on the wrong side of the garment, matching all the transferred markings. Pin together around the edges (above).

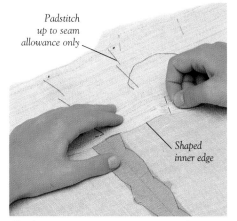

Padstitch up to seam allowance only
Shaped inner edge

2 ATTACH THE INTERFACING to the garment by sewing long, parallel padstitch in vertical rows, spacing the rows of stitching approximately 2 in (5 cm) apart (above). Catch the interfacing to the interlining only, and do not padstitch into any of the seam allowances.

Trim seam allowance

3 TRIM the interfacing seam allowances along the side seams, the shoulders, and the neck (above). Leave the seam allowance around the armhole edges intact. Catchstitch the trimmed interfacing edges and the shaped inner edge to the interlining.

INTERFACING A COLLAR

Acollar interfacing, applied only to the under collar, shapes the collar roll line. Rows of chevron padstitch give a more shaped collar, parallel padstitch a less shaped collar, or the two can be combined. The stand area is between the neckline seam and the roll line, while the fall lies between the roll line and the outer edge.

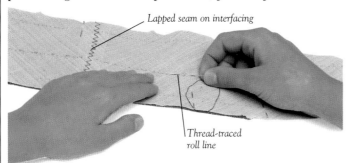

Lapped seam on interfacing

Thread-traced roll line

1 STITCH the under collar center back seam. Press open. Stitch the center back seam of the interfacing under collar with a lapped seam. Transfer the marked roll line onto the interfacing using thread tracing, and pin to the wrong side of the under collar. Baste both together along the roll line (above).

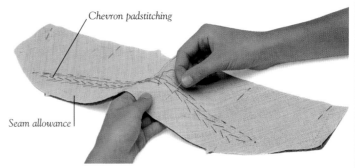

Chevron padstitching

Seam allowance

2 REMOVE THE BASTING. Padstitch the stand area only using short chevron padstitch, parallel padstitch, or a mixture of both. Catch only a thread or two of the fabric. Stitch parallel to the roll line, shaping the under collar over your hand (above). Do not padstitch the seam allowances.

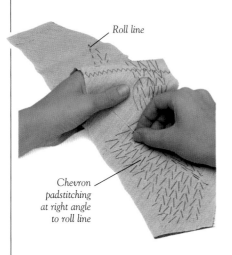

Roll line

Chevron padstitching at right angle to roll line

3 PADSTITCH the fall area of the collar using slightly longer padstitch than that used in the stand. Padstitch out at right angles from the roll line to the outer edge, following the grainline of the interfacing. Work the stitches quite loosely, shaping the under collar over your hand (left). Do not padstitch the collar seam allowances.

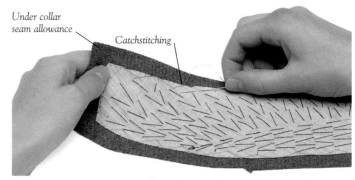

Under collar seam allowance

Catchstitching

4 REMOVE THE BASTING from the roll line. Trim away all the interfacing from the under collar seam allowance. Catchstitch the trimmed edges of the interfacing down onto the under collar, catching only a thread of the fabric below so that the stitching will not show on the right side (above).

MACHINE PADSTITCHING

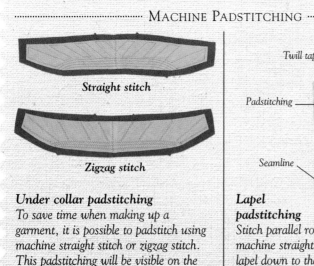

Straight stitch

Zigzag stitch

Under collar padstitching
To save time when making up a garment, it is possible to padstitch using machine straight stitch or zigzag stitch. This padstitching will be visible on the right side of the garment fabric.

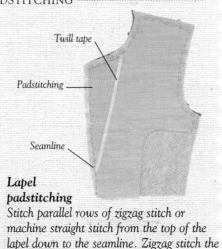

Twill tape

Padstitching

Seamline

Lapel padstitching
Stitch parallel rows of zigzag stitch or machine straight stitch from the top of the lapel down to the seamline. Zigzag stitch the twill tape, catching both edges.

Pin under collar to ham

5 PIN THE UNDER COLLAR around a tailor's ham (above). Pass a steam iron close above the collar roll line to set in the collar shape. (If the pressed and padstitched under collar is not to be attached right away, store it pinned around a rolled towel or tailor's ham to preserve its shape. Do not store flat.)

ASSEMBLING A COLLAR

A TOP COLLAR should always be cut slightly larger than the under collar so that it is large enough to hide the outer seam when the collar is completed and attached to a garment. If the pattern has not allowed for this, or if the fabric is very thick, the seam allowances on the outer edge of the top collar are made smaller for the same effect.

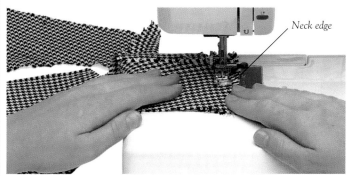

Chevron padstitching
Parallel padstitching
Diagonal stitch across point
Right sides together

1 PIN, BASTE, AND STITCH the under collar to the top collar, leaving the neck edge free. At each corner make one diagonal stitch across the point to avoid bulk. Ease the top collar onto the under collar. Trim and layer the seam allowances (above). Press the seam toward the under collar.

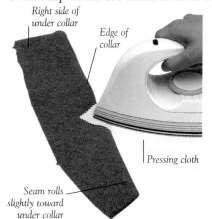

Right side of under collar
Edge of collar
Pressing cloth
Seam rolls slightly toward under collar

2 TURN the collar right side out, and pull out the corners. Using a pressing cloth, press the collar so that the seam rolls slightly toward the under collar. Press only the edges of the collar (left). Do not press out the roll. Fold the collar along the roll line, and press.

ATTACHING A FRONT FACING

A FRONT FACING should be cut slightly larger in the lapel area than the jacket front. If the pattern has not allowed for this, a smaller seam allowance is taken on the facing above the notch at the end of the lapel roll line. If using a checked or striped fabric, care should be taken to stitch the front facing exactly parallel to the fabric pattern.

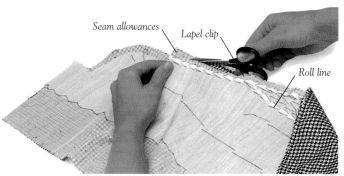

Neck edge

1 STAYSTITCH THE NECK EDGE SEAMLINES on the front and back facings. With right sides together, match, pin, and stitch the front facings to the back neck facing along the shoulder seamline (above). Press seams flat, then press them open and trim the seam allowance to half its width.

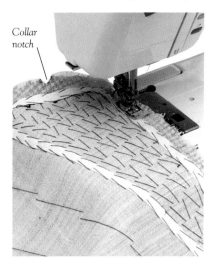

Collar notch

2 MATCH, PIN, and baste the front facing to the garment along the front opening and the lapel edges. Stitch, beginning at the collar notch at the junction of the collar and lapel (left). Stitch across the short edge of the lapel, then continue down the long edge of the lapel and the front opening edge of the jacket. Secure the threads.

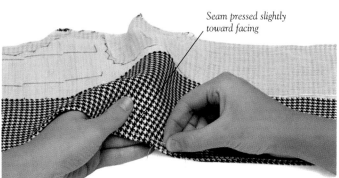

Seam allowances
Lapel clip
Roll line

3 CLIP INTO THE SEAM ALLOWANCE at the end of the lapel roll line. Above the lapel clip, layer the seam allowances so that the facing measures ¼ in (5 mm) and the garment measures ⅛ in (3 mm). Below the lapel clip, layer the garment seam allowance to ¼ in (5 mm) and the facing to ⅛ in (3 mm) (above).

Seam pressed slightly toward facing

4 PRESS THE SEAM ALLOWANCE above the lapel clip to the garment, and below it to the facing. Turn the facing right side out. Using a pressing cloth, press the seam above the lapel clip slightly toward the garment, and below it slightly toward the facing. Baste (above). Stitch the shoulder seams, and press open.

291

ATTACHING A COLLAR

WHEN ATTACHING A COLLAR to a jacket, the under collar is sewn to the neck edge of the garment, and the top collar to the neck edge of the facings. Both seams are then pressed open and stitched together. The edges of the collar and top edges of the lapels must be exactly the same on each side, and the shape of the collar should be held.

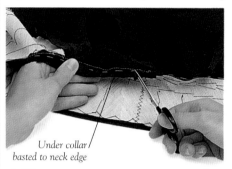

Under collar basted to neck edge

1 WITH RIGHT SIDES TOGETHER, match, pin, and baste the under collar to the neck edge along the seamline. Begin and end 1/16 in (2 mm) in from the front facing, aligning the facing seam with the neckline seam. Clip the seam allowance (above). Stitch with the garment right side up.

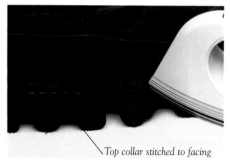

Top collar stitched to facing

2 PRESS THE SEAM FLAT, clipping and notching where needed. Stitch the top collar to the facing sections, as in the previous step, but stitching the top collar right to the beginning of the facing stitching. Press the seam flat (above), clipping and notching where needed.

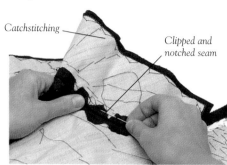

Catchstitching
Clipped and notched seam

3 TRIM THE SEAM ALLOWANCES to 3/8 in (1 cm), trimming the shoulder seam allowances away diagonally to reduce the bulk inside the jacket. Press the seams open over a tailor's ham, and catchstitch down both seam allowances on each of these seams (above).

Pinned side seam

4 WITH RIGHT SIDES together, match and pin the garment side seams. Machine stitch the side seams (above). Either try on the jacket or place it on a dress form (p. 14) to check the fit.

Back neck seam

Collar and lapel fall smoothly before pinning

5 ADJUST THE COLLAR and the lapels until both roll smoothly into place along the roll lines (above). Pin both in place along the collar and lapel roll lines. Pin just above the back neck seam.

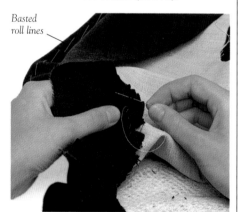

Basted roll lines

6 BASTE ALONG the pinned collar and lapel roll lines. Remove the pins. Pull up the back neck facing, and loosely blind hemstitch the facing to the garment neck seam (above). Remove the pins.

7 WORKING ON the buttonhole side of the front opening, finish the reverse side of the bound buttonholes on the facing (p. 241). Use small stitches, especially at the corners (above).

Button marking

8 FOLD BACK THE BUTTON SIDE of the facing 2 in (5 cm) from the front edge. Blind catchstitch the facing to the interfacing between the top and bottom button markings (above).

Rolled towel

9 REMOVE ALL THE BASTING. Put a rolled towel underneath the collar and lapels. Holding a steam iron close to the garment, steam the collar and lapels (above). Remove the towel when dry.

MAKING SLEEVES

THE SLEEVE FOR A CLASSIC TAILORED JACKET is usually cut in two pieces: the under sleeve and the upper, or top, sleeve. This gives the sleeve a good fit and allows for movement. When easing the crown of the sleeve into the armhole, as much ease as possible gives an attractive sleeve cap. The cap is supported by the sleeve heading (p. 294).

ASSEMBLING A MITERED TWO-PIECE SLEEVE

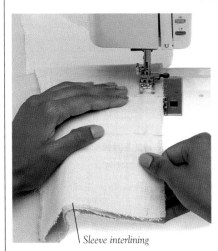

1 MATCH, pin, and stitch the front seam of the under and upper sleeve (left). Press flat, then open. Make the bound buttonholes (p. 241). Cut a strip of bias interfacing to the hem length by the depth, plus 1⅜ in (3.5 cm), and pin it ⅝ in (1.5 cm) below the hemline, avoiding the miter seam allowances.

Sleeve interlining

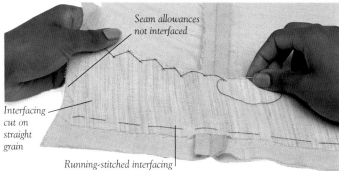

Seam allowances not interfaced

Interfacing cut on straight grain

Running-stitched interfacing

2 RUNNING STITCH the interfacing to the interlining only along the hem foldline, then catchstitch the upper edge (above). Cut an interfacing strip ½ in (12 mm) wider than the buttonhole side and ⅝ in (1.5 cm) wider than the vent foldline.

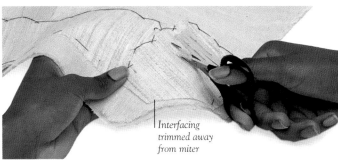

Interfacing trimmed away from miter

3 PIN ONE LONG EDGE OF THE STRIP ⅝ in (1.5 cm) beyond the vent foldline. Trim the interfacing away from the miter seam allowance. Running stitch the interfacing in place along the vent foldline. Catchstitch the free edges. Cut away the interfacing around the buttonholes (above). Finish off (p. 241). Turn over the vent edge of the under sleeve by ¼ in (5 mm).

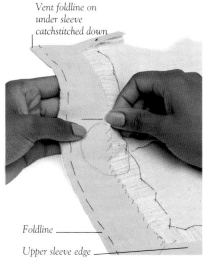

Vent foldline on under sleeve catchstitched down

Foldline

Upper sleeve edge

4 PIN the vent edge in position and catchstitch it down. Machine the mitered seam with right sides together. Trim across the corner, press the seam open and turn to the outside. Turn up the hem along the foldline. Baste in position ¼ in (5 mm) in from the foldline. Slipstitch the hem along the sides and the upper edge (left).

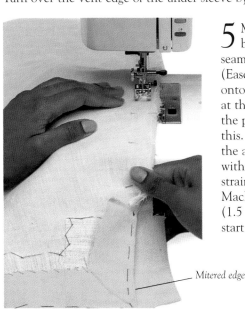

5 MATCH, PIN, and baste the back seam of the sleeve. (Ease the upper sleeve onto the under sleeve at the elbow area, if the pattern allows for this. The ease enables the arm to bend without placing any strain on the fabric.) Machine stitch to ⅝ in (1.5 cm) from the start of the vent (left).

Mitered edge

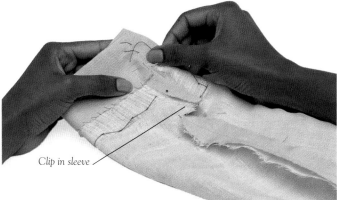

Clip in sleeve

6 PRESS THE SEAM FLAT, then press it open, clipping into the under sleeve seam allowance at the vent so that the seam lies flat. Position the vent edges so that the upper sleeve overlaps the under sleeve, and baste the vent in place diagonally (above). Mark the positions for the buttons before attaching the buttons to the garment (p. 235–236).

293

SETTING IN A SLEEVE

Pin underarm from front notch to back notch

1 SEW a double row of gathering stitches around the sleeve cap. Insert the sleeve into the armhole, right sides together. On the wrong side, match and pin the underarm seams together. Pull up the front to gather. Pin around the cap (left).

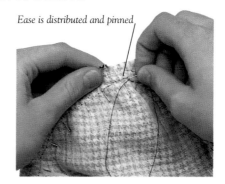

Ease is distributed and pinned

2 MARK with a pin ¼ in (2 cm) on each side of the shoulder seam. Pull up the back gathering stitches. Distribute the ease up to these pins, leaving the center free, and pin in place. Baste around the sleeve, using small stitches (left).

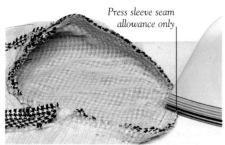

Press sleeve seam allowance only

3 CHECK THE FIT AND HANG of the sleeve by trying on the garment. With the jacket wrong side out, steam press on a flat surface. Carefully shrink away any ripples from the top of the sleeve seam allowance only (above).

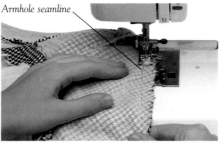

Armhole seamline

4 MACHINE STITCH AROUND the armhole seamline, stitching from the sleeve side. Stitch a second row of stitches inside the first, between the underarm notches (above), then trim the new seam allowance to ¼ in (6 mm).

Wider half of sleeve heading placed against sleeve

5 USING THE CROWN of the sleeve as the central point, center and pin the sleeve heading to the wrong side of the sleeve cap. Place the heading fold against the seamline. Pin (above), then whipstitch the fold to the seamline.

INSERTING SHOULDER PADS

SHOULDER PADS are made up from various triangular layers of interlining and padding materials such as flannel. The pads are used to shape and build up the shoulder area of a jacket. The pattern envelope usually suggests a suitable size of pad. A wide range of ready-made styles and shapes is available; the shapes change with the fashions.

MAKING SHOULDER PADS

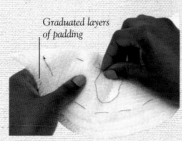

Pattern pieces meet at shoulder seam

1 *Tape the front and back pattern sections together along the shoulder seamline. Draw the required pad shape on the pattern paper (left). Trace, then cut the shape out of the flannel.*

Graduated layers of padding

2 *Graduate the flannel layers, and stitch together with long running stitch (left). For a thick pad, sandwich thin cotton padding between flannel.*

Widest point of pad

1 INSERT the pad into the jacket so it extends ⅜ in (1 cm) from the armhole seamline, with the widest point centered over the shoulder seam. Pin (left). Stitch the pad edge to the armhole seamline with loose running stitch.

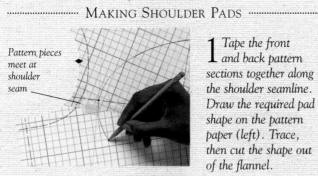

Top layer of pad

2 PULL BACK the facing, and blind hemstitch (p. 76) the end of the pad to the seam allowance. Bring the facing back down, and pin. Catchstitch (p. 76) the front facing to the shoulder pad, catching only the top layer (left).

HEMMING A JACKET

A JACKET HEM should be straightened by placing it on a dress form or on the wearer, and measured up from the floor (p. 204) before the jacket hem is trimmed. If the jacket is made from heavy fabric, to reduce bulk the bias strip along the hem is cut away from the seams, and the edges are tucked under the seam allowance.

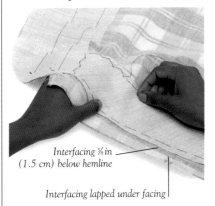

Interfacing ⅝ in
(1.5 cm) below hemline

Interfacing lapped under facing

1 CUT a bias strip of interfacings to the hem length, and 1⅜ in (3.5 cm) wider. Open out the facings, and pin the strip ⅝ in (1.5 cm) below the hemline. Using long running stitch, stitch the strip along the hemline. Catchstitch the free edges (left).

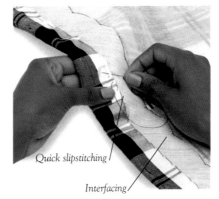

Quick slipstitching

Interfacing

2 TURN UP the hem along the hemline. Baste in place ¼ in (6 mm) from the fold. Trim the hem of the facing and the front of the garment that will be covered by the facing to ⅝ in (1.5 cm). Quick slipstitch (p. 74) the hem to the canvas only (left).

Facing slipstitched to hem

Pressing cloth

3 FOLD BACK the facing. Slipstitch the lower edge to the hem. Slipstitch the raw edge of the facing to the hem, using small stitches. (This edge can be turned under before slipstitching if using a lightweight fabric.) Press using a cloth to avoid shine (left).

WEIGHTING A HEM

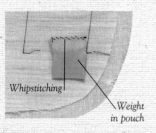

Whipstitching

Weight
in pouch

Stitch rectangles of fabric into small pouches. Drop a curtain weight into each, and slipstitch the edge closed. Whipstitch the pouches to the interfacing above the hemline at the seams and front opening.

MAKING A JACKET LINING

T HE CONSTRUCTION OF A JACKET is concealed by the lining. Lining fabric should match the outer fabric in weight, quality, and care requirements. Ease of wear is added by building in a pleat at the center back of the lining. After pinning the lining, the jacket must be tried on to check that the lining is not tight or pulling the jacket.

ATTACHING INTERLINING TO A LINING

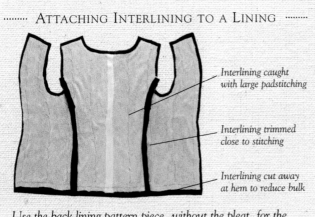

Interlining caught
with large padstitching

Interlining trimmed
close to stitching

Interlining cut away
at hem to reduce bulk

Use the back lining pattern piece, without the pleat, for the interlining back. Use the front lining pattern pieces, with the hem allowances cut away, for the interlining. Pin the interlining to the wrong side of the lining, and padstitch. Pin and stitch the darts through both layers. Slash them open, trim, and press open.

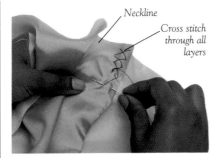

Neckline

Cross stitch
through all
layers

1 SEW the darts and the back seams. Baste the back pleat, and press to one side. Cross stitch the pleat for 1¼ in (3 cm) down from the neckline (left). Stitch a row of staystitching inside the seam allowance.

Front opening and
shoulder, neck, and
armhole edges are
staystitched

2 COMPLETE all the internal seams and the side seams. Press them flat then open, clipping and notching as needed (left). Turn and press under all the staystitched edges to the wrong side, except at the armholes.

ATTACHING A LINING

LINING HIDES THE INTERFACING construction and the raw edges inside a garment. It makes a jacket comfortable to wear and easy to put on and take off. The lining should be slightly larger than the garment so that it does not constrict its hang and cause wrinkles. After it is attached to the garment, the lining is handstitched in place.

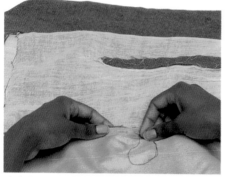

1 MAKE UP THE LINING (p. 295), and position it on the garment with wrong sides together. Match the lining and the garment side seams together, and pin. Using long running stitch, attach the lining seam allowance to the garment seam allowance (above). Do not stitch the lower 6 in (15 cm) of the garment.

Shoulder seam

2 MATCH ALL THE NOTCHES. Pin the unattached front and front shoulder seam lining to the garment. Allow the folded edge of the lining to hide the raw edge of the garment facing and the front shoulder seam. Pin the lining and the garment armholes together. Baste the shoulder lining in place (above).

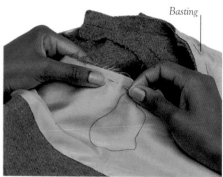

Basting

3 QUICK SLIPSTITCH (p. 74) the folded edge of the lining to the facing. Do not stitch the lower 6 in (15 cm). Pin the folded edge of the back neck lining over the facing so that it covers the shoulder edges. Quick slipstitch in place. Baste the back armhole layers together (above). Trim the armhole lining level with the garment.

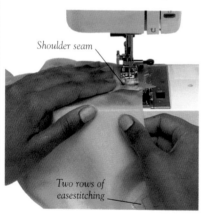

Shoulder seam

Two rows of easestitching

4 MAKE UP the lining sleeves, right sides together, and press the seams open. On the wrong side, stitch two rows of easestitching across the sleeve cap between the front and the back notches. Staystitch between the front and back notches of the underarm (left).

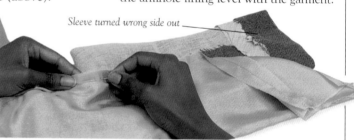

Sleeve turned wrong side out

5 TURN THE GARMENT through to the wrong side. Match and pin together the garment sleeve seam and the sleeve lining seam. Pin along the seam allowances. Using long running stitch, join the seam allowances (above). Do not stitch the lower 4 in (10 cm), measuring up from the hem edge of the sleeve.

Bottom of garment sleeve

Right side of lining

Easestitching

6 PUSH YOUR ARM THROUGH the shoulder of the sleeve lining and take hold of the bottom of the garment sleeve opening. Pull the lining over your arm and up the garment sleeve (above). The sleeve and the lining now lie wrong sides together, with the sleeve inside the lining.

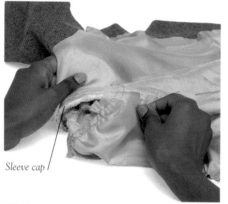

Sleeve cap

7 DRAW THE LINING up and over the sleeve cap. Pull up the easestitching to fit the sleeve lining around the armhole. Tuck the lining seam allowance under, clipping the garment underarm where necessary. Fold the lining over the basted armhole layers. Pin (above).

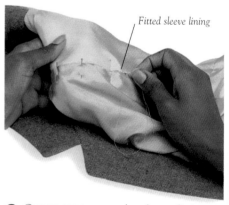

Fitted sleeve lining

8 QUICK SLIPSTITCH the sleeve lining around the armhole as pinned (above). Use small stitches, especially when stitching over the sleeve cap where the ease is positioned. Stitch only the lining, so that the stitches are not visible on the outside of the garment.

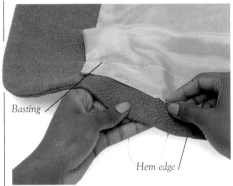

9 TURN UNDER the lining seam allowance. Press and pin to the garment hem edge, lapping the lining ⅝ in (1.5 cm) over the raw edge of the hem. If desired, baste the surplus lining 2 in (5 cm) above the lapped edge. Quick slipstitch in place (above).

Basting

Hem edge

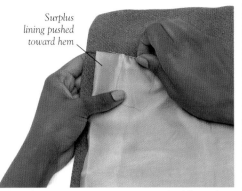

Surplus lining pushed toward hem

10 REMOVE THE BASTING holding the excess lining away from the hem edge. Finish quick slipstitching the front edges of the lining to the facing (above), and push all the surplus lining toward the hem to form a pleat. The pleat allows for the fabric to drop slightly after wear.

FINISHING A SLEEVE LINING

Pinned tuck

To allow for ease, pin a ⅜-in (1-cm) tuck around the sleeve lining 2 in (5 cm) from the bottom. Turn the edge of the lining under to lap the raw hem edge by ⅝ in (1.5 cm). Slipstitch (above). Unpin the tuck.

MAKING WAISTBANDING FOR PANTS OR SKIRTS

USING READY-MADE WAISTBANDING rather than simply applying interfacing to a waistband gives a very firm finish. Using waistbanding makes it easy to achieve an even, straight band, and some types are even guaranteed not to roll over. Waistbanding is available in only two widths: 1 in (2.5 cm) and 1½ in (4 cm).

Waistbanding

1 CHECK THAT THE WAISTBAND of the garment fits properly. Make any necessary alterations to the garment. Cut the waistbanding to the length of the waistband, plus the length of the underlap (above). Do not include the two end seam allowances in the calculation.

2 PIN THE WAISTBAND to the garment, matching all the notches. Place the underlap to the right side of the garment. Stitch the seam, and press as stitched. Press the seam allowances up into the waistband (above). Fold the waistband down over the garment.

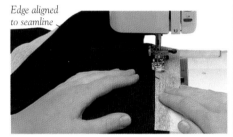

Edge aligned to seamline

3 FOLD THE WAISTBANDING over the seam allowances, with the waistbanding lying away from the garment. Stitch along the waistbanding edge through both seam allowances. Finish ⅝ in (1.5 cm) from the ends (above). Trim and layer the seam allowances.

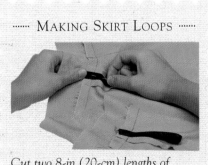

MAKING SKIRT LOOPS

Cut two 8-in (20-cm) lengths of ⅜-in (1-cm) tape. Fold each in half to form a loop, and pin hanging down from the waistband side seam (above). Attach when finishing the waistband.

Raw edge of waistband

4 FOLD THE WAISTBAND along the center foldline, right sides together. Pin. Stitch both of the waistband ends close to but not through the waistbanding. Trim the seams and the corners (above). Turn the waistband to the right side, and enclose the waistbanding.

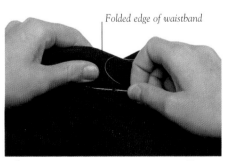

Folded edge of waistband

5 PULL THE END CORNERS square. Press the waistband down over the banding. Turn under the seam allowance along the unstitched edge, and press. Pin the fold even with the waistband. Slipstitch to the waistband seam (above). Press, and attach suitable fasteners (p. 260).

COUTURE DRESSMAKING TECHNIQUES

COUTURE DRESSMAKING places enormous importance on the choice of fabric and the attention to fine detail, both of which justify the expensive price tags placed on designer evening wear. Fabrics used for evening wear, such as velvet, satin, and chiffon, tend to slip and stretch, so care is needed when handling them. Velvet should be sewn in the direction of the nap. Seams should be basted with small stitches to prevent slippage during construction. Bodices without straps or shoulder fabric are supported with boning.

RELATED TECHNIQUES

Hand sewing stitches, p. 74
Taping seams, p. 89
Attaching interlining to
a garment, p. 105
Facing a neckline, p. 127
Marking a hemline, p. 204
Stitching an enclosed
lapped zipper, p. 252

ASSEMBLING A BONED BODICE

BONES CAN BE SEWN to the seam allowances or onto the firmest layer of interlining before this is attached. Each bone is inserted into a length of seam tape that must have a width measurement slightly wider than the bone. The tape can be purchased, or cut from lining strips. Two layers of interlining usually shape and support the bodice.

INTERLINING A BODICE

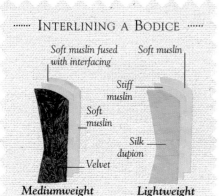

Soft muslin fused with interfacing
Soft muslin
Stiff muslin
Soft muslin
Silk dupion
Velvet

Mediumweight **Lightweight**

Most fabric used in evening wear is medium- or lightweight. To give a crisp, wrinkle-free appearance, the bodice fabric is backed by two layers of interlining. The base layer is the stiffest and falls next to the lining.

STITCHING UP A BODICE

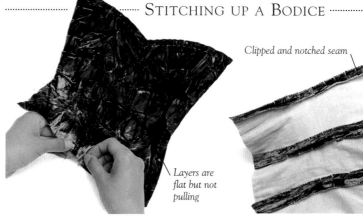

Clipped and notched seam

Layers are flat but not pulling

Tailor's ham

1 WORKING ON a flat surface, assemble the bodice pieces. Place the firmest interlining layer at the bottom of the layers, then the softest, and finally the outer fabric. Pin together, then baste along the seam allowance through all the layers (above). Press lightly.

2 STITCH ALL the bodice pieces together. Press the seams flat, and press open. Clip and notch the seam allowances to allow them to lie flat. To avoid flattening the bust shape, press the bust seam over a tailor's ham (above) or a rolled-up wad of calico.

BONING ON INTERLINING

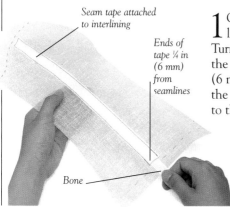

Seam tape attached to interlining

Ends of tape ¼ in (6 mm) from seamlines

Bone

1 CUT seam tape to the length of the bodice. Turn both short ends of the tape under by ¼ in (6 mm). Pin, then stitch the long edges of the tape to the interlining ¼ in (6 mm) from the seamlines. Cut the bone ¼ in (6 mm) shorter than the tape. Insert it into the tape (left).

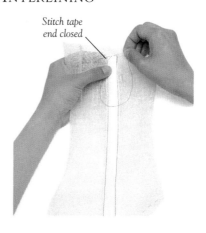

Stitch tape end closed

2 WHIPSTITCH the ends of the seam tape closed (left). Then attach the interlining to the bodice fabric as shown in Steps 1 and 2 (see above), with the bones facing in toward the body. Bodices boned with plastic should be pressed using a medium rather than a hot iron to avoid melting the bones.

BONING FINE FABRICS

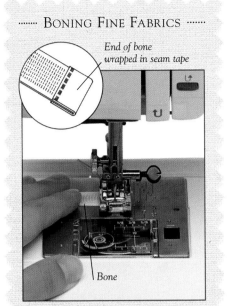

End of bone wrapped in seam tape

Bone

For boning bodices in fine fabrics or with fine linings where the sharp ends could break through, first wrap the ends of the bone with a layer or two of seam tape. Stitch in place (above) before inserting the bone into the channel on the interlining.

BONING IN A SEAM ALLOWANCE

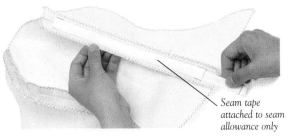

Seam tape attached to seam allowance only

TURN UNDER THE ENDS of the tape ¼ in (6 mm). Stitch the tape centrally over the seams with its ends ¼ in (6 mm) from the bodice top and bottom. Insert the bone into the channel (left). Then whipstitch the ends closed.

LINING A BODICE

Wrong side of bodice

Boning in seam tape

Lining

1 SEW THE LINING. With right sides together, pin and baste the lining to the bodice. Stitch the lining to the bodice top on the wrong side (above). (Attach any fastenings before the lining.)

Interlining

Catchstitching

2 TRIM AND LAYER the seam allowance, then clip and notch it. Catchstitch the top turn-down onto the garment (above). Turn right side out. Slipstitch the lower edge to the bodice.

INSERTING LACING

LACING CAN BE USED at the center front or the center back of a bodice. The required width of the gap to be laced is calculated first. Generally, gaps are no wider than 3¼ in (8 cm) at the back and (2 in) 5 cm at the front. If the pattern does not allow for it, this amount is deducted from the pattern before cutting out the fabric.

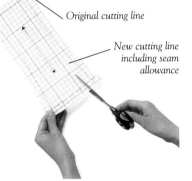

Original cutting line

New cutting line including seam allowance

1 ON the pattern, mark and cut off an area equal to half the desired width in from the original cutting line on each side of the center back or front (left). Cut out the bodice using the new pattern piece, and complete any boning as necessary (see opposite and above).

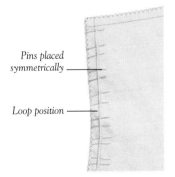

Pins placed symmetrically

Loop position

2 STITCH A ROW of stitching down the new seamline to act as a guide, ⅝ in (1.5 cm) in from the edge. Mark the desired loop spacing with crosswise pins placed on both sides of the opening. Begin and end with a ¾ in (2 cm) gap at the points where the top and bottom seamlines intersect.

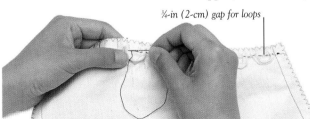

¾-in (2-cm) gap for loops

3 MAKE NARROW LOOPS (p. 248–249), cut into 1¾-in (4.5-cm) lengths. Baste, matching pin markings (above). Stitch across the ends of the loops. Attach the lining (see above). Make up a lace (Step 4), or thread with a ribbon.

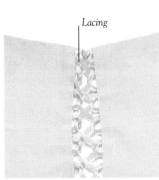

Lacing

4 CUT AN 3¼-in (8-cm) wide strip by the length needed to lace the bodice. Fold the strip lengthways, right sides together. Stitch the ends and side, leaving a ⅝-in (1.5-cm) seam allowance. Leave a 2¼-in (6-cm) gap in this seam to turn the lace through. Slipstitch the seam closed, then thread the lace.

299

MAKING A BIAS SKIRT PATTERN

THIS PATTERN IS SUITABLE for lightweight, flimsy fabrics and is used frequently for evening gowns; it works well long or short. Cutting on the bias causes the skirt to skim the hips and then flare out gently at the hem. A skirt cut on the bias is usually lined and may have a layer of net chiffon, or organza on top to add to the flared effect.

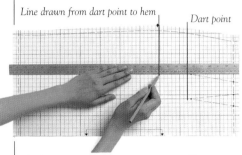

Line drawn from dart point to hem
Dart point

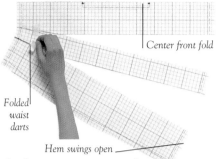

Center front fold
Folded waist darts
Hem swings open

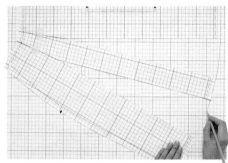

1 A BIAS SKIRT PATTERN is usually adapted from a straight skirt pattern that has two darts at the waist. On the front of the original pattern only, draw two lines parallel to the side seams of the pattern, starting at the dart points and continuing to the hem (above).

2 CUT THE LINES up to the dart point, then fold the waist darts out to cause the hem to swing out. Pin at the desired width (above). Fold a piece of pattern tissue in half, place the center front of the original pattern on the fold, and tape or pin in place.

3 DRAW THE NEW HEM OUTLINE on the tissue, using a continuous line to join the pattern pieces at hem and waist level (above). Cut out the new skirt shape. Detach the original pattern. Mark a bias grainline on the new pattern, bisecting the center front at a 45-degree angle.

MAKING BIAS RUCHING

RUCHING IS ALWAYS CUT on the bias to give the fabric more elasticity. This technique is used extensively in couture dressmaking. Small areas, such as waistlines or bustlines, can be ruched, or a whole bodice can be treated in this way. Be prepared to spend some time arranging the gathers. Take care to avoid pulling them too tightly.

Dress form
Area between basting lines to be ruched

Long edges basted under

1 LAY THE GARMENT OUT, or place it on a dress form, and decide on the area to be ruched. Mark one row of basting along the top and bottom of this area (above). Measure the length and depth of the area.

2 CUT A STRIP OF FABRIC on the bias twice as deep as the marked area by its length (above). (The bias strip depth depends on fabric weight. Chiffon is cut three times as deep as the marked area.)

3 BASTE BOTH LONG EDGES of the fabric strip under by 1¼ in (3 cm). Stitch two rows of gathering stitches across one short end, and gather it up to fit across the marked garment area (above).

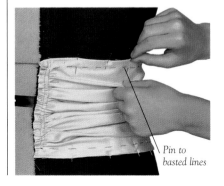

Pin to basted lines

4 PIN the gathered end of the ruching to the garment at one side of the opening. Keeping the garment pulled tight on the dress form, stretch the ruching around the body of the garment. Pin the ruching to the basted lines (left).

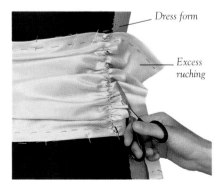

Dress form
Excess ruching

5 AFTER stretching the ruched fabric around the dress form, handstitch two rows of gathering stitches across the ends to fit the ruching. Pull up the threads, and pin. Trim any excess ruching next to the gathering (left).

Ruching must be even

6 POSITION the gathers in the ruching. Working around the garment one section at a time, pin the gathered ruching in place at the side back, side, side front, and center front (left). Position the pins between the folds of the fabric.

7 TAKE the garment off the dress form, and stitch the ruching loosely between each pinned gather. The stitches must be very small, each catching only one thread of the ruching (left). Remove the thread tracing. The ruching at the opening is covered by the facing or zipper.

MACHINE-ROLLED HEMMING ON FINE FABRICS

A MACHINE-ROLLED HEM is a very narrow, rolled hem suitable for all fine, sheer fabrics such as chiffon, silk, organza, georgette, and satin. It is an ideal hem for a circular or flared skirt, and for a chiffon scarf. The finished depth of the hem should be no more than ⅛ in (3 mm). One row of machine edgestitching is visible on the right side.

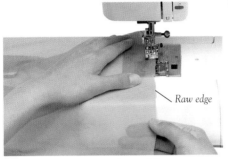

Raw edge

1 ALLOW FOR A ⅜ in (1 cm) hem. Machine stitch the skirt hem ¼ in (6 mm) in from the raw edge to stop the hem from stretching (above). (Loosen the tension if the fabric is puckering.)

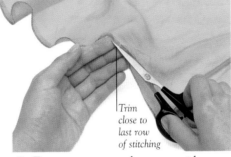

Trim close to last row of stitching

2 FOLD THE HEM to the wrong side along the first row of stitching, and edgestitch. With a pair of small, sharp scissors, trim the hem close to the bottom row of stitching (above). Press.

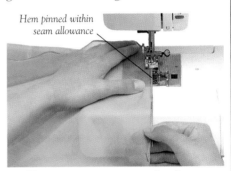

Hem pinned within seam allowance

3 TURN THE HEM UP again by ⅛ in (2 mm), pin, and stitch close to the fold (above). (If the hem is on the straight grain instead of on the bias, the first row of stitching [see Step 1] can be omitted.)

CUTTING A NECKLINE ON THE BIAS

THIS TYPE OF NECKLINE adds a stylish finish to a strapless evening gown. It is often cut using contrasting textured or colored fabric. The finished appearance is that of a turned-back band around the neckline of a garment. It is simply constructed from a bias strip that allows it to fit closely around the top of the bodice.

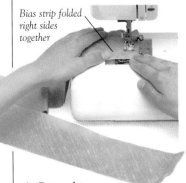

Bias strip folded right sides together

1 CUT a bias strip the length of the neckline, by twice the finished width plus the seam allowances. Machine stitch the short ends (above).

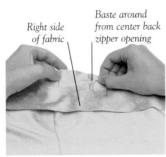

Right side of fabric *Baste around from center back zipper opening*

2 TURN THE BAND to the right side. Lightly press the seams, but not the foldline. Baste the raw edges of the band together. Pin and baste the raw edges of the band to the garment (above).

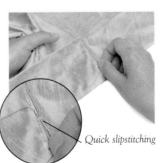

Quick slipstitching

3 FINISH THE TOP of the garment as required with a lining or facing. Understitch the seam to help the lining to roll to the inside. Quick slipstitch the ends to the garment center back (above).

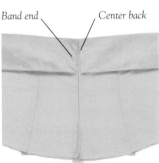

Band end *Center back*

4 DO NOT PRESS the top of the band. It should be allowed to roll over the top of the garment and will sit snugly against the bodice.

MAKING ROSETTE DECORATIONS

FABRIC ROSETTES can be used to decorate evening and wedding gowns. Easy to make, the finished rosettes are attached singly or in clusters of various sizes. They may be made from the same fabric as the garment or from a contrasting one. Fabrics with body, such as taffeta, organza, velvet, and heavy silk satins, give the best results.

28 in (70 cm)

4 in (10 cm)

1 CUT A STRIP of fabric on the bias, about 28 in (70 cm) long by 4 in (10 cm). (Alternatively, join short strips of fabric along the straight grain.) Fold the strip in half lengthwise with wrong sides together, and trim both ends to form a curve. This will neaten the finished rose.

Zigzag-stitched edge

2 WITH WRONG SIDES together, zigzag stitch the raw edges of the strip along the long edges. Handstitch or machine stitch a row of gathering stitches along the long edge and the curved ends, ¼ in (5 mm) from the edge (above). Leave the gathering thread loose at one end.

Loosely gathered strip is tightly rolled at center

3 PULL ON THE ROW of gathering stitches, and push the gathers along to the far end. The far end should be slightly gathered since this will be the center of the rose and will be tightly rolled. Begin to roll up the strip. Stitch through the base to hold the rolled-up center (above).

Secure base with small stitches

4 CONTINUE to roll up the strip, stitching through the base to fix the new layers (left). As the gathers progress to the outer petals, gather the fabric more tightly, so that the petals spread out. When the strip has been completely rolled, secure the outer edge with a few more stitches. Finish off the gathering thread, and cut.

Baste edge by hand

Staystitching

Required finished diameter

Turn under allowance

5 TO FINISH the base of the rosette, cut a circle of fabric large enough to fit over the gathered end, plus ¼ in (5 mm) to make a turned-under edge. Staystitch the circle inside the edge. Fold under along the staystitching, and baste the fabric down around the edge (left).

Use seam ripper to remove basting

Tightly gathered outer petals

Base

6 WITH WRONG SIDES together, center the circle of fabric over the gathered base of the rosette. Secure the circle by whipstitching in position over the gathered edges, then carefully remove the basting (above).

SECURING ROSETTES

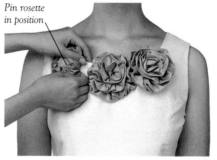

Pin rosette in position

FIRST DECIDE ON THE POSITION of the cluster. Place the garment either on a dress form or on the wearer, and position the roses on the fabric to achieve the desired result. Pin in position (above). Handstitch each of the rosettes securely to the garment, stitching through the base at the center of the circle.

INSERTING PEARL RODS

Pearl rods

Rosette

Pearl rods are purchased ready-made from bead shops and haberdashery suppliers. Usually available only in white, they can be dyed to match a garment using commercial dyes. To insert, roll the fabric strip around a cluster of pearl rods when starting to coil the rosette. Stitch in place.

MAKING DECORATIVE BOWS

DECORATIVE BOWS are used mainly on evening and bridal wear, and sometimes on girls' dresses. The size of the bows depends on personal taste, but small bows often decorate the shoulder area, while a large bow can be placed at the center back of the waist. The fabric can be interlined with net or tulle to form a stiff bow.

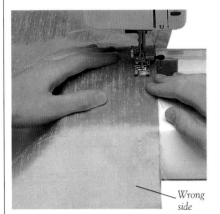

Wrong side

1 DECIDE ON the size of the finished bow. Cut a rectangle of fabric on the straight grain twice the width by twice the length of the desired finished bow, including seam allowances. With right sides together, fold the fabric in half lengthwise, and stitch along the length (left).

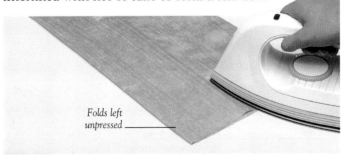

Folds left unpressed

2 TURN THE STITCHED TUBE OF FABRIC to face right side out. Center the seam on the underside of the tube. Press the seam gently, being careful not to press thea outside folds of the strip, which should remain soft and rounded (above).

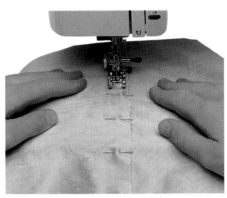

3 BRING THE SHORT ENDS of the tube to the center on the underside of the fabric. Overlap the ends by ⅜ in (1 cm), and pin. Stitch these ends along the center of the strip to form a wide, circular band (above).

Uncompleted tie end

Turn right side out

4 DECIDE on the shape and size of the tie ends. Make a pattern, and cut two tie ends. With right sides together, pin and stitch both tie ends, leaving the short edges open. Trim and finish the edges. Pull the ends through to the right side (above).

Underside of bow

Tie ends

5 PRESS the turned tie ends, and overlap the finished short ends by ⅜ in (1 cm). Pin and stitch. Pin the lapped seam of the tie ends over the center back of the bow. Baste in place (above).

Stitch gathers through all layers

6 USING a strong, single thread or a doubled thread, stitch long – about ¾-in (2-cm) – gathering stitches at the center of the bow, leaving the same size spaces in between each stitch. Pull up the gathering thread tightly to form the bow (above). Secure the thread ends.

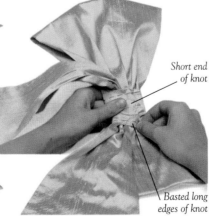

Short end of knot

Basted long edges of knot

7 CUT OUT THE KNOT to the required width plus two ⅜-in (1.5-cm) overlaps, by the bow center length plus allowances. Baste the overlaps under the knot, and slipstitch the short ends to the underside of the bow. Wrap the knot around the bow. Join the ends with a lapped seam (above).

········· DETACHABLE BOW ·········

Hook will prevent bow from drooping

On the underside of the bow, stitch hooks at the top of the knot, and at the top corners of the bow (above). Attach matching thread loops to the garment. Repeat this process at each corner of the tie ends.

MENDING

REPAIRING WORN or torn fabric will extend the useful life of a garment or furnishing. An accidental tear or hole can be mended neatly by darning or patching and, if the repair is done well, the fabric can appear almost as good as new. The simple repair of a zipper or the replacement of worn elastic will salvage an otherwise unwearable item. The basic needlework techniques that are described in depth throughout the book can also be applied in mending. The application of some of these techniques is shown in the steps below.

REMOVING MACHINE STITCHES

MENDING sometimes involves removing machine stitching along seamlines. Using a seam ripper makes the job quick, but care must be taken because it is easy to cut the fabric. Once the stitching has been removed, any stray threads should be cut or trimmed, and the seam should be steam pressed to remove the line of stitching holes.

SEAM RIPPER METHOD

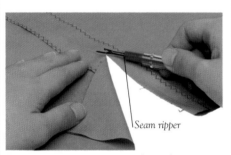

Seam ripper

PULL THE SEAM APART and, working with the point of the seam ripper on the bottom and the ball on the top, insert its point between the fabric edges and cut upward to sever the thread (above).

SCISSORS METHOD

USE FINE, POINTED SCISSORS to ease out the machine stitching and cut a loop every few stitches along the seam (above). Pull the seam apart and snip away all the stitching between the two pieces of fabric.

FINE MACHINE STITCHES

Work a pin or needle under a stitch to ease it out (above), then cut it. Ease out and cut every second or third thread loop. Ease the seam edges apart and remove all the threads.

DARNING A HOLE

A DARNING MUSHROOM, A PIECE OF CARDBOARD, or the hand not used for sewing can support and slightly stretch fabric, while a hole is darned with a long darning needle and a thread that matches the fabric in weight. If the hole is large, a piece of net or muslin can be placed underneath, and the darning worked through this.

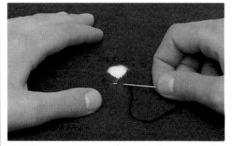

1 WORK small running stitches around the hole or the area where the fabric has worn away (above). The stitches will strengthen the edge of the darning area, and ensure that knitted fabrics do not run.

2 WORK A SERIES of close, parallel rows of long, flat running stitches over the hole to fill in all the outlined area (above). Do not make the stitches too loose, or pull them too tight at the edges.

3 WORKING AT A RIGHT ANGLE to the filling stitches, weave the thread in and out of alternate rows of stitches (above), catching the garment fabric at each side and filling in the outlined area.

MENDING A SEAM

IT IS BEST TO MEND A SEAM on the inside with matching thread. Before the repair is begun, any short pieces of thread are pulled out and any long threads are trimmed close to the seam. If the thread has snapped, restitching the seam will solve the problem. However, if the fabric has torn, the seam must be reinforced before it is repaired.

REPLACING STITCHING ALONG A SEAMLINE

IF THE STITCHING has simply come undone, trim off any loose ends of thread. Using short, straight machine stitches (above), or small hand backstitches, replace the missing stitches, working on the inside of the seam. To secure, overlap the existing stitching with the new stitching at both ends of the seam.

REPAIRING FABRIC RIPPED AT A SEAMLINE

Iron-on patch

IF THE FABRIC HAS RIPPED along the seamline, first repair the tear in the fabric with an iron-on patch. This should be cut to a suitable size so that it covers the tear neatly but is not too bulky (see Mending a Tear, below). Restitch the seam, sewing over the patch and slightly to one side of the original line of stitching (above).

MENDING AN UNDERARM SEAM

When mending an underarm seam, first repair the seam. Then cut a lightweight, diamond-shaped patch, and press under the edges. Pin and stitch the patch over the underarm seam, stitching around the edges and along each seamline (above).

MENDING A TEAR

THE MOST COMMON METHOD of reinforcing a tear is to use a patch on the inside. Alternatively, a patch can be put over the tear with handstitching; this is weaker than machine zigzag stitching, but less conspicuous. The thread color should be matched as closely as possible to the garment fabric color for a neat, invisible repair.

REINFORCING AND STITCHING

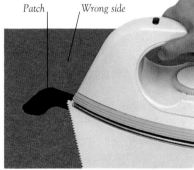

Patch   *Wrong side*

1 CUT A PIECE of double-sided, fusible webbing just large enough to cover the tear. Using a steam iron, fuse the webbing to a fabric patch of the same size. Position the patch on the wrong side of the tear and, working on the right side, pull the torn edges together gently. Using a pressing cloth, press to fuse the webbed patch to the fabric (left).

2 IF THE FABRIC around the tear is very worn, stitch over the torn edges on the right side, using machine three-step zigzag stitch (left) or overcast stitch. Either stitch across both edges of the tear at once, or stitch over each side separately. (If the tear is in an area of the garment that receives little wear, the fused patch may be a sufficient means of repair by itself.)

MENDING A TEAR IN A SHEER FABRIC OR SOFT JERSEY

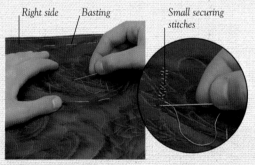

Right side   *Basting*   *Small securing stitches*

An iron-on patch would be too thick on sheer fabric or soft jersey. Instead, place a piece of stiff paper beneath the tear. Baste it in position to hold the fabric edges together. Darn across the tear, inserting the needle through the tear and bringing it up on one side, then down through the tear and up on the other side (above). Work with small stitches, and do not pull tightly. Once the repair is finished, remove the basting and the paper.

PATCHING A HOLE

A FABRIC PATCH should, if possible, be taken from the garment material – perhaps from a hem or facing – or matched as closely as possible. Fused patches are used for thick fabrics such as denim, where a hemmed edge would be too bulky and would not lie flat. Patches with turned-under edges are for light- to mediumweight fabrics.

FUSED PATCH

Fusible web

Right side   *Patch*

Right side   *Patch*

1 TRIM AWAY THE RAGGED EDGES of the hole. Cut a patch at least ⅝ in (1.5 cm) larger all around than the hole. Cut a piece of paper backed fusible web the same size. Cut a hole out of the web, making it the same size as the garment hole (above).

2 PRESS TO FUSE ONE SIDE of the web to the wrong side of the patch, then remove the paper from the other side. Place the patch over the right side of the garment hole. Using a pressing cloth, fuse the patch in position (above).

3 WORKING on the right side, machine stitch around the raw edge of the fused patch, using a close zigzag stitch (p. 77) (above). Alternatively, use either a three-step zigzag stitch (p. 77) or an overcast stitch (p. 74).

PATCH WITH TURNED-UNDER EDGES

1 TRIM THE HOLE OR WORN AREA of the fabric into a square or rectangle, and snip a short, diagonal cut at each corner (above). Cut out a patch 1 in (2.5 cm) larger all around than the hole.

2 FINISH THE PATCH EDGES by pressing them to the right side. Working on the wrong side, place the patch right side down over the hole. Baste and handstitch the patch in position (above).

3 WORKING ON THE RIGHT SIDE, turn the raw edges of the garment fabric under to the inside and slipstitch the folded edges to the patch (above). Then remove the basting and press.

REPAIRING ZIPPERS

IF A RUNNER SLIPS OFF THE TEETH OF A METAL ZIPPER, it is possible to make a temporary repair. Once it is broken, a metal zipper is generally weakened and may break again, so it should be replaced as soon as possible. A nylon zipper under stress can gape and pull apart. As with a metal zipper, cutting and rethreading serves only as a temporary repair.

1 PULL THE RUNNER close to the zipper base. On the side without the runner cut the tape between two teeth ¼ in (6 mm) from the base (above). If a tooth is missing, pull the runner below the gap.

2 FEED the zipper teeth above the cut or gap on the zipper into the open side of the runner. Pull up the runner. If the zipper is not correctly aligned and no longer lies flat, pull the runner down. Repeat process until the zipper teeth interlink correctly and the zipper lies flat.

3 PULL THE RUNNER back up along the zipper. Just above the cut or gap, overcast or zigzag stitch across the zipper teeth to hold the two sides together and to form a stop for the runner (above).

REPAIRING FABRIC UNDER A BUTTON

CONSTANT USE may eventually cause the threads that secure a button to tear a hole in the fabric. After the button is removed, this hole must be repaired and reinforced before the button can be restitched. For a small hole, fusible mending tape in a matching color can be used as a means of reinforcement. To repair a large hole or a lightweight fabric, a piece of matching fabric is used. The tape or patch should be trimmed in a circle or oval shape.

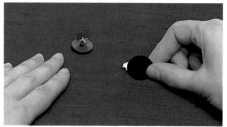

1 CUT A PIECE of mending tape into a circle or oval shape (above) and fuse it over the hole on the wrong side of the garment. (Alternatively, baste a small patch to the wrong side of the garment.)

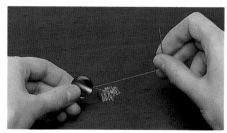

2 ON THE RIGHT SIDE of the garment, work machine or running stitches in rows across and slightly beyond the patch, stitching through both patch and fabric. Replace the button (above).

REPAIRING A BUTTONHOLE

A BUTTONHOLE MAY TEAR AT ONE END when it is accidentally snagged or if it is continually under stress on a tight-fitting garment. Before the end of a buttonhole is repaired, it should be reinforced on the wrong side with a small, fusible patch in a matching color. A carefully executed buttonhole repair should be almost invisible.

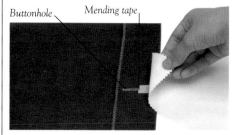

Buttonhole *Mending tape*

1 TRIM AWAY any loose threads or frayed fabric ends using a pair of small, sharp scissors. To reinforce the area under the end of the buttonhole, use a pressing cloth to fuse a patch of mending tape to the wrong side of the fabric (above).

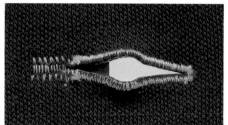

2 USING MATCHING THREAD, work rows of small running stitches across the worn area at right angles to the buttonhole, taking care to incorporate the fused patch underneath, and stitching as firmly and as neatly as possible.

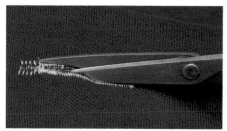

3 RESTITCH THE END of the buttonhole through the patch, lapping the ends of the new stitching over the previous stitching. (Alternatively, restitch along the entire buttonhole.) Then recut the end using small, sharp scissors (above).

REPAIRING ELASTIC

REPLACING THE ELASTIC in a simple casing channel is an easy repair. The process is more complicated on some ready-made garments where the elastic and casing are held together by multiple rows of stitching. In this case, because the fabric may be cut inadvertently as the stitches are removed, the whole casing should be replaced.

Wrong side of casing

1 REMOVE A SMALL OPENING in one of the casing seams using small, sharp scissors (above). (Alternatively, remove an opening at the base of the casing.) Then cut the new piece of elastic to fit the waist snugly but comfortably, and add an extra 1 in (2.5 cm) for the join.

Old elastic *New elastic*

2 CUT ACROSS THE OLD ELASTIC, and join the new piece of elastic to one end with a safety pin (above). Gently pull the old elastic from the opposite end of the opening, so that the new elastic is drawn through the entire length of the casing. Unpin and discard the old elastic.

Opening

3 CHECK THAT THE ELASTIC is lying flat within the casing, overlap the ends of the elastic, and overcast or whipstitch them together. Close the opening in the seam by slipstitching (above). To prevent the elastic from rolling, stitch along each vertical seam through the casing.

GLOSSARY

Abutted seam Seam used to join two fabric pieces edge to edge, sometimes used with a lightweight fabric underlay; generally used for joining interfacing and interlining to eliminate bulk.

Acetate Shiny synthetic fabric that drapes well (*see* p. 59).

Acrylic Woven or knitted synthetic fabric (*see* p. 56).

Alpaca Woolen fabric (*see* p. 51).

Anti-fray spray Convenient sewing aid for sealing cut edges of fabric without the need for stitching or other finishing.

Armhole Garment opening for the arm and sleeve.

Arrowhead stitch Small, triangular stitches worked either by hand or by machine across a seam to add strength at a point of possible strain (e.g., at the top of a pleat on a tight-fitting skirt).

Awl Sharp-pointed tool used for piercing small holes in fabric ready for the insertion of eyelets or buttonholes.

Backstitch Strong handstitch with a double stitch on the wrong side, used mainly for seaming as an alternative to machine stitching.

Banding Method of finishing a raw edge by applying a wider strip of fabric than that used for binding. The strip extends beyond the raw edges and can be used to add length to a garment.

Bar tack Short, straight row of reinforcing stitching worked by hand or machine and used to strengthen points of strain on a garment, especially in areas subject to strain where splitting could occur (e.g., at a pocket top or end of a zipper opening).

Basting Long running stitches made by hand or machine to hold fabric in position temporarily prior to the final stitching, or to hold the garment sections together before they are fitted.

Belt carrier Loop made from a strip of fabric or a thread chain, which is used to support a belt; generally inserted at the side seams of a garment.

Belt stiffening Flexible supporting fabric that is applied to the inside of a belt to provide stiffness and maintain the shape of a belt (fusible interfacing is generally used to achieve the amount of stiffening required).

Bent-handled shears Fabric-cutting tool; the angled lower blade allows fabric to lie flat as it is cut.

Bias Diagonal line on fabric that is on neither the lengthwise nor the crosswise grain. The "true" bias is the diagonal line formed at a 45-degree angle when the lengthwise grain is folded to the crosswise grain.

Bias binding Strips available ready-made or cut on the bias grain of fabric; used to give a neat finish to hems and seam allowances.

Bias binding maker Tool used to create bias binding by folding under raw edges of a fabric strip.

Binding Method of finishing a raw edge by enclosing it in a strip of fabric. Also a notion (e.g., bias binding, ribbon, or twill tape) used for practical purposes such as finishing a raw edge or strengthening a seam.

Blanket stitch Handstitch worked along the raw or finished edge of fabric to decorate or finish.

Blind catchstitch Handstitch worked as for catchstitch, but with the hem edge folded back before stitching, so that hemming is invisible from the right side.

Blind hemstitch This tiny handstitch is used to attach one piece of fabric to another (e.g., a facing to a seam allowance). Also a machine stitch consisting of two or three straight stitches and one wide zigzag stitch, used to stitch hems invisibly and to produce shell tucks.

Bobbin Round holder beneath the needle plate of a sewing machine, on which thread is wound; can be made from plastic or metal.

Bodice Upper-body section of a garment. On strapless evening dresses the seams of the bodice are supported by boning.

Boning Narrow nylon or plastic strip used for stiffening and shaping close-fitting garments; most often used in the bodices of strapless evening dresses; ends can be covered to protect fine fabrics.

Bouclé Synthetic fabric (*see* p. 58).

Brushed cotton Thick cotton fabric (*see* p. 47).

Bustline Horizontal line running across the back and around the fullest part of the bust; important measurement when sizing or altering a pattern.

Buttonhole Opening through which a button is inserted to form a fastening. Buttonholes are most often machine stitched with a close zigzag or satin stitch, but they may also be worked by hand or finished in different ways (e.g., bound or piped).

Buttonhole stitch Overedge handstitch that is used to finish and strengthen the raw edges of a buttonhole.

Button loop Decorative fastening, usually attached between facings or at the edge of a garment; can be made in different ways. See **Frog fastening** and **Narrow loop**.

Button shank Stem between a button and fabric, which can be part of the button or constructed with thread, and which allows room for the buttonhole side of the item to fit under the button when joined; often used on thick fabric.

Calico Cotton fabric (*see* p. 45).

Cambric Cotton fabric (*see* p. 45).

Cap See **Sleeve cap**.

Catchstitch Hand-worked hemming stitch used to join the edges of interfacings or facings to the inside of an item. This stitch is always worked from left to right.

Cashmere Fine, soft, woolen fabric (*see* p. 49).

Plastic bobbin – see Sewing machine accessories, p. 17

Casing Tunnel of fabric created by parallel rows of stitching, through which elastic or a drawstring cord is threaded (e.g., at the waist of a skirt or pants, or to draw in the waist of a dress or casual jacket).

Center line Vertical center of the bodice, skirt, or yoke section of a garment; marked on the relevant pattern pieces.

Challis Woolen fabric (*see* p. 50).

Chambray Plain-weave cotton fabric (*see* p. 43).

Charmeuse Delicate satin-weave synthetic fabric (*see* p. 58).

Cheesecloth Loosely woven, cotton fabric (*see* p. 45).

Chiffon Silk fabric (*see* p. 55).

Chinese ball button Made by looping a length of cord or fabric tubing into a tight ball; used in conjunction with a frog fastening.

Chintz Cotton fabric (*see* p. 43).

Clip Small cut at the edge of fabric to indicate a pattern marking such as a foldline, center front line, or dart position. Seam allowances can also be clipped to achieve a point when turned to the right side (e.g., a collar point), or to allow a smooth curve to form (e.g., a collar or scalloped edge).

Coating Heavy, woolen fabric (*see* p. 49).

Complex French curve Measuring tool similar to the French curve, but also used to measure straight edges on pattern pieces. It has buttonhole guides and seam allowance slots.

Corduroy Napped cotton fabric (*see* p. 47).

Cotton Made from the fibrous hairs covering the seed pods of the cotton plant, which are woven into fabric that is soft, durable, and inexpensive, cotton is used for a wide range of dressmaking and home-furnishing purposes. It is available in many weights.

Cotton velvet Napped cotton fabric (*see* p. 47).

Couching Method of securing a cord or other item to a fabric by working small handstitches over the top of the item.

Crease Line formed by pressing a fabric fold.

Crepe Woolen fabric (*see* p. 49).

Crepe-backed satin Synthetic fabric (*see* p. 58).

Crepe de Chine Smooth, silk fabric (*see* p. 54).

Crepon Synthetic fabric (*see* p. 56).

Crinkle cotton Cotton fabric, also called crepon (*see* p. 44).

Crinkle fabric Finely pleated and creased synthetic fabric (*see* p. 60).

Cross stitch Handstitch used for practical purposes (e.g., holding pleats and folds in position prior to machine stitching); also used for decoration.

Crosswise fold Widthwise fold of fabric made at the fabric cutting stage. It is used to accommodate either wide or unusually shaped pattern pieces.

Crosswise fold with nap Fabric with a nap is folded at the cutting stage with wrong sides together and cut along the fold. The top layer is then turned around so that the nap runs in the same direction on both layers of fabric, and the pattern piece is cut.

Crosswise grain Direction of the widthwise (weft) threads on a fabric, running from selvage to selvage crossing the straight grain of the fabric.

Curtain weight Weight inserted into a curtain hemline in order to improve the hang of the fabric and prevent billowing; it is also sometimes used in tailoring.

Curved seam Machine-stitched seam with two differently shaped edges which, when joined, shape an area of a garment (e.g., over the bust, in at the waist, and out at the hips); also referred to as a princess seam.

Custom tailoring Traditional method of sewing a well-fitting garment. A layered arrangement of reinforcing and structuring fabrics is handstitched and steamed into place underneath the finished garment; this allows the shape of the garment to be held in place permanently.

Cutting line Solid, printed line on a pattern piece used as a guide for cutting (a multisize pattern has several cutting lines on the relevant garment pieces).

Cutting mat Mat with a grid design that allows precise measuring and cutting; used to protect a work surface during fabric cutting.

Damask Cotton fabric (*see* p. 46).

Darning mushroom A mushroom-shaped wooden tool placed beneath an area of fabric to be darned to facilitate stitching lengthwise and crosswise over the hole.

Dart Tapered, stitched fold of fabric used on a garment to shape the fabric around the contours of the body. Darts (e.g., French dart and contour dart) are used mainly on women's clothes to provide fullness at the bust and hips, and shape at the waist; small darts also shape the back shoulders and elbows of tailored garments. Darts are formed using different methods.

Denim Hardwearing cotton fabric (*see* p. 46).

Devoré velvet Patterned silk fabric (*see* p. 54).

Double coating Reversible woolen fabric (*see* p. 50).

Double jersey Woolen fabric with ribs running in different directions on either side (*see* p. 51).

Drape Property of fabric, enabling it to fall into graceful folds; not all fabrics drape so before buying fabric for an item, check the drape. Also a specific arrangement of folds, controlled by gathers, pleats, or tucks, in a garment or curtain.

Dress form Realistic body shape used for the fitting of garments, and especially useful for tailored garments where a perfect fit is essential; available in one size or as an adjustable form.

Dressmaker's carbon Paper available in a number of colors, used in conjunction with a tracing wheel to transfer pattern markings.

Dressmaker's pencil Chalk pencil with an erasing brush at one end, used to mark lines (e.g., darts or tucks) on fabric.

Drill Cotton fabric (*see* p. 47).

Dupion Silk fabric (*see* p. 55).

Ease Distribution of fullness without the formation of gathers or tucks when one section of a seam is joined to another, slightly shorter section (e.g., at the sleeve cap on a set-in sleeve).

Easestitch Long machine stitch, worked in either a single or a double row, used to ease in fullness where the distance between notches is slightly greater on one seam edge than on the other (e.g., for shaping an elbow). *See also* **Gathering**.

Edgestitch Can be worked as an alternative to zigzag stitch on fine fabric; used to finish hems and facings to prevent fraying by turning under the raw edge and stitching a small hem. Can also be worked on the right side of an item, close to a finished edge, seam, or edge of a fold.

Enclosed edge Raw fabric edge that is sandwiched or concealed within a seam or binding; finishes and strengthens an item.

Eyelet Embroidered cotton fabric (*see* p. 45).

Fabric rosette – see Making rosette decorations, p. 302

Facing Layer of fabric positioned on the inside of a garment and used to finish raw edges (e.g., at a neckline, front or back jacket opening, or sleeve); it can be interfaced for weight. On a shaped garment edge, the facing is cut to the same shape, attached to the item by machine stitching, folded to the wrong side, and then handstitched flat to the lining or fabric for a neat finish.

Faille Synthetic fabric (*see* p. 57).

Feather stitch Machine stitch used to join up two abutting, nonfraying edges (e.g., on a suede fabric); also used as a decorative embroidery stitch and in quilting.

Fibers Natural or manmade filaments from which yarns are spun; the yarns are then made into a variety of fabrics.

Flannel Woolen fabric (*see* p. 48).

Flat-fell seam Machine-stitched, self-enclosed seam that is flat, strong, and hardwearing; generally used on sportswear.

Flock Synthetic fabric (*see* p. 59).

Fly Finished opening that conceals a zipper or buttons; generally used on shorts and pants.

French curve Measuring tool whose edge is used to make curved adjustments on a pattern area (e.g., on an armhole or neckline). *See also* **Complex French curve**.

French seam Machine-stitched, self-enclosed seam with a strong, neat, and narrow finish; used only on straight fabric edges. This seam is ideal for use on sheer fabrics where seam allowances are visible. *See also* **Mock French seam**.

French tack Stitching used to hold two layers of fabric loosely together; generally used to link a free-hanging lining to the main hem of an item to hold the lining in position. The stitching is worked between the two hems, so is invisible from both sides.

Frog fastening Decorative fastening made from a length of narrow tubing or cord, which is arranged into four overlapping loops and stitched at the center. Used in conjunction with a decorative Chinese ball button, generally on a jacket or long dress coat.

Front bands Fabric strips used to finish the entire length of the front opening edges of a garment.

Fur fabric Synthetic fabric also referred to as fake fur; can be brightly colored (*see* p. 61).

Fusible interfacing Chemically treated, nonwoven interfacing designed to be fused to another fabric with the heat of an iron; available in different weights.

Fusible web Soft, adhesive web used for fusing fabrics together; a hot iron is used for bonding.

Gabardine Waterproof, wool-blend or wool fabric (*see* p. 49).

Gathered self-bound seam A seam used to stitch a gathered edge to a straight edge. *See also* **Self-bound seam**.

Gathering Two parallel rows of running stitch or loose machine stitch; long threads are left attached on both ends of the gathering and the excess fabric is pulled up from one or both ends and used to draw in fabric for fit, or for decorative ruffled effect.

Georgette Silk fabric (*see* p. 55); also produced as a polyester.

Gingham Checked cotton fabric (*see* p. 42).

Glazed cotton Cotton fabric; also referred to as chintz (*see* p. 43).

Grain Lengthwise and crosswise direction of threads in a woven fabric. When these threads are at right angles, the fabric is said to be on the "true" grain.

Grainline Line that follows the grain of a fabric (a straight arrow on a pattern piece indicates that the pattern should lie parallel to a straight edge).

Grosgrain Stiff, ribbed, synthetic fabric (*see* p. 57).

Gusset Small, shaped piece of matching fabric set into a slash or seam for added ease of movement (e.g., at the underarm of a sleeve that would otherwise be tight).

Habutai Silk fabric (*see* p. 55).

Handkerchief linen Sheer, lightweight linen (*see* p. 52).

Heading Fabric tuck above a casing, or at the top edge of a curtain. Also a narrow edge above a gathered ruffle.

Buckle kit – see Covering a buckle, p. 177

Heading tape Wide fabric tape containing loops that is stitched to the top of a curtain for the insertion of hooks. The tape is drawn up to make softly gathered pleats in the fabric, and the curtain is attached to a rod using hooks inserted into woven pockets on the heading tape.

Heavy-duty stitch Very strong handstitch used to join together two layers of heavy fabric.

Hem Finished lower edge of an item (e.g., the bottom of a garment or curtain, or the lower edge of a straight sleeve). Hems can be finished by hand or machine in various ways, the method used depending on the weight and nature of the fabric (e.g., a hand-rolled hem is ideal for sheer fabrics, while a double-stitched hem gives support to extra-wide hems or heavy fabrics). Hem finishings can be invisible on the right side, or be made into a decorative feature.

Hem allowance Amount of fabric allowed for turning under to make up a hem. Depth of hem allowance can vary, depending on the style or function of the item.

Hemline Foldline along which a hem is marked and the hem allowance folded to the wrong side for stitching; the finished lower edge of an item.

Hemstitch Handstitch, worked as either a vertical or a slanting hemstitch, used for invisible hemming on the wrong side of a garment or home furnishing item; also used for securing inside edges (e.g., on a collar or cuffs).

High bust Measurement taken above the full bust, under the arms, and around the back and chest; if this measurement is more than 2 in (5 cm) larger than the full bustline measurement, a garment pattern size should be selected by the high bust.

Hipline Horizontal line that runs around the fullest part of the hips; when choosing an appropriate pattern size for pants or a skirt, this measurement should be taken into account, rather than that of the waist. Important measurement for altering a pattern.

Needle and thread – see Hand-sewing needles, p. 10

Hook-and-eye fastener Two-piece metal fastening used to fasten overlapping edges on fabric areas where a neat join is required (e.g., on a waistband). Can have painted finishes to coordinate with fabric.

Integrated or self-facing Used at a straight garment edge, this type of facing is cut as one with the garment, then folded to the inside.

Interfacing Specially designed fabric placed between garment and facing fabrics to give added stiffening, shaping, and support at specific areas (e.g., on a waistband, collar, or cuffs). It is made in light-, medium-, and heavyweights to match the garment fabric being used. Nonwoven interfacing is ideal for general use; woven canvas interfacing is used for tailoring. *See also* **Fusible interfacing**.

Interlining Layer of muslin or fluffy, lightweight fabric placed between lining and garment fabrics to add warmth or bulk; often used in tailored jackets and coats, or in drapery to add body.

Jacquard fabric Patterned synthetic fabric (*see* p. 59).

Jersey Knitted, crease-resistant, cotton fabric (*see* p. 42).

Knit fabric Stretchable fabric made of loosely interlocking threads (e.g., soft jersey). Seams on a knit fabric must be stitched with ease to prevent the stitches from breaking; they may require taping (e.g., at the edge of a hip pocket that may stretch with wear).

Lace Cotton fabric (*see* p. 45).

Lamé Synthetic fabric (*see* p. 61).

Lapel Section of a jacket or shirt that is turned back between the top button and collar.

Lapped seam Used on non-frayable fabrics (e.g., suede), where the seam allowance of one edge is placed over the edge to be joined, then topstitched close to the overlapping edge.

Lawn Cotton fabric (*see* p. 44).

Layering Trimming of fabric layers at a seam allowance to different widths, to remove bulk and enable the seam to lie flat.

Layout Guide to the position in which pattern pieces are laid on a fabric ready for cutting.

Leather Animal hide (*see* p. 61).

Lengthwise grain Direction of the lengthwise (warp) threads on a woven fabric, which run parallel to the selvages. As it is less likely to stretch than the crosswise grain, the lengthwise grain is used as the straight grain wherever possible.

Linen Produced from the natural fibers of the flax plant, linen is woven in a range of weights and qualities to make fabrics that are cool and highly absorbent.

Lining Underlying fabric layer used to give a luxurious, neat finish to an item, as well as concealing the construction details of a garment and providing structural support. A lining also adds weight to the drape of a garment and makes it comfortable to wear.

Liquid gold Metallic synthetic fabric (*see* p. 61).

Liquid marking pen Marking tool available in two types. With one type, the marks disappear after 48 hours; the other washes out.

Lockstitch Also known as loop stitch, this is a handstitch used to join two fabric layers.

Loop stitch See **Lockstitch**.

Loop turner Hooked tool used for turning thin tubes (as belt loops) from the wrong side to the right side.

Machine basting Long, loosely tensioned machine stitching used to hold fabric in position temporarily before final stitching.

Machine foot Generally referred to as a presser foot, this part of a sewing machine is lowered onto fabric to hold it in position on the needle plate during stitching, and guides the needle smoothly through the fabric. Different feet are available for a range of purposes, including beading, piping, and inserting zippers.

Madras cotton Lightweight cotton fabric (*see* p. 43).

Measuring stick Used to check grainlines; also used to mark a straight hemline before turning up and stitching in place.

Microfiber Durable synthetic fabric (*see* p. 57).

Mitered corner Diagonal seam formed when fabric is joined at, or shaped around, a corner (e.g., where the hems meet at the corner of a vent in a sleeve, or at the base of a curtain). After stitching, any excess fabric is normally cut away on the underside.

Mock French seam Used as for a French seam, but on a curved fabric edge. See **French seam**.

Mohair Woolen fabric (*see* p. 51).

Moleskin Cotton fabric (*see* p. 46).

Multisize pattern This has cutting lines for a range of sizes printed on each pattern piece.

Multistitch See **Three-step zigzag stitch**.

Muslin Cotton fabric (*see* p. 44).

Nap Soft pile fabric surface made by short fibers that brush in one direction (e.g., velvet or corduroy). The nap should run in the same direction on all pieces of an item.

Narrow loop Fastening formed from a narrow fabric tube; generally used with round or domed buttons as a decorative fastening.

Safety pins – see Pins, p. 10

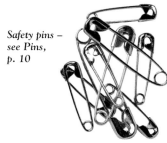

Narrow loop carrier Loop formed from a narrow tube of fabric, and stitched to a waistband or inserted in the garment side seams to support a belt.

Neckband Piece of fabric cut to match the neckline and used to make a shaped band.

Neckline Part of a garment that lies around the neck; this may vary in style from a simple faced neckline to a bound neckline or a front placket opening.

Needle grabber Sewing aid with a textured surface, used during handstitching to pull a needle through thick or unyielding fabric.

Needle threader Simple device with a looped wire that pulls thread through the eye of a needle.

No-crease wool See p. 51.

Noil Silk fabric (*see* p. 53).

Notch Outward-facing, V-shaped (or double V-shaped), transferable marking on a pattern, which indicates alignment with another piece for seaming purposes.

Notion Any haberdashery article, other than fabric, used in the construction of an item. The notions required for making a garment are listed on the pattern envelope and include interfacing fabrics, bindings, fasteners, tapes, ribbons, elastics, and trims.

Nylon See **Pure nylon**.

One-way design Pattern, stripe, or check that repeats in one direction along the length of a fabric. When using a one-way design, all pattern pieces must be placed on the fabric so that the design is the correct way up on each piece.

Organza Silk fabric (*see* p. 54).

Overcast stitch Overedge handstitch used to finish raw fabric edges.

Overedge stitch Preset machine stitch, worked over the edge of a seam allowance, which stitches and finishes a very narrow seam in one complete action; generally used on sheer fabrics where seam allowances are visible.

Overlap Part of a garment construction that is designed to extend over another part (e.g., a hook-and-eye waistband opening or a sleeve cuff) to hide a fastening.

Pad stitch Used predominantly in tailoring to fasten canvas interfacing firmly to a fabric (e.g., on a jacket collar). When the stitches are worked short and close together (as in short chevron padding stitch), the fabric is shaped three-dimensionally; when long and spaced apart (as in long parallel padding stitch), the stitches hold the interfacing to the fabric.

Partial fold Method of folding fabric; one section of the fabric forms a folded double layer, and the other forms a single layer.

Pattern markings Symbols printed on a pattern to indicate the fabric grain, the placement of a pattern piece on the fold (straight line with bent arrows at each end pointing toward pattern foldline), and construction details such as notches, darts, buttonholes, and tucks. Pattern markings are transferred to fabric using a marking medium (e.g., a dressmaker's pencil) or thread markings (e.g., tailor's tacks).

Pickstitch Decorative surface handstitch, generally used on collars, which can be used as an alternative to topstitching.

Pile Raised loops or tufts on the surface of a fabric (e.g., on velvet). The pile should run in the same direction on all pieces of an item.

Pinking shears Cutting tool with serrated blades, used on fray-resistant fabrics (e.g., woolen fabrics) to finish a seam allowance with a zigzagged finish.

Piping Trim made from bias-cut strips of fabric, used either flat or with an inserted cord to form round piping; used on a range of items, especially home furnishings.

Pivoting Technique used to stitch a sharp corner. The machine is stopped with the needle in the fabric, the foot is raised, and the fabric turned. The foot is then lowered and stitching continued.

Placket Finished opening used in a garment to make it easy to put on and to ensure a good fit (e.g., at the neckline and cuffs).

Placket bands Fabric strips used to finish the two sides of an opening, stopping partway down the bodice; usually formed from two strips, but may sometimes be cut as one piece.

Pleat Even fold of fabric, often partially stitched down, used to take in fullness; most commonly used on skirts and dresses to shape the waistline, but also worked on curtain headings and bed valances, and as a decorative feature on sleeves and blouses. Various types of pleat (e.g., knife pleat, box pleat, or inverted pleat) are formed using different methods.

Pleater Machine used to gather and stitch fabrics quickly for smocking or elasticizing. The fabric is wound through a series of hand-activated rollers that pleat the fabric, which is then stitched by a row of needles threaded with cotton or elastic.

Pocket bag The inside of a concealed pocket that hangs down inside a garment.

Pocket flap This folds down to cover the opening of a pocket. It may be made as one piece with the pocket (e.g., on a patch pocket), when the flap simply folds down on the right side of the pocket, or made separately from the pocket and stitched on above it.

Pocket welt Generally used on a slashed pocket, this is stitched to the lower edge of the pocket opening and stands up to cover it.

Point presser Tool for pressing seams and points in small areas (e.g., on a collar).

Point turner Sewing aid with a pointed end, which is used to push out points (e.g., on a collar) to create a neat, sharp finish.

Polar fleece Synthetic fabric (*see* p. 58).

Polyester crepe Lightweight synthetic fabric (*see* p. 57).

Poly linen Linen-look synthetic fabric (*see* p. 58).

Poplin Cotton fabric (*see* p. 43).

Pounding block Weighted tool, used to pound creases into heavyweight fabric after steaming.

Preshrunk fabric Fabric treated in the manufacturing process so that it will not shrink during subsequent laundering.

Presser foot *See* **Machine foot.**

Pressing cloth Clean cloth placed over fabric to prevent marking during pressing, or when only a minimum of heat is required. The cloth may be dampened for steam pressing woolen fabrics.

Prickstitch Small, spaced backstitch worked by hand, used mainly to work invisible stitching when inserting a zipper.

Princess seam *See* **Curved seam.**

Pure nylon Non-absorbent synthetic fabric (*see* p. 59).

PVC fabric Tough, nonporous, synthetic fabric (*see* p. 60).

Quick slipstitch Handstitch used to join two folded, abutting edges; also known as even slipstitch.

Raw edge Cut fabric edge that – in most cases – requires finishing by straight stitching, zigzag stitching, or another method (e.g., anti-fray spray) to stop the edges from unraveling.

Rayon Plant cellulose, regenerated to form fibers. Rayon fabrics are absorbent and comfortable to wear.

Reinforcement Use of underlay, extra rows of stitching, or a patch of fabric to strengthen an area of a garment that will be subjected to strain (e.g., a buttonhole).

Reverse stitching Straight machine stitching that is worked backward for a short distance at the beginning and end of a seam to secure the threads before cutting off (most sewing machines have a button that can be pressed to reverse the stitching).

Reversible fabric Fabric woven so that either side may be used as the right side (e.g., damask).

Right side Outer side of a fabric, designed to appear as the visible part of a finished garment or home furnishing. The right side is important when cutting out and sewing items; instructions are given in the pattern envelope.

Rotary cutter Tool with interchangeable, round blades, used to produce precise, straight edges when cutting fabric. It should be used with a cutting mat.

Rubber fabric Latex material (*see* p. 60).

Ruching Several lines of stitching worked to form a gathered area.

Ruffle Decorative gathered trim, made from a single or double layer of fabric. Ruffles may be gathered in different ways to form different finishes (e.g., with a heading, with double edges, or as a circular ruffle at a garment neckline).

Running stitch Handstitch used for seaming and gathering (for gathering, two parallel rows of stitching are normally worked). Running stitch is quick to work but not as strong as backstitch.

Satin stitch Worked by hand or machine, this is formed by neat, parallel stitches worked closely together to entirely cover an area of fabric. Satin stitch is used to reinforce the short ends of a buttonhole, as well as for purely decorative purposes.

Seam allowance Amount of fabric allowed for on a pattern where sections of an item are to be joined together by a seam; generally this amount is ⅝ in (1.5 cm).

Seam edge This is the cut edge of a seam allowance.

Seam gauge Adjustable sewing-machine attachment that is fixed to the needle plate and used as a guide for sewing straight seams.

Seamline Line designated for stitching a seam; this is generally a distance of ⅝ in (1.5 cm) from the seam edge.

Seam ripper Hooked cutting tool used to open or undo seams and areas of detailed work, such as buttonhole stitching.

Seam roll Tool used to aid in the pressing of shaped garment areas.

Seam taping Stitching of seam tape, bias binding, or twill tape to a seam to stabilize the seam and prevent stretching.

Seersucker Striped and puckered cotton fabric (*see* p. 43).

Self-bound seam Machine-stitched, self-enclosed seam often used on lightweight fabrics that do not fray readily.

Self-enclosed seam Seam in which raw edges are enclosed by stitching to form a neat, narrow finish. French and mock French seams, flat-fell seams, and self-bound seams are all examples of self-enclosed seams.

Self-stay Made from a strip of the garment fabric itself and used as for a separate stay or to reduce bulk.

Selvage Finished edge on a woven fabric, which runs parallel to the warp (lengthwise) threads.

Sequin fabric *See* p. 60.

Serger Machine used for quick and efficient stitching, trimming, and edging of fabric in a single action; used mainly to finish seams while sewing to give a professional finish to a garment.

Serger attachments Tools that can be attached to a serger which enable the machine to perform a greater range of functions. These are normally purchased separately.

Sew-in interfacing Canvas used to shape a garment, generally in tailoring, attached by stitching. Available in different weights, depending on the garment fabric.

Shank *See* **Button shank.**

Shantung Silk fabric (*see* p. 55).

Sheer fabric Fine, transparent fabric (e.g., chiffon) often used for delicate items such as scarves.

Shirring Form of machine gathering used to take in fullness, stitched in rows across fabric; often worked with a cotton top thread and shirring elastic bobbin thread to allow for stretch.

Shoulder pad Fabric-covered or uncovered foam pad used to shape and support a garment shoulder. See **Tailored shoulder pad.**

Silk Threads spun by silkworms and woven in varying weights to create fabrics that are cool, absorbent, and luxurious in feel.

Small scissors – see Cutting tools, p. 11

Silk-cotton mix See p. 53.

Silk-linen mix See p. 53.

Silk satin See p. 53.

Silk-wool mix See p. 53.

Single jersey Knitted woolen fabric (see p. 51).

Slanting hemstitch See **Hemstitch**.

Sleeve board Small, narrow board, often attached to an ironing board, used for pressing seams and narrow sections of a garment.

Sleeve cap Section at the top of a sleeve that is intersected by the shoulder seam.

Sleeve heading Narrow strip of padding used to fill out a sleeve cap and to create a roll of fabric at the top of a sleeve.

Slipstitch Hand-worked hemming stitch that is used to attach a folded fabric edge to another layer. See also **Quick slipstitch**.

Skirt marker Adjustable rule for the accurate marking of a hem, consisting of an upright ruler and a squeeze bulb filled with chalk.

Smocking Even rows of stitching used to gather in fabric fullness and shape squares of fabric, worked before a garment is made up.

Snaps These are available in black, silver, or a clear finish, and are used where a lightweight, invisible fastening is needed.

Spandex Lightweight stretchable synthetic fabric (see p. 61).

Spool pin Pin that holds the spool of thread at the top of a sewing machine, ready to be fed through the machine and down to the needle.

Sports net Cotton fabric (see p. 44).

Stay Small piece of fabric or tape sewn to a specific area of an item purely for reinforcement (e.g., at the point of a slash, or under a bound buttonhole).

Staystitching Straight machine stitching worked just inside a seam allowance to strengthen it and prevent it from stretching or breaking (e.g., on loosely woven or soft jersey fabrics).

Stitch-in-the-ditch Short length of stitching used to create stability (e.g., at the side seams of a waistband to hold elastic flat and prevent it from rolling).

Stitch ripper Small tool with a curved leading edge, used to cut delicately and precisely through a stitch or through stitching.

Stitch tension On a sewing machine this dial controls the degree of tightness or looseness of the top spool and bobbin threads when interlocking to make a stitch. When upper and lower tensions are balanced, the threads are drawn equally into the fabric.

Straight grain Indicated by a straight placement arrow on a pattern piece, this shows where to place the fabric so that it is parallel to the selvage; this grainline has the least give. See also **Lengthwise grain**.

Straight stitch Plain machine stitch used for seaming, staystitching, understitching, and topstitching.

Stretch stitch Strong, straight machine stitch, worked with two stitches forward and one backward so that each stitch is worked a total of three times.

Suiting linen See p. 52.

Synthetic fabric Fibers produced chemically from combinations of gas, petroleum, alcohol, water, and air woven into fabrics that are affordable, durable, hardwearing, and crease-resistant (although not very absorbent).

Taffeta Silk fabric (see p. 54).

Tailored shoulder pad Pad of soft batting sandwiched between layers of felt or interfacing, used to give shape along the shoulders of a jacket or coat.

Tailor's chalk Available in several colors, this is used to mark fabric and is removed from the fabric surface by brushing.

Tailor's ham Tool used for pressing shaped areas of a garment (e.g., the collar of a tailored coat).

Tailor's tacks Loose thread markings used to transfer symbols from a pattern to fabric and worked in a contrasting thread with the pattern pinned to the fabric.

Tartan Plaid woolen fabric (see p. 49).

Terry cloth Cotton fabric (see p. 47).

Thimble Made of metal or plastic, this protective cap fits over a finger during handstitching, and aids in pushing the needle through unyielding fabric.

Three-step zigzag stitch Machine stitch, used as zigzag stitch, but with a flatter finish; also known as tricot and multistitch.

Ticking Cotton fabric (see p. 46).

Top collar Outer fabric section of a garment collar.

Topstitching Row (or double row, worked with a double-topstitching needle) of straight stitching worked on the right side of an item, close to the finished edge, to provide a neat, decorative appearance; can also be worked in a contrasting color of thread.

Tracing wheel Tool used in conjunction with dressmaker's carbon to transfer pattern markings to fabric.

Tricot See **Three-step zigzag stitch**.

Tuck Stitched fold of fabric formed along the straight grain; used to take in fullness (e.g., to shape a waistline), or to provide a decorative feature on a range of garments including children's clothes, summer tops, and wedding dresses. Various types of tuck (e.g., pin tuck, spaced tuck, or shell tuck) can be formed using different methods.

Tweed (modern and traditional) Woolen fabric (see p. 50).

Under collar Inner fabric section of a garment collar.

Underlap Edge of a garment that extends under another edge (e.g., at the opening of a cuff or at a waistband).

Underlay Strip of fabric placed on the underside of the main fabric to provide reinforcement (e.g., underneath a buttonhole or in mending).

Underlining Layer of soft fabric cut to the same shape as, and placed beneath the, garment fabric before seams are joined or interfacing is applied; used mainly on tailored garments.

Understitching Line of machine stitching through facing and seam allowances invisible from the right side; this helps an edge seam to roll naturally to the wrong side, and the facing to lie flat. On fine fabrics or areas difficult to reach by machine, it may be worked by hand using prickstitch through the facing and seam allowances.

Venetian Woolen fabric (see p. 50).

Vent Lapped opening (e.g., in the hem and sleeve openings of a tailored jacket or coat).

Vertical hemstitch See **Hemstitch**.

Vinyl Synthetic fabric (see p. 60).

Viscose Synthetic fabric (see p. 57).

Voile Cotton fabric (see p. 44).

Waistband Band of fabric (often stiffened to prevent stretching and buckling) attached to the waist edge of a garment to give a neat, stable finish. Styles include straight, decoratively shaped, and stretch waistbands.

Waistline Horizontal line around the waist at which a ribbon or cord sits naturally above the hips. Also the waist edge of a garment, which may be finished with a facing, casing, or ribbing, or to which a waistband may be added; an important measurement when altering a pattern.

Warp Lengthwise threads or yarns of a woven fabric.

Washed silk See p. 54.

Wax chalk Marking medium for woolen fabrics, available in black or white, and removed by pressing with a pressing cloth.

Weft Threads or yarns that cross the warp of a woven fabric.

Welt See Pocket welt.

Whipstitch Strong, overedge handstitch used for joining two flat edges together.

Winceyette Cotton fabric (see p. 46).

Wool Natural, spun fiber, available in a range of weights, textures, and weaves. Woolen fabrics drape well and are soft, absorbent, water-repellent, and elastic. Wool is a preferred fabric for tailoring.

Worsted Woolen fabric (see p. 48).

Wrong side Reverse side of a fabric (e.g., the flat side of pile fabric or the unprinted side of printed fabric), which should be on the inside of a finished item. Markings should always be made on the wrong side of the fabric to prevent them from showing on the finished item.

Zigzag blind hemstitch Machine stitch similar to blind hemstitch, consisting of three narrow zigzag stitches followed by one wide zigzag stitch.

Zigzag stitch Machine stitch of variable length and width used to finish the raw edge of a seam allowance on frayable fabrics; a commonly used machine stitch.

Zipper Widely used fastening available in different types, weights, and lengths. Chain and coil zippers are used for a range of purposes; concealed zippers are generally used on skirt and dress openings; heavier, longer, separating zippers are suitable for jackets. Zippers are stitched in different ways depending on their position on a garment (e.g., a lapped zipper is used at the top of a seam, and an enclosed zipper within a seam).

Zipper fly Extension outside a garment that covers the zipper and the zipper teeth.

Zipper guard Fabric facing that protects undergarments and skin from the zipper teeth.

Zipper foot Narrow machine foot with a single toe. This foot is adjustable and can be positioned to sit either to the right or left of the needle. It enables the needle to stitch close to the teeth when inserting a zipper.

Stitching tape – see Sewing and Fabric Aids, p. 14

INDEX

ACKNOWLEDGMENTS

························· REVISED EDITION ·························

Special thanks to:

Cloth House, 98 Berwick Street, Soho, London W1F 0QJ (tel: 020 7287 1555) for supplying a wide range of fabrics; Coats Crafts UK for yarns and sewing accessories; The Holding Company, 241–45 Kings Road, London SW3 5EL (tel: 020 7352 1600) for props; Janome UK for the sewing machine; Jasmine, 65 Abbeville Road, London SW4 (tel: 020 8675 9475) for clothes and props;

Joe Allen Bespoke Couture, 20 Cross Street, London N1 2BQ (tel: 020 7704 1040) for beautifully made clothes and the loan of other items for photography; MacCulloch and Wallis, 25–26 Dering Street, London W15 1AT (tel: 020 7629 0311) for special fabrics; Malabar Cotton Company, 31–33 South Bank Business Centre, Ponton Road, London SW8 5BL (tel: 020 7501 4200) for wonderful cottons and silks.

························· ORIGINAL EDITION ·························

Special thanks to:

Barneys Textile Centre, The Berwick Street Cloth Shop, Borval Fabrics, James Hare Silks Ltd., Janome UK Ltd., John Kaldor Fabric Maker UK Ltd., MacCulloch and Wallis (London) Ltd., Newey Goodman Ltd., Rose and Hubble Ltd.,Graham Smith Fabrics Ltd.

Dorling Kindersley would also like to thank:

Text and technical consultation Chris Jefferys; Clare Carter; Lisa Rose and Martin Shoben of the London Centre for Fashion Studies.

Specialist advice The staff of MacCulloch and Wallis (London) Ltd.; Maureen McGuigan and the staff of Janome UK Ltd.; Valerie Wootton; Charyn Jones.

Providing props for photography:
Fabrics Barneys Textile Centre, London; The Berwick Street Cloth Shop, London; Borval Fabrics, Pudsey; House of Faiman, London; Denholme Velvets Ltd., Bradford; Hanson's Discount Fabrics, Sturminster Newton; Harris Fabrics Ltd., Milton Keynes; James Hare Silks Ltd., Leeds; John Kaldor Fabric Maker UK Ltd., London; MacCulloch and Wallis (London) Ltd., London; Rose and Hubble Ltd., London; Graham Smith Fabrics Ltd., Keighley.

Haberdashery and other sewing accessories Adjustoform Products Ltd., Ashford (dress forms); Coats Crafts UK, Darlington (threads); Entaco Ltd., Studley (needles); Fiskars UK Ltd., Bridgend (scissors, pinking shears, rotary cutters); John Lewis Partnership, London (ironing board covers and haberdashery); Newey Goodman Ltd., Tipton (needles, pins, buttons, and other haberdashery); Perivale-Gütermann Ltd.,

Greenford (threads); Simplicity Patterns Ltd., Glasgow (patterns); Stockman London Ltd., London (tailor's hams); Vilene Interlinings, Halifax (interfacings); William Whiteley & Sons, Sheffield (leather shears); YKK (UK) Ltd., London (zips).

Sewing machines and machine accessories Janome UK Ltd., Stockport; Princess Pleaters, Hereford.
Steam irons Domena Ltd., Haywards Heath.
Hand care The Body Shop/Bodyshop Colourings, London; The Garden Pharmacy, London.

Editorial assistance Jo Finnis, Adèle Hayward, Sasha Heseltine, Jacky Jackson, Emma Lawson.
Design assistance Emma Boys, Jackie Dollar, Rachel Gibson, Darren Hill, Robert Newman, Mark Wilde.
DTP assistance Jason Little, Raúl López Cabello.

Sewing Debbie Brett, Kathleen Copeland-Nyberg, Jean Coombs, Gwen Diamond, Penny Hill, Beryl Miller, Val Parker, Heather Purcell, Jane Skinner, Pam Southwell.
Tailors Alan Cannon Jones, Tony Walker.

Hand modelling Karima El-Ahmadi, Linda Birungi, Mary Clare Blake, Ana Börner, Lisa Broomhead, Alex Chiacchiararelli, Ana Jansson, Helen Oyo, Chacasta Pritlove, Vicki Rimmer, Lisa Rönnbäck, Amanda Sparling, Renée Teo.

Additional photography (p. 42–59) Sue Baker.
Photographic assistance Sarah Ashun, Gary Ombler.
Gallery artworks Bernhard Gussregen.
Additional artworks Karen Cochrane.
Paper patterns John Hutchinson.

Glossary Jane Royston.
Index Hilary Bird.